THE WALKING MUSE

THE WALKING MUSE

HORACE ON THE THEORY OF SATIRE

Kirk Freudenburg

PRINCETON UNIVERSITY PRESS   PRINCETON, NEW JERSEY

Library of Congress Cataloging-in-Publication Data
Freudenburg, Kirk, 1961–
The walking muse : Horace on the theory of satire /
Kirk Freudenburg.
p.   cm.
Includes bibliographical references and index.
ISBN-0-691-03166-5 (cloth)
1. Horace, Satirae. 2. Horace—Aesthetics. 3. Verse satire, Latin—
History and criticism—Theory, etc. 4. Comic, The, in literature.
5. Aesthetics, Ancient. 6. Rome in literature. I. Title.
PA6393.S8F7   1992
871'.01—dc20   92-8534

For Judi Ann Freudenburg

Contents

Acknowledgments

THIS BOOK is a thoroughly revised, expanded version of my 1989 doctoral dissertation at the University of Wisconsin. Though the members of my dissertation committee (Barbara Fowler, Paul Plass, Fannie Lemoine, and John Scarborough) have not been closely involved with subsequent revisions, I would like to thank them formally for their earlier advice and encouragement. I am especially grateful to Professor Lemoine, who suggested that I read Joel Relihan's 1985 dissertation on the history of Menippean satire, the most recent in a long line of fine works on satire to emerge from the University of Wisconsin (something in the waters of Lake Mendota, I suppose). Other department members who offered help along the way include Jim McKeown, Jeffrey Wills, John Bennet, and B. B. Powell.

My greatest debt, of course, I owe to my dissertation advisor, Denis C. Feeney, for his time, scholarly savvy, and diligence in providing incisive criticisms of my work. He, more than anyone, has taught me to be confident in my ideas. Among those who have played similar roles in the past, I am especially grateful to Norman Nagel, my mentor at Valparaiso University, for his inspiration and his many insights into the power of words, and to Kevin Herbert of Washington University, who gave me not only the opportunity to pursue the classics but an excellent model to follow as well.

Others who kindly agreed to read the book and provide criticisms include Elaine Fantham, Kenneth Reckford, Susan Braund, and Michael Wigodsky. Their vigilance saved me from many errors and misjudgments. Any that remain, of course, are entirely my own.

For preparation of the final manuscript I owe sincere thanks to John Eble, a fine editor, scholar, and friend. Thanks also to Marjorie Pagan for technical assistance, and to my colleagues in the classics department at Kent State University for their continued encouragement. The Kent State University Research Council generously provided two grants supporting this project.

Finally I thank my wife, Judi, who has contributed more to this project (and to my sanity) than she will ever know or admit. To her I dedicate this book.

THE WALKING MUSE

CHAPTER ONE

Horatian Satire and the Conventions of Popular Drama

INTRODUCTORY REMARKS: ANCIENT RHETORIC AND THE PERSONA THEORY

"The poet's work may be a mask, a dramatized conventionalization, but it is frequently a conventionalization of his own experiences, his own life. If used with a sense of these distinctions, there is use in biographical study."[1] Since the days of the great "Personal Heresy" debate, which pitted C. S. Lewis of Oxford against E. M. Tillyard of Cambridge, critics of personal poetry have struggled to strike a balance between the opposing claims of art and autobiography.[2] The concept of the poet's mask, the persona, while generally accepted in theory, still suffers from much neglect in the actual practice of criticism. It troubles us, for it leads to the ironic realization that all personal poetry, such as satire, elegy, and lyric, is essentially impersonal, or at least personal only in a restricted sense, for the poet chooses to create and project a specific image of himself as speaker just as he would create any other character to play a role in his fictional poetic world. This remarkable irony is central to a proper understanding of Horatian and all Roman satire: the speaker who delivers his criticisms in the first person is not the poet himself but the poet in disguise. Like the modern stand-up comedian who claims, "a funny thing happened to me on the way to the show," he invents a second life for himself, a conventionalized, often ridiculous existence, which may or may not bear any significant resemblance to his own life experience. In the end, Horace's satiric persona is no more the real Horace than

[1] R. Wellek and A. Warren, *Theory of Literature* (New York: Harcourt, Brace, 1942), 72.
[2] See E. M. Tillyard, *The Personal Heresy: A Controversy by E. M. Tillyard and C. S. Lewis* (London: Oxford University Press, 1965). Seminal articles by classicists include H. Cherniss, "The Biographical Fashion in Literary Criticism," *University of California Publications in Classical Philology* 12 (1943–44): 279–91; A. W. Allen, " 'Sincerity' and the Roman Elegists," *Classical Philology* 45 (1950): 145–60; and G. Highet, "Masks and Faces in Satire," *Hermes* 102 (1974): 321–37. The best bibliographical survey concerning the persona in Roman satire is M. M. Winkler, *The Persona in Three Satires of Juvenal* (Hildesheim: Olms, 1983), 1–22.

is "Maudie Pritchert" the real Jonathan Winters or "Karnak the Magnificent" the real Johnny Carson. He is simply one of the satirist's favorite masks, the moralistic preacher adapted from diatribe and comedy.

This approach to Roman satire, despite its iconoclastic ring, is by no means an innovation of modern theory. It is important to realize that the Roman poets themselves were fully inured to this way of thinking about their work. We recall from Catullus 16 that the speaker saw fit to berate his critics, Aurelius and Furius, for daring to draw from his poems conclusions about his own life. He counters, "For it is proper that the devoted poet himself be chaste, though this is not required of his verse" (16.5–6).[3]

Neither Catullus nor Horace can be credited with inventing the practice of speaking through a mask, for as the term *persona* (the actor's "mask") suggests, the practice was well known to them from drama.[4] Even more influential was the use of the first-person mask in rhetoric. Every Roman schoolboy was expected to master the practice of characterization for the sake of projecting a positive, trustworthy image (*ethos*) of himself as speaker and a highly negative image of his opposition. The evidence of ancient theory suggests that the training involved could be quite tedious.[5] Aristotle, for example, at *Rhetoric* 2.1395a2–5 relates that storytelling (μυθολογεῖν) and the use of maxims (γνωμολογεῖν) are suited to older speakers, especially those from the countryside. They impress upon the listener the notion of time-worn experience, and thus they carry no conviction in the mouth of a younger speaker. At 3.1413a, however, discussing the comic use of metaphor, Aristotle relates, "Hyperboles are juvenile, as they indicate vehemence . . . that is why such expression is inappropriate in the mouth of an older man."[6] Unlike his ancient counterpart, the modern reader tends either to overlook such details or to assign them a significance much less than they deserve. For the ancient reader, hy-

---

[3] Compare Ovid *Tristia* 2.354: *crede mihi, distant mores a carmine nostro: / vita verecunda est, Musa iocosa mea* ("Trust me, my morals and song are completely different: my lifestyle is reverent, my muse sportive"). Martial 1.4.8 draws the same distinction: *lasciva est nobis pagina, vita proba* ("My book is insolent, my life-style virtuous").

[4] Compare Anderson: "Horace did not invent this method of speaking through a mask in satiric potery. As a little reflection should indicate, the satirist speaking in the first person is merely an extension of dramatic and rhetorical practices long known, according to which any actor or orator must assume the character appropriate to his speech." W. S. Anderson, *Essays on Roman Satire* (Princeton: Princeton University Press, 1982), 29–30.

[5] At *Ad Herennium* 4.49.63–4.53.66, for example, the topic of characterization is treated under the headings *Effictio, Notatio,* and *Sermocinatio.*

[6] Quoted from D. Russell and M. Winterbottom, *Ancient Literary Criticism: The Principal Texts in New Translations* (Oxford: Clarendon Press, 1972), 155.

perboles project youth and vehemence whereas maxims create the impression of age and country simplicity. Both contribute significantly to the unseen *ethos* of the speaker.

Problems associated with the separation of art from autobiography are especially acute in the case of Roman satire, for it is the poet's aim to invite trust, to project sincerity and candor. As a result, his words convince us, and we are all too willing to believe that the speaker and the poet are one and the same. Here again, every detail is significant. Hermogenes, writing in the second century A.D., discusses the various means available to the orator in the formation of an *ethos* characterized by simplicity (*On Types* 324):

> "Simple" also are thoughts that appear to border on the vulgar. These are found when one speaks about vulgar or ordinary matters. For example, in the speech against Stephanus for false witness, we have the phrase "showered the nuts over him," and again "strip the rose-garden." In the Appeal against Eubulides, we find the speaker saying that his mother used to sell ribbons in the market.[7]

This last detail reminds us that Horace, too, chose to stress his father's humble station in life even though it is obvious that he grew up in most privileged circumstances.[8] The repeated *libertino patre natus* of 1.6, in conscious emulation of Bion (ἐμοῦ ὁ πατὴρ μὲν ἦν ἀπελεύθερος), creates a specific image of the speaker in the mind of the ancient reader: a man of humble origins, he has never learned the subtleties of deceit.

As he continues his discussion of characterization (*On Types* 325), Hermogenes draws the following illustration from Xenophon's *Cyropaedia* 2.3.9: " 'Simple' also are thoughts occurring in arguments drawn from irrational animals. 'The ox strikes with his horn, the horse with his hoof, the dog with his mouth, the boar with his tusk.' "[9] The passage is immediately reminiscent of Horace's *Satires* 2.1.51–55:

> Come, consider with me how every creature frightens its enemies with its most powerful weapon, as nature herself compels: the wolf attacks with its tooth, the bull with its horn. How so, unless by instinct? Entrust

[7] Ibid., 573. The last example cited by Hermogenes shows the rhetor's penchant for viewing not only incidental remarks, but the actual facts of the case as material for the development of character. Demosthenes' speech *Against Eubulides* leaves no doubt that Euxitheus's mother was in fact a seller of ribbons in the marketplace. Yet, as a student of *ethopoeia*, Hermogenes knows that some autobiographical facts are to be glossed while others, such as Euxitheus's devotion to his poor, hardworking mother, are to be amplified and embellished in order to fashion a positive moral image of the speaker.

[8] On this point, see especially D. Armstrong, "*Horatius Eques et Scriba: Satires* 1.6 and 2.7," *Transactions of the American Philological Association* 116 (1986): 255–88.

[9] Russell and Winterbottom, *Ancient Literary Criticism*, 575.

Lefty [Scaeva] the Prodigal with a long-lived mother and it won't be his
pious right hand that does the dirty deed. Neither does the wolf attack
with hoof, nor does the bull bite.

Horace has given the motif a humorous twist. As Hermogenes indicates, the illustration is highly suggestive, projecting the distinct image of the homespun, moralizing rustic who simply cannot deceive.
We trust him fully. He, like the Lucilius of *Satires* 2.1, entrusts us with
his secrets, as he would his closest friends, and as a result we find it
very hard to question his sincerity and to believe that he is in fact a
product of fiction. Satire deceives, for more than any other genre it
demands an autobiographical explanation.[10]

Although recent scholarship has sought to redefine the speaker's
role in the satires by drawing the necessary distinction between autobiography and art, a clear, coherent picture of Horace's satiric persona is still much needed. The works of W. S. Anderson and J. Zetzel
have advanced far in the right direction.[11] What is needed is a more
comprehensive approach, one that respects the enormous possibilities of tiny details. In undertaking this study I take Aristotle as my
guide, especially mindful of his advice on the topic of characterization, knowing that Horace was like-minded in such matters: at *Rhetoric* 3.1417a15–17, Aristotle expresses the opinion that the narrative
portion of a forensic speech "should be expressive of character, and
will be so if we know what produces this effect." He gives the example
of the Socratic dialogues, which he considered particularly expressive
of moral character. He then adds: "Other things indicative of character are the concomitants of different sorts of character, like for instance, 'He went on walking as he spoke,' an act that shows insolence
and boorishness of character."[12] The detail is too slight to merit much
notice, but for Aristotle the act of speaking while walking was all-
telling, a tiny detail of enormous significance. For Aristotle, as for his
many adherents in rhetoric and drama, good character portrayal required extreme subtlety. He concludes, at 3.1417b: "And introduce
yourself at once as having a certain character so that the audience can
contemplate you as such, and do the same with your adversary, but

---

[10] Geoffrey Harrison has recently argued that *Satires* 2.1.30–34, which has so often
been taken as a straightforward defense of autobiographical satire, is, in fact, a mock
defense of satire and a disparagement of Lucilius's artistic talents. See G. Harrison,
"The Confessions of Lucilius (Horace *Sat.* 2.1.30–34): A Defense of Autobiographical
Satire?" *Classical Antiquity* 6 (1987): 38–52.

[11] See Anderson, *Roman Satire*, 13–49; and J.E.G. Zetzel, "Horace's *Liber Sermonum*:
The Structure of Ambiguity," *Arethusa* 13 (1980): 59–77.

[12] Quoted from Russell and Winterbottom, *Ancient Literary Criticism*, 164.

without being obvious."[13] Good character portrayal is well hidden and works under the surface by nuance, the glancing reference, the well-chosen word. Horace was extremely well versed in earlier theory, both Greek and Latin. Like Theophrastus, Menander, and Terence before him, he well knew the value of concealing the mechanisms of theory (*celare artem*). It is with this understanding that I approach the task of defining Horace's satiric persona.

To begin this study, I limit myself to the first four satires of Book 1, the so-called diatribe satires, for here alone has Horace developed an image of the speaker fully consistent from satire to satire.[14] *Satires* 1.5 introduces a new speaker, and 1.6 yet another. The speaker of the diatribe satires does return from time to time, primarily in Book 2, where he appears in the guise of Ofellus, Damasippus, and Davus. He was a favorite character of Horace, resurrected again in several of the *Epistles* and fondly remembered as the one outstanding figure of his earlier work. This speaker, I maintain, is clear and self-consistent. His full color can be appreciated only by close study of the minute details that went into his portrayal.

Among those who made an art of character portrayal, the writers of popular comedy were regarded by theorists and practitioners alike as unequaled masters of their craft.[15] Horace, I maintain, shared this view, and he consciously shaped his satiric persona along lines sug-

---

[13] Ibid., 165.

[14] *Satires* 1.1–1.3 have traditionally been referred to by the commentators as the "diatribe satires," although there is little consensus as to what exactly the term diatribe means. A useful definition is that of D. A. Russell: "a lecture or discourse on a moral theme, marked by a combination of seriousness with humour and a certain vividness and immediacy in language." D. A. Russell, *Plutarch* (New York: Charles Scribner's Sons, 1973), 29, n. 25. This definition is broad enough to include the works of authors as diverse as Bion, Teles, Horace, and Epictetus. *Satires* 1.4 does not fit this definition because it does not address a specific moral issue, yet I use the term *diatribe* in reference to 1.4 because the literary issues at hand are treated by the same fictional moralist, a distinctly Bion-like character, of *Satires* 1.1–3. Standard works on diatribe include A. Oltramare, *Les origines de la diatribe romaine* (Lausanne: Payot, 1926), and B. Wallach, "A History of the Diatribe from Its Origin up to the First Century B.C. and a Study of the Influence of the Genre upon Lucretius III, 830–1094" (Ph.D. diss., University of Illinois, Urbana-Champaign, 1974). Other useful studies include J. Kindstrand, *Bion of Borysthenes*, Studia Graeca Upsaliensia 11 (Uppsala, 1976), 97–99; G. Fiske, *Lucilius and Horace: A Study in the Classical Theory of Imitation*, University of Wisconsin Studies in Language and Literature 7 (Madison, 1920), 117–19; G. Highet, *The Anatomy of Satire* (Princeton: Princeton University Press, 1962), 40; and H. D. Jocelyn, "Diatribes and Sermons," *Liverpool Classical Monthly* 7, no. 1 (1982): 3–7.

[15] Quintilian, at *Institutes* 10.1.69, recommends the careful study of Menander in the training of the orator largely on the basis of his skills in characterization: *ita est omnibus rebus, personis, adfectibus accommodatus* ("so perfectly adapted to all circumstances, characters and emotions"). See also Hermogenes *On Types* 323–24.

gested by various characters known to him from the comic stage. He admits as much at the end of *Satires* 1.4 where, in sketching the famous portrait of his father, which is, in fact, a version of his own satiric persona, he adapts his picture to a wholly fictional model: the satirist, like his father, is the comic *doctor ineptus*, displaying all the humorous loose ends of Terence's Demea.

This is not the type of image that a standard moralist would choose to convey. It is an image that undermines old assumptions concerning Horace's satiric mission; too often the *Satires* are regarded as entirely serious in their didactic intent, and Horace himself is accepted as a second Bion with an equally serious ethical mission, much in line with Augustus's efforts at moral reform. The satirist's overt ineptitude, just alluded to, argues against this approach. The notion of an inept persona, shaped at least as much by comedy as it was by Hellenistic moralizing, calls for a new understanding of Horace's work. Zetzel said it well: "Whatever we feel the final aim of the poet is, it is surely not simple-minded moral or literary judgments; it is, among other things, the creation of a complex and demanding poetic world."[16] This world, we shall see, brings with it all the trappings of the comic stage.

THE PERSONA OF THE DIATRIBE SATIRES AND THE INFLUENCE OF BION

Horace's *Satires* contain numerous references to the beliefs and day-to-day experiences of the speaker that may, in fact, bear little resemblance to the beliefs and experiences of Horace himself. Only rarely can such autobiographical details be checked against references to the life of the poet outside of the poetry itself, and thus, the lines separating art from autobiography must always remain somewhat obscure. We can never know, for example, whether Horace actually made the trip to Brundisium described in 1.5, was confronted by the bore of 1.9, or was trained in the lessons of satire by his father, as he suggests in 1.4. We can be sure, however, that even if these events belonged to Horace's experience, they have been conventionalized—some, at least, to an extreme degree—for each invites comparison with characters and events well known to Horace's audience from earlier literature. The life experiences of Horace have been thoroughly sifted. Those contained by his poems, regardless of their "sincerity," have been carefully selected from among an infinite number

---

[16] Zetzel, "Horace's *Liber Sermonum*," 73.

of like experiences for the specific purpose of creating an image of the satirist and the world that surrounds him. Satire, in other words, is not a log of personal experience, the votive tablet described in 2.1; for the satirist has, at all points, carefully chosen and worked his "personal" experiences along conventional lines in order to carve out a place for his work within the larger literary tradition familiar to his audience.

W. S. Anderson was the first to recognize and take seriously the conventional nature of Horace's satiric persona, noting the inherent incongruity that separates the persona from what must have been Horace's character in real life:

> He strikes us as a considerably older man, possessing the wisdom of experience, serenely above the materialistic pursuits of his fellow men, capable of a self-irony which only the profoundest self-restraint and self-analysis will permit. How much effort must have gone into the creation of that character by a young man not quite thirty, I leave to the reader's imagination. The main point is that Horace produced a Socratic satirist probably quite unrepresentative of himself.[17]

Anderson's Socratic satirist represents perhaps the clearest and most reasonable attempt yet made to encapsulate the persona of Book 1. Even so, the analogy with Socrates fails in two significant respects: first, it falsely assumes that the satirist maintains a single consistent persona throughout Book 1. Although the Socratic analogy has some claim to accuracy in the case of the diatribe satires, it cannot account for the several unique images of the satirist projected in *Satires* 5, 7, 9, and the renegade 8. Second, even within the diatribe satires, the Socratic analogy shows certain limitations, most notably in its failure to account for the satirist's nondialectical approach. Unlike Socrates, the satirist pontificates. His interlocutor is a shadowboxer, totally void of personality, outside of time and place; he functions as a rhetorical convenience. He is neither a peer nor a pupil; he is an adversary, an ignorant voice from the crowd. This type of teacher/adversary relationship Oltramare defined as the singular characteristic that separates true diatribe from its ancient counterpart, the Socratic dialogue, and thus he aligns Horace's early satires with a different, yet related tradition.[18] The case for Socrates, therefore, is severely limited. If it is to be maintained at all, it must be adjusted not to the image of Plato's Socrates, but to the caustic, censorious Socrates cherished by

[17] Anderson, *Roman Satire*, 29.
[18] "The debate with a fictive interlocutor is the most obvious of diatribe's formal characteristics. . . . it is the one premiere trait which distinguishes diatribes from Socratic dialogues." Oltramare, *Diatribe romaine*, 11.

the Cynic tradition.[19] Even beyond this, there is a degree of ineptitude displayed by the satirist of the diatribe satires for which no analogy with Socrates, Bion, or any other moral philosopher can account.

Taking a different approach, Zetzel has analyzed Horace's satiric persona within a larger treatment of the structure of Book 1, arguing that the progressive structure of the book is apparent through the gradual development of the speaker:

> We begin with a voice that is all but disembodied, except for the fact that he is addressing Maecenas on a philosophical topic. This lack of detail lasts through the first three poems, but from the introduction of Horace's father in the fourth, through the explicitly autobiographical narratives of 5–7 to the statements about Maecenas and his friends and their social and literary beliefs that occupy the last two poems, we gain an increasingly vivid idea of the speaker. In a sense, the book is a progressive revelation, a development of a persona, and also a description of the speaker's progress from outside the circle of Maecenas to inside it.[20]

Zetzel, though wedded to the notion of a single persona, has improved upon Anderson's thesis by arguing that the reader's perception of the speaker, consistent through *Satires* 1.4.103, shifts significantly thereafter. Such an analysis, although it gives due weight to the changing perceptions of the reader, misleads when it insists that the lack of autobiographical detail in the diatribe satires makes for a "disembodied" speaker. As pointed out, explicit autobiographical reference is not essential to good characterization, which relies on the tiniest quirks of diction, illustration, and thought to convey an image of the speaker. When these details are given their due weight, there can be no question as to the clarity of the image projected. In contrast to Zetzel's view, it is my contention that the persona of the diatribe satires is the most sharply developed and consistent speaker in the *Satires*. Once this character has been fully delineated, the influences that stand behind its creation will become clear, and new models will be suggested to replace the analogy of Socrates.

The revelation of the speaker of the diatribe satires is immediate. His features are drawn in full color in the very first lines of *Satires* 1.1 (1.1.1–3):

> Qui fit, Maecenas, ut nemo, quam sibi sortem
> seu ratio dederit seu fors obiecerit, illa
> contentus vivat, laudet diversa sequentis?

[19] For the Cynic version of Socrates, see A. A. Long, "Socrates in Hellenistic Philosophy," *Classical Quarterly* 38 (1988): 151.

[20] Zetzel, "Horace's *Liber Sermonum*," 68–69.

> How come, Maecenas, no one lives content with his own lot in life—
> whether given by reason or thrust upon him by chance; rather he praises
> those who follow other paths?

The lines present an odd mixture of colloquialism with philosophical
terminology: *Qui fit* and *nemo* do not belong to the language of poetry
but to prose and everyday speech.[21] *Ratio* and *fors*, though not restricted to philosophical usage, are made specific to Stoic and Epicurean attitudes toward fate in line 2, and thus we have the immediate
impression of the self-made philosopher.[22] His casual disavowal of
knowledge in line 2 the ancient reader regarded as highly suggestive.
Pseudacron notes *ad Satires* 1.1.2:

> He has briefly touched on two sects; for, when he says reason [*ratio*], he
> touches upon the Stoics, when he says chance [*fors*], the Epicureans. The
> Stoics say that all events take place by fixed reason while the Epicureans
> say it is by chance.[23]

The satirist neither knows nor does he much care about the theoretical issues involved with his question. His flippant disregard for abstract speculations of the Stoics and Epicureans, coupled with his
vivid, self-made style, points immediately to the Cynic, the popular
moralist of Greek diatribe. He begins *Satires* 1.1 with a discussion of
mempsimoiria ("discontent with one's lot in life"), one of the most overworked themes of Cynic diatribe.[24] He follows suit in *Satires* 1.2, treating the theme of sexual desire (*amor*), and 1.3, on friendship and anger (*amicitia* and *ira*). All are illustrated in the loose, prolix fashion of
a moralizing rustic, and nowhere does the satirist indulge in abstract
speculation, except for the sake of parody.

The satirist is a philosopher, but not a philosopher who demands
respect for being original, well read, or polished. His rhetoric, like
his philosophy, is homespun. He has a penchant for animal similes
(1.1.32–40), maxims (1.149–50, 1.3.68), and storytelling (1.1.95–

---

[21] On the colloquial character of *qui fit* and *nemo*, see Zetzel, "Horace's *Liber Sermonum*," 69 and n. 51, who follows P. Lejay and F. Plessis, *Oeuvres d'Horace* (Paris, 1911;
repr. Hildesheim: Georg Olms, 1966), 10, and B. Axelson, *Unpoetische Wörter: Ein Beitrag zur Kenntnis der lateinischen Dichtersprache*, Skrifter Utgivna av Vetenskaps-Societeten i Lund (Lund, 1945), 76.

[22] Note that *ratio* "grants" (*dederit*) a certain way of life whereas *fors* simply "tosses it
one's way" (*sibi . . . obiecerit*). The verbs chosen contrast Stoic notions of the λόγος as a
conscious providential force with the haphazard clashing of atoms propounded by the
Epicureans.

[23] My translation here, and all subsequent references to Pseudacron, is based on
O. Keller, *Pseudacronis Scholia in Horatium Vetustiora*, vol. 2 (Stuttgart: Teubner, 1967).

[24] On the theme of *mempsimoiria* and its background in diatribe, see especially Oltramare, *Diatribe romaine*, and Fiske, *Lucilius and Horace*, 219–28.

100), all of which, Aristotle informs us, are characteristic not of the professional rhetorician but of the old country sage.[25] These illustrations, ill-suited to a cleverly devised oration, are not tactfully arranged. They are gathered in an addled, long-winded fashion, which frequently calls attention to itself: "Lest I detain you," *ne te morer*, 1.1.14; "It's not a long story," *non longa est fabula*, 1.1.95; "I return to the point from which I digressed," *Illuc, unde abii, redeo*, 1.1.108; "That's enough for now," *iam satis est*, 1.1.120, and so on. These are not the traits of the young Horace, the sophisticate, trained in the finest schools at Athens and numbered among the friends of Maecenas. Rather, these traits suggest age (perhaps age that borders on senility), the want of formal training, and a disturbing lack of social refinement.

The speaker of the diatribe satires is the sworn enemy of subtlety and nuance. He boasts of his *libertas* in *Satires* 1.4, defending his right to lampoon. He is frequently obscene. Social conventions, for example in matters of sex, mean little to him. He speaks his mind as a good Cynic, whatever the consequences. He projects the image of a man with a mission, out to convert. At times he is pushy and oppressive: *nonne vides*, "Don't you see?" 1.4.109; *fateare necesseset*, "You must confess." He is given to overstatement: "How come, Maecenas, *no one [nemo]* lives content with his own lot," 1.1.1; "*All* singers have this vice," *omnibus hoc vitium est cantoribus*, 1.3.1. Unlike Socrates, who claims not to "know" anything, the satirist is often disrespectful of his hearer and dogmatic; he does not seriously engage his listener in a dialectical process, he harangues. At 1.1.25–26 he makes clear that he regards himself as a teacher, his audience as students, whom he compares with little children who refuse to learn unless given a cookie. All of this was readily apparent to the ancient reader. From the opening lines of *Satires* 1.1, the image projected was perfectly clear. The analogy with Socrates, in this case, is far too flattering.

There is nothing serene about the self-confidence displayed by the satirist. It is obvious that we are to think of him as stopping his man-in-the-street, calling attention to himself, drawing a crowd. Occasional objections are raised by nameless fools, forcing the satirist to think on his feet, shifting his argument to the immediate needs of the conversation. Within such a setting one hardly expects an impeccable logical structure. The term *sermo* ("conversation"), as many have suggested, approximates the Greek διατρίβη, a highly rhetorical, popularized form of the philosophic dialogue that imitates the free form of conversation. A predictable, well-considered logical form has no

---

[25] See Aristotle *Rhetoric* 2.1395a2–5.

place in diatribe. Oltramare relates of diatribe that "the tone of exhortations is always urgent and puffing; the diatribist overwhelms his adversary with a flood of incongruous ideas; he follows out his arguments with little apparent logical connection."[26]

In order to write poetry that approximates diatribe, Horace must follow suit, building in to his arguments all of the unpredictable transitions of conversation. This "conversational logic," so foreign to the best lessons of rhetorical and poetic theory, is a central feature of the diatribe satires.[27] Its influence we see in the elusive, transitional logic of *Satires* 1.1, which has been severely criticized for its alleged failure to relate neatly its two central themes, *mempsimoiria* and *avaritia*. Much scholarship on this satire has attempted to find some natural connection between these themes in order to vindicate the satire as a well-crafted, logical unit.[28] There is no reason, however, to assume that formal precision is what Horace intended, and the best scholarship on this question, rather than doing away with the satire's failings, has attempted to approach the problem from the assumption that Horace had some explicit purpose in choosing to relate these two themes in such a haphazard fashion. The key question raised here is whether Horace is more interested in arguing logically the trite themes of Cynic diatribe, in which case he shows average competence, or in creating the persona of the moralist well known to his audience from Greek popular philosophy. Judged by the latter standard, *Satires* 1.1

---

[26] Oltramare, *Diatribe romaine*, 14.

[27] On the "conversational" style of the diatribe satires, see Zetzel, "Horace's *Liber Sermonum*," 70; M. Coffey, *Roman Satire* (London: Methuen, 1976), 70; and D. Armstrong, *Horace* (New Haven: Yale University Press, 1989), 31.

[28] See, for example, C. Knapp, "Horace, *Sermones* 1.1," *Transactions of the American Philological Association* 45 (1914): 91–109. Fraenkel demonstrates that Horace was not the first to relate these two themes. Rather, drawing upon Teles and the seventeenth Hippocratic *Epistle,* he proves that these two themes were commonly treated together by the Hellenistic popular philosophers, such as Bion. He makes this point, however, not to apologize for the structure of 1.1. He still recognizes the "clumsy formula of transition," which was noted so often before, claiming that it was employed for the purpose of avoiding "the impression of giving a lecture or preaching a sermon: he wants to talk, as a gentleman will talk in congenial company." See E. Fraenkel, *Horace* (Oxford: Clarendon Press, 1957), 94. How a clumsy transition makes one appear a gentleman I do not know. The opposite, I believe, is actually the case. Hubbard, like Fraenkel, recognizes a certain design inherent in the clumsy transition, an attempt at a "disunified unity" (my paraphrase) disjoined in appearance only. Thus, Hubbard maintains, Horace shows himself apt at what Lucilius is not. See T. Hubbard, "The Structure and Programmatic Intent of Horace's First Satire," *Latomus* 40 (1981): 305–21. This thesis is attractive, though encumbered by Hubbard's painfully elaborate ring-structure proposal. See also J. Bodoh, "Unity in Horace's *Sermo* 1.1," *L'Antiquité Classique* 39 (1970): 164–67, which also argues that the failed logic of the poem is deliberate.

succeeds brilliantly. Its rough logic, as David Armstrong has pointed out, has been intentionally crafted to serve the larger designs of the poet:

> In *Satires* 1.1, by the simple three-part form he has imposed, Horace gives the reader from the start a sample of the form that his hexameter poetry will perfect: a logic of transition that imitates the free form of conversation by its quick, apparently unconnected transitions of thought, but always repays the reader with a sense of progression and coherent argument in the end.[29]

The influence of Greek popular philosophy upon the persona of the diatribe satires is apparent at every turn. Horace himself, years after their initial publication, called attention to the Cynic inspiration of his *Satires*, referring to them as "diatribes like those of Bion" (*Bioneis sermonibus, Epistles* 2.2.60). Following this suggestion, scholars have long sought to establish the precise nature of the influence of popular philosophy upon the diatribe satires. Already in Oltramare's day the topic was nearly exhausted, and so there is no need to repeat the process here.[30] Although there can be no doubt that the diatribe satires invite comparison with Greek popular philosophy, the question remains, to what end do they invite such comparison? Until very recently, commentators on the *Satires* have universally assumed that Horace borrows the themes and illustrations of Bion for the expressed purpose of duplicating his moral mission, becoming a voice of reform in a decadent age. In making this assumption, however, they have failed to recognize that Horace has not simply borrowed the lessons of Bion and adapted them to a Roman context; rather, he has become Bion. Thus, it is with some surprise that Oltramare notes: "The poet pushes his imitation of popular moralists all the way to the literal reproduction of their expressions and their habitual plays on words," traits attached deeply to the Cynic persona, independent of any specific moral agenda.[31] The satirist is himself a fictional creation based upon the persona that the works of Bion project. It is my contention that the many parallels that exist from persona to persona would have us read the diatribe satires not as true ethical treatises but as fiction, complex works of art intended as art.

A summary review of certain fragments of Bion, now made accessible by Kindstrand's excellent edition, will serve to underscore the

[29] Armstrong, *Horace*, 31.

[30] See Oltramare, *Diatribe romaine*, 138, for a list of old German works on the topic of diatribe in the *Satires* of Horace. Chief among these is R. Heinze, "De Horatio Bionis Imitatore" (Ph.D. diss., Bonn, 1889).

[31] Oltramare, *Diatribe romaine*, 146.

conventional nature of Horace's Cynic persona.[32] Like the satirist, Bion is a moralizer. His individual treatises, similar to the first three satires of Book 1, each treat a separate moral theme, as can be observed in the two preserved titles "On Wrath" and "On Slavery" (Περὶ τῆς Ὀργῆς and Περὶ Δουλείας).[33] Bion does not approach these issues from the standpoint of the traditional *sapiens*. At F10 he expresses his disdain for logic chopping. F15 allies Bion with the Skeptic Pyrrho against the Stoic notion of "moral progress" (προκοπή).[34] We recall that the speaker of the diatribe satires sustains an ongoing polemic against Stoic dogmatists, such as Fabius and Crispinus. In F9A and F9B, Bion attacks the Platonic concept of ἀνάμνησις, a theoretical concept totally irrelevant to his ethical concerns. Diogenes nicely summarizes Bion's attitude toward organized systems of learning (Diogenes Laertius 4.57): καὶ ὅλως καὶ μουσικὴν καὶ γεωμετρίαν διέπαιζεν ("and he made thorough sport of letters and mathematics"). The philosophy of Bion, like that of the satirist, is entirely nontheoretical, based on simple ethical questions taught from everyday experience, belying the fact that both were extremely well trained in the more abstract branches of philosophy taught by the Hellenistic schools. Like the satirist, Bion sought to project the image of the self-made, common-sense philosopher. Even his brand of Cynicism was self-made, far milder than that espoused by his master, Crates.[35]

Both Bion and the satirist use illustrations drawn from the sphere of everyday life to project an image of country simplicity. The diction is often highly colloquial, as at F1A, where Bion describes his father as τῷ ἀγκῶνι ἀπομυσσόμενος, which compares directly to the description of Lucilius as *emunctae naris*, "his nose wiped clean," at 1.4.8. F42A and F42B compare the rich with money purses, which are worth only as much as they have on the inside. Likewise, at F68, Bion draws his famous comparison between the life of man and a banquet, exactly as the satirist at 1.1.117–19. Although we have no actual fables extant among the fragments of Bion, we find several comparisons with animals, as at F21, where he claims that one must be careful in the way that one meets with external circumstances, just as one is careful of

---

[32] The *testimonia* and *fragmenta* of Bion have been gathered, edited, and annotated by Kindstrand, *Bion*, whose numbering I shall follow throughout.

[33] These works, otherwise unknown, are mentioned in T9A, T9B, and T10.

[34] On the Skeptics and their relation to the Cynic school, see Kindstrand, *Bion*, 53–78, especially nn. 53 and 55. For further attacks on organized systems of learning, see F5A, F6, and F15.

[35] I use the term *Cynic* advisedly in the case of Bion, realizing its severe limitations. For full justice to the complexities of Bion's philosophical viewpoint, see Kindstrand, *Bion*, 56–78.

the way in which one catches a snake.[36] F31A compares Arcesilaus, the founder of the Middle Academy (see T12) to a mouse that nibbles through the grain sack when it finds nothing else to eat. Besides animal similes, Bion is also particularly fond of maxims, such as "friends have all things in common" (κοινὰ τὰ φίλων, T3); "wealth controls all" (τὸν πλοῦτον νεῦρα πραγμάτων, F46); and "old age is a haven of troubles" (τὸ γῆρας . . . ὅρμον εἶναι κακῶν, F62).[37] All of these are characteristic of the speaker of the diatribe satires as well and project the image of the homespun, moralizing rustic. After all, it is the farmer who must deal with snakes in the garden and mice at the grain sack.

At F17 Bion relates that he is a vegetarian; he drinks only water and needs only a few leaves to make up his bed.[38] The satirist, adhering to the same tradition, makes drinking from a pure small spring analogous to a life according to nature at 1.1.51–60. His diet, he would have us believe, consists of bread and vegetables.[39] Other parallels worthy of note are Bion's extreme self-confidence as he approaches his listener from a position of moral superiority, and his reliance on personal abuse.[40] Yet, for all of his vehemence and *sale nigro*, as Horace himself captions Bion's abuse, he is able to see and expand upon the humorous side of man's foolish nature.[41] Occasionally he can even laugh at himself. All of these parallels, I contend, suggest that Horace has not simply borrowed the themes and illustrations of Bion for the sake of duplicating his moral mission, as is so often assumed; rather he has become the Cynic moralizer in every aspect of his character.

DIATRIBE IN THE AGE OF HORACE

The themes and illustrations of Cynic diatribe were simple and trite; the diction was colloquial, and the logic humorously loose. Such roughhewn moralizing hardly seems the proper material for imitation by a refined poet trained in the best poetic traditions of his day

[36] On the use of fables and animal similes in Cynic literature, see Fiske, *Lucilius and Horace*, 223 and n. 12; and Kindstrand, *Bion*, 32 and n. 48.

[37] Cf. also F1 and F58. On the use of maxims, or "proverbs" in Cynic literature, see Kindstrand, *Bion*, 32–33, especially nn. 50 and 51.

[38] Against extravagant food, cf. also F81. Just as in the case of Horace, we have no way of knowing whether these were the actual practices of Bion.

[39] Compare especially *Satires* 1.1.73–75 and 1.6.111–12. On food, water, and wine in Greek popular philosophy, see Oltramare, *Diatribe romaine*, 50, and Kindstrand, *Bion*, 216–20.

[40] See especially F7 and F31A.

[41] Good examples of this are seen at F38A and F47A.

and writing for a discriminating select audience. Yet this is exactly what we are presented with in the first four satires of Book 1. The image conveyed, that of a refined Callimachean street preacher, is incongruous, suggestive not of serious moralizing but of parody. In contrast to much previous scholarship, I maintain that the diatribe satires are completely detached from the true spirit and intent of the ethical treatises that they imitate. They are, in fact, a burlesque of Greek popular philosophy, which had grown fully ripe for parodic treatment by Horace's day and certainly long before.

There is nothing particularly innovative about Horace's choice of Bion as a model for his early satires. Charting the use of Greek popular philosophy in early Roman literature, Oltramare has identified the strong influence of diatribe in authors as diverse as Plautus, Lucretius, and Cato, and slighter influence in the case of many others. Pseudacron, *ad Epistles* 2.2.60, suggests that the Romans themselves recognized Bion's direct influence upon Lucilius, whose diatribes in Book 26, Udo Scholz has recently suggested, parallel exactly the sequence of themes treated by Horace in the first four satires of Book 1.[42] In the very idea of adapting diatribe to a Roman context, therefore, Horace's diatribe satires have little claim to originality, for the evidence available indicates that the practice was well established at Rome since the early second century B.C.

The days immediately prior to the publication of Horace's *Satires* represent the most prolific and creative period in the history of diatribe in its various manifestations at Rome. Among the most notable productions of the period were the *Menippean Satires* of Varro, dubbed by others as the "Cynic Satires."[43] J. Relihan has recently made a very convincing case for the self-parodic side of all Menippean satire, beginning with the works of Menippus himself.[44] In an approach similar to my position regarding Horace, Relihan has argued that Menippean satire is, in fact, a parody of learning and

[42] Pseudacron writes: "With malicious, bitter jests, that is, with satire. [His *sermones*] are, moreover, the arguments of Bion the philosopher, with which he exposes the stupidity of the common crowd. The poems of Lucilius nearly coincide with this" (*Lividis et amaris iocis, idest satyra. sunt autem disputationes Bionis philosophi, quibus stultitiam vulgi arguit, cui paene consentiunt carmina Luciliana*). Pseudacron's Latin, here, is vague and subject to several possible interpretations. For the thematic parallels that link *Satires* 1.1–4 to Lucilius Book 26, see U. Scholz, "Der Frühe Lucilius und Horaz," *Hermes* 114 (1986): 335–65. For cautionary notes against Scholz's view, see J. Christes, "Der frühe Lucilius und Horaz: Eine Entgegnung," *Hermes* 117 (1989): 321–26.

[43] See Aulus Gellius *Noctes Atticae* 2.18.7.

[44] See J. Relihan, "A History of Menippean Satire" (Ph.D. diss., University of Wisconsin at Madison, 1985).

dogma that takes as its primary target the speaker himself.[45] This approach, of course, turns much earlier scholarship on the *Menippean Satires* on its head, since it calls into question the serious ethical intent of the work and the very integrity of the speaker. The *Iambs* of Callimachus, contemporary with the seriocomic works of Menippus, D. Clayman has recently shown, exhibit precisely the same traits:

> Callimachus' *Iambi* seem at home in the general context of Hellenistic moralizing literature. His decrying of wealth in *Iambi* 3 and 12, his attack on a corrupt schoolmaster in *Iamb* 5 and a pimp in *Iamb* 11 fit, formally at least, into this modern moralizing trend in literature. Like the Cynics, Callimachus woos his audience with puns, parody, mock debates, ghosts rising from the dead, trees that talk, obscenity, anything, in short, that his considerable imagination could conceive. Callimachus' intent, however, is not to create legitimate diatribes and moralizing choliambs, but to parody them.[46]

Clayman goes on to suggest that Callimachus's *Iambs* "would not have met with the approval of Bion or Phoenix," alluding to the fact that, already in the early third century B.C., the practitioners of diatribe fell into two distinct camps: the serious dogmatic moralists, such as Phoenix of Colophon, and their parodists, such as Menippus, Callimachus, and later Varro, who exploited the humorous potential of severe moralizing. Horace, I maintain, belongs to the second camp.

The first century B.C. had more than its fair share of dogmatists and pedants, in whose hands diatribe became ripe for parody. Among the most lamentable manifestations of diatribe in Roman literature were the *Apocryphal Letters* of Diogenes and Crates, dated to the first century B.C. and later. Unlike the diatribe satires, these letters appear to have little or no redeeming literary value. It is likely that they were written as practice pieces to be used by schoolboys as part of their rhetorical training.[47] Among the various philosophical sects, Philodemus's *De Ira* and *De Morte* provide evidence for the use of diatribe among the Epicureans.[48] Even more important is Book 3 of *De Rerum Natura*, in which diatribe is adapted to hexameter poetry very much in the tradition of Lucilius, though with little humor in evidence. B. Wallach has argued that the themes, arguments, and sty-

[45] Ibid., vii.

[46] D. Clayman, *Callimachus' Iambi*, Mnemosyne Supplement 59 (Leiden: E. J. Brill, 1980), 70.

[47] On the *Apocryphal Letters* of Diogenes and Crates, see Oltramare, *Diatribe romaine*, 21.

[48] See B. Wallach, *Lucretius and the Diatribe against the Fear of Death: De Rerum Natura III 830–1094*, Mnemosyne Supplement 50 (Leiden: E. J. Brill, 1976), 8.

listic devices of Book 3 "all indicate that Lucretius must have been familiar with the Cynic-Stoic genre and that he knew the work of Bion of Borysthenes, to whom the development of the diatribe as a genre probably is due."[49]

Lucilius, Lucretius, and Horace all wrote hexameter adaptations of the diatribes of Bion. Although Horace is explicit about his debt to Lucilius, he is completely silent about Lucretius, with whom he must have been familiar. Indeed, parallels between the *De Rerum Natura* and the various works of Horace are often striking and have been used to show some fellow feeling on the part of Horace, an erstwhile Epicurean, for the philosophical mission of Lucretius.[50] *Satires* 1.1 alone shows a number of close parallels. Besides similarities in diction and style common to didactic poetry in hexameters, we see the life of man compared to seafaring and warfare (1.1.4–7), exactly as at *De Rerum Natura* 2.1–6;[51] discontent (μεμψιμοιρία), the initial theme of *Satires* 1.1, was used by Lucretius at *De Rerum Natura* 3.1060–70, and the teacher who hands out cookies to his pupils is immediately reminiscent of the physician's honeyed cups (*De Rerum Natura* 1.936–50); the themes *intra fines naturae* and *finis quaerendi* have obvious Lucretian parallels (see *De Rerum Natura* 5.1432–33), along with the *conviva satur* of 1.1.119, which strongly resembles *De Rerum Natura* 3.938 and 960.

Other parallels could be cited. These alone suffice to suggest that the influence of the *De Rerum Natura* upon the diatribe satires is fairly obvious. It must be remembered, however, that both authors had recourse to Bion, Lucilius, Varro, and numerous other writers who made use of the same themes, which were part of a common pool, making it virtually impossible to trace a given theme to a specific source. The banquet of life theme, for example, which concludes *Satires* 1.1, several scholars have taken as a direct reference to the *De Rerum Natura*.[52] This may well be true. It is worth noting, however, that, before Lucretius, the analogy was used by Aristotle, Epicurus, Chrysippus, Bion, and many others to whose works Horace certainly

[49] Ibid., 11.

[50] See especially N. DeWitt, "Epicurean Doctrine in Horace," *Classical Philology* 34 (1939): 127–34; and C. Murley, "Lucretius and the History of Satire," *Transactions of the American Philological Association* 70 (1939): 380–95. For more recent notes on Horace's Epicureanism, see R. Nisbet and M. Hubbard, *A Commentary on Horace: Odes Book 1* (Oxford: Clarendon Press, 1970), 376–79.

[51] For dictional parallels, see Murley, "Lucretius," 392. On the themes of seafaring and warfare in diatribe, see Oltramare, *Diatribe romaine*, 122 and theme 52.

[52] See, for example, Murley, "Lucretius," 383–84, and J. Glazewski, "*Plenus Vitae Conviva*: A Lucretian Concept in Horace's *Satires*," *Classical Bulletin* 47 (1971): 85–88.

had recourse.[53] The safer inference is that both Lucretius and Horace drew from the same pool; they were part of the same trend of vigorous experimentation in the various forms of diatribe so characteristic of late republican literature. Even if one is to assume that Horace borrowed much directly from Lucretius, it would be wrong to conclude with Mendell that Horace regarded his work in the same vein as the *De Rerum Natura*, "as a popular presentation of philosophy," or that the *De Rerum Natura* in its turn must be given a significant place in the history of satire, as Murley has argued.[54] This is to make far too much of Lucretius as satirist and Horace as a moralist.

Diatribe, in the age of Horace, was pursued by pedants, dogmatic philosophers, and their parodists. The evidence of the *Satires* themselves suggests that Horace was one such parodist and that the persona of the diatribe satires was drawn along lines suggested by a well-known contemporary type. The first personal reference made in the *Satires*, other than the dedication to Maecenas, is to a certain windbag named Fabius, a Stoic philosophical writer (1.1.13–14):

> cetera de genere hoc adeo sunt multa, loquacem
> delassare valent Fabium.

Other illustrations of this type—so many are they—could wear out the windbag Fabius.

Of interest here is the manner in which the satirist hints that the illustrations that open the satire, all quite typical of diatribe, might well be found in the works of Fabius. The lampoon, as a result, cuts both ways; for in attempting to distance himself from the garrulous works of Fabius, the satirist has, in fact, underscored the comparison. The same is true of the lampoon that concludes the satire (1.1.120–21):

> Iam satis est. ne me Crispini scrinia lippi
> compilasse putes, verbum non amplius addam.

That's enough for now. And lest you think that I have pilfered the bookcases of bleary-eyed Crispinus, I will add not another word.

Here again, as at 1.1.13–14, the satirist has caught hold of himself after rattling off his illustrations at length. He begs not to be compared with Crispinus, who, Pseudacron relates, was not only a dogmatic Stoic but a writer of verse. As before, the lampoon implies that the audience perceived some obvious connection between the satirist's moralizing and that of Crispinus. There is a self-parodic side to

---

[53] For the history of this theme, see Kindstrand, *Bion*, 281–82.

[54] See Murley, "Lucretius," 394, and C. Mendell, "Satire as Popular Philosophy," *Classical Philology* 15 (1920): 138–57.

this lampoon in its suggestion that the satirist has himself slipped into the very incompetence that he derides. No one seriously doubts that *Satires* 2.3 and 2.7 should be regarded as parodies of Stoic diatribe, specifically the works of Stertinius and Crispinus, because they are put into the mouths of a wastrel-turned-Stoic and a converted slave. Yet, in the diatribe satires of Book 1, when a voice claiming to be Horace makes use of precisely the same diction, themes, and illustrations in a most awkward fashion, the parody escapes us. Logical failings, dictional quirks, and the like are written off as the rough edges of youth: Horace will hit his stride in the *Odes*, where his impetuosity and anger subside, giving him the chance to write really fine verse. Such apologies fail to respect the double tradition of diatribe, which, by 35 B.C., in its revival among the Stoic and Epicurean dogmatists, had once again grown ripe for parody. Horace certainly saw the humorous, parodic possibilities suggested in the works of Crispinus, Fabius, and Stertinius, and he strongly hints in *Satires* 1.1. and elsewhere that this is exactly the direction he chose to take.[55]

THE PERSONA AND SELF-PARODY

We have seen already the colorful extremes of the satirist's Cynic persona: he is a convert, a social misfit, and addled sermonizer. Such character traits, while certainly humorous, are fully in keeping with the seriocomic spirit of a Bion or Phoenix, serious moralizers who consciously sought to avoid every hint of social savvy and abstract sophistication. In themselves such extremes do not seriously detract from the philosopher's ethical mission. Rather, like the humorous loose ends of Socrates, bare feet and all, they suggest simplicity and freedom, inspiring trust in the listener. There is a second side to the satirist, however, a degree of gross ineptitude that far exceeds the norms of self-irony demanded by the Socratic dialogue or Cynic diatribe. His lessons, caricatures of real learning, are humorously flawed, and they demand that we not take him too seriously as a moralist. As a philosopher he is inept, fickle, and unable to handle the traditional themes and illustrations entrusted to him. His shortcomings, obvious at every turn, suggest that he is himself the chief object of satire.

At several places in the first four satires of Book 1, the satirist

[55] Consider Pseudacron's note *ad Satires* 1.1.120: *Sufficit ergo, inquit, me de avaris dixisse, hoc est me Stoice locutum esse* ("I have said enough," he says, "about the greedy"; that is, "I have spoken enough in a Stoic manner"). See Keller, *Pseudacronis Scholia*, 15.

makes claims that, taken separately, seem reasonable, yet, when considered together, appear overstated, false, or contradictory. An important case in point concerns the satirist's declared mission as a moral reformer. In the opening lines of *Satires* 1.4 the satirist defends the public, censorial function of his work by claiming that satire, after the manner of Lucilius, is the legacy of Old Comedy.[56] The claim is certainly simplistic and one-sided for Horace's day, bearing little relation to the satirist's actual practices in the first three satires of Book 1.[57] Yet the claim does have some theoretical respectability, and, if we indulge the satirist, we can accept his simple equation: Old Comedy = Public Censure against Criminals = Lucilius. As the satire proceeds, however, the satirist makes a case for himself that directly contradicts this equation. At 1.4.65–74 he claims that criminals have nothing to fear from him as they do from the libel mongers Sulcius and Caprius; his works are not available to the general public, for he recites them only to a few select friends, behind closed doors, and that only when compelled.[58] The public, censorial function of satire is completely absent, and no amount of indulgence can reverse the obvious contradiction. The satirist, it seems, cannot be trusted. Even with effort, it is difficult to take him at his word and regard him as a serious moralist.

More obvious than the internal contradictions of *Satires* 1.4 is the satirist's blatant incompetence in handling the traditional themes and illustrations of diatribe. *Satires* 1.1, for example, opens with the *mempsimoiria* theme. The point of this motif in traditional diatribe was to show men longing for ways of life clearly and naturally opposite from their own, as at Pseudo-Hippocrates *Epistle* 17:[59]

[56] On the association of Old Comedy to censorship, an idea not original to Horace, see Fraenkel, *Horace*, 126, n. 2; C. Van Rooy *Studies in Classical Satire and Related Literary Theory* (Leiden: E. J. Brill, 1966), 148 and 174, n. 16; and R. LaFleur, "Horace and *Onomasti Komodein*: The Law of Satire," *Aufstieg und Niedergang der römischen Welt* 2.31.3 (1981) 1795, nn. 9 and 10.

[57] Horace pays respect to the artistic abilities of the Old Comic poets by referring to them as *poetae* (*Satires* 1.4.1), a term he uses very carefully throughout the satire. A second reference to Old Comedy at *Satires* 1.10.14–17 again treats matters of poetic style (see Chapter 2). Even Cicero, who generally took a hard line against the open attack of Old Comedy (see *De Re Publica* 4.10–12), was able to appreciate Aristophanes as a poet (see *De Legibus* 2.15.37, and 3.1.19). Even so, the satirist's claims at 1.4.1–5 are rather simplistic and one-sided in their emphasis on invective directed against "thieves, adulterers, and murderers." How, for example, would Aristophanes' *Frogs* or *Clouds* fit into this scheme?

[58] I owe this observation to Zetzel, "Horace's *Liber Sermonum*," 62–64. See also P. Langford, "Horace's Protean Satire: Public Life, Ethics, and Literature in 'Satires II'" (Ph.D. diss., Princeton University, 1989), 22–25.

[59] Cited by Fraenkel, *Horace*, 93.

ἡγεμόνες καὶ βασιλέες μακαρίζουσι τὸν ἰδιώτην, ὁ δὲ ἰδιώτης ὀρέγεται βασιλείης,
ὁ πολιτευόμενος τὸν χειροτεχνεῦντα ὡς ἀκίνδυνον, ὁ δὲ χειροτέχνης ἐκεῖνον ὡς
ἐυτονεῦντα κατὰ πάντων.

Generals and kings praise the commoner's life, while the commoner
strives for royal power. The politician praises the craftsman's life, free
from danger, while the craftsman praises the politician, since he is free
to do whatever he wishes.

The theme treats opposite extremes and the futility of envy: the
craftsman leads a dull existence, the politician a dangerous one, so
that, in avoiding the one extreme, the fool who despises his own life
makes straight for its opposite. Horace uses this same theme quite
effectively in *Odes* 1.1. In *Satires* 1.1., however, the theme is severely
distorted (*Satires* 1.1.1–12):

> Qui fit, Maecenas, ut nemo, quam sibi sortem
> seu ratio dederit seu fors obiecerit, illa
> contentus vivat, laudet diversa sequentis?
> 'o fortunati mercatores!' gravis annis
> miles ait, multo iam fractus membra labore.
> contra mercator navem iactantibus Austris
> 'militia est potior. quid enim? concurritur: horae
> momento cita mors venit aut victoria laeta.'
> agricolam laudat iuris legumque peritus,
> sub galli cantum consultor ubi ostia pulsat.
> ille, datis vadibus qui rure extractus in urbem est,
> solos felicis viventis clamat in urbe.

How come, Maecenas, no one lives content with his own lot in life—
whether given by reason or thrust upon him by chance; rather he praises
those who follow other paths: "Oh those lucky sea merchants," says the
soldier, heavy in years, his body now broken by great toil. Yet the merchant, when his ship is tossed by wind from the south: "Military life is
better. Why, you ask? A battle stirs. The outcome is immediate, either
death or pleasant victory." The jurisconsult praises the farmer when,
right before sunrise, his client rattles at the door. The farmer, however,
when he has posted bond and is dragged from the country into the city
claims that citydwellers alone are happy.

In each case, the satirist, against all precedent, makes his characters
choose a way of life that contains the very problems they seek to
avoid: the soldier desires the life of the merchant, supposing that he
alone is secure and carefree. Yet, ever since Solon and throughout

the history of diatribe, seafaring was associated with shipwreck, folly, and distress.[60] We expect the soldier to choose a style of life in clear contrast to his own, but, as D. Blickman has recently shown, the motifs of military service and seafaring were virtually synonymous in Horace's day. They had become symbols of "the misery that results from an ignorance of the proper aims of life."[61] The soldier's choice, then, is laughable. Likewise the merchant should, according to the best precedents of diatribe, long for a simple country existence, as at *Odes* 1.1.15–18:

> luctantem Icariis fluctibus Africum
> mercator metuens otium et oppidi
> laudat rura sui.

The merchant, fearing the west wind as it fights the Icarian waves, praises the relaxation and country setting of his old hometown.

In *Satires* 1.1, however, the merchant praises military life, arguing that death comes quickly to the soldier, even though we have just been informed that the complaining soldier is heavy in years (*gravis annis*) and long-suffering. The jurisconsult wishes that he were a farmer so that he could sleep late in the mornings—again a laugh—and the farmer is somehow convinced that a day in court represents city life at its most elegant. Overall, the traditional logic of the *mempsimoiria* theme has been severely skewed. We laugh at the illustration and at the moralist himself, who has so blatantly mishandled it.

Parody of the conventions of diatribe is again apparent at *Satires* 1.2.68–72, where the satirist tries his hand at the Cynic convention of personification.[62] Bion seems to have used this device frequently and to great effect. For example, at F17 he allows circumstances, τὰ πράγματα, to take on a human voice and address its detractor (3–5):

> τί μοι μάχη; μή τί σοι κέκλοφα; οὐ πᾶν τὸ
> προσταττόμενον ὑπὸ σοῦ ποιῶ; οὐ τὴν
> ἀποφορὰν εὐτάκτως σοι φέρω;

---

[60] For an early version of the *mempsimoiria* theme, see Solon fragment 1, especially lines 43–46, on the greed and folly of seafaring.

[61] D. Blickman, "Lucretius, Epicurus, and Prehistory," *Harvard Studies in Classical Philology* 92 (1989): 179.

[62] "Personifications of abstract concepts are common in Greek literature, especially in philosophy of a more popular kind, such as the Cynic, as it must be considered as a very effective way of attracting listeners." Kindstrand, *Bion*, 213. See Kindstrand's notes *ad* F17 for numerous examples of the device in Greek popular philosophy.

Why do you struggle against me? I have not deceived you, have I? Am I not doing all that you command? Am I not bringing you a healthy profit?

In the same fragment he allows poverty, πενία, to take on a voice and address its detractor in much the same vein. In both cases, the abstraction addresses its accuser (τὸν ἐγκαλοῦντα), chides him for being a fool distraught by his own greed, and proceeds to give sound advice on living within nature's bounds. At *Satires* 1.2.68–72, the satirist has retained the basic shape of the motif, but he has radically altered its contents:

> huic si muttonis verbis mala tanta videnti
> diceret haec animus "quid vis tibi? numquid ego a te
> magno prognatum deposco consule cunnum
> velatumque stola, mea cum conferbuit ira?"
> quid responderet? "magno patre nata puella est."

Imagine that the man experiencing such evils should hear his dick's voice: "What is it you want? When my dander is up do I demand of you a cunt wrapped in a stole, descended from a mighty consul?" What would he respond? "The girl has an influential father."

No matter how earnestly the satirist may seem to intend the lesson at hand, one cannot escape the fact that he has here presented the picture of a man arguing with his own penis. Unlike the personifications of Bion, the picture is simply too absurd and distracting to command sober reflection on the part of the reader.[63] The satirist has taken the old Cynic convention to an extreme, and with a straight face he pretends to maintain his earnest didactic intent.[64] This brilliant piece of parody takes as its primary target the satirist himself.

Earlier in the same satire the satirist makes several other humorous gaffes that call into question his competence as a moralizer. At *Satires* 1.2.35 he again crosses the boundary between the seriocomic and the burlesque by putting the extremely coarse term, *permolere* ("grind away at"), into the mouth of none other than Cato the Elder.[65] We can assume that the Stoic sermonizers were in the habit of quoting their favorite in a more reverent vein. In the lines that follow, the

[63] "Horace's talking penis is apparently unique in ancient poetry, although Lucilius (fragment 237) had been gross enough to picture one weeping." Armstrong, *Horace*, 35.

[64] In contrast to Fiske, *Lucilius and Horace*, 265, I see no reason for regarding Porphyrion's note on line 68—*muttonem pro virili membro dixit Lucilium imitatus*—as referring to the personification of the *mutto*, but simply to the use of the term itself.

[65] On the tone of *permolere*, see J. Adams, *The Latin Sexual Vocabulary* (Baltimore: Johns Hopkins University Press, 1982), 152–55.

satirist attempts to apply the theme *modus in rebus* where it simply cannot work by suggesting that freedwomen (*merx in classe secunda*, 47) somehow strike a balance between two extremes of sexual behavior, that is, prostitution (1.2.31–36) and adultery with high-class matrons (1.2.37–46). He quickly realizes that his handy moral formula—virtue equals the extremes of vice divided by two—will not work in this case, and he reverts to arguments that, in good Cynic fashion, strongly favor sex with women of the lowest class.

The satirist, it is obvious, is no *sapiens*. He cannot handle the themes and illustrations of Greek popular philosophy. Much less can he handle topics that demand a certain degree of theoretical knowledge, as he demonstrates at *Satires* 1.3.96–124, where he attempts to employ an Epicurean proof on the emergence of human laws against the Stoic paradox, "all sins are equal." The exposition that results is humorously flawed. It is intended as a parody of Epicurean doctrine, a "mock history of the social contract," not as an effective argument against the Stoics.[66] In the space of fewer than twenty lines, the satirist treats a full range of themes, such as the origins of animals and language, the building of cities, and the invention of laws, all of which Lucretius treated at great length in Book 5 of his *De Rerum Natura*.[67] The satirist piles them together in a haphazard fashion only to conclude (*Satires* 1.3.107–12):

> (nam fuit ante Helenam cunnus taeterrima belli
> causa, sed ignotis perierunt mortibus illi
> quos Venerem incertam rapientis more ferarum
> viribus editior caedebat, ut in grege taurus).
> iura inventa metu iniusti fateare necesse est,
> tempora si fastosque velis evolvere mundi.

For even before Helen the cunt was the most dreadful cause of war. But in those days men died in obscurity; randomly gratifying their lusts like beasts, they were cut down by a stronger rival, as happens with bulls in the herd. If you are willing to page through the seasons and annals of the world, you will be forced to admit that laws are established in the fear of injustice.

The philosophical discussion ends in bathos. *Causa*, a term packed with meaning and regarded with due reverence by Epicureans, the

---

[66] Armstrong, *Horace*, 40.

[67] See especially *De Rerum Natura* 5.925–1457. I. M. Le M. DuQuesnay, "Horace and Maecenas," in T. Woodman and D. West, eds., *Poetry and Politics in the Age of Augustus* (Cambridge: Cambridge University Press, 1984), 32–33, and n. 58, traces other possible verbal echoes of Lucretius in *Satires* 1–4. Noting the broad philosophical range of many such passages and the apparent irony of others, it is very difficult to make a case for Horace's Epicureanism on the basis of the diatribe satires.

satirist equates with *cunnus*, and somehow—the connection is not clear, thus the parentheses—he uses this observation to bolster his conclusion that human laws result from the fear of injustice.[68] This is parody of the broadest sort. The satirist has severely botched the illustration at hand and, as a result, trivialized the erudition of Stoics and Epicureans alike. Once again, the chief source of humor rests in self-parody, the satirist's own incompetence.

SELF-PARODY AND THE INFLUENCE OF THE COMIC STAGE

Despite the many tendencies shared between the *Satires* and Greek popular philosophy, there is a second side to the satiric persona, a degree of overt incompetence which both destroys his credibility as a moralizer and seriously questions any direct analogy with Bion, Socrates, or any other true moral philosopher. The diatribe satires are, in fact, parodies of diatribe, after the manner of Callimachus, Menippus, Varro, and certainly others. Yet a third influence is suggested in the very nature of the satirist's incompetence, which is multifaceted, highly conventionalized, drawn along lines well known to Horace from the stage of popular comedy.

It is precisely in the various expressions of self-parody and ineptitude, where the Bion equation fails, that Horace reveals the strong influence of comedy upon his *Satires*. The many facets of the satirist's incompetence Horace has carefully selected and crafted in accordance with a well-known comic type. The clearest illustration of this we see at *Satires* 1.3.29–34:

> iracundior est paulo, minus aptus acutis
> naribus horum hominum: rideri possit eo quod
> rusticius tonso toga diffluit et male laxus
> in pede calceus haeret: at est bonus, ut melior vir
> non alius quisquam, at tibi amicus, at ingenium ingens
> inculto latet hoc sub corpore.

He is rather hot-tempered, and ill-suited to modern social sensibilities. One might laugh at his toga, which hangs bumpkinlike, even worse than his haircut, and his shoe, which hangs terribly loose on his foot. Yet, he is a good man—you will find none better—and a devoted friend, whose uncultured exterior hides a vast intelligence.

Commentators on this passage have long puzzled over the identification of the character described. Their traditional aversion to the idea

---

[68] On *causa* as a catchword for Epicurean theory, see K. Freudenburg, "Lucretius, Vergil, and the *Causa Morbi*," *Vergilius* 33 (1987): 59–74.

that the satirist here describes himself is based on the false assumption that Horace and the satiric persona are one and the same.[69] Thus, given a choice, they have preferred the more sophisticated image projected elsewhere, such as the Epicurean playboy of the *Odes*, to the graceless bumpkin described here. Yet, as we have seen, the satirist has a distinct bumpkinlike side to his personality, which fits this image quite nicely. Admitting, then, that all is fiction, we should readily admit the possibility that the unnamed misfit of *Satires* 1.3.29–34 is none other than the satirist himself.

A similar passage at *Epistles* 1.1.94–97 makes the identification with the speaker quite certain:

> Si curatus inaequali tonsore capillos
> occurri, rides; si forte subucula pexae
> trita subest tunicae vel si toga dissidet impar,
> rides.

If I show up with lopsided hair, clipped by an unsteady barber, you laugh. If the shirt under my new tunic is tattered, or if my toga hangs askew, you laugh.

Here there is no doubt that the speaker refers to himself. The similarities connecting this passage with *Satires* 1.3.29–34 are striking, especially considering the petty nature of the details described. A closer look at *Epistles* 1.1, however, shows that such details are far from insignificant; they manifest an attempt by Horace to recreate with utmost precision the persona he projected so many years before in the diatribe satires of Book 1.

The opening lines of *Epistles* 1.1 allude to past literary efforts of the speaker (*Epistles* 1.1.1–3):

> Prima dicte mihi, summa dicende Camena,
> spectatum satis et donatum iam rude quaeris,
> Maecenas, iterum antiquo me includere ludo?

Maecenas, told by my earliest muse and now to be told by my last, do you seek again to shut me within my old school, though the crowds have seen enough of me and I have been discharged from the arena?

---

[69] Typical is the view of A. Kiessling and R. Heinze, *Q. Horatius Flaccus: Satiren* (Berlin: Weidmannsche Verlagsbuchhandlung, 1961), 51: "One should not think that Horace intends this as a description of himself." Commentators universally reject the scholiast's suggestion that the satirist refers to Vergil. Concerning the case for the satirist himself, see especially Lejay and Plessis, *Oeuvres d'Horace*, 77–78, and R.S.W. Hawtrey, "The Poet as Example: Horace's Use of Himself," in Carl Deroux, ed., *Studies in Latin Literature and Roman History*, vol. 1, Collection *Latomus* 164 (Brussels: Latomus Revue d'Études Latines, 1979), 249–56. Both Hawtrey and Lejay assume that these lines refer to traits of Horace himself, rather than to the persona he has created.

The retired gladiator analogy is maintained only briefly, and it quickly becomes apparent that the "old school" to which the speaker returns is his old persona. Once again he takes on the role of the old Cynic moralizer preaching in hexameters.[70] He is no *sapiens*, committed to the teachings of any particular sect (see *Epistles* 1.1.13–15). He addresses the very themes he addressed in *Satires* 1.1–3 (*Epistles* 1.1.33–36, *avaritia, cupido, amor*, and 90–93, *mempsimoiria*). He uses fables (73–75), and maxims (20, 41–42, and 52), just as the satirist of the diatribes.[71] He has the same uneven haircut, the same ill-fitting clothes, and, we are tempted to assume, the same pair of floppy shoes (see 94–98, quoted previously). Perhaps most important of all, he has the satirist's eye for the folly of human behavior (98–105), and the same penchant for self-parody.

Fifteen years or so after his initial appearance, Horace has recreated his old persona in painstaking detail, right down to his silly haircut and ill-fitting clothes. The picture is precisely that of *Satires* 1.3.29–34. David Armstrong has recently suggested that throughout *Satires* 1.3, not just in lines 29–34, we are to think that the satirist describes himself; he is the drunkard of lines 90–94 who pisses on the dinner couch, breaks an antique goblet, grabs a piece of chicken from the wrong side of the plate, and so on.[72] The suggestion is attractive, for this is just the type of behavior we have come to expect of the speaker, who is something of a social menace.[73] Horace himself, in all likelihood, never pissed on Maecenas's couch, and he probably dressed quite well. He certainly could afford to. These subtle

---

[70] On the overall importance of Cynicism in Book 1 of the *Epistles*, see J. Moles, "Cynicism in Horace *Epistles* 1," *Papers of the Liverpool Latin Seminar* 5 (1985): 33–60.

[71] Note that *Epistles* 1.1.20 may be a clever reference to *Satires* 1.5.82–85.

[72] See Armstrong, *Horace*, 37–41. Compare *Miles Gloriosus* 648–56, where Periplectomenus contrasts his own refined habits with the loathesome table manners of Apulians: "I am from Ephesus. I wasn't born in Apulia [*Ephesi sum natus, non enim in Apulis*]. . . . I never fondle someone else's girl at a dinner party, nor do I make a grab for the appetizers, or snatch the cup out of turn." The description is the playwright's own tour de force in the conventions of character portrayal (*ethopoeia*). Palaestrio congratulates Periplectomenus (and thereby, Plautus) at line 763 for being "a good man when it comes to describing bad manners" (*Bonus bene ut malos descripsit mores*), calling attention to the studied nature of his descriptions of character. Horace, an Apulian by birth, may well intend us to see himself in the Plautine role suggested in *Satires* 1.3.29–34.

[73] At *Satires* 1.3.63–66 the satirist draws attention to his lack of social charm:

> simplicior quis et est qualem me saepe libenter
> obtulerim tibi, Maecenas, ut forte legentem
> aut tacitum impellat quovis sermone molestus:
> "communi sensu plane caret" inquimus.

There is one who is rather straightforward—as often I would willingly present myself to you, Maecenas—so that the pest goads with some sort of chatter one who is reading or at rest: "The man clearly lacks social tact," we say.

details, while worthless as autobiography, Horace's audience regarded as highly connotative bits of fiction, cleverly devised to suggest literary antecedents behind the creation of the satiric persona.

An interesting parallel to the satirist's persona is seen in the rustic or bumpkin, ἄγροικος, of Theophrastus (*Characters* 4.1–5):

ὁ δὲ ἄγροικος τοιοῦτός τις, οἷος κυκεῶνα πιὼν εἰς ἐκκλησίαν πορεύεσθαι, καὶ τὸ μύρον φάσκειν οὐδὲν τοῦ θύμου ἥδιον ὄζειν, καὶ μείζω τοῦ ποδὸς τὰ ὑποδήματα φορεῖν, μεγάλῃ τῇ φωνῇ λαλεῖν . . . καὶ ἀναβεβλημένος ἄνω τοῦ γόνατος καθιζάνειν, ὥστε τὰ γυμνὰ αὐτοῦ φαίνεσθαι.

The bumpkin is the sort who, having just downed his onion brew, walks into the public assembly and asserts that myrrh smells no sweeter than garlic, and he wears sandals too big for his feet. He chatters with a loud voice . . . and he sits down with his clothes pulled up above the knee, so that he leaves his privates exposed.

It is commonly assumed that Theophrastus's character sketches both influenced and themselves owe a great deal to the influence of the comic stage.[74] The sketch of the boor, as Ussher has noted, clearly shows this influence. Antiphanes, Anaxilas, Philemon, and Menander all wrote comedies entitled *The Boor* (Ἄγροικος), and certainly others must have employed the theme as well.[75] The boor in comedy was traditionally a rustic, untrained in the sophisticated ways of city life. Compare the rustic Kleainetos in Menander's *Georgos* (97K):

εἰμὶ μὲν ἄγροικος, καὐτὸς οὐκ ἄλλως
ἐρῶ, καὶ τῶν κατ᾽ ἄστυ πραγμάτων οὐ
παντελῶς ἔμπειρος.

I am a rustic, I will not deny it, and I am entirely unskilled in the ways of the city.

The obvious point of interest, here, lay in the close parallels between this type and the persona of the satirist. Both are social misfits, loud and unrestrained, maintaining at the same time a certain attractive simplicity and honesty. Both wear their garments in a humorous, rustic manner and, once again, we see the floppy shoe.

The floppy shoe I regard as one of those tiny details of enormous significance that I mentioned at the beginning of this chapter. Ever

---

[74] See especially T.B.L. Webster, *Studies in Menander* (Manchester: Manchester University Press, 1950), 197–217, *An Introduction to Menander* (Manchester: Manchester University Press, 1974), 43–55; R. G. Ussher, *The Characters of Theophrastus* (London: Macmillan, 1960), 3–14; and R. L. Hunter, *The New Comedy of Greece and Rome* (Cambridge: Cambridge University Press, 1985), 148–49.

[75] For references, see Ussher, *Theophrastus*, 55, n. 2, and T. Kock, *Comicorum Graecorum Fragmenta*, vol. 2 (Leipzig: Teubner, 1880–88) 12.

since Aristophanes, it seems that various bumpkins and buffoons of comedy were portrayed in shoes much too big for their feet. Besides making for a ridiculous appearance, oversized shoes would have caused a loud, uneven "galumphing" sound as the character crossed the stage, adding an element of farce to the scene. Evidence for the convention we see at *Knights* 315–21, where Aristophanes takes aim at Cleon (the Paphlagonian), claiming that he was once a shoemaker, and a very dishonest one at that:

SS: εἰ δὲ μὴ σύ γ᾽ οἶσθα κάττυμ᾽, οὐδ᾽ ἐγὼ χορδεύματα,
    ὅστις ὑποτέμνων ἐπώλεις δέρμα μοχθηροῦ βοὸς
    τοῖς ἀγροίκοισιν πανούργως, ὥστε φαίνεσθαι παχύ,
    καὶ πρὶν ἡμέραν φορῆσαι, μεῖζον ἦν δυοῖν δοχμαῖν.

NT: νὴ Δία κἀμὲ τοῦτ᾽ ἔδρασε ταὐτόν, ὥστε καὶ γέλων
    πάμπολυν τοῖς δημόταισι καὶ φίλοις παρασχεθεῖν·
    πρὶν γὰρ εἶναι Περγασῆσιν, ἔνεον ἐν ταῖς ἐμβάσιν.

SS: I don't know my sausages if you don't yourself know the shoe trade. You're the one who used to sell shoes to rustics, ripping them off by making crooked cuts of leather from a miserable hide. The shoe seemed sturdy but, before being worn for a day, it was ten inches too wide.

NI: Yes, by god, he did the very same thing to me, so that I have become a laughingstock throughout the city to friends and fellow citizens alike. For before I got to Pergasae I was swimming in my shoes.

Oversized shoes were, apparently, the stock-in-trade of rustics (τοῖς ἀγροίκοισιν) and various other fools of the comic stage, such as the Sausage Seller and Nicias themselves. Horace certainly knew of this convention. He refers to it at *Epistles* 2.1.170–74, where he uses the metaphor of running to take aim at Plautus's loose compositional technique:

> aspice Plautus
> quo pacto partis tutetur amantis ephebi,
> ut patris attenti, lenonis ut insidiosi,
> quantus sit Dossennus edacibus in parasitis,
> quam non adstricto percurrat pulpita socco.

Look at how Plautus presents the part of the young lover, the strict father, and the faithless pimp. See what a buffoon he is among the greedy parasites and how he runs across the stage with a floppy shoe.[76]

[76] On the satirist as parasite, see my comments in Chapter 4. Compare Harpax's description of the slave Pseudolus at *Pseudolus* 1219–20: "He has a large head, sharp eyes, a ruddy face, and tremendous feet [*admodum magnis pedibus*]."

References such as these indicate that the satirist's floppy shoe is far from insignificant, for it explains something about the spirit in which the persona of the diatribe satires was intended. Along with his uneven haircut and ill-fitting clothes, the floppy shoe of *Satires* 1.3.31–32 bears direct reference to the conventions of the comic stage, rendering the satirist a bumpkin or buffoon.[77] As a moralist, then, we would expect some rather unbalanced, self-parodic sermonizing from this character, exactly as we have it in the diatribe satires of Book 1. He invites laughter, both at the dogmatism he so curiously mishandles and at himself as an inept moralizer.

The idea of blending the characters of the Cynic moralizer and the bumpkin or buffoon was, in all likelihood, not original to Horace but was itself the legacy of popular comedy. Already in Bion's day it appears that the Cynic moralizer had made his way onto the comic stage. A scene from Menander's *Pilots*, for example, portrays an unnamed moralizer preaching to a young man on the elusive value of material wealth (301K):

τἀργύριον εἶναι, μειράκιον, σοι φαίνεται
οὐ τῶν ἀναγκαίων καθ᾽ ἡμέραν μόνον
τιμὴν παρασχεῖν δυνατόν, ἄρτων, ἀλφίτων,
ὄξους, ἐλαίου, μείζονος δ᾽ ἄλλου τινός;
ἀθανασίας δ᾽ οὐκ ἔστιν, οὐδ᾽ ἂν συναγάγῃς
τὰ Ταντάλου τάλαντ᾽ ἐκεῖνα λεγόμενα ·
ἀλλ᾽ ἀποθανεῖ καὶ ταῦτα καταλείψεις τισίν.

Young man, do you suppose that money can purchase anything beyond the basic necessities of bread, meal, vinegar, and oil? Immortality has no price, not even were you to stockpile the legendary talents of Tantalus. But you will die and leave these things to others.

Although the character is unnamed, his type is well known: his moral superiority, reverence for poverty and simple foods, his reference to the proverbial wealth of Tantalus and the death of the rich fool all point to the Cynic moralizer.

The lines that separate the Cynic moralizer from the bumpkin or buffoon were severely blurred on the stage of New Comedy. Julius Pollux, a scholar and rhetorician of the second century A.D. who has left significant notes on the costumes of comedy, records at *Onomasticon* 4.119: πήρα, βακτηρία, διφθέρα ἐπὶ τῶν ἀγροίκων ("a wallet, walking stick, and travel bag belong to rustics").[78] Pollux goes on to note that parasites were characterized in much the same way, with the ad-

---

[77] The *dossennus* reference of *Epistles* 2.1.170–74 equates Plautus to the "hunchback," a stock character in the Atellan farces.

[78] See C. Saunders, *Costume in Roman Comedy* (New York: AMS Press, 1966), 135.

dition of a strigil and oil flask. These, of course, are the traditional appurtenances of the beggar Cynic as well. Saturio, playing the role of the buffoon/parasite in the *Persa*, stresses his likeness to the Cynic philosopher (*Persa* 123–26):

> cynicum esse egentem oportet parasitum probe:
> ampullam, strigilem, scaphium, soccos, pallium,
> marsuppium habeat, inibi paullum praesidi,
> qui familiarem suam vitam oblectet modo.

The parasite must really be a beggar Cynic: let him have his flask, his blade, his cup, shoes, cloak and wallet, with just enough therein to provide for his own family comfort.

As Philip Corbett has recently shown, in the tradition of New Comedy at Rome, the Cynic beggar and the parasite/buffoon were virtually synonymous:

It would seem that, by Horace's time, the professional *Scurra* is to be linked with the Cynic beggar philosopher, who is also an *imi subselli vir*. He has then, by this time, been relegated to the position of the *parasiti ridiculi* of Plautus, who were also, by their dress and language, to be associated with the Cynic tradition of humour.[79]

Horace was well aware of the comic tradition linking Cynic philosophers to professional jesters. At *Satires* 1.1.23–27, for example, he makes a mock apology for his penchant for jest in the illustration of serious moral issues: "Furthermore, lest I ramble on with laughter like one who rattles off jokes [*ne sic, ut qui iocularia, ridens / percurram*] . . . let us seek serious issues with all jesting left behind." The speaker implies that he has sunk nearly to the level of professional jesters, the *scurrae* of the comic stage who earned their bread by jests and were in possession of some of the world's earliest jokebooks. Rather than deny the comparison, the mock apology actually underscores the impression that the satirist is, in essence, a comic figure. He is drawn in the full brilliant colors of the typical Cynic beggar, bumpkin, or buffoon well known to Horace's audience from the stage of popular comedy.

COMIC SELF-DEFINITION IN *SATIRES* 1.4

Viewing the speaker of the diatribe satires as a character from comedy explains the speaker's many humorous inadequacies as a moral-

---

[79] P. Corbett, *The Scurra* (Edinburgh: Scottish Academic Press, 1986), 64.

izer. Like his several counterparts on the comic stage, he is the typical *doctor ineptus*, the moralizer who, as Cynic, rustic, or buffoon, takes himself far more seriously than his abilities will allow. Horace knew this motif, and he alludes to its programmatic significance in *Satires* 1.4, where he recasts his own satiric persona in the portrait of his father. This portrait, which is only superficially intended as a moral validation of satire, speaks directly to the question of Horace's understanding of the relationship of comedy to satire.

It was E. Leach who first lent substantial proof to the suspicion that the portrait of the satirist's father in 1.4 is nothing more than a clever poetic fiction;[80] he is the traditional comic *pater ardens*, cleverly adapted from the character of Demea in the *Adelphi* of Terence. The verbal parallels, the convictions, and characteristics shared between Demea and the satirist's father make the literary influence upon the portrait of 1.4 undeniable. This realization is, initially at least, a bit troubling, for the satirist's father, who seems so real, is regarded with love and respect by his son. We would like to think that such a character did exist in the decadent last days of the Roman Republic and that Horace's work was, just as he says, in some way the result of his teaching. Against this, I would simply argue that the fictional nature of this portrait need not rule out the possibility of its programmatic intent. Quite to the contrary, we can safely assume that Horace had very good reasons for choosing Demea, among all the fictional models available to him, as the single best expression of his satiric persona; for the fact that both the satirist and his father have been adapted from popular comedy suggests that the analogy with comedy was somehow central to Horace's understanding of satire. Nowhere is this more evident than in the famous portrait of the Elder Horace.

The characteristics and attitudes shared between Demea and the satirist, both on his own and in the person of his fictional father, are many and striking. We note, for example, their shared moral and educational convictions. Like the satirist, Demea is a rustic, trained in the simple country wisdom taught by experience. He instructs his son

---

[80] E. W. Leach, "Horace's *Pater Optimus* and Terence's Demea: Autobiographical Fiction and Comedy in *Sermo* 1.4," *American Journal of Philology* 92 (1971): 616–32. See also Coffey, *Roman Satire*, 74 and 229, n. 49. Referring to *Satires* 1.4.105–26, David Armstrong asserts: "No educated listener in Horace's circle can have missed behind this seemingly autobiographical scene the allusion to *The Brothers* by the Roman comic playwright Terence, produced more than a hundred years earlier." Armstrong, *Horace*, 3. Although several scholars have taken seriously the fictional nature of the satirist's portrait of his father, I can cite no commentator on Horace who has integrated this into a larger understanding of Horace's satiric program. Somehow, it seems, comic fiction is central to Horace's understanding of satire, and this is precisely what the portrait of the Elder Horace is designed to convey.

to look at the world around him and see in the lives of others models (*exempla*) for his own moral conduct (*Adelphi* 414–416):

> nil praetermitto; consuefacio; denique
> inspicere tamquam in speculum in vitas omnium
> iubeo atque ex aliis sumere exemplum sibi.

I pay attention to everything. I have taught [my son] to do the same. In sum, I tell him to reflect upon the ways of all, just as he would look into a mirror, and to take from them a model for his own behavior.

The passage, as Leach and others have indicated, strongly resembles *Satires* 1.4.105–15. No educated reader of Horace's day would have failed to make the connection. The "mirror of life" analogy, as a well-worn motif of Greek popular philosophy, clearly refers Demea's teaching to the traditions of Cynic diatribe.[81] Like the Elder Horace, who also shows distinct traits of the Cynic, he is a self-made wise man. As he relates to his slave Syrus, he keeps to the country, eschewing the more relaxed methods of his alter ego, Micio, to raise his son in accordance with the *mos maiorum* (*Adelphi* 411–12):

DE: salvos sit! spero, est simili' maiorum suom.
SY: hui.
DE: Syre, praeceptorum plenust istorum ille.

DE: Bless him! He is his father's son.
SY: Bravo!
DE: Syrus, that boy is well stocked with those precepts.

Again, the passage bears comparison with the portrait of the satirist's father (*Satires* 1.4.115–19):

> sapiens, vitatu quidque petitu
> sit melius, causas reddet tibi: mi satis est si
> traditum ab antiquis morem servare . . .
> possum.

The philosopher will tell you what to seek and what to avoid, he will relate physical causes. For me it's enough to preserve the morals handed down from your ancestors.

Here the satirist's father shows his Cynic coloring. In similar fashion to *Satires* 1.1.2, he flippantly disregards the abstract speculations of the Stoics, who claimed to teach a science of moral choice, "what to seek and what to avoid" (*vitatu quidque petitu sit melius*), and the Epi-

---

[81] I owe this observation to Oltramare, *Diatribe romaine*, 73–74.

cureans, experts in the physical causes (*causae rerum*).[82] His lessons, like those of Demea, consist of *exempla* drawn from everyday experience. They are designed to dissuade his son from the painful mistakes of his contemporaries. Here again the Elder Horace betrays his comic temperament: he preaches against wasting one's inheritance (*Satires* 1.4.109–11), the engaging of prostitutes (113–15), and adulterous love affairs, a virtual catalog of the traditional sins of the young comic lover. Horace, tongue-in-cheek, implies that he too has a fictional past, and he gives us to suspect that, like Ctesipho, his counterpart in the *Adelphi*, he has not always been the obedient son he pretends to be.

From these few references, we begin to see just how carefully Horace has chosen a fictional model for his father and, in the end, for himself as satirist. Besides their shared educational convictions and their rustic, Cynic coloring, both Demea and the satirist share a distinct penchant for ineptitude. Donatus has observed that Demea commands little respect as a serious moralizer: he advises his son, *ut idioticus et comicus pater, non ut sapiens et praeceptor* ("as an uneducated man, typical of comedy, not as a philosopher and teacher").[83] Given the ancient consensus on Demea, we must wonder at Horace's choice of a model for his father. The comparison, while perfectly suited to the persona of the diatribe satires, is by no means the loving tribute to the Elder Horace it pretends to be.

Throughout the play, Demea boasts about the superiority of his

---

[82] The satirist, at *Satires* 1.4.126–29, defends his father's use of personal *exempla*:

> avidos vicinum funus ut aegros
> exanimat mortisque metu sibi parcere cogit,
> sic teneros animos aliena opprobria saepe
> absterrent vitiis.

As a neighbor's funeral stuns gluttons when sick and compels them with the fear of death to spare themselves, so reproaches directed against others often deter young minds from vice.

The Elder Horace here again shows the distinct markings of a Cynic. Compare Demetrius *On Style* 3.170:

> Χρήσονται δέ ποτε καὶ οἱ φρόνιμοι γελοίοις πρός τε τοὺς καιρούς, οἷον ἐν ἑορταῖς καὶ ἐν συμποσίοις, καὶ ἐν ἐπιπλήξεσιν δὲ πρὸς τοὺς τρυφερωτέρους, . . . τοιοῦτος δὲ ὡς τὸ πλέον καὶ ὁ Κυνικὸς τρόπος.

And sometimes even deep thinkers make use of jests on the right occasions, such as at feasts and drinking parties, and in rebukes directed against those who live too sumptuously . . . this is, for the most part, the Cynic fashion.

On *vitatu quidque petitu sit melius* as a Stoic ethical concern, compare Seneca *Epistles* 66.6.

[83] I owe this observation to R. L. Hunter, "Horace on Friendship and Free Speech," *Hermes* 113 (1985): 490.

own stern pedagogy over the more relaxed methods of his brother. At 417–19, he rehearses his program with his wily slave Syrus:

> DE: hoc facito. SY: recte sane. DE: hoc fugito. SY: callide.
> DE: hoc laudist. SY: istaec res est. DE: hoc vitio datur.
> SY: probissime.

> DE: You should do this. SY: Certainly. DE: And avoid this. SY: Well said.
> DE: This is to be considered praiseworthy. SY: By all means true.
> DE: And this is to be considered a vice. SY: Magnificent!

The slave quickly tires of Demea, who has something about him of the pedantic boor, and before the scene ends, Syrus, with his kitchen utensils in hand, makes a mockery of the pedagogical methods he has just praised (423–27):

> et quod queo
> conservis ad eundem istunc praecipio modum:
> "hoc salsumst, hoc adusumst, hoc lautumst parum;
> illud recte: iterum sic memento." sedulo
> moneo quae possum pro mea sapientia.

> And, as far as I am able, I teach my fellow slaves in this very same method: "This needs salt! That's undercooked! This hasn't been washed! That's well done, remember to do it that way next time!" I make what admonitions I can according to my own special skills.[84]

It must be remembered that the satirist, too, rehearses the pedagogical methods of his father in much the same vein (134–36):

> rectius hoc est;
> hoc faciens vivam melius; sic dulcis amicis
> occurram; hoc quidam non belle: numquid ego illi
> imprudens olim faciam simile?

> This is more honest. I'll be better off with that. This will endear me to my friends. That was ugly conduct of so and so. Could I, without thinking, someday do the same?

The general shape of this passage—the repeated short bursts of thought, each introduced by *hoc*, as well as its placement within the larger context of a father's stern moralizing—suggests that Horace

---

[84] The slave who employs sophisticated technical terms in the sphere of his everyday existence is a basic comic type. For an early parallel compare Aristophanes *Frogs* 971–91.

has fashioned his father, in very specific terms, after the model of Terence's Demea.

As the plot unfolds, it becomes apparent that Demea's methods have been entirely unsuccessful. His son Ctesipho, whom he has kept on the farm, is subject to vice to the same extent as his city-bred brother, Aeschinos. And so, as Demea continues to boast of his "superior" methods, not knowing what the audience knows, he simply makes a fool of himself. For example, at 392–97, the slave Syrus, who has such fun parodying Demea's pedagogical methods at 423–27, ironically invites Demea to make a fool of himself:

> SY: nimium inter vos, Demea,
> (non quia ades praesens dico hoc) pernimium interest,
> tu, quantus quantu's, nil nisi sapientia es,
> ille somnium. num sineres vero illum tuom facere haec?
> DE: sinerem illum? aut non sex totis mensibus
> prius olfecissem quam ille quiquam coeperet?

> SY: There is a great difference between you and your brother, Demea—I say this not because you are present—a tremendous difference. You are wisdom herself, through and through. Your brother is a fool. You wouldn't allow that other son of yours (Ctesipho) to do such things, would you?
> DE: Allow him? Why, wouldn't I have sniffed out the problem six months before it even started?

The audience knows that the exact opposite is true, and so Demea's boast serves only to highlight his incompetence. His failings are matched only by his extreme pride and self-confidence. He is an absurd character, high-minded, sincere, but an utter failure as a moralist. Such are the typical features of the comic *doctor ineptus*.

These very traits make Demea the perfect model for the satiric persona of the diatribe satires, for he too is the typical *doctor ineptus* of comedy. Like Demea, he plays the role of the stern, rustic pedagogue, whose failings are apparent to all but himself. He is, in the end, a character of fiction, and Horace clearly intended him as such. Seeing the satirist in this way, we come to understand something of the spirit in which the diatribe satires were intended: in creating his persona in *Satires* 1.1–4, Horace has drawn an analogy between the practitioners of diatribe—thinking primarily of the severe Stoic preachers of his day, such as Fabius and Crispinus—and their buffoonlike counterparts, the stern rustic moralizers of the comic stage.[85]

[85] On Horace's firsthand knowledge of the Cynic or Stoic popular preacher, see Fiske, *Lucilius and Horace*, 229; D. R. Dudley, *A History of Cynicism* (London: Methuen,

The satirist, then, is a moralizing buffoon, a brilliant blend of two distinct types. All along he has shown his comic coloring—in his blatant mishandling of the themes of popular philosophy, his funny haircut, floppy shoes, and so on. At the end of *Satires* 1.4, however, he makes the comic analogy explicit in the person of his father. Judging from what we know of the satirist, we begin to understand just how important this analogy with comedy is to Horace's satiric program. The reference to Terence's *Adelphi* is perfectly chosen. Much more than a clever allusion, it is the satirist's own self-definition: he is himself a fictional creation playing a part in a comic play. For Horace, it seems that the lines that separate comedy from satire are all but transparent.

THE COMIC PERSONA AND HIS COMIC WORLD

Horace is a dramatist. Not only has he fashioned a dramatic persona for himself as satirist, he has created an entire comic world as his stage.[86] The best illustration of this point is found in *Satires* 1.2, which is the most thoroughly dramatic of the diatribe satires. Closer analysis of this piece indicates just how heavily Horace has leaned on the analogy with comedy, its themes, type characters, and techniques, in the formation of his *Satires*.

The dramatic occasion of *Satires* 1.2 is the death of Hermogenes

---

1937), 117–24; and Oltramare, *Diatribe romaine*, 72. See also E. Rawson, *Intellectual Life in the Late Roman Republic* (Baltimore: Johns Hopkins University Press, 1985), 53. Rawson is probably correct in asserting that Horace had no firsthand knowledge of Cynic street preachers.

[86] Bion, too, may have been strongly influenced by what he saw on the comic stage. Diogenes claims of Bion (T11): ἦν δὲ θεατρικὸς καὶ πολὺς ἐν τῷ γελοίως διαφορῆσαι ("He was theatrical and entirely given over to humorous lampoon"). Fiske, in contrast to Kindstrand, takes the term θεατρικός to refer to Bion's manner of illustrating his themes; compare Kindstrand, *Bion*, 49–50, and Fiske, *Lucilius and Horace*, 188. The most natural interpretation of the term may also be its correct one, that is, "of the theater," meaning that Bion drew his humorous illustrations from the comic stage. We know for a fact that Bion was, along with his contemporary, Menander, a student of Theophrastus, see Kindstrand, *Bion*, 11. His penchant for malicious lampoon, however, suggests that he learned his theatrical practices from Old Comedy. Kindstrand (p. 50) adds a final note to his interpretation of T11: "The meaning of θεατρικός with reference to Bion seems therefore to be that he used a highly rhetorical style with all the different Gorgian figures and that he thus sought to attract and amuse the mob rather than to give serious philosophical instruction." It is quite possible that Bion, like his contemporary Menippus, with whom he is often classed as a new breed of hedonist Cynic, was more interested in self-parody and vivid performance than he was in serious moralizing.

Tigellius, a famous singer who was a particular favorite of the dogmatic Stoic (or Stoics) addressed in *Satires* 1.3.[87] Tigellius is lampooned as a spendthrift at the beginning of 1.2, and much of the humor that is directed against him concerns the circuslike atmosphere surrounding his death. The flute girls, quack doctors, beggars, mimes, and buffoons are all distressed over his death because he was such a dear friend. The short concluding quip, *Quippe benignus erat* ("He certainly was a *kind* man," line 4), plays on the humorous double meaning of the adjective *benignus*, which means both "kind" and "generous." The lampoon is very clever. It cuts both at Tigellius and his so-called friends, lowlifes who mourn only the loss of a steady income. Tigellius is drawn in the colors of an Old Comic wastrel. Compare Cratinus fragment 12KA (Aristophanes fragment 583), where a scholiast of Lucian Iov. trag. 48 p.83,16R. relates of Callias:

ὁ μὲν Καλλίας οὗτος, ὡς Κρατῖνος ᾿Αρχιλόχοις φησίν, ῾Ιππονίκου υἱὸς ἦν, τὸν δῆμον Μελιτεύς, ὡς ᾿Αριστοφάνης ῞Ωραις, πλούσιος καὶ πασχητιῶν καὶ ὑπὸ πορνιδίων διαφορούμενος καὶ κόλακας τρέφων.

This Callias, as Cratinus relates in his *Archilochoi*, was the son of Hipponikos, a member of the Melitean deme. According to Aristophanes' *Horai*, he was a rich pervert who wore himself out on little whores and subsidized flatterers.

Like Tigellius, Callias is stigmatized for the company he keeps. His "friends" consist of various hired lowlifes who feed off of his loose habits. Apparently the picture of Tigellius that opens *Satires* 1.2 is conventionalized.

The satirist moves on to discuss an opposite type, the miser of lines 4–6, who is every bit as extreme in his vice as Tigellius. Lines 7–11 treat the young prodigal given over to "eating up his inheritance." He is pursued by Fufidius (12–18), the loan shark who makes life hard for young men who, in spite of their stern fathers (*duris patribus*, 17), have overextended themselves. By this point, the satirist has created the impression that he works within a very strange world indeed—a world of extremes only, where one is either a miser or a spendthrift, with nothing in between. Yet this world is not altogether

---

[87] Compare *Satires* 1.3.129–30 where some unnamed Stoic dogmatist claims: *ut, quamvis tacet, Hermogenes cantor tamen atque / optimus est modulator.* For the possibility that the Hermogenes of 1.2 and that of 1.3 are, in fact, two different men, see Fraenkel, *Horace*, 86; N. Rudd, *The Satires of Horace* (Cambridge: Cambridge University Press, 1966), 292–93; and DuQuesnay, "Horace and Maecenas," 55–56.

unfamiliar, for all the characters presented have their obvious counterpart on the comic stage. The miser was a traditional comic character (compare Euclio in the *Aulularia*), as was the prodigal son (Philolaches in the *Mostellaria*), the moneylender (Misargyrides in the *Mostellaria*), and the harsh fathers (Menedemus in the *Heauton Timoroumenos*). The various characters of the opening lines who so greatly grieve at the loss of Tigellius are reminiscent of the comic parasites, doctors, and cooks who feed off the wealth of the gullible rich. Thus, by line 18, the reader has gained the distinct impression that the satirist, as he describes the world about him, is actually referring to the well-known world of the comic stage.

The passage in lines 18–22 strongly confirms this impression:

> at in se
> pro quaestu sumptum facit; hic vix credere possis
> quam sibi non sit amicus, ita ut pater ille, Terenti
> fabula quem miserum gnato vixisse fugato
> inducit, non se peius cruciaverit atque hic.

"But surely he spends money on himself in proportion to his income." "You'd scarcely believe how much he hates himself. He's like that father whom Terence showed on stage, the one who lived miserably after his son ran off. Even he never tortured himself as badly as this man."

Not only do these lines discuss a comic theme, but they are delivered in a manner very reminiscent of rapid comic dialogue. Lejay writes:

> Horace does not allow his interlocutor to complete his sentence. Likewise in comic dialogue an interlocutor will often interrupt and attach to the end of a verse an exclamation which produces the elision of the final syllable of the preceding word. One should suppose, then, that this is pronounced when the other character has not yet finished speaking and that the two syllables coincide.[88]

Lejay goes on to draw several comparisons with similar passages in Terence. He shows that not only does the passage discuss a comic theme, it is itself delivered as a piece of comic dialogue. The lines separating real life and life on the comic stage have become severely blurred. With ease the satirist connects real life with the stage fiction from Terence's *Heauton Timoroumenos*. The comic analogy is not intended parodically, but as a natural reference to life as it has been described in lines 1–19.

The satirist draws his illustrations from a comic world. It is a world of extremes only, as we see in the characters of Maltinus, Rufillus,

---

[88] Lejay and Plessis, *Oeuvres d'Horace*, 40.

and Gargonius (25–30), who embody the principle "there is no mean" (*nil medium est*, 28). The Cato of line 31 is a comic character, fashioned after the manner of Solon in Philemon's *Adelphi*.[89] The passage in lines 37–46 treats the question of adultery and its consequences. Fiske has suggested that the motif is adapted from a scene in Book 7 of Lucilius, in which the husband of a guilty woman takes vengeance upon her by castrating himself.[90] The Lucilius scene plays upon a basic comic assumption, namely, that women cannot restrain themselves sexually, and that the husband's self-castration is, therefore, an appropriate comic punishment. The *testa/testis* wordplay within the Lucilius passage also contains a probable comic reference. Compare, for example, *Miles Gloriosus* 1416–17, where Pyrgopolynices addresses Periplectomenus and Cario, who threaten him with castration as a punishment for adultery:

> PY: Et si intestatus non abeo hinc, bene agitur pro noxia.
> PE: Quid si is non faxis?
> PY: Ut vivam semper intestabilis.

> PY: And if I do not leave here "unattested," the injury is deserved.
> PE: And what if you don't leave?
> PY: May I live forever "intestate."

Cario demands one mina of gold in return for the braggart's *salvis testibus* (1420).[91] The situation we see in *Satires* 1.2.37–46, that of the adulterer abused by slaves, is the same as that of *Miles Gloriosus* 1413–20. Both this passage and its more immediate model in Lucilius's Book 7 show strong traces of comic coloring.

The passage in lines 37–62 compares opposite extremes in sexual behavior (high-class adultery versus the pursuit of chorus girls and prostitutes). It concludes (59–62):

> an tibi abunde
> personam satis est, non illud quidquid ubique
> officit evitare? bonam deperdere famam,
> rem patris oblimare, malum est ubicumque.

---

[89] The motif of the elder statesman condoning the use of prostitutes by young men is apparently borrowed from a passage in Philemon's *Adelphi* (3KA). See Lejay and Plessis, *Oeuvres d'Horace*, 33–34. The statesman in Philemon's version is Solon, who may or may not share Cato's penchant for coarse sexual diction (i.e., the Cato of *Satires* 1.2) depending on how one fills the lacuna at the beginning of line 12. Compare Bentley, ἐστυκότως; Kock, . . . πως; and Capps, λυποῦν τι.

[90] Fiske, *Lucilius and Horace*, 259.

[91] For other instances of the *testa/testis*, see W. Parker, *Priapea: Poems for a Phallic God* (London: Croom Helm, 1988), 92–93.

Or perhaps you are perfectly content to avoid the dramatic role without
avoiding the actual deed that harms irrespective of class. To destroy your
good reputation, to ruin your father's estate is evil in every case.

The satirist addresses a certain Marsaeus, who praises himself for
never having bedded a married woman, though he has squandered
his entire inheritance on the chorus girl Origo (55). Once again, the
speaker views the world around him as a comic stage. He never considers the possibility of a happy, loving marriage, which has no place
in comedy, where it is assumed that young men fall in love with prostitutes and chorus girls, braggarts chase after married women, and
old men lament the henpecking suffered at the hands of their unat-
tractive, heavily dowered wives. The satirist derides Marsaeus for
avoiding one stage role (*personam*, 60), that of the adulterer, only to
play another, that of the wastrel youth (61–62).[92]

The scene that follows, 64–72, is one of the most humorous and
oddly dramatic illustrations found in the corpus of Roman satire, a
curious blend of the Cynic "talking abstraction" and the *exclusus amator* motif of comedy. Villius, an illicit lover of Fausta, the daughter of
Sulla, stands outside the door of her house, beaten and slashed, while
she carries on inside with a second lover, Longarenus.[93] Suddenly, his
penis gains the ability to talk and an argument ensues. The *animus
muttonis* is quick to point out that the *matrona*, for all of her wealth, is
not worth the effort. The satirist concludes with the Cynic commonplace that nature has a wealth of its own, which is free for the spend-
ing and does not carry with it the pains of matronly wealth.[94]

Lines 83–113, once again, represents a blend of Cynic ideology
with comic illustration. Lines 84–85 appears to be an adaptation of
Alexis 98K:

---

[92] We note the satirist's tendency to view life as a stage in the *mempsimoiria* theme of
Satires 1.1. Jupiter says (16–18): "*iam faciam quod vultis. eris tu, qui modo miles, / mercator;
tu, consultus modo, rusticus. hinc vos, / vos hinc mutatis discedite partibus.*" Jupiter plays the
part of a stage director: "You, over here! And you, over here!" (*hinc vos, vos hinc*).
Mutatis paritibus ("with parts exchanged") certainly refers to stage roles; compare the
ὥσπερ ἐν δράματι ὑποκριτὰς ἀποδύσας of Maximus of Tyre, discussed by Fiske, *Lucilius
and Horace*, 219–20, and Bion's μὴ οὖν βούλου δευτερολόγος ὢν τὸ πρωτολόγου πρόσωπον
(F16A, 4–5). Both passages clearly connect the stage metaphor to the *mempsimoiria*
theme.

[93] DuQuesnay, "Horace and Maecenas," 34–35, gives a curious political slant to this
passage.

[94] *Dives*, "wealthy" (74), is, of course, figurative, but it is humorously treated in its
literal sense (compare *dispensare*, "pay out," in line 75) in order that nature may compare favorably to the "wealthy" matron. These lines also recall Epicurus (Diogenes
Laertius 10.144): ὁ τῆς φύσεως πλοῦτος καὶ ὥρισται καὶ εὐπόριστός ἐστιν. See Fiske, *Lucilius and Horace*, 249.

καλὸν ἔχει
τοῦ σώματός τι. τοῦτο γυμνὸν δείκνυται.

If she has some good physical feature, she shows it uncovered.

Several commentators have noted that the larger context of this passage is parallel to a scene in Philemon's *Adelphi*, where Solon displays the distinct traits of the Cynic moralizer.[95] The main theme of the satire, *in medio virtus* (29), is a Cynic ideal that informs the satirist's attitude toward sex, another commonplace of New Comedy.[96] The passage in lines 96–100 also displays an obvious comic reference. The satirist argues that rich matrons, unlike prostitutes, are unapproachable because of the many obstacles that stand in one's way (98–100):

> custodes, lectica, ciniflones, parasitae,
> ad talos stola demissa et circum addita palla,
> plurima quae invideant pure apparere tibi rem.

There are attendants, the litter, hairdressers, parasites, a stole that hangs down to the ankles and a jacket on the outside, so many things that begrudge a clear view of the item.

Megadorus, a bachelor, makes a similar complaint against society women in Plautus's *Aulularia*. He complains that husbands of his day must abide the abuse of their heavily dowered wives, who boast (500–502):

> enim mihi quidem aequomst purpuram atque aurum dari,
> ancillas, mulos, muliones, pedisequos,
> salutigerulos pueros, vehicla qui vehar.

It's only fair that I receive purple and gold, slaves, mules, stable boys, footmen, errand boys and a car to ride in.

Megadorus continues (508–10):

> stat fullo, phrygio, aurifex, lanarius;
> caupones patagiarii, indusiarii,
> flammarii, violarii, carinarii;

Standing in line are the cleaner, dyer, goldsmith, and wool weaver; those huckster embroiderers, underwear manufacturers, dyers in red, purple and brown.

---

[95] On the Cynic and comic features of *Satires* 1.2.84–101, see Fiske, *Lucilius and Horace*, 253–54.

[96] For the theme ἡδὺ πᾶν τὸ μέτριον in New Comedy, compare Alexis 216K and Antiphanes 258K.

The list goes on for many lines.[97] The satirist's view toward society women has clear precedents in the complaints of the elderly, hen-pecked husbands of popular comedy.

The world of *Satires* 1.2 is a comic stage, and so it is only fitting that the satire should end with what is very nearly a full-blown comic scene: the husband returns unexpectedly from the country; the lover runs for his life while the wife and her *conscia* grieve for themselves, the one for her dowry, the other for her legs. The scene plays upon the audience's knowledge of similar scenes from the comic stage. The motif of the adulterer's escape was especially popular in mime, which modeled its characters on those of regular comedy.[98] Ovid, at *Tristia* 2.497–500, gives the basic elements of the motif:

> Quid si scripsissem mimos obscena iocantes
> qui semper vetiti crimen amoris habent,
> in quibus assidue cultus procedit adulter
> verbaque dat stulto callida nupta viro?

> What if I had written mimes with their obscene jokes, which always have illicit love as their theme, in which the handsome adulterer keeps coming back on stage and the clever bride deceives her foolish husband?

At Juvenal *Satires* 6.41–44, the satirist chides his friend, Postumus, on the occasion of his engagement:

> quid fieri non posse putes, si iungitur ulla
> Ursidio? si moechorum notissimus olim
> stulta maritali iam porrigit ora capistro,
> quem totiens texit perituri cista Latini?

> Do you suppose that anything is impossible if Ursidius takes a wife? What next if he, once the most notorious of adulterers, a man who has hid in as many closets as Latinus with his life on the line, is now sticking his stupid neck out for the marital halter?

Latinus was a famous mime actor under Domitian. He apparently played the role of the handsome adulterer many times.[99] The basic

---

[97] Note that the passage is also reminiscent of the opening lines of *Satire* 1.2. For a general review of the *uxor dotata* motif in comedy, see Hunter, *New Comedy*, 90–92.

[98] For a similar comic scene, see the *Mercator*, where it is the *matrona* who returns from the countryside to find her husband involved in an affair. In the *Miles Gloriosus*, Pyrgopolynices is caught red-handed with a married woman. The end of *Satires* 1.2, as J. McKeown and E. Fantham have noted, is probably connected much more closely to mime. See J. McKeown, "Augustan Elegy and Mime," *Proceedings of the Cambridge Philological Association*, n.s. 25 (1979): 71–84; and E. Fantham, "Mime: The Missing Link in Roman Literary History," *Classical World* 82 (1989): 153–63.

[99] See McKeown, "Augustan Elegy and Mime," 72–73.

features of the Adultery Mime are clear: there is a bedroom scene; the husband returns unexpectedly; the lovers scramble; the wife stalls for time and the lover takes cover under the bed or in a closet; the wife dupes the husband, who probably has amorous desires of his own; the lover makes a fast escape in a disheveled state.

The same scene has been played out hundreds of times in modern movies and on television (we think of the lover in boxer shorts, tripping over his pants, which keep falling down to his ankles). The scene that Horace imagines is highly farcical and shows all the traits of similar scenes known from comedy and mime. Certain details give this away. For example, it is mentioned in passing that the husband is returning "from the country" (*vir rure*, 127). In other words, it is assumed that the tryst takes place in the city, where, in comedy, vices tend to flourish, and that the rich matron's husband has a country estate.[100] The *conscia*, as here, is frequently used in comedy as the facilitator of an illicit love affair.[101] The *uxor dotata* was a well-known comic type and explains nicely the glancing reference *doti deprensa* (131). Likewise, comic slaves commonly express concern for their legs when they are in trouble, thus explaining the oblique reference in 131.[102] The satire ends with the lover running for his life, vainly trying to keep his tunic from falling. Horace adds the significant note, "one must escape with bare foot" (*fugiendum est ac pede nudo*, 132), implying that the lover has lost one shoe. We see him hobble as he runs. The scene is full of illustrations of this type, which are animated and highly visual. The entire scene is greatly compressed, so that such oblique details make sense only by reference to similar scenes well known to Horace's audience from the stage of popular comedy. Obviously, it is not a scene that most members of Horace's audience would recall from their own personal experience.

THE SUBTLETY AND DEPTH OF THE COMIC ANALOGY

Horace's penchant for drama, so apparent in *Satires* 1.2, is consistent throughout the *Satires*. In *Satires* 1.4, the first of the so-called programmatic satires, the satirist makes a strong case for the analogy with comedy as he several times refers to the techniques and style of comedy in his defense of satire. The same is true of *Satires* 1.10. Seeking to define his work from a theoretical standpoint, Horace consis-

[100] On the city/country contrast in comedy, see Hunter, *New Comedy*, 109–13.
[101] Compare Milphidippa in the *Miles Gloriosus*, a type whom we find at least as early as the *Hippolytus* of Euripides.
[102] Compare Plautus *Poenulus* 886, and *Asinaria* 475–79.

tently finds his best models in comedy. At *Satires* 1.4.56–57, the satirist goes so far as to claim, *his, ego quae nunc, / olim quae scripsit Lucilius* ("these verses, the type that I now write and that Lucilius used to write"), referring to the scene that directly precedes in lines 48–53, a comic vignette complete with *pater ardens*, faithless *meretrix*, and *exclusus amator*.[103]

Even after the comic persona of the diatribe satires exits the stage, it is clear that the analogy with comedy is still uppermost in Horace's mind. In *Satires* 1.4 the satirist defends his use of mundane themes and colloquial diction by reference to comedy, and in 1.5 he carries these claims into practice. Here we have Maecenas, sent on an important political mission in the face of impending civil war. We might expect some rather grand moralizing from the satirist, a sermon on the wrongs of civil strife, a description of the contending parties, the fleet of Sextus Pompey, or the heroism of Maecenas. Instead, we hear about mosquitoes and frogs, drunken sailors, upset stomachs, the bad bread of Canusium, and much more that is equally petty. These trivialities are related with a colloquial flair strongly reminiscent of comedy. Priapus in *Satires* 1.8 shows strong affinities with the wily slave of comedy, and the bore of *Satires* 1.9 was regarded already by Porphyrion as a *character dramaticus*.[104] The trend continues into Book 2. Elizabeth Haight has argued that each of the satirist's interlocutors in Book 2 resembles a Menandrean type.[105] Especially worthy of note are the various *doctores inepti*—Damasippus in 2.3, Catius in 2.4, and Davus in 2.7. Damasippus is a reconstituted version of the satirist of the diatribe satires, a moralizing buffoon in Stoic guise. Catius is a glorified comic cook or *cenae pater*. He has a clear comic counterpart in the braggart Epicurean cook of Damoxenos's *Syntrophoi*.[106] He trivializes his Epicurean learning by preaching a philosophy of fine dining, which, he claims, rivals the best teachings of Pythagoras, Socrates, and Plato combined: he teaches the "art of fine dining" (*ars cenarum*, *Satires* 2.4.35), the "nature" of mushrooms, fish, and birds (20–21 and 45). He cautions against the moral depravity of wines im-

---

[103] For the veiled reference to the *exclusus amator* at *Satires* 1.4.48–52, see R. Thomas, "New Comedy, Callimachus, and Roman Poetry," *Harvard Studies in Classical Philology* 83 (1979): 191–93.

[104] See H. Musurillo, "Horace and the Bore: The *Character Dramaticus* of Sat. 1.9," *Classical Bulletin* 40 (1964): 65–69.

[105] See E. Haight, "Menander at the Sabine Farm, *Exemplar Vitae*," *Classical Philology* 42 (1947): 147–55. Kiessling and Heinze, LeJay, and others have identified *Satires* 2.3.259–71 as an adaptation of Terence *Eunuchus* 46–49 and 57–73.

[106] See Damoxenos fragment 2KA.

properly mixed (24–26), and he loathes philosophers of other schools who restrict their natural talent (*ingenium*) to the baking of cakes (47).

Slave characters named Davus are typical of New Comedy. Even if Horace actually possessed a slave who went by this name, the Davus of *Satires* 2.7 shows the distinct traits of the wily slave of comedy. Like his counterpart Damasippus in *Satires* 2.3, he is an inept Stoic moralizer who chides the satirist for various moral failings. At lines 56–61 he contends:

> metuens induceris atque
> altercante libidinibus tremis ossa pavore.
> quid refert, uri virgis ferroque necari
> auctoratus eas an turpi clausus in arca,
> quo te demisit peccati conscia erilis,
> contractum genibus tangas caput?

> You are led into her house frightened. Your bones rattle as your fear wrangles with your desires. What's the difference between going off to be branded with torches and butchered by the sword and being locked in a stinking closet where the maid, in on her mistress' crime, has hidden you, contorted, your head pressed against your knees?

Davus, like the speaker of the diatribe satires, sees the world around him as a comic stage. Horace, the criminal, has become the typical playboy adulterer of the Adultery Mime. *Satires* 2.8, the last and perhaps latest piece in the collection, brings on stage Nasidienus, another version of the typical comic *cenae pater*. The story is related by a contemporary writer of comedies, Fundanius, and so, as we would expect, it is highly charged with comic technique. The scene is complete with parasites, a buffoon, a braggart Epicurean cook, and a last-minute escape, all played out beneath the *aulaea* ("tapestries"), also the name applied to the backdrop of a comic play.[107]

This review, however cursory, suggests that the comic analogy was central to Horace's understanding of satire and that *Satires* 1.2 is by no means unique in its bold dramatic coloring. Rather than making further illustrations of the same point, by now quite obvious, I conclude this chapter by drawing attention to two of the subtler manifestations of the satirist's comic technique.

The first illustration concerns the use of "significant" names in the *Satires*, that is, names chosen on the basis of etymological deriva-

---

[107] I discuss comic aspects of *Satires* 2.8 in Chapter 4 in relation to the *mimus nobilis* theme.

tion.[108] Aristotle, writing in the period of Middle Comedy, notes that the device was particularly favored by writers of comedy, who fully appreciated its value for character delineation (*Poetics* 9.1451b12–14):[109]

ἐπὶ μὲν οὖν τῆς κωμῳδίας ἤδη τοῦτο δῆλον γέγονεν· συστήσαντες γὰρ τὸν μῦθον διὰ τῶν εἰκότων, οὕτω τὰ τυχόντα ὀνόματα ὑποτιθέασιν.

This (that poetry deals with the universal) has become clear in the case of comedy; for comedians, once they have arranged their plot from what is probable, in the same way assign to their characters whatever names occur to them.[110]

Some examples of suitable comic names are Aristophanes' Philokleon and Bdelykleon ("Cleon Lover," "Cleon Hater"), or Strepsiades ("Elusive," that is of his debts). Plautus, much more so than Terence, was fond of descriptive names, such as Pyrgopolynices ("Storm Trooper"), Artotrogus ("Bread Gobbler"), and Acroteleutium ("Knockout"), all of the *Miles Gloriosus*.

One important instance of a significant name that has eluded the commentators on Horace is that of Balbinus at *Satires* 1.3.40.[111] The verb *balbutire*, which is etymologically related to the Roman family name Balbus, "stammering," means to wheedle with loving endearments, "baby talk," in other words. The etymology of the name Balbinus fits nicely the character of line 40. He finds the mole of his lover, Hagna, quite attractive. It can be no accident that the verb *balbutire* occurs for the first and only time in the *Satires* only eight lines later and in exactly the same context (*Satires* 1.3.47–48):

> hunc varum distortis cruribus, illum
> balbutit scaurum pravis fultum male talis.

[108] The topic of significant names in the *Satires* has been treated at length by Rudd. See Rudd, *Satires of Horace*, 132–59.

[109] In Antiphanes' *Poiesis*, Comedy personified praises the easy life of Tragedy, whose characters and themes have all been decided beforehand (Antiphanes fragment 191K, 17–21): "But I don't possess these conveniences; rather, I must invent all new names [ἀλλὰ πάντα δεῖ εὑρεῖν ὀνόματα καινά], new events, new speeches, and besides things that have happened earlier, the present circumstances, the conclusion and the preface."

[110] Aristotle proceeds to contrast Comedy's use of τὰ τυχόντα ὀνόματα ("whatever names occur") with the τὰ γενόμενα ὀνόματα ("the actual names") of tragic characters. On these lines, see G. Else, *Aristotle's Poetics: The Argument* (Cambridge, Mass.: Harvard University Press, 1957), 308–09.

[111] Palmer is the exception: "*Balba-verba* are the lisping words of lovers: hence Hor. gives the name Balbinus to a doating lover, 1.3.40"; A. Palmer, *The Satires of Horace* (London: Macmillan, 1883), 306–7.

This one with the crooked legs he calls "bandy," and that one who can
barely stand with his bad ankles he calls "gimpy."[112]

The father glosses over the imperfections of his son by means of
his sweet and somewhat childish terms of endearment. The verb *balbutire*, like English "babble" which it closely resembles in sound and
meaning, perfectly conveys the sound and sense of a lover's whee-
dling chatter. Whether real or fictional, Balbinus does exactly what his
name suggests, much in the manner of a comic *dramatis persona*.
Hagna (Greek Άγνη) is a common *libertina* name that, ironically
enough, means "pure," or "chaste." It is the perfect name for a lover
of Balbinus, for thus, in line 40, we have an oblique reference to the
traditional comic predicament of the doting lover and his forbidden,
somewhat reluctant *meretrix*. The reference is well hidden. Like the
simple *rure* of 1.2.127, and the *patribus duris* of 1.2.17, it calls for savvy
on the part of the reader, who must at all times relate the world of
Horatian satire to the fictional world of popular drama.[113]

A final example I take from *Satires* 1.3.129–33, where the satirist
plays upon the humorous possibilities of the Stoic paradox *sapiens est
rex*. The dogmatic Stoic boasts:[114]

> ut, quamvis tacet, Hermogenes cantor tamen atque
> optimus est modulator; ut Alfenus vafer, omni
> abiecto instrumento artis clausaque taberna,
> tonsor erat, sapiens operis sic optimus omnis
> est opifex solus, sic rex.

As Hermogenes, though silent, is still the worlds greatest singer and mu-
sician; as crafty Alfenus, even after he set aside every tool of his trade
and closed his shop, was still a barber, so is the wise man the best practitioner of every craft, he alone is king.

[112] Lines 44–48 of *Satires* 1.3 plays on the humorous possibilities of various Roman
cognomina: Balbus (40), Paetus and Pullus (45), Varus (47), Scaurus (48).

[113] Another possible "significant name" overlooked by Rudd, perhaps rightly, is that
of Ummidius (*Satires* 1.1.95). The one striking fact about Ummidius is that he has no
moderation (*nil medium est*). His name may reflect this (Ummidius = *in* + *medius*). This
being the case, it is quite humorous that his *libertina* should kill him in the manner that
she does (100): *divisit medium*.

[114] The reading *sutor* for *tonsor* in line 132 is attested by Porphyrion and all manuscripts except the Blandinius vetustissimus, which in this instance, as elsewhere, alone
preserves the correct reading. *Tonsor*, the more difficult reading, serves as a humorous
paraprosdokian because the Stoic sage was frequently compared not with a barber but
with a shoemaker. Thus the substitution. C. Brink, "Horatian Notes IV: Despised
Readings in the Manuscripts of the Satires Book 1," *Proceedings of the Cambridge Philological Association*, n.s. 33 (1987): 22–25, makes a good case for the reading *tonsor*.

By this boast the speaker has made a fool of himself, and so, the satirist claims, playful young boys will pull on his beard and cause him to "explode and bark" (*rumperis et latras*, 136). The question remains, how exactly has the dogmatic Stoic made a fool of himself?

Porphyrion relates that Alfenus set aside his manual trade in order to become a lawyer. He may well be the Alfenus of Catullus 30, P. Alfenus Varus, the famous consular and jurisconsult honored by Vergil at *Eclogues* 6.6–12 and 9.26–29.[115] There is nothing particularly funny or inept about the fact that a barber should become a lawyer, that is, unless one approaches the claim with a few comic assumptions. In comedy, the verb *tondere*, nearly as often as it means simply to cut or clip, connotes deceit and intrigue, in the sense of to fleece, or rip off.[116] Thus, the *tonsor* is the typical comic con artist or thief. In lines 129–33 of *Satires* 1.3, the Stoic has inadvertently lampooned his lawyer friend in much the same vein that lawyers are ridiculed today: "Alfenus, even though he has sold his shop to become a lawyer, is still the same old *shearer* [that is, crook] that he always was." The joke relies on a comic metaphor, "the spoken slang of low life" so common to the diction of Plautus and Terence.[117] Without the comic reference, which is quite subtle, the joke is completely lost. Here again, the lines that separate comedy from satire have been severely blurred.

The Alfenus joke, like the reference to Balbinus at *Satires* 1.3.40, illustrates the working of the comic analogy at its very subtlest and best. The satirist's penchant for conventionalizing human experience runs deep; it is a key to his perception of satire. In the pages that follow, I intend to show that this penchant for comic illustration is matched by a unique Horatian theory of satire that directly refers his practices as satirist to the theory and practice of comedy.

[115] On the identification of Alfenus, see Nisbet and Hubbard, *Horace*, 227–29.

[116] See, for example, *Mercator* 526 and *Bacchides* 242.

[117] On *tondere* as a metaphor for deceit and intrigue in Roman Comedy, see E. Fantham, *Comparative Studies in Republican Latin Imagery* (Toronto: University of Toronto Press, 1972), 102–4.

CHAPTER TWO

Aristotle and the Iambographic Tradition: The Theoretical Precedents of Horace's Satiric Program

INTRODUCTION: THE THEORY OF AN ARISTOTELIAN HORACE

It has been nearly a century since G. L. Hendrickson first argued that the satirist's self-defense in *Satires* 1.4 is not based on the actual criticisms of some contemporary literary adversary but is rather a fictional apology that serves to define Horace's satiric program within the context of ancient theory.[1] Hendrickson, very much ahead of his time, distinguished clearly between the conventions of satire and the life of the satirist:

> I do not believe that Horace is here justifying himself before the harsh criticisms of a public which felt aggrieved and injured by his attacks, nor do I believe that the contents of the satire and the criticisms of himself which it presents are drawn from life.[2]

It is indeed unlikely that Horace should have met with the type of criticism he describes in *Satires* 1.4, where, he would have us believe, he defends himself against the charge of having made violent, malicious attacks against his contemporaries. As Rudd and others have pointed out, most of the persons named in the first three satires of Book 1 were either dead, fictional, or too insignificant to merit much notice.[3] The lampoons themselves are harmless and rather oblique. They show little evidence of any overt hostility on the part of the satirist, the charges he must address in 1.4.

Hendrickson has proposed a second approach to the satirist's self-defense:

> It is, on the contrary, a criticism of theory put concretely. The charges of an imaginary critic, describing Horace as an envenomed and unspar-

---

[1] See G. L. Hendrickson, "Horace, *Serm.* 1.4: A Protest and a Programme," *American Journal of Philology* 21 (1900): 121–42.

[2] Ibid., 124.

[3] On the names in the *Satires*, see especially Rudd, *Satires of Horace*, 132–59; LaFleur, "The Law of Satire," 1801–2, gives a short bibliographical survey of the topic.

ing satirist—in terms such as literary criticism employed concerning Lucilius and Aristophanes—give the poet opportunity to utter his protest against this character which tradition had attributed to satire.[4]

The charges addressed, in other words, have been contrived to serve the larger, programmatic designs of the satirist. In reviewing his claims from the standpoint of ancient theory, Hendrickson has made a strong case for the Aristotelian side of the satirist's self-defense. He argues that, in *Satires* 1.4, Horace establishes his Aristotelian credentials against a much narrower preconception of his work, which equated all satire with the coarse, bitter invective of the Old Comic poets and Lucilius. His work, Hendrickson maintains, manifests the best principles of Aristotle's liberal jest. "Thus, after a few tentative efforts in a more or less distinctly Lucilian manner, as it would seem, Horace early came into his own humane and kindly point of view."[5] Horace quickly abandons any real pretensions to the role of the Old Comic poet and, in *Satires* 1.3 and 1.4, he champions Aristotle's theory of the liberal jest against the traditions of Old Comedy and the iambic idea. Such is the traditional view of Horace, the Aristotelian satirist.

Hendrickson's analysis of *Satires* 1.4 remains basic to an understanding of Horace's satiric program and has been followed with only slight modifications by Lejay, Fiske, Puelma-Piwonka, and many others who have found in *Satires* 1.4 a clever adaptation of Aristotle's theory of the liberal jest.[6] Certainly the most recent and exhaustive treatment of this topic is Alison Parker's 1986 dissertation, "Comic Theory in the Satires of Horace," which neatly collects the available evidence for Aristotelian ethical, rhetorical, and poetic theory in the *Satires*, focusing not only on the programmatic claims of *Satires* 1.4, 1.10, and 2.1, but also on the practice of Aristotelian jest in the nonprogrammatic satires.[7] Parker has proposed that Horace's Aristotelian leanings are evident in the very structure of Books 1 and 2, which progress toward a *telos* of artistic and moral refinement defined by Aristotle's theory of the liberal jest.[8] Parker's work, while it certainly

[4] Hendrickson, "Horace, *Serm.* 1.4," 124.

[5] Ibid., 137.

[6] See, for example, Lejay and Plessis, *Oeuvres d'Horace*, xlvii–l; Fiske, *Lucilius and Horace*, 277–306.

[7] Alison R. Parker, "Comic Theory in the Satires of Horace" (Ph.D. diss., University of North Carolina at Chapel Hill, 1986).

[8] Parker summarizes her case for the Aristotelian structure of the *Satires* as follows: "All of the poems of the second half of Book 2, I would suggest, can be called artistic improvements over their counterparts of the first half: 2.2 and 2.4 rant, whereas their respective mates, 2.6 and 2.8, reflect, and even 2.5 shows significant Aristotelian prog-

owes much to Hendrickson, is the most imaginative of its kind and it leaves little doubt that Horace has freely adapted Aristotelian theory to his definition of satire.

Two recent articles by R. L. Hunter and M. Dickie have underscored a second, distinctly anti-Aristotelian side to Horace's satiric theory, which has never received serious consideration among commentators after Hendrickson, whose narrow Aristotelian focus, by necessity, excluded the possibility of any real fellow feeling between Horace and the exponents of the iambic idea.[9] Both Hunter and Dickie have argued that Aristotle's theory of the liberal jest, although it plays a definite role in forming Horace's views on satiric humor, is simply too tidy to account for all of the evidence. It fails to integrate Horace's statements concerning his debt to Old Comedy and the *Lucilianus character*, which are not intended ironically, but as genuine programmatic claims. Hendrickson and his followers have assumed that Horace only dabbles with the iambic idea in his early satires, never intending it too seriously, and that, as he matures, he moves steadily away from the theory and practice of *nominatim* attack. Yet, connections with Lucilius and/or Old Comedy are explicitly drawn in each of the programmatic satires, and nowhere, in spite of much scholarship that argues otherwise, does the satirist attempt to disavow their influence upon his work.

New approaches must be sought to reconcile Horace's views on Old Comedy and the iambic idea to his decidedly Aristotelian leanings on the topic of satiric humor. In this chapter, I argue that, far from presenting a bland, uniform approach to the question, Horace draws his theoretical tenets from two irreconcilable camps, namely, the Peripatetic tradition followed by Cicero, and the tradition of the *Iambos*, which Horace knew primarily from Lucilius, but also from iambic poetry, Old Comedy, and Cynic moralizing. The result is a hybrid theory that, against all precedent, seeks to maintain the integrity of both traditions. Horace wants it all: as a theorist, he combines the best features of two otherwise hostile traditions to create his own unique perception of satiric humor; and as an artist, he writes in the best traditions of ancient comedy, both Old and New.

---

ress over 2.1 by its fuller embrace of the dialogue form. Just as in Book 1 Horace had portrayed a movement toward greater civilization in art through his triadic structure, so in Book 2, with its pairs, the poet reminds us that art, like language, is never static, but continually labors toward a *telos*." Parker, "Comic Theory," 132.

[9] M. Dickie, "The Disavowal of *Invidia* in Roman Iamb and Satire," *Papers of the Liverpool Latin Seminar* 3 (1981): 183–208; and Hunter, "Horace on Friendship," 480–90.

ARISTOTLE'S THEORY OF THE LIBERAL JEST

Aristotle's theory of the liberal jest arises in Book 4 of his *Nicomachean Ethics* from a discussion that concerns the mean in human behavior at times of relaxation and play, which, Aristotle reluctantly concedes, "seem to be a necessary part of life."[10] Against the virtues of the εὐτράπελος, the clever gentleman, Aristotle weighs the deficiencies of the ἄγροικος, the humorless boor, and the excesses of the βωμόλοχος, the buffoon. The boor he mentions only in passing, objecting that he is "useless in playful conversation, for, though he understands nothing, he takes offense at everything." From what we have seen of the boor in Chapter 1, it is likely that Aristotle knew this character from the stage of comedy.

The buffoon, while he knows the value of humor, is given over to the opposite extreme (*Nicomachean Ethics* 4.1128a33–1128b2):

ὁ δὲ βωμολόχος ἥττων ἐστὶ τοῦ γελοίου, καὶ οὔτε ἑαυτοῦ οὔτε τῶν ἄλλων ἀπεχόμενος, εἰ γέλωτα ποιήσει, καὶ τοιαῦτα λέγων ὧν οὐθὲν ἂν εἴποι ὁ χαρίεις, ἔνια δ' οὐδ' ἂν ἀκούσαι.

The buffoon cannot keep from jesting, and, if he can cause a laugh, he spares neither himself nor anyone else. And he says the sort of things the polite gentleman never says, and other things that he refuses even to hear.

Here again, Aristotle defines the vicious extreme by analogy with a character known to him from the comic stage.[11] The buffoon knows no limit. He is a slave to his own humor, and his ridicule spares no one, not even himself. He offends by both the sheer number of his jests as well as by their vulgarity. Aristotle goes on to argue that the polite gentleman will always display tact (ἡ ἐπιδεξιότης), which allows him, in contrast to the buffoon, to say and hear only certain things in jest. Tact implies education, refined judgment, the ability to weigh one's options carefully in any given situation and to choose the virtuous middle course. We see in Aristotle's treatment of the buffoon, the attempt to define certain standards of behavior in regard to jest. He seeks a restrained middle course, which will both preserve and advertise the dignity of the speaker, who must at all times take care to avoid the vicious extremes of comic stage characters.

[10] For Aristotle's theory of the liberal jest, see *Nicomachean Ethics* 4.1127b33–1128b4.
[11] On the buffoon as an Old Comic stage character, see *Nicomachean Ethics* 4.1128a13–25.

The *Nicomachean Ethics* sketches out only the broadest outlines of Aristotle's theory of the liberal jest, which, we have good reason to suspect, was treated in much greater detail in the lost second book of his *Poetics*.[12] Aristotle records at *Rhetoric* 3.1419b2–9:

Περὶ δὲ τῶν γελοίων, ἐπειδή τινα δοκεῖ χρῆσιν ἔχειν ἐν τοῖς ἀγῶσι, καὶ δεῖν ἔφη Γοργίας τὴν μὲν σπουδὴν διαφθείρειν τῶν ἐναντίων γέλωτι τὸν δὲ γέλωτα σπουδῇ, ὀρθῶς λέγων, εἴρηται πόσα εἴδη γελοίων ἐστὶν ἐν τοῖς περὶ ποιητικῆς, ὧν τὸ μὲν ἁρμόττει ἐλευθέρῳ τὸ δ' οὔ. ὅπως οὖν τὸ ἁρμόττον αὑτῷ λήψεται. ἔστι δ' ἡ εἰρω-νεία τῆς βωμολοχίας ἐλευθεριώτερον· ὁ μὲν γὰρ αὑτοῦ ἕνεκα ποιεῖ τὸ γελοῖον, ὁ δὲ βωμολόχος ἑτέρου.

Concerning jests, since they seem somewhat useful in debates, and Gorgias is right when he says that it is necessary to ruin your opponents' seriousness with a laugh and their laughter with seriousness, how many types of jests there are has been defined in the *Poetics*, of which some befit the free man, others not. The speaker will see to it that he chooses the jest that suits him. Irony is more suited to the free man than buffoonery, for the one (the free man) makes a joke on his own account, the other (the buffoon) on account of someone else.

Aristotle takes his cue from Gorgias, who apparently had much to say on the topic of humor in oratory. The orator knows the value of jest as an emotional appeal. He also knows its limits. As a public speaker, he resembles the stage actor who strives to convey a specific *ethos*, and, like the clever gentleman of *Nicomachean Ethics* Book 4, he will at all times avoid the role of the comic buffoon, whose humor knows no respectable bounds.

Aristotle's statements at *Rhetoric* 3.1419b2–9 suggest that he maintained no clear distinction between rhetorical and poetic theory on the topic of liberal humor. For a list of the types of jokes available to the orator and their ethical significance, he simply refers his reader to *Poetics* Book 2, now lost.[13] Connections with *Nicomachean Ethics*

---

[12] The question concerning the existence of this treatise is, I realize, a difficult one. Modern scholarship has, at times, disputed the existence of Aristotle's second book, but the most recent studies of this topic have come out strongly in favor of the notion that the *Poetics* originally had two books. See especially G. Else, *Plato and Aristotle on Poetry* (Chapel Hill: University of North Carolina Press, 1986), 185–95; and R. Janko, *Aristotle on Comedy* (Berkeley: University of California Press, 1984), 63–66. Both Else and Janko argue strongly for the existence of a second book. Compare the much earlier, negative conclusion of A. P. McMahon, "On the Second Book of Aristotle's *Poetics* and the Source of Theophrastus' Definition of Tragedy," *Harvard Studies in Classical Philology* 28 (1917): 1–46. I concur with Janko that, "The evidence for a continuation to the *Poetics* of some sort, in which comedy was discussed, is overwhelming" (p. 66).

[13] On the relative dating of these two works, see G. Kennedy, "Two Contributions to Aristotelian Studies," *American Journal of Philology* 111, na 1 (1990): 86–91.

Book 4 are also obvious, indicating that, on the topic of liberal humor, Aristotle's poetic, rhetorical, and ethical theories were all cut from the same cloth. The *topos* was extremely flexible, adapted (initially at least) to various uses from the field of rhetoric;[14] thus, it is from later rhetorical theory that we are able to gain fuller insight into Aristotle's thinking on the liberal jest.

The immediate history of Aristotle's theory is virtually impossible to trace because, with the possible exceptions of the Coislinian Treatise and several brief statements in Demetrius, almost nothing survives of ancient rhetorical, ethical, and poetic theories of humor from before the first century B.C.[15] This is especially distressing because we know from later sources that famous theorists, such as Demetrius of Phaleron, Theophrastus, Eratosthenes, and Aristophanes of Byzantium, to mention only a few, all wrote large-scale treatises on the topic of poetic humor.[16] As a result, very little can be said about specifically Hellenistic developments on the theory of the liberal jest. The lines that separate Aristotle from later Hellenistic theory concerning this topic will always remain obscure.

The rhetorical works of Cicero are by far the most important source for Aristotle's liberal jest in later theory. Specific references are *De Oratore* 2.216–90, and *Orator* 87–90. *De Officiis* 1.103–4 approaches the *topos* from a purely ethical standpoint, but the conclusions reached are fully consistent with those of rhetorical theory. Other perhaps less important sources for the study of this topic are Quintilian's *Institutes* 6.3, and many scattered references in Plutarch, especially his *Quaestiones Conviviales* and the *Comparatio Aristophanis et Menandri*.

---

[14] Consider Aristotle's reference to Gorgias as an authority on humor at *Rhetoric* 3.1419b2–9, just quoted in the text.

[15] R. Janko has made a very detailed study of the *Tractatus Coislinianus* and concludes that the original source of this work was the lost Book 2 of Aristotle's *Poetics*. Janko departs radically from what he refers to as the "Bernaysian orthodoxy," which argues that the work is that of a late compiler who sought to reconstruct the lost Book 2 from scattered references to comedy found in the *Poetics*, *Rhetoric*, and *Nicomachean Ethics*. Lane Cooper has done precisely this in his *An Aristotelian Theory of Comedy, with an Adaptation of the Poetics and a Translation of the Tractatus Coislinianus* (New York: Harcourt, Brace, 1922). Janko's thesis has not met with much success. For other, more traditional views of the treatise, see G.M.A. Grube, *The Greek and Roman Critics* (Toronto: University of Toronto Press, 1965), 144–49; and D. A. Russell, *Criticism in Antiquity* (Berkeley: University of California Press, 1981), 152, 204–6. Grube, not unlike Janko, is rather alone in maintaining that Demetrius's *On Style* belongs to the early third century B.C. See Grube, *Greek and Roman Critics*, 110, and *A Greek Critic: Demetrius On Style* (Toronto: University of Toronto Press, 1961), 39–56.

[16] For some idea of the broad scope of Hellenistic scholarship on the topic of poetic humor, see Janko, *Aristotle on Comedy*, 44–52.

Mary Grant's 1924 monograph, "The Ancient Rhetorical Theories of the Laughable," remains the standard work on humor in ancient theory.[17] Grant has shown that Aristotle's theory of the liberal jest, which was treated but incidentally in his extant works and much more fully in *Poetics* Book 2, laid the foundation of all further discussion of humor in oratory. Cicero's discussion of the *topos*, most notably at *De Oratore* 2.216–90, is very full and well illustrated, much more so than *Nicomachean Ethics* 4 and the scattered references to jest in the *Rhetoric* and *Poetics*, suggesting that he was well versed in later Hellenistic theories of humor.

Apart from expanding the *topos* and adding refinements in definition, it is quite clear that the Hellenistic handbook writers on rhetoric, followed by Cicero, made no significant advance upon Aristotle's theory of the liberal jest. Cicero, for example, at *Orator* 88, cautions against the improper use of jest in a manner highly reminiscent of Aristotle:

> Illud admonemus tamen ridiculo sic usurum oratorem, ut nec nimis frequenti ne scurrile sit, nec subobsceno ne mimicum, nec petulanti ne improbum, nec in calamitatem ne inhumanum, nec in facinus ne odi locum risus occupet.

> Nonetheless, we make the following admonition: the orator will use jest in a manner that is not too profuse, lest he come off as a buffoon. To avoid the mime actor's role, he will avoid obscenity. Nor will he take relish in abuse, like a rogue, and he will not laugh at disaster, which is inhuman. He will not laugh at crime, lest laughter take hatred's place.

Here again, stage characters are used as illustrations of vice. Cicero argues, very much in line with Aristotle, that the *ridiculum* (Aristotle's τὸ γελοῖον) must be used in moderation. Excess, like that of the buffoon and the mimic, is a sign of bad moral character. This type of illustration is especially suited to a Roman context, where the characters of comedy and mime were played by slaves or men of no social status. Their "illiberal" humor, it was assumed, was somehow a condition of their slave status. The "free" citizen (*liber*, Aristotle's ἐλεύθερος), though he enjoys the broad humor of comic slaves and buffoons, in formal discourse of any kind will cultivate a type of humor suited to his liberal temperament.

The comparison of the orator to stage characters is perfectly understandable within a Roman context, where the term *actor* refers not only to the dramatic actor, but also to the plaintiff in a legal suit. Like

[17] See M. A. Grant, *The Ancient Rhetorical Theories of the Laughable*, University of Wisconsin Studies in Language and Literature 21 (Madison, 1924).

his counterpart on the stage, the Roman orator made his case in the open air from a platform surrounded by an audience (the *corona*) whose members felt free to express their feelings by applause, catcalls, or silence. Like the dramatic actor, the orator needed to play to his audience, eliciting various emotions at the proper time, in the proper degree, and in a manner suited to his character. Both Aristotle and Cicero agree that laughter has its proper place in oratory as an appeal to the emotions of the listener and, more important, to the judge presiding over the case. Unlike his master, Plato, Aristotle conceded the necessity of emotional appeal in an effective deliberative speech (*Rhetoric* 2.1378a20–23):

ἔστι δὲ τὰ πάθη, δι' ὅσα μεταβάλλοντες διαφέρουσι πρὸς τὰς κρίσεις, οἷς ἕπεται λύπη καὶ ἡδονή, οἷον ὀργὴ ἔλεος φόβος καὶ ὅσα ἄλλα τοιαῦτα, καὶ τὰ τούτοις ἐναντία.

It is through the emotions that men, changing their course, differ in regard to their judgments. The emotions are accompanied by pain and pleasure; such are wrath, pity, fear, and all other such things and their opposites.

Compare the claims of Julius Caesar Strabo, Cicero's Roman exemplar of the liberal jest, at *De Oratore* 2.236:

Est autem, ut ad illud tertium veniam, est plane oratoris movere risum; vel quod ipsa hilaritas benevolentiam conciliat ei, per quem excitata est . . . vel quod ipsum oratorem politum esse hominem significat, quod eruditum, quod urbanum, maximeque quod tristitiam ac severitatem mitigat et relaxat, odiosasque res saepe, quas argumentis dilui non facile est, ioco risuque dissolvit.

Moreover, to enter upon my third point, it is clearly the orator's duty to inspire laughter, either because lightheartedness itself wins over goodwill for the one through whom it is stirred . . . or because it signifies that the orator himself is a polished gentleman, that he is learned, urbane, and most of all because it softens harshness, loosens severity, and because often unpleasant topics, which are difficult to answer by proofs, it brushes off with laughter and jest.

Although he admitted the necessity of emotional appeal in oratory, in response to the pure philosopher's disdain for irrational appeal, Aristotle set specific limits on the practice. Emotional proofs, though effective and necessary, he regarded as somewhat hazardous, for they expose the true moral character of the speaker.[18] Jest, therefore,

---

[18] Aristotle claims at *Rhetoric* 2.1377b22–24: ἀνάγκη μὴ μόνον πρὸς τὸν λόγον ὁρᾶν,

must be used with tremendous caution. Compare Julius Caesar Strabo's statements concerning imitative jest at *De Oratore* 2.242:

> Atqui ita est totum hoc ipso genere ridiculum, ut cautissime tractandum sit. Mimorum est enim ethologorum, si nimia est imitatio, sicut obscenitas. Orator surripiat oportet imitationem ut is qui audiet, cogitet plura, quam videat; praestet idem ingenuitatem et ruborem suum, verborum turpitudine et rerum obscenitate vitanda.

> However, this entire type of jesting must be treated with extreme caution, for if the imitation is too much, it becomes just like the obscenity of mime actors who mimic the character traits of others. The orator should simply hint at mimicry, so that the hearer might imagine more than he sees; likewise, he must testify to his own good breeding and modesty by avoiding foul language and obscene gestures.

An emotional appeal reveals the character of the speaker, showing that he is possessed of certain qualities that the listener, it is supposed, will find attractive. Thus, emotional appeals, such as the imitative jest, must be used with great caution, for mimicry reveals a low moral character, the excesses of the mime actor, just as subtlety reveals the educated liberal temperament. The disposition of the listener will directly depend on the type of humor the orator chooses to use.

A third quotation from Julius Caesar Strabo's discourse on humor again reflects the direct influence of Peripatetic theory. He summarizes his case as follows (*De Oratore* 2.247):

> Temporis igitur ratio, et ipsius dicacitatis moderatio et temperantia et raritas dictorum distinguet oratorem a scurra, et quod nos cum causa dicimus, non ut ridiculi videamur, sed ut proficiamus aliquid, illi totum diem et sine causa.

> Calculation of the proper occasion, therefore, and moderation of the abuse itself, as well as the temperance and infrequency of jests, will distinguish the orator from the buffoon; and the fact that we speak with good cause, not so that we might resemble wiseacres, but that we might make some improvement. Those do it all day long and without cause.

The watchwords of the liberal jest are *ratio*, that is, calculation of the proper time, place, and audience for jest, and *moderatio*, Aristotelian μεσότης. As Julius Caesar Strabo continues his discourse, he predicates these as the virtues of rhetorical jest in a host of categories, such as the language used, subjects treated, and persons addressed. Grant

---

ὅπως ἀποδεικτικὸς ἔσται καὶ πιστός, ἀλλὰ καὶ αὐτὸν ποιόν τινα καὶ τὸν κριτὴν κατασκευάζειν ("Not only must the speaker see to it that his speech is demonstrative and convincing, but he must also present both himself and the judge as being of a certain character").

has treated this discourse in some detail, and it is unnecessary to rehearse her findings here. Suffice it to say that *De Oratore* 2.216–90 represents the full flowering of Peripatetic theory. In spite of his refinements in definition and his exhaustive manner of illustration, Cicero has made no great advance upon the theories outlined in the *Nicomachean Ethics*.

ARISTOTLE ON OLD COMEDY AND THE IAMBIC IDEA

Poetry, rhetoric, and drama, in their more sublime or ridiculous moments, are all capable of eliciting strong emotions. Plato, a strict rationalist, found this very troubling and dangerous, and thus, we recall from Book 10 of the *Republic*, he actually excluded dramatic poets, both tragedians and comedians, from his ideal state. At *Republic* 10.605a–b he states his case:

> καὶ γὰρ τῷ φαῦλα ποιεῖν πρὸς ἀλήθειαν ἔοικεν αὐτῷ, καὶ τῷ πρὸς ἕτερον τοιοῦτον ὁμιλεῖν τῆς ψυχῆς, ἀλλὰ μὴ πρὸς τὸ βέλτιστον, καὶ ταύτῃ ὡμοίωται · καὶ οὕτως ἤδη ἂν ἐν δίκῃ οὐ παραδεχοίμεθα εἰς μέλλουσαν εὐνομεῖσθαι πόλιν, ὅτι τοῦτο ἐγείρει τῆς ψυχῆς καὶ τρέφει καὶ ἰσχυρὸν ποιῶν ἀπόλλυσι τὸ λογιστικόν.

> Yes, for he [the tragedian] resembles him [the painter] in making base things into the truth; and in appealing to the inferior part of the soul and not to the best part he also resembles him. And so we now rightly refuse to accept him into a city-state that is to be well ordered because he encourages and nurtures this part of the soul and, in making it strong, he destroys the soul's rational element.

Emotions are irrational, a blight on the soul which, like the unruly horse of the *Phaedrus*, must be whipped into obedience by the soul's highest element (the charioteer), which is pure reason. Tragedy, however, elicits powerful emotions such as pity, causing them to gain a stronger hold on the soul. At 606b Socrates claims, "For once you have fed your pity and made it strong toward those sufferings [that is, artificial sufferings on the tragic stage], it is not easily restrained in your own sufferings." Tragedy, in short, is bad for the soul.

On the same basis, Plato excludes comic poets from his ideal state (*Republic* 10.606c):

> Ἆρ᾽ οὐχ ὁ αὐτὸς λόγος καὶ περὶ τοῦ γελοίου, ὅτι ἂν αὐτὸς αἰσχύνοιο γελωτο-
> ποιῶν, ἐν μιμήσει δὴ κωμῳδικῇ ἢ καὶ ἰδίᾳ ἀκούων σφόδρα χαρῇς καὶ μὴ μισῇς ὡς
> πονηρά, ταὐτὸν ποιεῖς ὅπερ ἐν τοῖς ἐλέοις; ὃ γὰρ τῷ λόγῳ αὖ κατεῖχες ἐν σαυτῷ
> βουλόμενον γελωτοποιεῖν, φοβούμενος δόξαν βωμολοχίας, τότ᾽ αὖ ἀνίης καὶ ἐκεῖ

νεανικὸν ποιήσας ἔλαθες πολλάκις ἐν τοῖς οἰκείοις ἐξενεχθεὶς ὥστε κωμῳδοποιὸς γενέσθαι.

Does not the same reasoning apply to humor as well; that is, if the jesting that you yourself would be ashamed to practice you listen to, in comic representation or in private performance, thoroughly enjoying yourself, and you do not hate them as evil, are you not doing the very thing you did in the case of pity [that is, tragedy]? For that which you, by reason, fearing the reputation of a buffoon, were holding inside, the part of you that wants to play the clown, you then release, and before you know it, you have made it strong, so that often, carried away, you become a comedian at home.

Comedy fosters irrational license, buffoonery, deep within the soul. Once it has taken hold, Plato fears, it is not easily eradicated. Here we see the beginnings of a theoretical prejudice against Old Comedy, with its abusiveness and broad farce, marked by the term βωμολοχία. Aristotle, to some extent at least, shared this prejudice with his master. It is a prejudice based in Plato's radical concept of human emotions and the divided nature of the human soul.

Plato bans the writers of tragedy and comedy from his ideal state, allowing them to return only if they can demonstrate that their work possesses some higher function than giving pleasure. Emotions are stirred by drama. The emotion Plato associates with tragedy is pity (τὸ ἐλεεινὸν). The audience takes pleasure in the experience because the situation, while disastrous, is entirely aritificial. Such pleasure, Plato contends, erodes reason.

At *Philebus* 48, Plato makes a concerted effort to define precisely the type of pleasure, that is, the specific emotional response he associates with comedy.[19] The *Philebus* addresses the nature of pleasure. Once again, Plato takes a disparaging view of dramatic poetry, arguing that pleasures evoked at a dramatic performance are "mixed" rather than "pure" (ἡδονὰς ἐν λύπαις οὔσας ἀναμεμιγμένας). Pure pleasures Plato defines as those associated with reason and the pursuit of reality, such as the pleasure felt in solving an abstract mathematical or ethical question. All other pleasures, he argues, are inferior, because they are mixed with pain, and they tend only to distract one from the pursuit of reason. Such is the case with the type of pleasure elicited by a performance on the comic stage (*Philebus* 48A):

Τὴν δ' ἐν ταῖς κωμῳδίαις διάθεσιν ἡμῶν τῆς ψυχῆς, ἆρ' οἶσθ' ὡς ἔστι κἂν τούτοις μῖξις λύπης τε καὶ ἡδονῆς;

[19] On the *Philebus* and the emotional theory of Plato and Aristotle, see W. W. Fortenbaugh, *Aristotle on Emotion* (London: Duckworth, 1975). This is a basic study of these issues to which I am much indebted.

As for the disposition of our souls at comic performances, don't you know that even here our pleasure is mixed with pain?

The pleasure of comedy is not pure pleasure, but an alloy of pleasant and painful emotions, which signify a corrupt moral character. The specific pain that Plato associates with comedy is envy (φθόνος), and the pleasure, though not designated by the technical term ἐπιχαιρεκακία, is obviously malice. Plato has Old Comedy in mind when he describes comic laughter at *Philebus* 50a as that ἐπί τοῖς τῶν φίλων γελοίοις ("directed toward the laughable traits of our friends"), in other words, the lampoon of contemporaries. Although the *Philebus* was written at a time when public lampoon was restricted on the comic stage, Plato has maintained a dramatic unity of time in voicing his sentiments through Socrates.[20] Plato is overtly hostile to Old Comedy. His intolerance again stems from his theory of the divided soul. Thus at *Republic* 10 and in the *Philebus* we see the beginnings of a theoretical prejudice against Old Comedy that would play a significant role in later poetic theory. For Aristotle, like Plato, chose to expand upon one trait of Old Comedy, that is, the iambic idea, and to show that this type of humor is rooted in bad moral character.[21] The vicious emotions that were commonly associated with the will to harm Plato pinpointed as envy and malice, which are the charges addressed in *Satires* 1.4.

Aristotle inherited from his master a deep sense of apprehension toward emotional appeal, which greatly influenced his theories of drama and rhetoric. In order to make a place for drama within the life of the educated gentleman, Aristotle must somehow come to grips with Plato's objection that the dramatic poets do nothing but incite dangerous, irrational pleasures. To do this, Aristotle introduces the possibility of a "rational" emotional response, that is, emotions

[20] The need to maintain the dramatic unity of time may have prevented Plato from theorizing about the humor of his own day through the mouth of Socrates. Thus, the *Philebus* refers only to the negative character of Old Comedy. Even so, Grube correctly asserts that, "It is curious that Plato, so adept at humour, irony, sarcasm and even farce, should have reflected so little on the nature of the comic." Grube, *Greek and Roman Critics*, 65.

[21] Plato's suspicion toward all types of emotional appeal is especially obvious in his early works. Later in life he was prepared to make some slight concessions to the needs of human emotions. Already at the end of the *Philebus*, for example, he makes a case for the unmixed, "rational" pleasures. Again in the *Symposium*, he concedes that a strong, passionate ἔρως may have a positive function: when channeled and trained by reason, sexual desire can act to inspire the lover toward the ultimate, abstract vision of beauty. At *Laws* 653–54, Plato actually suggests the positive value of a musical education, a rather obvious departure from the strictures of *Republic*, Book 10. See Grube, *Greek and Roman Critics*, 61–65.

trained by reason.[22] At *Nicomachean Ethics* 2.1106b21–22, Aristotle argues that one must cultivate the mean in emotional response, just as in one's actions:

τὸ δ' ὅτε δεῖ καὶ ἐφ' οἷς καὶ πρὸς οὓς καὶ οὗ ἕνεκα καὶ ὡς δεῖ, μέσον τε καὶ ἄριστον, ὅπερ ἐστὶ τῆς ἀρετῆς.

But it is nessecary [to feel these emotions] at the right time, on the right occasions, toward the right people, for the right purpose and in the right manner, which is the middle degree and the best, the mark of virtue.

In other words, emotions, when properly educated, take on a rational color. The educated gentleman does not seek to eradicate emotions but to train them according to reason. He learns to feel pity and fear in the appropriate circumstances and in the proper degree.

Aristotle's theory of "rational" emotions attempts to address the narrow rationalism of Plato, his radical conception of pleasure and emotions that called for the elimination of all types of emotional appeal. The theory allowed Aristotle to make a case for the value of rhetoric and drama in the life of the educated gentleman. It requires little effort to see just how vastly different are the separate approaches to rhetoric of the *Gorgias*, where the professors of rhetoric are treated as unprincipled hucksters and flatterers, and Aristotle's *Rhetoric*. We are in two altogether different worlds. Grube summarizes Aristotle's achievement:

There were then, as we saw, two approaches to literary theory in the late fifth and fourth centuries; the philosophical and the rhetorical. Aristotle may be said to have brought them together in the *Rhetoric*. This is the last work we possess from the hand of a philosopher, and he makes this fusion with considerable success.[23]

Working in the shadow of his master, Aristotle must account for the emotional appeal of drama in some positive way if he is to reintroduce the writers of drama into his state, the final challenge of *Republic* Book 10. Aristotle took this challenge seriously, and we see his attempts to wrestle with the emotional appeal of drama in his famous definition of tragedy (*Poetics* 6.1449b24–28):

ἔστιν οὖν τραγῳδία μίμησις πράξεως σπουδαίας καὶ τελείας μέγεθος ἐχούσης, ἡδυσμένῳ λόγῳ, χωρὶς ἑκάστῳ τῶν εἰδῶν ἐν τοῖς μορίοις, δρώντων καὶ οὐ δι' ἀπαγγελίας, δι' ἐλέου καὶ φόβου περαίνουσα τὴν τῶν τοιούτων παθημάτων κάθαρσιν.

---

[22] See Fortenbaugh, *Aristotle on Emotion*, 9–22, for Aristotle's theory of emotion and its implications for his theory of drama.

[23] Grube, *Greek and Roman Critics*, 102.

Tragedy then is the imitation of action that is serious and complete, possessing magnitude, by means of language made pleasant by ornaments used separately in each of the various parts of the play. It represents men in action and does not use narrative. Through pity and fear it accomplishes the catharsis of these and similar emotions.

Aristotle's theory of tragic catharsis, whatever he means by the term, addresses the problem of the emotional appeal of tragedy.[24] Catharsis, whether it "purges," "relieves," or "cleanses" the emotions, is definitely intended as a positive experience. I suspect that tragic catharsis refers to the artificial training of the emotions to respond in accordance with reason—that is, at the proper times, for the right purpose, and toward the right people. After all, Aristotle was very careful to restrict the immoral and the irrational from the stage of tragedy, making a good cathartic experience one that is morally uplifting and justified by reason. Whatever the case may be, we see in his theory of catharsis something of how Aristotle came to terms with Plato's old objections to emotional appeal, which seem, to some extent, to have been the very incentive behind the theory of tragic catharsis.

Although most of what Aristotle has to say on the topic of comedy is now lost to us, we can be reasonably sure that he, in some way, made a case for the positive side of comedy's emotional appeal. If the Coislinian Treatise has any merit, he adapted his theory of catharsis to the comic stage as well. The number and type of emotions purged are uncertain, and several reasonable attempts have been made to define them.[25] Plato defined pity as the chief tragic emotion, and Aristotle followed suit. It is reasonable to suspect, then, that he also followed Plato in defining the comic emotions as envy (φθόνος) and malice (ἐπιχαιρεκακία).

The main point here is that Aristotle, in contrast to Plato, developed a theory of comedy that rendered it valuable from a moral and educational standpoint. He does not propose to ban comedy, not even Old Comedy, from his ideal state. At *Politics* 7.1336b1–23 he argues that αἰσχρολογία, obscene, abusive language, ought to be banned by the lawgiver. It is a sign of slavishness (ἀνελευθερία), a dan-

---

[24] Janko, *Aritstotle on Comedy*, 139–51, gives a thorough bibliographical survey of Aristotle's theory of tragic catharsis, to which should be added Else, *Plato and Aristotle on Comedy*, 152–62.

[25] On comic catharsis, see Janko, *Aristotle on Comedy*, 143–47; and Lane Cooper, *Aristotelian Theory of Comedy*, 67. Various proposals have been made for the emotions purged. See especially D. W. Lucas, *Aristotle: Poetics* (Oxford: Clarendon Press, 1968), 288; Grube, *Greek and Roman Critics*, 146–47; and L. Golden, "Comic Pleasure," *Hermes* 115 (1987): 165–74.

ger to the young and uneducated. But he goes on to make an exception of certain religious cults, iambic poetry, and comedy, adding, however, that only the mature, educated gentleman ought to be allowed to attend such functions. Their education, he claims, will render them immune to the harmful effects of obscenity and abuse (ἀπὸ τῶν τοιούτων γιγνομένης βλάβης ἀπαθεῖς ἡ παιδεία ποιήσει πάντας). Although he never goes so far as to ban such performances, he seems to have harbored some prejudice against Old Comedy and the iambic idea, at least in its more violent manifestations, preferring the subtler humor of later comedy. This point, however, is easily distorted. We recall that Aristotle was especially fond of Aristophanes, whose later plays show the less aggressive traits of Middle Comedy. Janko has suggested that Aristophanes "constituted a mean for A., between excessive buffoonery and plays that had become rather tame and serious."[26]

Aristotle made some exceptions for Old Comedy, especially in its less abusive forms, yet he definitely preferred the comedy of his own day.[27] At *Nichomachean Ethics* 4.1128a20–25, Aristotle draws a very telling analogy between the excessive behavior of the buffoon and the Old Comic hero.[28] The difference between slavish jest and that of the educated gentleman he explains as follows:

ἴδοι δ᾿ ἄν τις καὶ ἐκ τῶν κωμῳδιῶν τῶν παλαιῶν καὶ τῶν καινῶν· τοῖς μὲν γὰρ ἦν γελοῖον ἡ αἰσχρολογία, τοῖς δὲ μᾶλλον ἡ ὑπόνοια· διαφέρει δ᾿ οὐ μικρὸν ταῦτα πρὸς εὐσχημοσύνην. πότερον οὖν τὸν εὖ σκώπτοντα ὁριστέον τῷ λέγειν μὴ ἀπρεπῆ ἐλευθερίῳ, ἢ τῷ μὴ λυπεῖν τὸν ἀκούοντα, ἢ καὶ τέρπειν;

And one can see [the difference] in the case of comedies, the old and the new. For in the case of old comedies, obscenity was a source of laughter,

[26] See Janko, *Aristotle on Comedy*, 206. Compare Platonius's assessment of the Old Comic poets, which is based ultimately in Aristotelian principles: "Aristophanes attained to the mean character between these men. For he is neither too abusive, like Cratinus, nor is he too pleasant, like Eupolis. Rather, he possesses toward wrongdoers the excessiveness of Cratinus as well as Eupolis's understated charm." See Cratinus Testimonia 17KA.

[27] Against the prevailing consensus of Aristotelian scholarship, M. Heath has argued that Aristotle's statements on liberal humor at *Nicomachean Ethics* 2.1108a23–26 and 4.1128a4–1128b3 are not applicable to his theory of comedy, which, he claims, is fully consistent with Aristophanic practice. See M. Heath, "Aristotelian Comedy," *Classical Quarterly* 39, no. 2 (1989): 344–54. Although I disagree with Heath on several points of detail, I fully concur that Aristotle's theory of comedy has been too narrowly interpreted. His liberal jest could accommodate quite comfortably even the comedies of Aristophanes and the iambs of Archilochus (see my nn. 8, 16, and 40).

[28] On these lines, see Heath, "Aristotelian Comedy," 344. In spite of Heath's objections, it seems clear that Aristotle indicates a preference for the restrained style of later Athenian comedy.

while for the new it is, rather, innuendo. These things differ greatly in regard to suitable behavior. Therefore, shall we define the man who ridicules well by his saying that which is not unsuited to the free man, or by his not inflicting pain upon the listener, but that he actually charms him?

Here Old Comedy is associated directly with bad moral character. Like the buffoon, the Old Comic hero directly abuses his enemy. He causes pain (λυπεῖν) with his obscene lampoons. Proper jest, Aristotle argues, prefers innuendo, the clever, harmless jest, which actually pleases its object. The ability to lampoon in a proper manner, once again, requires a great deal of education and tact. The εὐτραπελός, the quick-witted gentleman, strikes the proper balance between boorishness and buffoonery. Proper training makes the difference (*Rhetoric* 2.1389b): ἡ γὰρ εὐτραπελία παπαιδευμένη ὕβρις ἐστίν ("for clever jest is insolence that has been educated"). Aristotle does not categorically dismiss the element of lampoon from gentlemanly humor, as one might expect. Rather, he makes room for a new type of lampoon, one that reflects the restrained liberal temperament of its agent.

In his famous discussion on the origins of comedy at *Poetics* 4.1448b34–5.1449b9, Aristotle argues that comedy, like tragedy, developed toward a *telos* of artistic and moral perfection. The evidence of *Poetics* 3.1448a24–29 suggests that Aristotle placed Aristophanes rather near the end of this development.[29] Even so, his prejudice against Old Comedy and the iambic mode of humor in general comes across quite clearly. He argues that, early in the history of poetic humor, poets divided themselves off into two different groups according to their own natural tendencies (*Poetics* 4.1448b25–28):[30]

οἱ μὲν γὰρ σεμνότεροι τὰς καλὰς ἐμιμοῦντο πράξεις καὶ τὰς τῶν τοιούτων, οἱ δὲ εὐτελέστεροι τὰς τῶν φαύλων, πρῶτον ψόγους ποιοῦντες.

Those who were more serious represented the fine deeds of fine men. Those of less substantial character represented the deeds of baser individuals, first of all composing lampoons.

At *Poetics* 4.1448b27, Aristotle consigns the iambic poets to the second class, that of the εὐτελέστεροι, "those of less substantial character." The adjective carries definite negative moral connotations. Aristotle considered the writers of iambs most distant from the *telos* of liberal humor.

It was Homer who first took strides to separate humor from lam-

---

[29] See Janko, *Aristotle on Comedy*, 206 and 211.

[30] For a close analysis of Aristotle's argument, see Else, *Plato and Aristotle on Comedy*, 186–92.

poon, and thus he merits special attention within a discussion of the history of comedy (*Poetics* 4.1448b35–38):

ὥσπερ δὲ καὶ τὰ σπουδαῖα μάλιστα ποιητὴς Ὅμηρος ἦν, μόνος γὰρ οὐχ ὅτι εὖ ἀλλὰ καὶ μιμήσεις δραματικὰς ἐποίησεν, οὕτως καὶ τὰ τῆς κωμῳδίας σχήματα πρῶτος ὑπέδειξεν, οὐ ψόγον ἀλλὰ τὸ γελοῖον δραματοποιήσας.

And just as Homer was the supreme poet of serious matters—for he was unique not only because he composed well, but also because he made representations of a dramatic nature—thus also he was the first to sketch out the form of comedy by not composing invective, but dramatic poems on the laughable, as such.

In the area of poetic humor, Homer's innovations were dual in nature: as opposed to the earlier ψόγος, which Aristotle uses here in a semitechnical sense to denote an elementary, nondramatic form of invective, Homer composed a poem, dramatic in nature, that drew its humor not from personal abuse but from the laughable as such (τὸ γελοῖον).[31]

Aristotle goes on to praise Crates, the Athenian poet of Old Comedy, for much the same reason (*Poetics* 5.1449b5–8):

τὸ δὲ μύθους ποιεῖν ['Επίχαρμος καὶ Φόρμος] τὸ μὲν ἐξ ἀρχῆς ἐκ Σικελίας ἦλθε, τῶν δὲ 'Αθήνησιν Κράτης πρῶτος ἦρξεν ἀφέμενος τῆς ἰαμβικῆς ἰδέας καθόλου ποιεῖν λόγους καὶ μύθους.

Plot composition [Epicharmus and Phormus] first came from Sicily, while among the Athenians Krates was the first to free himself from the iambic idea and compose generalized dialogues and plots.

Movement toward the comic *telos* involves the rejection of the iambic idea, which, in Aristotle's thinking, concerns both plot structure and direct personal invective. His prejudice against the iambic idea is apparent.

Aristotle's famous definition of comedy arises within the context of

---

[31] On the formal connotations of the term ψόγος, see Heath, "Aristotelian Comedy," 346–47. Heath objects to the idea that the ψόγον of *Poetics* 4.1448b37 carries any sense of personal abuse. The "iambic idea" of *Poetics* 5.1449b9, normally taken as a reference to named abuse, he restricts to plot structure, an interpretation he supports by reference to *Poetics* 9.1451b8–9. Yet it is clear from *Poetics* 9.1451b12–15 that the "universal" (καθόλου) practices of later comedy Aristotle regarded not only as innovations in plot structure, but also as a movement away from *nominatim* attack. He contrasts contemporary comedians who used "random names" (τὰ τυχόντα ὀνόματα) with "the iambic poets who write about specific individuals" (οἱ ἰαμβοποιοὶ περὶ τὸν καθ' ἕκαστον ποιοῦσιν). Generalized plots extend to generalized, fictional characterization. The two concepts are inseparable in Aristotle's thinking.

his larger discussion on the evolution of humor from its most primitive forms—phallic songs, iambics, and Old Comedy—to the more refined humor he knew from the comic stage of his own day. The definition is in no way intended to cover Greek Comedy in general, certainly not Old Comedy. Rather, it describes comedy as Aristotle knew it from his own experience, sometime in the mid to late fourth century B.C. Aristotle writes (*Poetics* 5.1449a32–37):

Ἡ δὲ κωμῳδία ἐστὶν ὥσπερ εἴπομεν, μίμησις φαυλοτέρων μέν· οὐ μέντοι κατὰ πᾶσαν κακίαν, ἀλλὰ τοῦ αἰσχροῦ, οὗ ἐστι τὸ γελοῖον μόριον. τὸ γὰρ γελοῖον ἔστιν ἁμάρτημά τι καὶ αἶσχος ἀνώδυνον καὶ οὐ φθαρτικόν, οἷον εὐθὺς τὸ γελοῖον πρόσωπον αἰσχρόν τι καὶ διεστραμμένον ἄνευ ὀδύνης.

Comedy is, just as we have said, the representation of baser individuals, not, however, extending to total depravity; rather, the laughable is a division of the ugly, for it is a certain blunder and deformity that causes no pain and is not destructive. An immediate example is the laughable mask, which is something ugly and distorted, but without pain.

The stress on painlessness here is not intended to contrast the iambic idea with the laughable as such (τὸ γελοῖον), but to contrast the proper subject matter of comedy with that of tragedy;[32] unlike comedy, tragedy focuses not on slight defects of mind and body but on total corruption (κατὰ πᾶσαν κακίαν), which is very painful and destructive, such as murders, incest, and adultery. Though it is often taken this way, the point is not that the jest is totally without sting but, rather, that the gentleman's jest focuses only on slight physical and mental defects of the lampooned; it is the defects themselves, not the lampoons, that cause no harm to their possessor or to anyone else. In other words, one can be lampooned for being stupid or having big ears but not for being a murderer. Such jests, of course, will be rather painless for all concerned. Elsewhere we learn that the gentleman's jest at times of relaxation and play will cause its object no harm but will actually please him (see *Nichomachean Ethics* 4.1128a20–25, quoted previously). This is, in all likelihood, true of Aristotle's notion of comic jest as well.

The definition Aristotle gives here is clearly a definition of comedy that has reached its *telos*, where personal lampoon, if not ruled out altogether, has been at least severely restricted. The example Aris-

---

[32] "It is important to grasp that Aristotle's characterisation of the laughable in 1449a34–35 is meant to place comedy in opposition to tragedy, not one kind of comedy in opposition to another." Heath, "Aristotelian Comedy," 352.

totle uses to illustrate this point is the comic mask itself, which, though ugly and distorted, is nonetheless laughable. Here again, it is likely that Aristotle is thinking of comedy as he knew it from his own experience. Compare, for example, what Platonius says concerning the appearance of the comic mask in his treatise *On the Different Types of Comedies* (Περὶ Διαφορᾶς Κωμῳδίων, *Prolegomena de Comoedia* 1.57–61):[33]

ἐν μὲν γὰρ τῇ παλαιᾷ εἴκαζον τὰ προσωπεῖα τοῖς κωμῳδουμένοις, ἵνα, πρίν τι καὶ τοὺς ὑποκριτὰς εἰπεῖν, ὁ κωμῳδούμενος ἐκ τῆς ὁμοιότητος τῆς ὄψεως κατάδηλος ἦ· ἐν δὲ τῇ μέσῃ καὶ νέᾳ κωμῳδίᾳ ἐπίτηδες τὰ προσωπεῖα πρὸς τὸ γελοιότερον ἐδημιούργησαν δεδοικότες τοὺς Μακεδόνας καὶ τοὺς ἐπηρτημένους ἐξ ἐκείνων φόβους.

For in Old Comedy they likened the masks to the ones who were lampooned so that, before the actors even said anything, the one lampooned was recognized from the similarity of his appearance. But in Middle and New Comedy, they fashioned masks invented for caricature, fearing the Macedonians and the terrors they threatened.

The masks of Old Comedy, if Platonius can be trusted (and there is good evidence to suggest that he can), were portrait masks.[34] In all likelihood they exaggerated the humorous defects of the individual lampooned, such as a Cleon or an Alcibiades, in order to present a ridiculous, yet recognizable portrait. Old Comedy ridiculed not only by name (ὀνομαστί), but also by face. Middle and New Comedy, however, moved toward the ridicule of types (πρὸς τὸ γελοιότερον), both in name, character, and appearance. When Aristotle illustrates his point about the proper object of jest, defining the laughable (τὸ γελοῖον) by reference to the comic mask, he is thinking of the comic masks he knew from his own day, not the portrait masks of Old Comedy. Com-

---

[33] Quotations of the *Prolegomena de Comoedia* are taken from W.J.W. Koster, *Scholia in Aristophanem*, Fasc. Ia (Groningen: Bouma's Boekhuis, 1975).

[34] For the archaeological and literary evidence concerning the appearance of the mask of Old Comedy, see L. M. Stone, *Costume in Aristophanic Comedy* (New York: Arno Press, 1981), 19–59. Concerning the existence of the particularized "portrait" mask, she concludes: "The evidence here reviewed for portrait masks is certainly strong, though each of the individual cases listed here must be judged on its own merits. The reader should always bear in mind the difficulties and possible limitations of portrait masks. . . . On the whole, however, the creation of such masks seems to be possible, and the weight of the literary evidence makes it even probable. But the most persuasive argument is the emphasis on personal humor found throughout Aristophanic drama; physical caricature would indeed conform to the verbal lampooning which is such an integral element of Old Comedy" (pp. 38–39).

edy that has reached its *telos* dismisses the iambic mode of humor altogether, and this extends to the very dress of its characters.

Although the evidence for Aristotle's theory of comedy is sketchy and certainly difficult, his scattered references to comedy and to humor in general exhibit an overall consistency. At the very least, the following conclusions can be drawn: unlike Plato, Aristotle makes room for drama, even Old Comedy, within his ideal state. He never preaches against the ὀνομαστὶ κωμῳδεῖν per se, but against its less subtle, undramatized form in the old *iambos*, which directly inspired certain Old Comic poets. He was particularly fond of the more advanced Old Comic poets, such as Crates and Aristophanes, who had done much to soften the iambic character of Old Comedy by moving toward generalized plots played out by type characters. Even Archilochus could make some claim to refined liberal humor in Aristotle's thinking.[35] Other writers of iambs and Old Comedy, however, Aristotle considered the worst sort of scandal mongerers and gossips.[36] To some extent, at least, Aristotle nurtured the old prejudice of his master against Old Comedy. Although the educated gentleman could view such performances without suffering any damage to his soul, Aristotle clearly preferred the comedy of his own day, which was far less abusive. Comedy, like tragedy, had evolved toward a moral and artistic *telos*, defined by the liberal jest. It had become morally respon-

[35] Aristotle writes at *Rhetoric* 3.1418b24–30: "And as for moral character (ἦθος), since sometimes to speak of ourselves makes us liable to the charge of envy, wordiness, or contradiction, while to speak of another suggests abusiveness or boorishness, it is necessary to make another do the speaking, just as Isocrates does in his *Philippus* and *Antidosis*. Archilochus also censures in this way, for in his iambics he makes the father say of his daughter: 'There is nothing beyond expectation, nothing to be declared impossible.' " Concerning Aristotle's attitude toward Archilochus and Hipponax, Rosen has argued that, "the term ἰαμβικὴ ἰδέα, which Aristotle applied to certain Old Comic poets (*Poet.* 1448b31), has equal utility when applied to the poetry of Archilochos and Hipponax. It denotes the many features that recur in their poetry and help to define it, especially the antagonism between poet and ἐχθρός that occasioned the *psogos*. While this may at first sight seem self-evident, it is too often overlooked when commentators consider the identity of characters that appear in the iambos. For it means that, whether the poet sings of real, fictional or semi-fictional people, he must conform to the demands of a literary tradition. Even if we believe that the principal targets of abuse somehow represent real people, we need not assume that the stories told about them represent real events, since narrative details may be informed equally by generic considerations." R. M. Rosen, "Hipponax, Boupalos, and the Conventions of the *Psogos*," *Transactions of the American Philological Association* 118 (1988): 29–30.

[36] Aristotle describes the comic poets in very negative terms at *Rhetoric* 2.1384b9–11: "And men feel shame before those who preach against the faults of their fellow citizens [ἐπὶ ταῖς τῶν πέλας ἁμαρτίαις], such as the mockers and comic poets. For they are, in a sense, slanderers and gossips [κακολόγοι . . . καί ἐξαγγελτικοί]."

sible and could, under the proper circumstances, provide a valuable catharsis of the emotions.

THE ADVOCATES OF THE IAMBIC IDEA: OLD COMEDY, THE *IAMBOS*, AND CYNIC MORALIZING

Aristotle's theory of the liberal jest, in spite of its profound influence upon much later theory, was not without rivals in its day. The practitioners of the iambic idea, in its various forms, were themselves theorists by necessity, and they had much to say in defense of their practices. Their critics, in like manner with Plato and Aristotle, converted their scathing jests into signs of moral depravity, evidence for envy, malice, and a lack of self-control. The iambographers, in turn, made open abuse and obscenity a point of honor, a sign of honesty in the pursuit of a larger, public educational program designed to restore the moral fabric of their society. The writers of the *Iambos*, the Old Comic Poets, and, later, the Cynic moralizers all argued a consistent defense of the iambic idea, stressing their commitment to παρρησία (Latin *libertas*), the right of every free citizen to speak his mind in an open, democratic society. Lampoon, therefore, took on a noble moral dimension, which was alien to the thinking of Plato and Aristotle. Thus began a second, anti-Aristotelian approach to jest, which would profoundly influence Horace's thinking on the nature of satiric humor.

The parabasis to the *Acharnians* is perhaps the most famous example of the Old Comic poet's defense of his work.[37] Aristophanes had apparently run into some legal trouble in 426 B.C., soon after the production of his *Babylonians*, in which the Athenian statesman, Cleon, had met with some scorching abuse. At *Acharnians* 630–32 the chorus leader introduces Dikaiopolis's upcoming defense, which responds to

---

[37] Concerning the didactic intent of Old Comedy, see especially D. M. MacDowell, "The Nature of Aristophanes' *Acharnians*," *Greece and Rome* 30 (1983): 143–62; K. J. Dover, *Aristophanic Comedy* (London: B. T. Batsford, 1972), 49–53; and J. Henderson, "The Demos and the Comic Competition," in J. Winkler and F. Zeitlin, eds., *Nothing to Do with Dionysos?* (Princeton: Princeton University Press, 1990), 271–313. For arguments against the didactic function of the parabasis, see A. M. Bowie, "The Parabasis in Aristophanes: Prolegomena, *Acharnians*," *Classical Quarterly* 32 (1982): 27–40. A bibliographical survey of the question is found in Ian Storey, "Old Comedy 1975–1984," *Echos du Monde Classique* 31, n.s. 6 (1987): 21. See also R. Rosen, *Old Comedy and the Iambographic Tradition* (Atlanta: Scholars Press, 1988), 5–6 (n. 21) and 18–24. I am much indebted to Rosen's work, especially as it treats the public censorial function of the *iambos* and Cratinus's place within the iambographic tradition.

the charge that the poet harmed the city at a very crucial point in the Peloponnesian War:

διαβαλλόμενος δ' ὑπὸ τῶν ἐχθρῶν ἐν Ἀθηναίοις ταχυβούλοις,
ὡς κωμῳδεῖ τὴν πόλιν ἡμῶν καὶ τὸν δῆμον καθυβρίζει,
ἀποκρίνεσθαι δεῖται νυνὶ πρὸς Ἀθηναίους μεταβούλους.

Slandered by his enemies among the fickle Athenians, on the grounds that he lampoons our city and does violence to its people, it is now necessary to give answer to the inconstant Athenians.

The speaker goes on to reverse the charges, claiming that the comic poet is not a threat to the city but a great benefit. Aristophanes makes a humorous jibe against Athenian greed by promising that foreigners will come from far and wide, doling out large sums of cash to get a glimpse of the comic poet, "who risks the dangers of saying what is right among the Athenians" (ὅστις παρεκινδύνευσ' εἰπεῖν ἐν Ἀθηναίοις τὰ δίκαια). He then claims that even the great king of Persia respects his daring (647–51):

ὅτε καὶ βασιλεύς, Λακεδαιμονίων τὴν πρεσβείαν βασανίζων,
ἠρώτησεν πρῶτα μὲν αὐτοὺς πότεροι ταῖς ναυσὶ κρατοῦσιν·
εἶτα δὲ τοῦτον τὸν ποιητὴν ποτέρους εἴποι κακὰ πολλά.
τούτους γὰρ ἔφη τοὺς ἀνθρώπους πολὺ βελτίους γεγενῆσθαι.
κἂν τῷ πολέμῳ πολὺ νικήσειν, τοῦτον ξύμβουλον ἔχοντας.

And when the king was cross-examining the Spartan ambassadors, he asked them first which had the stronger navy, and next which had the poet who would address its many evils. For he said that those men were far braver and would be more victorious in war who possessed his counsel.

The irony of this passage does not obscure its serious intent: the comic poet advertises his value to society. He is a censor who addresses the evils of his city. His jests, though painful and unsparing, are made in a morally responsible manner. They aim at edification, the promotion of the overall welfare of the Athenian state. There is enough consistency in Aristophanes' apologetic claims from play to play to suggest that these sentiments accurately convey the poetic program for which he desired to be remembered. Whether he wrote each of his plays with these principles in mind is another question altogether.

At *Wasps* 650–51, Bdelykleon breaks the dramatic illusion in order to address the question of the purpose of comedy and the positive role of the comic poet:

χαλεπὸν μὲν καὶ δεινῆς γνώμης καὶ μείζονος ἢ 'πὶ τρυγῳδοῖς,
ἰάσασθαι νόσον ἀρχαίαν ἐν τῇ πόλει ἐντετοκυῖαν.

It is a difficult task and of marvelous intelligence, beyond even that of
comic poets, to heal an age-old disease engrained in the city.

The passage suggests a comparison between the Old Comic poet and
a physician; he attempts to cure the ills of the city, referring, in this
case, to the sickness of the Athenian judicial system exemplified by
Philokleon. Later in the parabasis (1015–50), the poet berates his audience for rejecting his efforts of the previous year, the original version of the *Clouds*. His enemies, the sophists and Cleon, he compares
to the various misshapen monsters destroyed by Heracles. The comic
poet is a second Heracles, ἀλεξίκακον, τῆς χώρας τῆσδε καθαρτήν ("the
protector from evil, the one who purges the land," 1043). He fights
on his city's behalf: ἀλλ' ὑπὲρ ὑμῶν ἔτι καὶ νυνὶ πολεμεῖ ("But even now
he wages war on your behalf," 1037). Again the analogy, while humorous, makes a case for the serious intent of the comic poet: like
the warrior or physician, he causes pain, but he does so only with a
view toward protecting or healing his city.

In the parabasis of his *Peace*, Aristophanes borrows heavily from
the parabasis of the *Wasps*, produced in the preceding year. Again,
he makes a case for ridicule that does more than elicit a laugh. He
distances his work from the low humor of rival comedies, which leveled abuse at slaves (*Peace* 748–53):

> τοιαῦτ' ἀφελὼν κακὰ καὶ φόρτον καὶ βωμολοχεύματ' ἀγεννῆ,
> ἐποίησε τέχνην μεγάλην ἡμῖν κἀπύργωσ' οἰκοδομήσας
> ἔπεσιν μεγάλοις καὶ διανοίαις καὶ σκώμμασιν οὐκ ἀγοραίοις.
> οὐκ ἰδιώτας ἀνθρωπίσκους κωμῳδῶν οὐδὲ γυναῖκας,
> ἀλλ' Ἡρακλέους ὀργήν τιν' ἔχων τοῖσι μεγίστοις ἐπεχείρει,
> διαβὰς βυρσῶν ὀσμὰς δεινὰς κἀπειλὰς βορβοροθύμους.

Having removed such trash and vulgarity and buffoonery, he created
for us a great art, and, having laid its foundation, he built it high with
lofty words and thoughts and lampoons, not the marketplace type. He
does not make fun of lowlifes and women, but, possessing the wrath of
Heracles, he puts his hand to significant men, braving the stench of their
hides and their filthy threats.

Again we see the comparison with Heracles, quoted directly from the
parabasis of the *Wasps*. Aristophanes suggests that he alone was responsible for making lampoon into a high art. He moved away from
the abuse of nameless lowlifes to take on men of real significance,

such as Lamachos and Cleon, whom he regarded as dangerous to the state and worthy of abuse.

Though he suggests otherwise, Aristophanes was not the first to introduce *ad hominem* abuse of Athens's leading citizens to the stage of comedy. The practice was long known to him from the works of Cratinus, whom Rosen and others have identified as the "pivotal figure" in the development of the iambic idea.[38] Later theorists drew a strong connection between the works of the earliest poets of Old Comedy, especially Cratinus, and the *Iambos*, which had become synonymous with personal abuse. Platonius, for example, says of Cratinus (*Cratinus Testimonia* 17KA):

Κρατῖνος ὁ τῆς παλαιᾶς κωμῳδίας ποιητής, ἅτε δὴ κατὰ τὰς ᾿Αρχιλόχου ζηλώσεις, αὐστηρὸς μὲν ταῖς λοιδορίαις ἐστίν· οὐ γάρ, ὥσπερ ὁ ᾿Αριστοφάνης, ἐπιτρέχειν τὴν χάριν τοῖς σκώμμασι ποιεῖ τὸ φορτικὸν τῆς ἐπιτιμήσεως διὰ ταύτης ἀναιρῶν, ἀλλ᾿ ἁπλῶς κατὰ τὴν παροιμίαν "γυμνῇ τῇ κεφαλῇ" τίθησι τὰς βλασφημίας κατὰ τῶν ἁμαρτανόντων.

Cratinus, the poet of Old Comedy, in emulation of Archilochus, is severe in his abuses. Unlike Aristophanes, he does not cloak his lampoons with charm, thereby removing the vulgar element from his reproach; rather, he levels his harmful jibes against wrongdoers in a straightforward manner, "with bald-headed abuse," according to the proverb.

Cratinus consciously emulates Archilochus. Like the iambic poet, he is associated with "blasphemous," literally, "harm-speaking" abuse.[39] Aristophanes is credited with softening this type of jest by adding an element of "kindness" or "charm" (χάρις). The claim that he "removes the vulgar element from reproach" (τὸ φορτικὸν τῆς ἐπιτιμήσεως . . . ἀναιρῶν) parallels nicely Aristophanes' own claims at *Peace* 748 (ἀφελὼς κακὰ καὶ φόρτον). Also, we recall from *Poetics* 5.1449b5–8 that Crates' dismissal of the iambic idea was a twofold innovation, both a reformation in plot structure and the rejection of direct, personal abuse. Platonius's notes on Cratinus suggest that he followed Archilochus not only in the severity of his abuse but also in the loose, unstudied structure of the ψόγος. He gives a grammarian's analysis: "He is well ordered in the introductions and elaborations of his dramas, but then he fills them out by tossing off his arguments and scattering them about in a haphazard fashion."[40]

---

[38] See Rosen, *Old Comedy*, 37.

[39] On Archilochus's reputation as a writer of "blasphemous" verse, see ibid., 13.

[40] For the writer of the anonymous *De Comoedia*, Cratinus was midway between Susarion and Aristophanes in the movement of Old Comedy from the iambic idea toward Aristotle's *telos* (see Cratinus Testimonia 19KA): "The Old Comedies differ among

The few fragments we possess of Cratinus suggest that he both perceived and advertised the influence of the iambic ψόγος upon his work. Fragment 6KA, taken from a play significantly titled the *Archilochoi*, speaks in praise of Archilochus, and other fragments show strong traits of the iambographic tradition. Aristophanes perceived some natural connection between Cratinus and the ritual *Iambos*. At *Frogs* 357 the chorus urges that those should stay away who have not been initiated in the Bacchic rites "of Cratinus's bull-eating tongue." What follows, as Rosen has pointed out, is a reenactment "of a Gephyrismos-like ψόγος," which gives a religious sanction to the practices of the comic poet.[41] Aristophanes understood his debt, as a writer of comedies, to the nondramatic forms of the *Iambos*, and he explicitly mentions Cratinus, an avowed emulator of Archilochus, in this connection. The anonymous *De Comoedia* suggests that, like Aristophanes and unlike earlier practitioners of Old Comedy, such as Susarion, Cratinus made his jests in a morally responsible manner (Cratinus Testimonia 19KA): "He [was the first] to add a beneficial element [τὸ ὠφέλιμον] to the fun of comedy, attacking wrongdoers and punishing them with, as it were, the public whip of his comedy."

Although the evidence is sketchy and certainly difficult, the fragments of Archilochus and Hipponax support the idea that the old Iambic poets understood and advertised the public, censorial function of their work. Hipponax, for example, frequently converts his enemy into a φαρμακός, the technical term for a man chosen as a public scapegoat, whose beating and exile would work some sort of "healing remedy" (compare φάρμακον) for the city.[42] At Degani fragment 26 he speaks of one who is to be lashed with fig branches in order to "cleanse the city" (πόλιν καθαίρειν).[43] Aristophanes, perhaps in direct imitation of Hipponax, makes his enemies into φαρμακοί at *Knights* 1405, *Frogs* 733, and fragment 655KA. At *Wasps* 650–51 he draws an analogy between the comic poet and a physician, and later in the

themselves, for the Attic writers who first framed the customary features of comedy brought their characters on stage in a haphazard fashion and laughter was their only consideration. But when Cratinus came upon the scene he established the number of characters at three, putting a stop to the disorder. And he added an element of benefit to the delight of comedy by lampooning wrongdoers, punishing them with the public whip of his comedy. But still, even he took part in the older fashion and of disorder from time to time." Again, concomitant with the movement from personal abuse to generalized humor is the movement away from the loose formal structure of the old ψόγος toward the universalized mimetic plot structure, which was the second half of Crates' innovation.

[41] See Rosen, *Old Comedy*, 24–28.
[42] For these observations I am indebted to Rosen (ibid., 21–24).
[43] See E. Degani, *Hipponactis Testimonia et Fragmenta*, Vol. 1 (Leipzig: Teubner, 1983).

same play (*Wasps* 1043) he makes himself the "cleanser" (καθαρτής) of the state. Although it is impossible to say whether Aristophanes drew these images directly from earlier iambic poetry, it is clear that, as a fellow writer of ψόγοι, he shared some sense of their public censorial function.

The later perception of the old iambic writers put an extreme emphasis on their penchant for biting invective. Their artistic qualities and their mastery of softer types of jest, which even Aristotle could appreciate, are almost never mentioned. Often the old iambic writers were compared to vicious animals: the bull that gores with its horn, the wasp that stings, snakes and dogs that bite. Callimachus, in his Γραφεῖον, draws the following portrait of Archilochus (Callimachus fragment 380 Pfeiffer): εἵλκυσε δέ δριμύν τε χόλον κυνὸς ὀξύ τε κέντρον σφηκός, ἀπ᾽ ἀμφοτέρων δ᾽ ἰὸν ἔχει στόματος ("He took from the dog's vicious wrath and the sharp sting of the wasp. He has the venom of both in his mouth"). At *Palatine Anthology* 7.71, the innocent wayfarer is warned to keep clear of Archilochus's tomb: "Depart in silence, traveler. Do not disturb the wasps that make their nest in this man's tomb."

The analogy with harmful beasts is not flattering and stems, perhaps, from a very conservative, Aristotelian view of poetic humor, which stresses the pain of invective without any reference to its positive moral function. As we have seen, the iambic poets and writers of Old Comedy preferred to compare themselves with physicians or warriors, who cause pain only to cure or protect. This view of the iambic idea, though it could claim no theoretical support in Plato or Aristotle, did not die out after the demise of Old Comedy but enjoyed a vigorous life in the Hellenistic period among the later practitioners of the *Iambos*. Theocritus's epitaph of Hipponax, for example, attests to a much more favorable view of the old iambic poets (*Palatine Anthology* 13.3):

Ὁ μουσοποιὸς ἐνθάδ᾽ Ἱππῶναξ κεῖται.
εἰ μὲν πονηρός, μὴ ποτέρχευ τῷ τύμβῳ·
εἰ δ᾽ ἐσσὶ κρήγυός τε καὶ παρὰ χρηστῶν,
θαρσέων καθίζευ, κἢν θέλῃς, ἀπόβριξον.

Here lies the poet Hipponax. If you are evil, do not approach the tomb. But if you are honest and worthy, take heart and have a seat, and, if you like, take a nap.

The epitaph assumes that only the evil man need fear the attacks of Hipponax. His reproaches are not haphazard, they are made in a morally responsible manner.

The same sentiment we see at *Epodes* 6.11–16, where Horace compares his invective to the work of the great iambic masters:

> cave, cave: namque in malos asperrimus
>   parata tollo cornua,
> qualis Lycambae spretus infido gener
>   aut acer hostis Bupalo.
> an, si quis atro dente me petiverit,
>   inultus ut flebo puer?

Watch out! Beware! For I brandish ready horns in my bitter rage against evildoers, just like that son-in-law once spurned by Lycambes or the bitter enemy of Bupalus. Now do you suppose that, if someone should attack me with malicious tooth, I will go unavenged and cry like a little child?

Horace associates his *Epodes* with the *Iambs* of Archilochus and Hipponax, who direct their invective against evildoers (*in malos*). He pictures himself as a bull on the attack, harassed by some petulant dog. In the opening lines of *Epodes* 6, he contrasts his attacks, which are justified, to those of his unnamed offender:

> Quid immerentis hospites vexas, canis
>   ignavos adversum lupos?
> quin huc inanis, si potes, vertis minas,
>   et me remorsurum petis?
> nam qualis aut Molossus aut fulvos Laco,
>   amica vis pastoribus,
> agam per altas aure sublata nives,
>   quaecumque praecedet fera.

Why do you harass undeserving strangers, a cowardly dog against wolves? Why don't you turn your empty threats this way, if you are able, and attack me, someone who will bite back? For just like a Molossian hound or the tawny Laconian, the shepherd's faithful support, with my ears upraised I will pursue through the deep snow whatever beast runs ahead.

The ignoble dog offends by making random attacks against the undeserving (*immerentes*). The Molossian or Laconian hound is faithful to its master, valued for steady service in shepherding and hunting.

The motif of the noble dog in *Epodes* 6 is significant, for it assumes a connection between the iambic poet and the Cynic moralizer, both known for their bitter lampoons. Cynics, of course, get their name from some perceived "doglike" quality in their character. The term probably began as a source of derision. The Cynics were chided for being no better than dogs: they lived outdoors, begged for food, barked at strangers, defecated and copulated in the streets. The dog analogy the Cynics quickly turned to their advantage. Diogenes Laertius records the following anecdote of Diogenes the Cynic (6.60): "When asked why he was called a dog, he said, 'I fawn upon those who provide for me, I bark at those who do not, and I bite evildoers'" (τοὺς δὲ πονηροὺς δάκνων). The Cynic, in other words, is not a begging mutt or rabid cur, but a noble watchdog that protects its master's house. The anecdote is humorous, but it once again points to the moral responsibility of Cynic lampoon. A second, even closer parallel to *Epodes* 6, we see at Diogenes Laertius 6.55:

> When asked what type of dog he was, he [Diogenes] said: "When I am hungry, I am a Maltese, but when I have eaten I am a Molossian. These the many, though praising them, do not dare accompany on the hunt because of the toil. Thus, neither are you able to live my life on account of the fear of the sufferings involved."[44]

The Cynic influence on Horace's self-definition in *Epodes* 6 is obvious, and we note with what ease he moves from the characterization of the iambic poet, the bull, to that of the Cynic, the noble Molossian hound. This is not uncommon, for by Horace's day, the Cynics, iambic poets, and the writers of Old Comedy had been reduced to a single class, noted for their shared commitment to παρρησία, Latin *libertas*, the free citizen's right to open abuse without fear of reprisal.

Gerhard has made a good summary of the Cynic creed:

> In contrast to the flattery of the κόλαξ, the Cynic speaks the truth in every circumstance so as to construct an antithesis between the concepts of ἀληθής and κόλαξ, and "life's greatest treasure" he regards as the courage for free speech, the typical παρρησία.[45]

The creed recalls the anecdote recorded of Diogenes the Cynic (Diogenes Laertius 6.69) that, when asked what was man's most beautiful possession (τί κάλλιστον ἐν ἀνθρώποις), he replied in one word: "παρρησία" The term embraces the idea of named assault, the frank statement of the truth regardless of persons.

The antithesis of Cynic parrhesia is flattery, telling one's friends what they most want to hear when, in reality, what they most need to

---

[44] Compare *Captivi* 85–87, spoken by Ergasilus the parasite: *prolatis rebus parasiti venatici / sumus, quando res redierunt, molossici / odiosicique et multum incommodestici* ("During the holidays we parasites are hunting hounds. When things return to normal we become Molossians, malicious mutts and dogs of distress"). On the Cynic background to this passage, see Oltramare, *Diatribe romaine*, 70.

[45] G. A. Gerhard, *Phoinix von Kolophon* (Leipzig: Teubner, 1909), 34.

hear is the painful truth. Horace at *Epistles* 1.18 advises his friend Lollius, the "most outspoken of men" (*liberrime*), to avoid the role of the buffoon, the "jester of the lowest couch" (*imi derisor lecti*, 10–11) whose obsequious flatteries resemble those of a "mime actor who acts the second part" (*partis mimum tractare secundas*, 14). The opposite type, although not specifically named, is obviously the Cynic, who insists on "barking out" (*elatrem*, 18) at whomever he pleases. As a result, the Cynic does not eat nearly as well as the flatterer, for he must offend his host should the need for reproach arise. The Cynic and the buffoon share much in common: like the parasites of New Comedy, they must beg their meals. They earn their bread by means of their aggressive wit. Yet they are opposites. Horace describes the difference in the anecdote of Aristippus, the spendthrift who courted Hellenistic kings and gave the following response to the criticisms of Diogenes the Cynic (*Epistles* 1.17.17–19): *namque / mordacem Cynicum sic eludebat, ut aiunt: / "scurror ego ipse mihi, populo tu"* ("Thus he (Aristippus) made fun of the harsh Cynic, as the story goes: 'I play the *scurra* for my own benefit, you on behalf of the people' "). The Cynic, though he resembles the buffoon in his poverty, dress, and mordant wit, differs in the intent of his jest, which serves a larger, public censorial function. Compare Aristophanes' statements at *Acharnians* 656–58:

> φησὶν δ' ὑμᾶς πολλὰ διδάξειν ἀγάθ', ὥστ' εὐδαίμονας εἶναι,
>
> οὐ θωπεύων, οὔθ' ὑποτείνων μισθούς, οὐδ' ἐξαπατύλλων,
>
> οὐδὲ πανουργῶν, οὐδὲ κατάρδων, ἀλλὰ τὰ βέλτιστα διδάσκων.

> He proposes to teach you many good things, to make you prosper. He does not flatter you nor does he bribe, cheat, play the scoundrel, or shower you with praise, but he teaches you what is best.

Aristophanes, like the later Cynics, proposes not to play up to his audience. He speaks his mind for a higher purpose than winning the dramatic contest. In the age of Diogenes, Bion, and Crates, free speech was greatly restricted. Flattery was the norm rather than the rule, and the Cynics, drawing upon the example of the Old Comic poets, sought to recover the full aggressive force of παρρησία, which they knew from the democratic Athens of more than a hundred years before.

Humor is the less hostile, "sweet" side of Cynic frankness. Diogenes once described his brand of moralizing with the following analogy:[46]

---

[46] On these lines see Gerhard, *Phoinix*, 41–42.

Οἱ μὲν ἰατροὶ τὰς τῶν ἐκλεικτῶν φαρμάκων πικρίας μέλιτι, οἱ δὲ σοφοὶ τὰς τῶν δυσκολωτέρων ἀνθρώπων ὁμιλίας ἱλαρότητι γλυκαίνουσιν.

As physicians sweeten the bitterness of their pills with honey, philosophers sweeten their instructions to peevish men with cheerfulness.

The Cynic mixes the bitter with the sweet, the serious with the laughable, to make his harsh lessons palatable to a larger, sometimes peevish audience. The physician analogy, as we have seen, has roots in the *Iambos* and Old Comedy,[47] and the same is true of the seriocomic moralizing described here, the *spoudaiogeloion*, which was the singular characteristic of Cynic moralizing, often credited to them as their unique invention. At *Frogs* 389–93, the chorus, devotees of Demeter, pray for victory in the ritual *Iambos*:

καὶ πολλὰ μὲν γέλοιά μ' εἰπεῖν, πολλὰ δὲ σπουδαῖα, καὶ
τῆς σῆς ἑορτῆς ἀξίως
παίσαντα καὶ σκώψαντα νι-
κήσαντα ταινιοῦσθαι.

Allow me to say many things in jest and many things in seriousness, and, having sported and lampooned in a manner worthy of your feast, let me, victorious, win the victor's wreath.

The chorus prays that they might win first prize for their "playing" and "lampooning." It is their duty to mix a great deal of humor (πολλὰ μὲν γέλοια) with a great deal of seriousness (πολλὰ δὲ σπουδαῖα). This is the earliest clear formulation of the *spoudaiogeloion*, the mainstay of Cynic moralizing that would play such a large role in shaping

---

[47] Diogenes Laertius (6.4) records the following anecdote of Antisthenes, once again bringing the physician analogy to the fore: ἐρωτηθεὶς διὰ τί πικρῶς τοῖς μαθηταῖς ἐπιπλήττει, "καὶ οἱ ἰατροί," φησί, "τοῖς κάμνουσιν" ("When asked why he lashed at his students so bitterly Diogenes replied, 'so do doctors lash at the sick' "). As popular as the physician metaphor may have been among the Cynics, it was not original to them. Aristophanes first attempted to describe the nature of his work in these terms. Once again we note a tradition shared between the Old Comic poets and the Cynics. The satirist places himself within this same tradition when he compares himself, as a Cynic moralizer, with a physician at *Satires* 1.4.126–29, and again at *Epistles* 1.1.33–40. This analogy is especially easy for the Cynic, working in Latin, to maintain because of the double meaning of *vitium*, which may mean either a moral "flaw" or "physical defect." Horace, once again, shows that he is very aware of the manner in which the Cynics approached their work and the types of illustrations they favored to relate this. This tradition has its basis in Old Comedy, and it is precisely in this tradition that the satirist chooses to place himself in *Satires* 1.4.

82 CHAPTER TWO

Horace's satiric mission.⁴⁸ Behind this notion is the idea that stinging lampoon, in spite of its humor, serves a purpose that goes beyond merely evoking a laugh. To use Horace's own analogy, humor is simply the sweet cookie, the bait used to introduce young boys to the serious matter of their ABCs.⁴⁹

Παρρησία, the stinging type, not the gentleman's jest preferred by Aristotle and his followers, was the one possession the Cynic truly prized. It was the legacy of the iambographic tradition, and it was recognized as such by the ancients. Diogenes Laertius describes Bion as "Theatrical and totally given over to cutting ridicule, using vulgar language against the affairs of life" (T11). Judging from the type of humor described, the stage reference, θεατρικός, must allude to the practices of Old Comedy. Demetrius also, at *On Style* 5.259, speaks of ἐν ταῖς κωμῳδίαις ("in comedies") and ὁ Κυνικὸς τρόπος ("the Cynic manner") as if they were synonymous, and Marcus Aurelius goes so far as to make Diogenes the Cynic a student of Old Comedy (*Meditations* 11.6):

ἡ ἀρχαία κωμῳδία παρήχθη, παιδαγωγικὴν παρρησίαν ἔχουσα καὶ τῆς ἀτυφίας οὐκ ἀχρήστως δι᾽ αὐτῆς τῆς εὐθυρρημοσύνης ὑπομιμνήσκουσα· πρὸς οἷόν τι καὶ Διογένης ταυτὶ παρελάμβανεν.

Old Comedy was introduced, having an instructive openness and suggesting modesty in an effective manner through its very plainness of language. To a similar end Diogenes adopted this as well.

Old Comedy and Cynic moralizing are bound by παρρησία, simplicity of language and a common pedagogic end. Though it seems quite likely, it is impossible to say whether Diogenes formulated his Cynic mission under the direct influence of Old Comedy. The intermediary of Socratic literature was certainly influential as well. Even so, the evidence suggests that there was a strong fellow feeling between the Cynics and the earlier practitioners of the iambic idea. At a time when freedom of speech was severely restricted on the stage of comedy, the Cynics sought to recall the Golden Age of Athenian παρ-

⁴⁸ Kindstrand, *Bion*, 47–49, discusses the influence of both Old Comedy and the Socratic tradition upon the Cynic concept of the *spoudaiogeloion*. For other general surveys, see also Grant, "Ancient Rhetorical Theories," 57–61; Fiske, *Lucilius and Horace*, 143–208; and L. Giangrande, *The Use of Spoudaiogeloion in Greek and Roman Literature*, Studies in Classical Literature 6 (The Hague: Mouton, 1972).

⁴⁹ See *Satires* 1.1.23–26, which Kiessling and Heinze regard as a "paraphrase of the concept of σπουδαιογέλοιον, which characterizes the κυνικὸς τρόπος in popular philosophy." Kiessling and Heinze, *Horatius Flaccus*, 7. See also Giangrande, *Spondaiogeloion*, 105–9.

ϱησία, exemplified in the works of Archilochus, Hipponax, and the writers of Old Comedy. They exploited this connection. By Horace's day, the writers of iambs, the Old Comic poets, and Cynic moralizers had become virtually synonymous, joined by their adherence to the *spoudaiogeloion* and the iambic idea.

The Hellenistic period saw the publication of numerous works on the topic περὶ τοῦ γελοίου, of which all have perished.[50] As a result, what little that can be said about Hellenistic theories of humor must be gleaned from later ethical and rhetorical tracts, the earliest of which date to the first century B.C. In spite of these difficulties, one trend that can be safely traced to the Hellenistic theorists is a significant shift away from the highly conservative principles of Plato and Aristotle on the topic of Old Comedy and the iambic idea in general. For example, preserved in most editions of the *Prolegomena to Comedy* are two substantial fragments of a much larger work by Platonius entitled *On Comedy* (Περὶ Κωμῳδίας). The surviving excerpts are entitled *On the Different Types of Comedies* and *On the Different Types of Characters* (Περὶ Διαφορᾶς Κωμῳδίων and Περὶ Διαφορᾶς Χαρακτήρων). Platonius, unfortunately, is simply a name assigned to these fragments, and no details concerning his life or the setting in which he produced his work can be safely reconstructed.[51] Still, as Karl Wendel and others have pointed out, Platonius's comments are taken from a very early source.[52]

[50] Julius Caesar Strabo, who doubts that there can be such a thing as a "theory" (*ratio*) of jest, relates at *De Oratore* 2.217 that he had seen a number of Greek books *de ridiculis*, all of which he found "insipid" or "witless" (*insulsi*). Their *insulsitas*, he adds, was the only thing he found in them worth laughing at.

[51] Even the roughest notion concerning the date of Platonius's remarks on comedy is elusive. Janko puts him in the fifth century A.D., but this is based purely on speculation concerning the name, Platonius, which may have something to do with the rise of Neoplatonism. See Janko, *Aristotle on Comedy*, 89.

[52] "The fact that, in the first section, New Comedy (νέα) is given only brief mention and plays no part in the definition of comedy and the defining characteristics of the Old and Middle, as well as the neat comparison of the three Comedians in the second section (the pattern of which is reminiscent of Dionysius of Halicarnassus and Quintilian respectively), indicates that Platonius made use of a very ancient source." K. Wendel, "Platonios," in A. Pauly, and G. Wissowa, eds., *Real-Encyclopädie der classischen Altertumswissenschaft* (Stuttgart: J. B. Metzler, 1894–1963), col. 2544. See also G. Kaibel, "Die Prolegomena ΠΕΡΙ ΚΩΜΩΙΔΙΑΣ," *Abhandlungen der Gesellschaft der Wissenschaften zu Göttingen* 2, no. 4 (1898): 3–70. Kaibel discusses some of Platonius's shortcomings as a critic, but nowhere does he question the fact that Platonius drew upon a very ancient source. He writes: "The clear, simple diction, the easy, unassuming sentence structure, the appropriate use of political terminology . . . it all testifies to a source of considerable age and to an author fully conversant with historical events" (p. 47).

The changing political conditions in late fifth-century Athens Platonius regards as the primary factor that prompted the shift from Old to Middle Comedy (*Prolegomena de Comoedia* 1.5–12):

τῆς ἰσηγορίας οὖν πᾶσιν ὑπαρχούσης ἄδειαν οἱ τὰς κωμῳδίας συγγράφοντες εἶχον τοῦ σκώπτειν καὶ στρατηγοὺς καὶ δικαστὰς τοὺς κακῶς δικάζοντας καὶ τῶν πολιτῶν τινας ἢ φιλαργύρους ἢ συζῶντας ἀσελγείᾳ. ὁ γὰρ δῆμος, ὡς εἶπον, ἐξῄρει τὸν φόβον τῶν κωμῳδούντων φιλοτίμως τῶν τοὺς τοιούτους βλασφημούντων ἀκούων· ἴσμεν γάρ, ὡς ἀντίκειται φύσει τοῖς πλουσίοις ἐξ ἀρχῆς ὁ δῆμος καὶ ταῖς δυσπραγίαις αὐτῶν ἥδεται. ἐπὶ τοίνυν τῆς Ἀριστοφάνους καὶ Κρατίνου καὶ Εὐπόλιδος κωμῳδίας ἀφόρητοί τινες κατὰ τῶν ἁμαρτανόντων ἦσαν οἱ ποιηταί.

When there was equality for all, the writers of comedy were without fear and were free to lampoon even the generals, the jurymen for judging wrongly, and, among the citizens, the greedy or those who lived in wanton luxury. For the people, so they said, removed the comic poets' fear as they eagerly listened to them blaspheme men of this sort. For we know that the common crowd has always been, by nature, hostile to the rich, taking delight in their misfortunes. In the case of the comedy of Aristophanes, Eupolis, and Cratinus, the poets were unsparing toward wrongdoers.

We see in this passage a significant shift from the Aristotelian view of Old Comedy. The sentiments expressed are, in fact, in keeping with what Aristophanes himself has to say concerning the moral significance of his work: the Old Comic poet is a protector of the city; his abuse is not exercised at random but is carefully directed at those who most severely threaten the welfare of the state, namely, the crooked judges and inept generals. There is no question of envy playing a role in the Old Comic poet's attacks, and no objections are raised against the obscenity and directness of Old Comedy. If anything, there seems to be some regret for these lost freedoms. Lampoons are made not against slight defects of character (ἁμάρτημά τι) but against the wrongdoers themselves (κατὰ τῶν ἁμαρτανόντων), dangerous enemies of the state. Linguistically, the alteration seems rather slight, but it marks a significant shift from the much narrower, Aristotelian view of Old Comedy and the iambic idea toward the view of the Old Comic poets themselves.

Platonius's comments on the development of comedy demonstrate that, at some time in the Hellenistic period, perhaps quite early, the iambic idea gained a certain degree of respectability among the theorists of humor, which it never enjoyed in the tradition of Plato and Aristotle. Writers in the iambographic tradition had defended their works in a consistent manner ever since the days of Archilochus and

Hipponax, yet only at a relatively late stage in the history of ancient criticism did these apologies attain to the status of "theory." It was through the influence of the Cynics, the Hellenistic advocates of παρρησία, that this shift came about.

From the initial statements of Platonius's Περὶ Κωμῳδίας (quoted earlier), we note that the Old Comic poets focused their censure not only upon crooked public officials, thus fulfilling their public censorial function, but also upon the "lovers of money" (φιλαργύρους) and "those who lived in wanton luxury" (συζῶντας ἀσελγείᾳ). Platonius claims that the common crowd naturally loves to see "rich men" (τοῖς πλουσίοις) meet with misfortune. He makes a similar shift at lines 44–47, where he contends that the "arguments" (ὑποθέσεις) of Old Comedy consist of the censure of generals and judges as well as "those who pile up cash illegally and those who live wicked lives" (καὶ χρήματα συλλέγουσιν ἐξ ἀδικίας τισὶ καὶ μοχθηρὸν ἐπανῃρημένοις βίον). In each case, Platonius has broadened the scope of the Old Comic poets' invective to include nonpolitical figures characterized by some type of moral vice. The vices mentioned are not flagrant abuses of the state and its laws, rather, they are the vices traditionally addressed in Cynic diatribe, namely, greed and luxury (philargyria and luxuria). It was Bion, we recall, not Saint Paul, who first made the love of money the root of all evil (F35A): βίων ὁ σοφιστής τὴν φιλαργυρίαν μητρόπολιν ἔλεγε πάσης κακίας εἶναι ("Bion the sophist said that the love of money was the capital city of all evil"). And Crates the Cynic, in similar fashion, argued that all evil came διὰ τρυφὴν καὶ πολυτέλειαν ("through luxury and extravagance"), terms that closely approximate the συζῶντας ἀσελγείᾳ of line 9.[53] For Platonius, the Old Comic poets made their jests in the manner of the later Cynics who, when the freedom to lampoon important political figures was no longer an option, directed their jibes at nonpolitical figures and against common vices, not specific crimes.

What makes all of this so suggestive and important for the present study is the fact that Aristotle's liberal jest, a theory of enormous significance in later criticism, had considerable rivals in the Hellenistic period. The commentators on Horace have never seriously considered that the Hellenistic critics were themselves sharply divided on the question of poetic humor. Horace, an expert in Greek poetic theory, knew of both traditions, the Aristotelian and the iambographic. In his programmatic satires, therefore, he must somehow establish a

[53] On the Cynic topos φιλαργυρία, see Kindstrand, Bion, 243–44; and Gerhard, Phoinix, 61–63, 267, and 279. On the topos of luxuria, Greek τρυφή, see Kindstrand, Bion, 218.

place for his work within these divergent and hostile traditions. This, we shall see, he does with remarkable success.

LIBERTAS IN THE AGE OF HORACE

Satires 1.4 proposes in its first lines to take up the topic of *libertas*, "freedom," a word the satirist applies to the Old Comic poets and Lucilius to denote primarily freedom of speech in the context of humorous, censorial poetry. Syme, DuQuesnay, and others have pointed out that the term was much broader in the 40s and 30s B.C., possessing definite political connotations inseparable from even a purely "nonpolitical," theoretical discussion of *libertas*, such as we see in *Satires* 1.4.[54] *Libertas* was an extremely volatile issue. It possessed the power to elicit the strongest emotions of scorn and regret in an age when old freedoms, some perceived, were threatened with extinction.

By 35 B.C., the latest possible date for the publication of *Satires* 1.4, the term *libertas* had taken on an elusive, highly rhetorical color as competing factions at Rome sought to claim the moral high ground for their political agenda. Freedom, like motherhood and virtue, is one of those noble abstractions that no one can rightly oppose, and so the term became the rallying cry for each of the various factions that took part in the civil strife of the late Republic. Caesar, for example, claims to have led his army against Rome, *ut se et populum Romanum factione paucorum oppressum in libertatem vindicaret* ("to set free himself and the Roman people, who were oppressed by a minority faction"). This is certainly a counterclaim made against the charge that he enslaved the Republic, for *libertas* was much more the watchword of the old republicans, such as Cato and Brutus, and the Pompeyans, who made the most of Pompey's kinship with Lucilius. Brutus, for example, advertised his connections with his ancestor, Lucius Junius Brutus, the tyrant slayer and traditional founder of the Roman Republic. In 43 B.C. he minted coins recalling the murder of Caesar on which, above the legend EID MAR (the Ides of March), he pictured a cap of liberty, the type worn by slaves when they were granted their freedom, flanked by two daggers, which symbolize the two assassins, Brutus and Cassius. Cicero, whom Antony charged

---

[54] On the political side of the term *libertas*, see R. Syme, *The Roman Revolution* (Oxford: Clarendon Press, 1939), 154–56 and 320–22; C. Wirszubski, *Libertas as a Political Idea at Rome during the Late Republic and Early Principate* (Cambridge: Cambridge University Press, 1950); and R. MacMullen, *Enemies of the Roman Order* (Cambridge, Mass.: Harvard University Press, 1966), 1–33.

with planning Caesar's murder, though he denies complicity in the plot, makes no apologies for the murder: "Will you never understand that you must decide whether those who carried out the deed are murderers or avengers of liberty?" (*vindices libertatis*, *Philippics* 2.12.30). Trebonius, the conspirator who detained Antony outside of the senate house while Caesar was being murdered, wrote violent verses attacking Antony in May 44 B.C. He took Lucilius as his model: *Deinde, qui magis hoc Lucilio licuerit assumere libertatis, quam nobis?* ("Then again, why should Lucilius be allowed to assume this type of free speech any more than we ourselves?").[55] Cato in similar fashion had tested the limits of free speech when he published his "Archilochean" edicts against Caesar in 59 B.C.[56]

Libertas, then, was a highly volatile issue in Horace's day and had been for quite some time. Any discussion of free speech, even from a purely theoretical standpoint, carried with it strong political overtones. In *Satires* 1.4, Horace, a friend of Maecenas and thereby a perceived enemy of old freedoms, proposes to lecture his audience on the topic of *libertas*. This is a very bold, almost foolhardy, undertaking. He must be especially careful in his criticisms of Lucilius, the exemplar of old republican *libertas* who had undergone a virtual apotheosis among the anti-Caesarians in the last days of the Roman Republic. Any overt criticism of Lucilian *libertas* would be construed as evidence for Octavian's hostility to old republican ideals, his desire to "enslave" the state. Unless he wishes to aggravate old wounds, which Octavian would rather see healed, Horace must tread lightly on this issue in *Satires* 1.4.

For the politically minded Stoics, such as Cato, *libertas* possessed a public dimension it never attained among the nonactivist Epicureans, who had debated on the topic of free speech since the third century B.C. Because their philosophy was formulated at a time when παρρησία was severely limited by the Macedonian monarchs, the Epicureans understood the term in a much more restricted, nonpolitical sense. Even so, certain ground rules for free speech were necessary for the smaller, enclosed community of the Garden. Παρρησία, for the Epicureans, became a private virtue or, at most, a "Garden" virtue, the counterpart of the cardinal Epicurean principle of friendship.

---

[55] *Ad Familiares* 12.16.3, on which see DuQuesnay, "Horace and Maecenas," 29–30. Heldmann has argued that the Trebonius Satire was not politically motivated, but was directed against Dolabella, Cicero's son-in-law, on moral grounds. See K. Heldmann, "Trebonius und seine Lucilische Satire aus dem Jahre 44 v.Chr.," *Symbolae Osloenses* 63 (1988): 69–75.

[56] On Cato's "Archilochean" verse, see L. R. Taylor, *Party Politics in the Age of Caesar* (Berkeley: University of California Press, 1949), 136–37.

The main source for a study of the *topos* of free speech among the Epicureans is Philodemus's *On Free Speech* (Περὶ Παρρησίας), which was written as the epitome of a series of lectures delivered in 78 B.C. by Zeno of Sidon, head of the Epicurean school at Athens. The text was found among the charred ruins of Philodemus's library at Herculaneum early in the nineteenth century, and though nearly five-sixths of the whole work is now lost and a full third of each surviving column has crumbled away, enough survives of the treatise for certain generalizations to be made.[57] Perhaps most important, it establishes a contemporary theoretical context for *Satires* 1.4, showing that the old Hellenistic debates over the topic of free speech were very much alive in Horace's day, still capable of making enemies of rival theorists.

Philodemus follows the course of Zeno's lecture in making παρρησία the counterpart of friendship, the duty of each member of the brotherhood of Epicurus to speak frankly concerning the faults of his friends. Anything short of this is flattery and a lie, a severe threat to an honest, scholarly community. Παρρησία, then, is a moral duty. It stems from genuine concern for a friend by one who is well aware of his own faults. Reproaches are well intentioned and gentle. They do not intend to harm but to teach. This type of thinking stems ultimately from Aristotle's discussion of the mean in social behavior at *Nicomachean Ethics* 2.1108a, where friendship constitutes the mean between flattery and nastiness, truthfulness lies between boastfulness and irony, and wittiness between buffoonery and rustic severity.

Philodemus, at Olivieri fragment 79, gives a peculiar Cynic slant to this type of mild, instructive censure among friends:

δύνηται [δ᾿] αὐτὸς ἢ δι᾿ ἡμῶν ἢ δι᾿ ἄλλου τῶν σ[υ]σχολαζόντω[ν θ]ε[ρ]απευθῆναι, μηδὲ συνεχῶς αὐτὸ ποιεῖν, μηδὲ κατὰ πάντων, μηδὲ πᾶν ἁμάρτημα καὶ τὸ τυχόν, μηδ᾿ ὧν οὐ χρὴ παρόντων, μηδὲ μετὰ διαχύσεως, ἀλλὰ συνπαθῶ[ς] τ[ὰς ἁμαρ]τίας ὑπο[λαμβάνειν καὶ μὴ καθυ[βρίζειν μηδὲ λοιδορεῖ]ν ἐπὶ . . .

And he himself might be cured either through us or through another of his fellow students. But one must not do it [censure] continuously, nor in every case. One must not censure every failure and success, nor matters pertaining to those not present. One must not censure with ridicule, but one should address faults with sympathy, without abuse and reproachfulness toward . . .

[57] Textual references are to Philodemus's ΠΕΡΙ ΠΑΡΡΗΣΙΑΣ, ed. A. Olivieri (Leipzig: Teubner, 1914). Olivieri's preface is, perhaps, the best introduction to the ancient *topos* and to Philodemus's treatment of it. Description of the physical condition of the papyrus I have taken from N. W. DeWitt, "Parresiastic Poems of Horace," *Classical Philology* 30, no. 1 (1935): 312–19.

Interesting here is the idea that παρρησία serves as a type of medical treatment, a "healing," directed against some minor fault or "defect," ἁμάρτημα. The analogy is suggested in the double meaning of ἁμάρτημα, which may apply to conditions of mind or body.[58] The physician analogy, as we have seen, was especially prominent among writers in the iambographic tradition, who justified the pain they caused by referring to it as a necessary healing process for the state. The metaphor comes into play again at Olivieri fragment 40, 44, 46, 64, 65, and elsewhere. It obviously played a large role in shaping the self-understanding of the Epicurean on the question of παρρησία.

Although Philodemus's treatise on free speech shows a certain affinity to Old Comedy and Cynic moralizing, its Aristotelian leanings are much more prominent. The fragment just quoted insists on a much softer brand of παρρησία than that espoused by the Cynics; it lays strong emphasis on limiting the frequency and aggression of one's censure. Censure of those who are absent is expressly prohibited. Olivieri fragment, column I draws several further limitations:

[ἀπὸ μὲν ἀστείας] πᾶς [τίς] ποτε εὐνοῶν καὶ συνετ[ῶς] κα[ὶ συν]εχῶς φιλοσοφῶν καὶ μέγας ἐν ἕξει καὶ ἀφιλόδοξος καὶ [δη]μαγωγὸς ἥκιστα καὶ φθόνου καθαρὸς καὶ τὰ προσόντα μόνον λέγων καὶ μὴ συνεκφερόμενος, ὥστε λοιδορεῖν ἢ πομπε[ύ]ε[ιν] ἢ [κ]αταβάλλε[ιν ἢ] βλάπτ[ειν], μηδ᾽ ἀσ[ε]λγε[ί]αις κα[ὶ κο]λακευτ[ι]καῖς χρώ[μενος τέχναις.]

Each man (who uses παρρησία) as a result of his urbane disposition does so with good intention, intelligently, continuously pursuing knowledge, entirely in control of himself, without conceit, little resembling the demagogue, free of envy, and addressing only pertinent matters, not in a state of high emotion so as to reproach or boast or destroy or harm. And he makes no use of florid and flattering devices.

The passage strongly resembles Julius Caesar Strabo's comments on the proper use of humor in oratory in Book 2 of the *De Oratore*. Philodemus takes a hard line against flattery and the use of artificial modes of speech, but beyond this, his precepts bear little resemblance to Cynic notions of παρρησία. The outright rejection of envy (φθόνος), aggressive railing (λοιδορεῖν), and harm (βλάπτειν) reads as a traditional Aristotelian reproach against writers in the iambographic tradition who, in contrast to the urbane pedagogue described previ-

---

[58] On ἁμάρτημα as a physical defect, compare *Prolegomena de Comoedia* XV.33: ὁ σκώπτων ἐλέγχειν θέλει ἁμαρτήματα τῆς ψυχῆς καὶ τοῦ σώματος ("The one who lampoons desires to censure defects of the soul and of the body"). Cicero translates this idea at *De Oratore* 2.239: *est etiam deformitatis et corporis vitiorum satis bella materies ad iocandum* ("There is sufficiently good material for jokes in ugliness and in the defects of the body").

ously, were much less afraid of the pain they might cause by their abuse.[59]

The single most distinctive feature of παρρησία in the iambographic tradition is its connection with aggressive lampoon and ridicule. This is strictly prohibited from the urbane παρρησία of the Epicureans. The only explicit reference to ridicule in Philodemus's treatise, "lampoon after the manner of comedians" (κ]ωμωιδοῦντ[ες σκώπτειν]) at Olivieri fragment 18, although it is difficult to decipher within its context, is certainly derogatory. The student is advised to "spit it out abruptly, as you would some strange food." It is a sign of bad moral character, παρρησία that stems from ill will.

Overall, Philodemus's approach to free speech is very Aristotelian. DeWitt has noted that "boisterous or violent condemnation, after the manner of the cynics, is severely condemned," while, in good Aristotelian fashion, emphasis is laid on gentleness, goodwill, restraint, and consideration of persons, time, and place.[60] Among other ancient sources, Cicero and Plutarch treat the topic on a relatively large scale, and in much the same vein as Philodemus.[61] Horace himself makes free speech a corollary of friendship at *Epistles* 1.18, where extremes in *libertas* are illustrated by two comic types noted for their aggressive humor, that is, the Cynic moralizer and the buffoon, who are equivalent to the δύσκολος and κόλαξ of *Nicomachean Ethics* 2.1108a23–31. Plutarch takes this type of thinking to an extreme in his *How to Tell a Friend from a Flatterer*, where, once again, buffoons and flatterers are posited as opposite types. Plutarch states plainly his objections to παρρησία that makes use of ridicule (*Moralia* 67E):[62]

Δεύτερον τοίνυν ὥσπερ ἐκκαθαίροντες ὕβριν ἅπασαν καὶ γέλωτα καὶ σκῶμμα καὶ βωμολοχίαν ἡδύσματα πονηρὰ τῆς παρρησίας ἀφαιρῶμεν.

Second, then, as if purging them away, let us remove all abusiveness, laughter, lampoon, and buffoonery, which are evil adornments of free speech.

For Plutarch, who follows the same theoretical tradition as Philodemus, humor and free speech do not mix well. His attitude toward Old Comedy is highly negative and unyielding (*Moralia* 68B-C):

[59] DeWitt regards Olivieri fragments 37, 38, and 52, among others, as proof of Philodemus's condemnation of Cynic parrhesia. See DeWitt, "Parresiastic Poems," 313, n.8.

[60] Ibid., 313.

[61] See especially *De Officiis* 1.128–48, and Plutarch's *How to Tell a Friend from a Flatterer*.

[62] For the affinities of Plutarch to Philodemus on the question of parrhesia, see Olivieri's notes to fragments 35, 37, 38, 46, 79, cols. Ia, IIa, IIb, IIIa, IIIb, XIa, XVb, XVIIa, XVIIIb, XXIVb, and Tab. XII.

It is true that the comic poets composed many things for their audience of a serious political nature. But the admixture of the laughable [τὸ γελοῖον] with scurrility [βωμολόχον] in them, just like mixing good food with a foul sauce, ruined their free speech and made it useless, so that the reputation of malice [κακοήθεια] and brutality [βδελυρία] is all that remains for its advocates. This type of humor is useless for speakers and audience alike. On other occasions, then, laughter and play are to be employed among friends. But free speech must possess seriousness and moral character [ἡ δὲ παρρησία σπουδὴν ἐχέτω καὶ ἦθος].

The sentiments are reminiscent of Aristotle in his sterner moments. Especially noteworthy is the mention of "the laughable as such" (τὸ γελοῖον), which Plutarch, following Aristotle, considers the one element of Old Comedy worthy of respect. Buffoonery, that is, excessive, harmful ridicule, destroys the overall effect of τὸ γελοῖον. For Plutarch, as for Plato and Aristotle, the practices of Old Comedy stem from bad moral character. Play and jest have no place in free speech among friends.

Although Plutarch's views on humor and free speech stem ultimately from Aristotle, his animus against Old Comedy and the iambic idea is much more pronounced than that of Aristotle, who understood the subtler side of Aristophanes' humor and art. Plutarch and Aristotle share a preference for Middle and New Comedy, but again, Plutarch takes Aristotle's principles to an extreme. In his treatise comparing Aristophanes to Menander (*Comparatio Aristophanis et Menandri*), Plutarch praises Menander, whose comedies "alone partake of wit without envy [ἀφθόνων ἁλῶν] and of good cheer." Aristophanes' comedies, however, he regards as "bitter and harsh, and they possess a ferocity that injures and bites [ἑλκωτικὴν δριμύτητα καὶ δηκτικὴν ἔχουσι]." The association of Old Comedy with envy stems ultimately from Plato's *Philebus*, and the reference to "biting" ferocity is reminiscent of later negative perceptions of Cynic moralizing. Although he preferred the softer practices of later comedy, Aristotle was indulgent toward Old Comedy, especially the comedies of Crates and Aristophanes, which dismissed the harsher elements of the iambographic tradition. Plutarch will have none of it. His position has definite roots in Peripatetic moral theory, yet parallels with *On Free Speech* of Philodemus suggest antecedents in Hellenistic theory of an even more conservative bent. It was, after all, in the Hellenistic period, when old freedoms were severely limited, that debates over the nature of free speech came to a head. The various philosophical schools, most notably the Cynics and Epicureans, whose views constituted opposite extremes, had much to say on the matter. These debates were renewed with much vigor in the last days of the Roman

Republic, when old freedoms associated with a bygone age were again threatened with extinction. Anti-Caesarians and conservative Stoics, such as Trebonius and Cato, were especially anxious to test the limits of *libertas* by writing verse in the iambographic tradition.[63] In so doing, they certainly adhered to a non-Aristotelian theoretical tradition, such as we saw in Platonius, which was much more indulgent toward the harsher aspects of iambographic poetry. Archilochus and Lucilius took on the status of champions of old republican *libertas*, and they were much emulated, especially among the anti-Caesarians. *Libertas* became their rallying cry.

It is within this political and philosophical milieu that Horace proposes to define the limits and proper use of *libertas* in *Satires* 1.4. It is a very timely and hazardous enterprise. Regardless of whether the satire was written in response to real criticisms, it is important to realize that, both in its political import and as a piece of poetic theory, *Satires* 1.4 belongs to a real polemical context.

ARISTOTELIAN THEORY IN *SATIRES* 1.4

Horace's theory of satire owes a great deal to Aristotle. G. L. Hendrickson made this clear nearly a century ago, and much good work has been done since to define the *Satires* as working models of Aristotle's theory of liberal humor. Scholarship on this question has focused primarily on *Satires* 1.4, in which, it seems clear, the satirist seeks to define himself as a good Aristotelian. Hendrickson's analysis, while it ignores a second iambographic side to the satirist's self-definition, is still basically sound. No one seriously doubts that the poet's defense is formulated from Aristotle's theory of the liberal jest. Yet, there is a curious, fictional and very Roman side to the satirist's self-defense contained in several allusions, some previously unnoted, to the stage of popular comedy. These allusions deserve special attention, for they once again underscore the key position of comedy in Horace's definition of satire.

In all criticism of poetic humor since Plato, the buffoon (βωμολόχος) exemplifies everything vulgar and inartistic in the practice of comedy, the most offensive type of humor. Even Aristophanes, whose comedies Plutarch regarded as prime instances of βωμολοχία, claims to have rid his comedies of buffoonery.[64] This is the charge Horace seeks to address in *Satires* 1.4. The charge makes sense, for the satirist

---

[63] On Trebonius's Stoic leanings, see Chapter 3, n. 109.
[64] See *Peace* 748–53, quoted in the text.

has, to this point, played the part of a Cynic moralizer, a stage role very similar to that of comic buffoons and parasites. At *Satires* 1.4.34–38, the satirist makes the comic reference perfectly explicit:

> faenum habet in cornu; longe fuge. dummodo risum
> excutiat, sibi non, non cuiquam parcet amico;
> et quodcumque semel chartis illeverit, omnis
> gestiet a furno redeuntis scire lacuque
> et pueros et anus.

> Get back! He has hay on his horn. As long as he shakes out a laugh, he will spare neither himself nor his friend. And once he has scribbled something out on his pages, he will hasten to tell all the slave boys and old biddies as they return from the bakeshop and water tank.

Scholars have long recognized in lines 34–36 a clear allusion to *Nicomachean Ethics* 4.1128a33–35, where the buffoon is described as a slave to laughter;[65] he spares neither himself nor his friends if he can cause a laugh (εἰ γέλωτα ποιήσει). In lines 37–38, however, Horace Romanizes the allusion by including traits known to him from the various buffoons of Roman popular comedy, namely the *scurra mimicus* and the *parasitus ridiculus*, both of which were noted for their faithlessness and scandalmongering. Compare *Curculio* 477–79, where the stage manager berates the lowlifes who hang about the water tank outside the city walls:

> confidentes garrulique et malevoli supera lacum,
> qui alteri de nihilo audacter dicunt contumeliam
> et qui ipsi sat habent quod in se possit vere dicier.

> The bold, garrulous, and malicious types you will find just past the water tank. They boldly abuse others for no reason, while they themselves show traits worthy of truthful censure.

The water tank is a specifically Roman allusion. The scandalmongers who hang about the water tank are a version of the *scurra mimicus*, noted for their lying, malice, and abusive humor. At *Trinummus* 199–202, Megaronides chides himself for having been taken in by scandalmongerers who show the same traits:

> nihil est profecto stultius neque stolidius
> neque mendaciloquius neque argutum magis,
> neque confidentiloquius neque periurius
> quam urbani assidui cives quos scurras vocant.

[65] See, for example, Hendrickson, "Horace, *Serm.* 1.4," 128.

> There is nothing more stupid or idiotic, nothing more deceptive or cunning, nothing more bold talking or cheating than those clever busybodies whom people call *scurrae*.

Hanging about with lowlifes; revealing the secrets of friends and enemies alike; scandalmongering at the water tank; these are the traits of the *scurra mimicus* who, as Corbett has suggested, had counterparts in the Cynic moralizers and the *parasiti ridiculi* of Roman New Comedy.[66] At *Satires* 1.4.34–38, therefore, Horace has Romanized the Aristotelian βωμολόχος, converting him to the *scurra* well known to his audience from the stage of mime.

At *Satires* 1.4.71–77, the satirist returns to the charge of scandalmongering. He describes his satiric practices in terms that define him as a good Aristotelian; he knows the need for restraint and he respects the proper time, place, and audience for lampoon. Against this image the satirist contrasts the practices of some unnamed critic. Once again, it is obvious that he has converted this critic, whether he is real or imagined, into a character of popular drama (*Satires* 1.4.81–89):

> absentem qui rodit, amicum
> qui non defendit alio culpante, solutos
> qui captat risus hominum famamque dicacis,
> fingere qui non visa potest, commissa tacere
> qui nequit, hic niger est, hunc tu, Romane, caveto.
> saepe tribus lectis videas cenare quaternos
> e quibus unus amet quavis aspergere cunctos
> praeter eum qui praebet aquam; post hunc quoque potus,
> condita cum verax aperit praecordia Liber.

The one who nibbles at an absent friend or offers no defense when another accuses him, the one who grasps at unrestrained laughter and the reputation of a lampooner, able to invent falsities and unable to keep a secret, this one is a menace. Beware of him, oh Roman! Often you will see such men at dinner parties sitting four to a couch. Of these one will spatter insults across the entire room, aspersing all but the host who provides the water. Afterward, when he is drunk and truthful Bacchus uncovers the hidden thoughts of his heart, even the host he insults.

The lines describe a typical *scurra mimicus* or parasite. He is faithless, a jester, and a liar. He betrays secrets entrusted to him by his friends.

---

[66] On the scandalmongering of the *scurrae* and *parasiti ridiculi*, see Corbett, *Scurra*, 29–32. These traits were also assigned to the amateur jesters of good family, the *Iuventus* mentioned by Livy in his history of drama at Rome. See Corbett, *Scurra*, 44–69.

He and his parasite companions sit four to a couch at dinner parties, a passing quip that implies that the host has not prepared for them. Like Balatro ("Buffoon") in *Satires* 2.8, they have crashed the party, brought in on the coattails of some influential friend. The buffoon makes humorous jibes against the entire crowd, though he tries his best not to insult the host, who pours the wine and keeps him well fed. After he has drunk a bit, however, even the host gets pasted. The adjectives *dicax* ("malicious," 83), and *urbanus* ("witty," 90) are terms commonly ascribed to the *scurra mimicus*. Corbett, who has done much good work on the topic of comic buffoons, concludes: "The professional *scurra*'s role in mime must then be that of a malicious, witty, gossiping, interfering, arrogant nuisance."[67] This is exactly the picture we have of Horace's critic at *Satires* 1.4.81–89.

As a parasite, he is also a hungry nuisance. Horace knew the type well. He understood that the *scurra*'s lying and faithlessness are consequences of his poverty. At *Epistles* 1.15. 26–32, Horace describes the plight of Maenius, a parasitic character known to him from Lucilius:

> Maenius, ut rebus maternis atque paternis
> fortiter absumptis urbanus coepit haberi,
> scurra vagus, non qui certum praesepe teneret,
> impransus non qui civem dinosceret hoste,
> quaelibet in quemvis opprobria fingere saevus,
> pernicies et tempestas barathrumque macelli,
> quidquid quaesierat ventri donabat avaro.

When he had courageously squandered the estates of his mother and father, Maenius acquired the reputation of a wit and a wandering *scurra*, keeping no fixed lodging and, when hungry, making no distinction between fellow citizen and enemy. Cruelly he trumped up scandals against whomever he pleased. He was a regular destroyer, whirlwind, and bottomless pit of market goods, and whatever he gained he gave as a votive offering to his greedy belly.

Maenius is drawn in the full colors of the traditional *scurra mimicus* or the parasite from the stage of comedy.[68] He is equivalent in every detail of his character to the scandalmongerers described at *Satires* 1.4.34–38 and 81–89, where, again, the satirist has pictured himself as living within a comic world. Unlike Aristotle, who inspired the analogy, Horace has not simply drawn a comparison between his crit-

---

[67] Ibid., 38.

[68] Fairclough notes *ad Epistles* 1.15.30, "The language is Plautine. Where food was concerned, he swept everything before him." H. R. Fairclough, *Horace: Satires, Epistles, Ars Poetica* (Cambridge, Mass.: Harvard University Press, 1929), 346.

ics and the characters he knew from the stage of popular comedy; rather, he has made them play a part in the fictional world of his *Satires*. They have actually become buffoons and parasites. We see them hanging about the water tank, begging meals, crashing parties, drinking to excess, flattering the host, and abusing their dinner companions. The comparison is itself very old and very Aristotelian. Its illustration in *Satires* 1.4, however, is uniquely Horatian. Horace, always skeptical of pedantic imitation of the Greeks, has thoroughly Romanized the illustration, alluding to practices known to his audience from the stage of Roman New Comedy and mime. Even more, he has dramatized the analogy, giving new life to an overworked theoretical metaphor. Unlike Aristotle, Horace does not discuss buffoonery as such; rather, he presents us with living buffoons who play out their farcical stage roles within his fictional comic world. Once again, we see that the analogy with comedy plays a central role in Horace's definition of satire.

HORACE'S THEORY OF SATIRE AND THE IAMBOGRAPHIC TRADITION

The opening statement of *Satires* 1.4, the first of the so-called programmatic satires, raises immediate problems for the theory of an Aristotelian Horace (*Satires* 1.4.1–5):

> Eupolis atque Cratinus Aristophanesque poetae
> atque alii quorum comoedia prisca virorum est,
> si quis erat dignus describi, quod malus ac fur,
> quod moechus foret aut sicarius aut alioqui
> famosus, multa cum libertate notabant.

> The poets Eupolis, Cratinus, and Aristophanes, and all the other men who wrote Old Comedy, if there was someone who deserved portrayal because he was a scoundrel and a thief, because he was an adulterer, murderer, or infamous in any other way, they publicly censured him with great freedom of speech.

These are the first words of the satirist as theorist. The sentiments expressed suit perfectly the persona of the cantankerous Cynic, fully committed to the brand of παρρησία he knew from the iambographic tradition. He will not be compromised. In good Cynic fashion, he claims to write satires in the same tradition as the great poets of the Old Comic stage, with Lucilius as his more immediate exemplar. He exalts their right to *libertas*, which he describes as the freedom to name and abuse the scoundrel, the thief, the adulterer, and the murderer.

Nothing could be farther from the spirit of Aristotle's liberal jest, for we have seen that Aristotle was careful to restrict lampoon to slight defects of character. At *Poetics* 5.1449a32–35 he argues that comedy, though it focuses on baser individuals, "does not extend to total depravity" (οὐ μέντοι κατὰ πᾶσαν κακίαν). We see the same thinking in Cicero, who argues that the orator "will not laugh at crime, lest laughter take hatred's place." The opening lines of *Satires* 1.4 make absolutely no concessions to these restrictions. If anything, they directly and intentionally contradict them. Compare, for example, the opening lines of *Satires* 1.4 with Aristotle's statements on the nature of extreme vice at *Nicomachean Ethics* 2.1107a9–13:

> Οὐ πᾶσα δ᾽ ἐπιδέχεται πρᾶξις οὐδὲ πᾶν πάθος τὴν μεσότητα· ἔνια γὰρ εὐθὺς ὠνό-
> μασται συνειλημμένα μετὰ τῆς φαυλότητος, οἷον ἐπιχαιρεκακία ἀναισχυντία
> φθόνος, καὶ ἐπὶ τῶν πράξεων μοιχεία κλοπὴ ἀνδροφονία.

> Not every activity admits of a virtuous mean, nor does every emotion. For certain things are composed immediately of badness, such as malice, shamelessness, and envy, and, in the case of activities, adultery, theft, and murder.

What strikes us here is that Horace has limited Old Comic censure to what Aristotle defined as the very worst types of crimes. Regardless of whether he intended these lines as an allusion to the *Nicomachean Ethics*, it must be admitted that the opening claims of *Satires* 1.4 are particularly ill-advised from the standpoint of Aristotelian theory: the scoundrel, thief, adulterer, and murderer of lines 3 and 4 possess fully the traits "extending to total depravity" that Aristotle was careful to restrict from the comic stage. The satirist makes no apologies for these practices, which he himself claims to follow.

As we have seen, there is nothing blatantly false in the idea that the satirist seeks to establish his Aristotelian credentials in *Satires* 1.4. Granting this, however, one must concede that this interpretation is only partially successful, and that the satirist's theoretical program may well be much more complex. Nowhere is this more evident than in the opening lines of *Satires* 1.4 (just quoted) a passage that, if anything, speaks directly against the restrictions of Aristotle's liberal jest. This statement makes little sense when set against the conservative, Aristotelian principles espoused later in the same satire. As a result, scholars have attempted, in various ways, to rescue Horace from these apparent contradictions. G. L. Hendrickson, who set the tone for nearly all subsequent interpretations of *Satires* 1.4, argued that the opening passage does not express Horace's own views but speaks for the "character which tradition had attributed to satire," to which Horace himself did not ascribe, but actually sought to displace in the remainder of *Satires* 1.4.[69] Parker, most recently, has argued much the same point. She writes in reference to the opening lines of 1.4: "We need not read 1.10 into 1.4 to perceive that Horace is being ironic, that he can only be setting up a straw argument, one that demands a refutation."[70] Arguing that Horace merely "pretends" to espouse a relationship between the Old Comic poets, Lucilius, and himself, Parker adds:

> He propounds in 1.4 an opinion of the Old Comedy that only a literary fool could hold—an opinion that brings to the fore all of that comedy's shortcomings in the eyes of an Aristotle without allowing it the virtues that so many scholars who followed could see so clearly. . . . At the end of his first book of satires, Horace delivers a firm rebuttal to the contention that the essence of Old Comedy lay in its vituperation.[71]

All of this assumes that Aristotle's liberal jest was the only valid approach to the topic of poetic humor known to the ancient theorists and that only a "literary fool" would dare suggest otherwise. As we have seen, however, Aristotelian theory did have significant rivals in the Hellenistic period, especially among the later practitioners of the iambic idea, and the opening sentence of *Satires* 1.4, far from conveying the air of ironic ineptitude, as Parker and others have maintained, speaks directly for this tradition. Quintilian's brief comments on the nature of Old Comedy at *Institutes* 10.1.65–66 are drawn from this same theoretical tradition:

> Antiqua comoedia cum sinceram illam sermonis Attici gratiam prope sola retinet, tum facundissimae libertatis est et in insectandis vitiis praecipua. . . . Plures eius auctores; Aristophanes tamen et Eupolis Cratinusque praecipui.

> Old Comedy alone preserves the pure grace of Attic speech, while it is especially noted for its eloquent freedom of speech in the denunciation of vice. . . . There are many authors of Old Comedy, the chief of whom are Aristophanes, Eupolis, and Cratinus.

Here again, the same poets are mentioned, the three great spirits of Old Comedy who had been canonized by the Hellenistic theorists.

---

[69] Hendrickson, "Horace, *Serm.* 1.4," 124.
[70] Parker, "Comic Theory," 44. See also Rudd, *Satires of Horace*, 88–90.
[71] Parker, "Comic Theory," 45.

Also, as in the opening lines of *Satires* 1.4, Old Comedy is noted for its free invective leveled against vice. Built into this discussion is the assumption that Old Comic abusiveness is morally responsible and in need of no apologies. This, of course, is good iambographic theory, a rival to Aristotle's liberal jest. Horace was certainly not the first to use it as a working model for Roman satire.[72] Seen in this way, it becomes very difficult to argue for the satirist's ironic ineptitude in the opening lines of *Satires* 1.4, the "straw argument" of those who argue for an Aristotelian Horace. Much more convincing is Dickie's final assessment:

> Horace says that the poets of Old Comedy, Eupolis, Cratinus and Aristophanes and the others, censured malefactors freely and that Lucilius is wholly dependent on them. However questionable this account of the intent of Old Comedy and of Lucilius' dependence on it may seem to us, what is important for the understanding of *Satires* 1.4 is that Horace adopts a view of Old Comedy, derived from Hellenistic literary theorizing, that makes Eupolis, Cratinus and Aristophanes the canonical poets of a genre whose defining characteristic was that of holding sinners up to opprobrium and that it is in that literary and moral tradition that he places himself.[73]

Platonius speaks for the same tradition when he makes "lampoon against the people, judges, and generals" the chief "goal" (σκοπός) of Old Comedy.[74] He mentions Aristophanes, Eupolis, and Cratinus as the premier writers of Old Comedy, noted for their "cutting abuse against wrongdoers" (ἀφόρητοί τινες κατὰ τῶν ἁμαρτανόντων). These wrongdoers, he suggests, include not only corrupt public officials, but also nonpolitical figures characterized by some type of moral vice. At *De Comoedia* 1.5–12 (quoted earlier in this chapter), Platonius makes a decidedly Cynic adjustment to his definition of Old Comic παρρησία, broadening the scope of invective to include vices traditionally addressed in Cynic diatribe. This shift toward nonpolitical invective represents not a softening of the iambic idea—the Cynics would not tolerate this—but a concession to the much more restrictive political conditions of the Hellenistic period.

---

[72] At some time in the first century B.C., perhaps under Varro's influence, as F. Leo has suggested, theories of Old Comedy were applied to the writing of satire. Diomedes definition of satire is derived from the same theoretical tradition in which Horace consciously places himself in the opening lines of *Satires* 1.4: *carmen maledicum ad carpenda vitia hominum archaeae comoediae charactere compositum.* See F. Leo, "Varro und die Satire," *Hermes* 24 (1889): 66–84.

[73] Dickie, "*Invidia*," 185–86.

[74] See *Prolegomena de Comoedia* 1.25–27, where Platonius plays on the rhyme of σκοπόν and σκώπτειν.

The satirist makes precisely the same shift at *Satires* 1.4.25–33, where he lists the objects of his satire. He describes them as *culpari dignos* ("worthy of censure," 25), which echoes the *dignus describi* ("worthy of portrayal") of line 3, putting the satirist in the same tradition as the poets of Old Comedy. The shift is rather dishonest, for without dismissing the idea that his satires attack criminals of the worst type, he takes us into the world of Cynic diatribe, where, from the street corner or market stall, the moralizer harangues and lampoons those given over to avarice, ambition, greed, and lust, which are hardly equivalent to murder, theft, and adultery. This shift, as Hunter has pointed out, at the same time takes the reader from the severe, public invective of Old Comedy to the softer practices of New Comedy and the actual world of Horace's *Satires*:

> When Horace returns in vv. 21ff. to the question of personal attack, after his consideration of Lucilius' stylistic weaknesses, he too alters the type of people involved from the criminals of vv.3–5. Although the echo of v.3 in *culpari dignos* (v.25) suggests that Aristophanes, Lucilius, and Horace stand in precisely the same tradition, Horace moves from crimes to "follies" of the kind with which all mankind is afflicted (*quemvis media elige turba*). To what extent vv.3–5 and 26–31 correspond has been much discussed, but it is clear that the latter verses take us into the world of New Comedy and Horace's own satires, without actually abandoning Old Comedy entirely.[75]

This last point is extremely important, for it suggests that Horace, as a theorist and practitioner of satire, does not simply dismiss one tradition in favor of another, as Hendrickson and many others have suggested;[76] he has, rather, created a dramatic world that draws upon the best features of Greek comedy, both Old and New, the iambographic and the Aristotelian. It is an absurd, impossible combination made very real in the world of Horace's *Satires*.

The second mainstay of the traditional Aristotelian interpretation of Horace's theory of satire is the idea that, in *Satires* 1.10, Horace directly renounces the iambographic views expressed in *Satires* 1.4, which he never really intended seriously.[77] This again is very mislead-

[75] Hunter, "Horace on Friendship," 486–87.

[76] The most recent reformulation of Hendrickson's thesis is K. Heldmann, "Die Wesenbestimmung der Horazischen Satire durch die Komödie," *Antike und Abendland* 33 (1987): 122–39.

[77] Others besides Parker have taken this same view. Rudd, for example, claims that in *Satires* 1.10, Horace "stands by his criticisms of Lucilius' style, but modifies what he said about his tone. While granting that Lucilius was witty, he now maintains that his wit was too often harsh and vulgar." Rudd, *Satires of Horace*, 94. Lafleur argues that

ing. The opening lines of *Satires* 1.10 speak directly against this thesis (*Satires* 1.10.1–6):

> Nempe inconposito dixi pede currere versus
> Lucili. quis tam Lucili fautor inepte est
> ut non hoc fateatur? at idem, quod sale multo
> urbem defricuit, charta laudatur eadem.
> nec tamen hoc tribuens dederim quoque cetera; nam sic
> et Laberi mimos ut pulchra poemata mirer.

Yes, I did say that the verses of Lucilius run with an ill-composed foot. Who is such an inept advocate of Lucilius that he will not admit this? But, the very same Lucilius, in the very same piece, was praised for rubbing down the city with much salt. Crediting him with this, however, I would not grant him the rest; for, in so doing, I would also have to marvel at the mimes of Laberius as fine poetry.

Here the satirist recalls that, in his earlier work, Lucilius was actually "praised" (*laudatur*) for "rubbing down" or "scouring" the city with much salt, that is, for his harsh, uncompromised *libertas*. Far from apologizing for his earlier assessment of the Lucilianus character, the satirist confirms his earliers views in very straightforward terms. He criticizes Lucilius for stylistic harshness, that is, his rough, unrelenting compositional style, not the harsh spirit of his invective. This is exactly the same approach taken in *Satires* 1.4, where the satirist praises Lucilius for his *libertas* but criticizes him for his overblown poetic technique. The passage that follows (*Satires* 1.10.7–14) argues that Lucilius lacks brevity and variety; he is too much given to the grand style (*tristi sermone*) of the epic poet and rhetor, and too little adept at the restrained humorous mode (*iocoso sermone*) of the educated wit, the *urbanus* who keeps his speech pared to a minimum. This entire argument, as I have argued elsewhere, is adapted from rhetorical theories of *compositio* and *varietas*, Greek σύνθεσις and ποικιλία, and it has little if anything to do with modes of humor.[78] This is

---

there is an evolution of poetic theory from *Satires* 1.4 to 1.10 and 2.1: "The three poems constitute a complex and evolving response to very real criticism and to pressures of a social, political, and legal, as well as a personal and artistic nature." He argues that in *Satires* 1.10 "Horace is actually rejecting the no longer acceptable attributes of his own satiric pose in the early poems." Lafleur, "Horace and *Onomasti Komodein*," 1826 and 1808. In contrast, I have argued for the inherent consistency of Horace's theoretical statements.

[78] See K. Freudenburg, "Greek Theories of Comedy and Style in the Satires of Horace" (Ph.D. diss., University of Wisconsin at Madison, 1989), 149–64, and "Horace's Satiric Program and the Language of Contemporary Theory in *Satires* 2.1," *American Journal of Philology* 111, no. 2 (1990): 187–203.

equally true of the passage that follows at *Satires* 1.10.14–17, where the satirist argues for a moderate blend of the *ridiculum* ("the amusing") and the *acre* ("the passionate"), taking the Old Comic poets as his stylistic exemplars. This passage is often taken as evidence for Horace's Aristotelian leanings, that is, his preference for the laughable (innuendo) versus the iambic idea (open abuse). This interpretation, however, breaks the clear flow of the argument, which treats matters of poetic style and modes of *sermo* and does not bear directly upon the question of open, personal abuse versus innuendo. The scholiast correctly regards the claim at line 17, "in this they [the Old Comic poets] are to be imitated," as a stylistic tenet: *id est venustate loquendi, ut auditores delectaret* ("that is, in the beauty of their everyday speech, so that one might charm the audience").[79] The verb *delectaret* is very telling; it refers the *hoc* of line 17 to the Old Comic poets' expertise in the middle or mixed style, whose function was *delectare* ("to charm") rather than *movere* ("to move"), the function of the grand style. The repeated *hoc* refers, then, not to *ridiculum* in the sense of "innuendo," but to the overall tenor of the preceding argument, which calls for a careful blend of rhetorical styles in the writing of satire.

Lucilian *libertas* was, in a sense, beyond criticism in 35 B.C. As we have seen, the political and social rhetoric of the late Republic was antipathetic to any softened or restricted version of old republican *libertas*, which had become the watchword of republicans and Caesarians alike. Any attempt by Horace to set limits upon Lucilian *libertas* would invite the scorn of the anti-Caesarians, lancing an old wound that Octavian would rather see healed. They would construe such criticisms as evidence for Octavian's tyrannical intentions toward the state. Lucilius was a republican hero whose bitter invective, like that of the Old Comic poets, spoke for vanishing freedoms. The old iambographic masters were much imitated in the late Republic, especially by the enemies of Julius and Octavian.[80] The critics in *Satires* 1.10 belong clearly to the anti-Caesarian camp. The opening of 1.10 suggests that they have construed *Satires* 1.4 as an assault on Lucilian *libertas*, which it is not, and so Horace is careful to point out in very straightforward terms that he has criticized Lucilius not on the basis of his *libertas* but only on the basis of style.

The names mentioned in *Satires* 1.10 are mostly obscure, but they show some interesting tendencies: Laberius, lampooned in line 6,

[79] H. J. Botschuyver, *Scholia in Horatium* (Amsterdam: H. A. Van Bottenburg, 1935), *ad Satires* 1.10.17.

[80] On the lampooning and political pamphleteering of the late Republic, see LaFleur, "Law of Satire," 1803–6.

wrote mimes offending Caesar;[81] Pitholaus, who is ridiculed at lines 21–23, wrote lampoons (*carmina maledicentissima*) against Julius Caesar; and Bibaculus, the *Turgidus Alpinus* of line 36, wrote harsh iambic verses against Octavian.[82] The anonymous "monkey" (*simius*) of line 18 is ridiculed as an avid fan of Calvus and Catullus, both of whom had written bitter invective against the Caesarians.[83] All told, this is entirely the wrong audience to address with criticisms of Lucilian *libertas*. Horace, in good Cynic fashion, defends the satirist's right to open invective in *Satires* 1.4. In *Satires* 1.10, in spite of much scholarship that argues otherwise, he makes precisely the same point. In no way does Horace deliver a "firm rebuttal" of his earlier views. Thus, in the two great programmatic satires of Book 1, the satirist twice assigns significant weight to the influence of Old Comedy upon his work. Because his statements show sound theoretical precedents, they are best taken as accurate, noncontradictory programmatic assertions. Regarding them seriously, we conclude that Horace saw himself, in the writing of satire, as writing in the same tradition as the great poets of the Greek Old Comic stage.

By now it is clear that Cynic moral literature and Old Comedy played a strong role in shaping Horace's satiric program. The case for the influence of the iambic poets is no less strong, for although Horace makes only one explicit reference to Archilochus as a model for satire at *Satires* 2.3.12, the satires themselves demonstrate that, for Horace, satire is very much a version of the Greek ἴαμβος. Martin West has pointed out that "the name ἴαμβος does not automatically imply a particular metre or metrical type. Iambic metre got its name from being particularly characteristic of ἴαμβοι, not vice versa."[84] The verbs ἰαμβίζειν and ἰαμβοποιεῖν mean simply "to lampoon," and it is in this sense that Catullus can rightly refer to his hendecasyllables as *iambi*.[85] In the same way, Horace is a writer of iambs, both in his *Epodes*, which fit the metrical qualification, and in the *Satires*, which

---

[81] On Laberius and Caesar, see Macrobius *Saturnalia* 2.7.

[82] The identification of *Turgidus Alpinus* (1.10.36) with M. Furius Bibaculus seems the best option given the similarities between *Satires* 1.10.36 and Horace's jibe against Furius, also a writer of historical epic, at *Satires* 2.5.39–41. The latter passage is much better attested as a reference to Furius Bibaculus. On the vexed question of poets named Furius, see M. Wigodsky, *Vergil and Early Latin Poetry, Hermes* Einzelschriften 24 (Wiesbaden: Franz Steiner, 1972), 148–50.

[83] On the lampoons of Calvus, Catullus, and Pitholaus, see Suetonius *Julius* 73 and 75. On Bibaculus, see Tacitus *Annals* 4.34.8 and Quintilian *Institutes* 10.1.96, where he is classed with Catullus and Horace as a writer of iambs.

[84] M. West, *Studies in Greek Elegy and Iambus* (Berlin: Walter de Gruyter, 1974), 22.

[85] See Catullus 36.5.

do not.[86] As a satirist, he could quite reasonably consider himself as writing in the same tradition as the great writers of Greek iambic poetry.

Horace was especially fond of Callimachus's *Iambs*, which, to some extent at least, served as a model for his first book of satires.[87] Parallels with the *Iambs* are especially frequent in the programmatic set pieces, *Satires* 1.4 and 1.10, suggesting that Horace assigned some theoretical significance to such allusions. Like Horace, Callimachus begins his *Iambs* with a series of parodies of popular moralizing literature, much of which he converts into a literary polemic against various inept, overly wordy poetasters of his day. The *philologoi* of *Iambs* 1 are the Callimachean counterpart to Horace's scholar-poets, Fabius, Crispinus, and others. *Iambs* 1 brings Hipponax back from the dead, but it is quite clear that he plays the role of a Cynic moralizer who harangues his audience on the street corner. At *Iambs* 1.32 he promises "I will not draw out the tale at length" (οὐ μαχρὴν ἄξω), which compares with the satirist's promises at 1.1.14 (*ne te morer*, "lest I detain you") and 1.1.95 (*non longa est fabula*, "it's not a long story"). Both speakers address their scholar-critics as if addressing fools from the crowd: at *Iambs* 1.29–30 Hipponax exclaims, "Baldy over there will waste his breath, huffing and puffing in order to keep a shirt on his back." The heavy breathing of the scholar-critic has its parallel in the overblown poetic practices of Crispinus, of whom the satirist says (*Satires* 1.4.19–21):

> at tu conclusas hircinis follibus auras
> usque laborantis, dum ferrum molliat ignis,
> ut mavis, imitare.

But you prefer to mimic goatskin bellows that howl away until the fire melts the iron.

Iambs 1, like *Satires* 1.4, responds to some real or imagined censure of the poet's iambographic practices. M. Dickie has shown that both

---

[86] One must keep in mind that Horace is also writing his *Epodes* in the late 30s B.C. One would be especially surprised, therefore, to find him, in either work, making any sweeping generalizations against the invective that was so characteristic of iambic poetry, Old Comedy, and Cynic moralizing.

[87] On the connections between the *Satires* and the *Iambs* of Callimachus, see especially C. M. Dawson, "The Iambi of Callimachus, a Hellenistic Poet's Experimental Laboratory," *Yale Classical Studies* 11 (1950): 138–40; A. Benedetto, "I giambi di Callimacho e il loro influsso sugli Epodi e Satire di Orazio," *Rendiconti dell'Accademia di Archeologia* 44 (1966): 23–69; Clayman, *Callimachus' Iambi*, 72–74; and R. Scodel, "Horace, Lucilius, and Callimachean Polemic," *Harvard Studies in Classical Philology* 91 (1987): 199–215. Except where I have indicated otherwise, all citations from Callimachus's *Iambs* are from Dawson.

Hipponax and the satirist respond to the charge of envy (φθόνος), which was the traditional attack on iambographers at least since the early fifth century B.C.:

> The tradition that it is *phthonos* or *invidia* that makes the iambic poet speak ill of others is to be seen most clearly in Pindar's second *Pythian*, where Archilochus is presented as an example of conduct to be avoided; he is the paradigm of those who out of *phthonos* denigrate others (52–96). Callimachus seems to be dealing with this view of iambic poetry in *Iamb* 1 when he has Hipponax, back from the dead, warn the assembled *philologoi* against feeling *phthonos* for each other.[88]

Likewise, Horace accuses his scholar-critics of envious backbiting, using descriptive terms such as "the ink of the black cuttlefish" (*nigrae sucus lolliginis*, 100) and "pure rust" (*aerugo mera*, 101), which have a long history as metaphors for envy and malice.[89] An even stronger link we see in the shared metaphor of *Iambs* 1.78–79 and *Satires* 1.4.33–34,[90] where both Hipponax and the satirist respond to the charge that their lampoons resemble the attacks of a raging bull. The gaping Corycean of *Iambs* 1.82–83, whose tongue wags like that of a drinking dog, symbolizes the eavesdropper and the faithless gossip.[91] He is the Callimachean counterpart to the scandalmongerer of *Satires* 1.4.36–38.

Outside of the programmatic satires of Book 1, *Satires* 1.8 shows perhaps the strongest connections with Callimachus's *Iambs*. Both *Iambs* 7 and 9 are narrated by talking, ithyphallic herms made of wood, the exact Greek counterpart to Horace's Priapus. The opening lines of *Iambs* 7 and *Satires* 1.8 both bring in the character of the carpenter and make humorous reference to the statue's dubious status as "god." Like *Satires* 1.8, *Iambs* 7 contains an *aition* that explains how the statue came to be worshiped at Ainos, with special reference to how the statue attained a curious break in its shoulder. Horace's Priapus has a split buttocks, which he explains by the humorous tale of Canidia and Sagana's foiled incantations. Both stories involve magical rites.[92] The opening passage of *Iambs* 9 also introduces an *aition*: "Oh long-bearded herm, why does your member point up to your beard and not to your feet?" As in *Satires* 1.8, immediate reference is made

---

[88] Dickie, "*Invidia*," 203.

[89] Ibid., 189–92.

[90] On the bull image, see also *Iambs* 13.52.

[91] On the character of the Corycean, see Dawson, "The Iambi of Callimachus," 19.

[92] Clayman notes that the remains of lines 43–44, κἠγὼ᾽π᾽ ἐκείναν . . . ταῖς ἐμαις ἐπῳδα[ῖς, "seem to imply that the Herm halted his own destruction by magical incantations." Clayman, *Callimachus' Iambi*, 37.

to the statue's ithyphallic condition, and here again, the herm has a mystical story to tell. Although Horace has thoroughly Romanized his version of the story, the Callimachean antecedents in *Iambs* 7 and 9 are quite obvious.

The strongest connections linking Horace's *Satires* to the *Iambs* of Callimachus are to be found in *Satires* 1.10. Several scholars have remarked on these connections, most notably R. Scodel, who has made an excellent case for their programmatic import. Scodel has shown that, by explicit reference to *Iambs* 13, Horace places himself firmly on the side of Callimachean aesthetic principles in the writing of satire. At the same time, however, he exerts his independence from these principles: "He implies that the true carrier of a tradition is not the slavish imitator but the poet who adapts his master in the same spirit in which the master adapted his own predecessors."[93] The following connections between *Satires* 1.10 and *Iambs* 13 are worthy of note: both pieces were, originally at least, the last in their respective collections, and both launch immediately into a defense of the poet's stylistic practices.[94] Each seeks to define a generic theory of style against rival theories of iamb and satire. They address theorists who have been censured earlier on in the work. Although the opening lines of *Iambs* 13 are highly fragmentary, Dawson has suggested that, in the reference to Mimnermus in line 7, "we may have here some reference to the concept of the need for brevity and variety in one's poems,"[95] which is exactly parallel to the course of the stylistic argument that opens *Satires* 1.10. Both pieces proceed to address the topic of poetic "blending": Callimachus defends his use of a mixed dialect and the blending of genres (*polyeideia*), which is characteristic of his *Iambs*;[96] Horace, who makes a case for stylistic blending at *Satires* 1.10.1–19, proceeds to argue against the practice of mixing Greek and Latin, which is an extreme version of Callimachus's blending theory. His critics subscribed to the practice, which, as good Callimacheans, they sought to endorse by reference to *Iambs* 13. They have adapted the analogy of wine mixing, the blend of Chian (Greek) with Falernian (Roman) at *Satires* 1.10.24, from *Iambs* 13.19–21, where Callimachus's critics claim that, if he persists in mixing dialects in his poetry, his friends will tie him up and "pour out his mixture"

---

[93] Scodel, "Callimachean Polemic," 215.

[94] On the case for the thirteenth *Iamb* as the last in its book, see D. Clayman, "Callimachus' Thirteenth *Iamb*: The Last Word," *Hermes* 104 (1976): 29–35.

[95] Dawson, "The Iambi of Callimachus," 123.

[96] I concur with Clayman who has argued that the charge of *polyeideia* "refers directly and exclusively to the *Iambi* themselves." Clayman, *Callimachus' Iambi*, 48.

(ἐγχεοῦσι τὴν κρᾶσιν).⁹⁷ In lines 31–35, Horace converts the Apollo of Callimachus's *Aetia* prologue into Quirinus, who warns him in a dream not to compose Greek verses. This conversion of Greek to Roman, like that of Hermes to Priapus in *Satires* 1.8, is very clever, for by it the satirist drives home his point about independent poetic *mimesis*: the slavish imitator of Callimachus—his critics, in other words—would have made Apollo give the warning. Quirinus, however, is a purely Roman deity. The illustration speaks against the type of starry-eyed philhellenism and Callimachean mimicry that the satirist seeks to deride. His satires, while they show clear precedents in Callimachus's *Iambs*, are a new, entirely Roman phenomenon. He shows this again in lines 40–45, where he ironically asserts that the *camenae*, Roman muses, not Greek, assign one genre per poet. This is precisely what Callimachus denies takes place at *Iambs* 13.26–32. Horace, while he subscribes to the one-genre-per-poet notion in neither theory nor practice, humorously suggests that he knows his Greek models quite well; he is, however, a capable judge, free to use them as he sees fit.

The *Iambs* of Callimachus make up but one of several strands of the iambographic tradition that Horace weaves into the texture of his *Satires*. Much good evidence exists to counter the idea of a strictly Aristotelian Horace, for, both in theory and style, the *Satires* display all of the diversity suggested in the term *satura*. Certainly Horace is a good Aristotelian, subscribing to the theory of the liberal jest in creating the distinctly New Comic world of his *Satires*. At the same time, however, he is a writer in the iambographic tradition: the Old Comic poet, the writer of iambs, and the Cynic who vaunts his right to name and abuse his enemies. The combination is impossible and absurd, for, as Plutarch's comparison of Aristophanes and Menander suggests, the iambographic and Aristotelian traditions are hostile. They simply will not mix. Yet this is exactly what Horace has done.

As a last illustration of this point, consider the opening passage of *Satires* 2.3, where the Stoic convert, Damasippus, berates the satirist for writing so little and so infrequently (*Satires* 2.3.11–13):

> quorsum pertinuit stipare Platona Menandro,
> Eupolin Archilocho, comites educere tantos?

To what end did you bring along such great companions, why did you pack Plato along with Menander, and Eupolis with Archilochus?

---

⁹⁷ I follow Pfeiffer's supplement of κρᾶσιν in line 20. See R. Pfeiffer, *Callimachus*, Vol. 1: *Fragmenta* (Oxford: Clarendon Press, 1949), 206.

The list is rather odd and self-contradictory: Plato and Menander, that is, Socratic dialogue and Greek New Comedy, simply do not belong in a list that includes Eupolis and Archilochus, an Old Comic Poet and a writer of iambs. These models, however, have been perfectly chosen, for they are the very models Horace has sought to emulate all along. Here again, he proves that he is much more than a good Aristotelian. Hunter concludes:

> Horace . . . has not rejected the Old in adopting the New; he is both Aristophanes and Menander or, as he suggests in Sat. 2.3.11–12, both Eupolis and Menander. Such a literary stance allows Horace the maximum freedom to include widely diverse material in his *sermones*; it was, in other words, just the stance he needed.[98]

Horace's programmatic claims in *Satires* 1.4 and 1.10 combine the best features of two otherwise hostile theories of humor. He is determined to have it all. Such a literary stance represents a unique Horatian contribution to ancient theories of poetic *libertas*, which, at the same time, adds significantly to our understanding of the relationship of comedy to satire.

[98] Hunter, "Horace on Friendship," 490.

CHAPTER THREE

The *Satires* in the Context of Late Republican Stylistic Theory

HORACE'S LITERARY RIVALS IN *SATIRES* 1.1–1.4

Despite the claims of *Satires* 1.4, Horace satirized almost no living contemporary of real significance in the first three satires of Book 1.[1] Rather, he reserved his best and most frequent lampoons for certain obscure literary rivals, contemporary theorists and poets who, he suggests, were every bit as wicked in their poetic practices as the various misers, wanton profligates, adulterers, thieves, and murderers mentioned in *Satires* 1.4: they were poemicides who piled word upon word with the relish of misers, sorting and stacking heaps of silver. Fabius, Crispinus, Fannius, Hermogenes Tigellius, Caprius, and Sulcius were real, living contemporaries, rival theorists, poets and writers of diatribe whose works, Horace suggests, subscribed to no aesthetic standards accepted in his day. He parodies their poetic practices in the diatribe satires of Book 1, portraying them as renegade poetasters guilty of the wildest abuses of style.

This is the standard view of Horace's opponents in the opening satires of Book 1.[2] Not a single fragment of their works has survived against which to check this view. As a result, the scholiasts and nearly all subsequent commentators on the *Satires* have accepted the satirist's assessment of his rivals without question. It is very strange, however, that Horace should invest so much time and energy criticizing opponents who he would otherwise have us believe deserve no attention whatsoever. At *Satires* 1.4.71–76 he even suggests that their works were read much more widely than his own. It is with good reason then that we suspect that Horace has fabricated a very lopsided impression of his literary rivals.

As a writer of lampoons in the iambographic tradition, the satirist is perfectly free to distort the image of his opponents. Aristophanes,

---

[1] This is the general concensus of scholars since Fraenkel, who remarked that the characters lampooned in *Satires* 1.3 are "mere ghosts," Fraenkel, *Horace*, 88. For a brief bibliographical survey of the topic, see Zetzel, "Horace's *Liber Sermonum*," 74, n. 16.

[2] See, for example, Oltramare, *Diatribe romaine*, 126–52; and Rudd, *Satires of Horace*, 133–43.

for example, grossly misrepresents Euripides, whom he portrays in several places as the lowest type of flighty poetic huckster with no claim to critical feeling. Contrary to nearly all that Aristophanes says of him, however, we know from other sources, chiefly from Euripides' works themselves, that Euripides was an exceptional artist who commanded much respect in his day from the most critical element in Athenian society. This may well be true of Horace's rivals as well, but the works that might prove this have vanished for good. It is the intention of this chapter, then, to redress at least some of the wrong assumptions made against Horace's opponents by restoring the real cogency of their critical tenets. I begin by examining characters such as Fabius and Crispinus individually, expanding upon significant details from the text and scholia which would help place Horace's statements against them within their larger theoretical context. The evidence suggests that Horace's opponents were extremely well versed in ancient theories of style, favoring especially the obscure tenets of Stoic (or quasi-Stoic) compositional theory that had clearer counterparts in the rhetorical theories of the so-called Atticists, such as Brutus and Calvus. These theories, though they appealed to the literary sensibilities of some of the most learned and critical members of Roman society, were antipathetic to the more traditional ideals of style favored by Aristotle, Demetrius, Cicero, and Horace himself. In spite of their flippant dismissal in the diatribe satires, it is clear that Horace's distorted view of his literary rivals belies the real validity and intensity of the contemporary debate to which his criticisms refer. It is this I seek to restore in the pages that follow.

As we unscroll the *Satires*, we meet first with a certain Fabius at *Satires* 1.1.14, a contemporary literary figure for whom Horace has reserved the honor of his first lampoon. Horace begins his first satire by launching immediately into a tirade on the theme of *mempsimoiria*, a favorite topic of diatribe for which, the scholiasts suggest, Fabius had become quite famous. Verging on bombast, the satirist checks himself (1.1.13–14): *cetera de genere hoc adeo sunt multa, loquacem / delassare valent Fabium* ("other things concerning this type, so many are they, could wear out the windbag Fabius"). The scholiasts remark on these lines:

> He mentions Fabius Maximus, who as an advocate of the Pompeian party wrote several books pertaining to Stoic philosophy. He was extremely garrulous. "If," he says, "I were to enumerate all the human types [*omnia genera hominum enumerarem*] who praise another's office more than their own, not only would I bring weariness upon everyone else, but I would also wear out Fabius."[3]

[3] Botschuyver, *Scholia in Horatium*, 258.

The scholiasts suggest that the *genere hoc* of line 13 refers to personality types (*genera hominum*). Fabius, apparently, was a philosopher and public speaker who made the various "classes of men" a particular area of his expertise, writing at length and quite loosely, if Horace is believed, on the various types of behavior pertaining to each class. He addressed these matters from a decidedly Stoic standpoint. His political leanings, as well, the scholiasts considered worthy of note. The *nomen*, Fabius, suggests that he was of good patrician stock, and so his alignment with Pompey is not surprising.

Although his theme recalls Fabius, the satirist is quick to deny any comparison with his Stoic rival in terms of style. He refers to him as *loquax*, "long-winded," an assessment that is recast in the scholiasts' *facundissimus*. We are left to conclude that Fabius was a pedantic boor who harangued an unwilling audience on the well-worn themes of Stoic ethics. This is the standard view of Fabius favored by most commentators on the satires.[4] Against this image the satirist contrasts his own refined practices (1.1.14–15): *Ne te morer, audi / quo rem deducam* ("lest I detain you, hear how I *reduce* the matter at hand"). In the term *deducam*, the satirist alludes to the *deductum carmen*, which makes the art of poetry analogous to spinning thread, that is, the poet resembles the spinner who carefully twists and spins a large tuft of carded wool into a fine, narrow thread. The satirist, unwilling to harangue his audience at length, "reduces" his theme to the simple stage metaphor of lines 15–22.[5]

In the lines that follow, the satirist expresses concern that, by using this illustration, he will be considered a mere jokester who has nothing really serious to say. He follows with his famous plea for the *spoudaiogeloion*, lines 24–26, which addresses the objections of a Fabius from whose practices the satirist claims to depart in lines 14–15. In line 27, he humorously promises to devote himself to a much more "serious" line of inquiry: *sed tamen amoto quaeramus seria ludo* ("but let us look into serious matters with all jesting set aside"). The line that follows is heavily spondaic. The thick, liquid texture of its sounds perfectly conveys the sluggish toil of the "rugged" plow (*duro aratro*), which turns the "weighty" earth (*gravem terram*), and so on, suggesting a return to the severity and drudgery demanded by the likes of Fa-

---

[4] Rudd compares Fabius to Crispinus: "The 'gas-bag' Fabius represents the same type. He was one of those speakers who hit the nail on the head with such relentless persistency that the wood eventually splits." Rudd, *Satires of Horace*, 133.

[5] On the notion of the *deductum carmen* and the analogy with spinning, see Horace *Epistles* 2.1.225, Vergil *Eclogues* 6.5, and Quintilian *Institutes* 4.1.60. See also S. Hinds, *The Metamorphosis of Persephone* (Cambridge: Cambridge University Press, 1987), 21–22; and C. Brink, *Horace on Poetry: Epistles Book II* (Cambridge: Cambridge University Press, 1982), 242.

bius. The whole train of thought constitutes a humorous rejection of the type of serious, unrefined Stoic sermonizing to which the satirist has, to this point, attached the name of Fabius alone. Other names follow as the scroll is drawn out.

Drawing *Satires* 1.1 to a close, the satirist lampoons by name several personalities well known to his audience, such as Nomentanus (101) and Tanais (105), of whom only Crispinus (120), is derided for his literary aspirations. The conclusion of *Satires* 1.1 is abrupt (1.1.120–21): *Iam satis est. ne me Crispini scrinia lippi / compilasse putes, verbum non amplius addam* ("That's enough for now. Lest you suppose that I have pilfered the bookcases of bleary-eyed Crispinus, I will add not another word"). Horace has reserved the honor of the first and final lampoon of his opening satire for contemporary writers, whom he somehow regarded as his rivals. The ending is humorous. The terse, *iam satis est*, suggests that the satirist's stylistic principles as a writer of *satura*, a term that carries the sense of fullness and sufficiency, match the ethical pronouncements he has made concerning moderation and knowing one's limits. Unlike Crispinus, whose works exemplify the opposite creed, *nil satis est*, Horace, the *conviva satur* of line 119, is able to say "enough now," or better yet, "it's satire now," and happily leave off from writing. This is especially ironic because Crispinus we know as an expert in matters of Stoic ethics.[6]

At *Satires* 1.4.13–16 the satirist derides Crispinus's poetic pretensions:

> Ecce
> Crispinus nummo me provocat: "accipe, si vis,
> accipiam tabulas. detur nobis locus, hora,
> custodes. videamus uter plus scribere possit."

Look! Crispinus is calling me out with a wager: "If you please, take your writing tablets and I'll take mine! Name the place, the time, and the referees, and we'll see which one of us is able to write more."

The challenge to see who can write "more" verses links Crispinus to the loose, unpolished practices of Lucilius described in the lines immediately preceding.[7] The repeated *accipe/accipiam* in lines 14 and 15 underscores his insistence; he simply demands to be regarded as a fool. On these lines Porphyrion notes: *Mimetico autem charactere provocantem ad scribendum Crispinum ostendit* ("Moreover, he presents Cris-

---

[6] The scholiasts record: "Plotius Crispinus was an expert in philosophy who wrote songs so learned and with such insight that he was called *aretelogue* [*ut aretalogus diceretur*], that is, a narrator of virtues." Botschuyver, *Scholia in Horatium*, 263.

[7] Pseudacron notes, "Just like Lucilius, he wrote many verses, but of poor quality" (*Hic similiter ut Lucilius multos, sed malos versus faciebat*).

pinus calling him out to write in the character of a mime actor"). Horace converts Crispinus into a type character known to his audience from the stage of mime. Like the bore of *Satires* 1.9, whose abrupt arrest itself is drawn from the mime tradition, Crispinus prides himself on the very features of his work that we know the satirist despised, namely, his loose, rapid-fire composition.[8] Likewise, his pushiness compares nicely with the characterization of Damasippus, who uses much the same approach to his unwilling hearer in *Satires* 2.3: *nunc accipe* (46), *accipe* (66 and 307). Like Crispinus, he draws his precepts from the *Chrysippi porticus et grex* ("the porch of Chrysippus and his herd"), while the sheer length of his diatribe highlights the unruliness of his moralizing. Horace's slave, Davus, indulges in a similar harangue in *Satires* 2.7. Horace, threatening punishment by various means, halts his abuse, but not before we have learned that Davus took his Stoic precepts from the doorkeeper of Crispinus.[9] We see yet another reference to Crispinus's Stoic sentiments at the end of *Satires* 1.3, where he is chided for being the lone *stipator* ("lackey") of some unnamed Stoic dogmatist.[10] All of this adds up to a picture very similar to that of Fabius. Both men are noted for their gross ineptitude as stylists and the severe Stoic sentiments that constitute the subject matter of their work.[11] DuQuesnay has suggested that Crispinus and Fabius may have shared similar political leanings as well:

> The political allegiance of most of the other targets is difficult to ascertain. Fabius the Stoic (1.1.14; 1.2.134) *Pompeianas partes secutus*, according to Porphyrio, who also tells us that the *nomen* of that other Stoic, Crispinus, was Plotius: that fact suggests the possibility of a link with another of the proscribed, L. Plotius Plancus. Both of these scraps of information tend to support the earlier speculation that Stoicism had a special connection with the Pompeian-Republican cause.[12]

The satirist's primary literary targets are not inept clowns, as he would have us believe; rather, they are prominent members of Ro-

---

[8] On the mimetic coloring of the bore of *Satires* 1.9, see Fantham, "Mime," 158–59.

[9] "Hold back your hand and your rage while I set forth the things the doorkeeper of Crispinus taught me" (*manum stomachumque teneto, / dum quae Crispini docuit me ianitor edo, Satires* 2.7.45). There is some evidence that the Stoics lampooned by Horace learned and practiced an unruly brand of diatribe, which they knew from Chrysippus. See *Stoicorum Veterum Fragmenta* 2.27; and Wallach, "Diatribe," 177–89.

[10] Porphyrion *ad Satires* 1.3.137–38 refers to Crispinus as a "devotee of Stoic teaching" (*disciplinae Stoicae sector*).

[11] Horace compares Crispinus's delivery to the incessant howling of the blacksmith's bellows, at *Satires* 1.4.19, to which Pseudacron adds: "By this he demonstrates that Crispinus writes howling bombast" (*Per hoc ostendit Crispinum inflate scribere et turgide*).

[12] DuQuesnay, "Horace and Maecenas," 54.

man society who merit the frequent attention they receive in the opening satires of Book 1. As Stoics and anti-Caesarians, they adhered to standards of style perfectly acceptable within their own group but radically different from those cherished by Horace and the friends of Maecenas.

The next significant literary figure encountered in reading the *Satires* consecutively is the singer, Hermogenes Tigellius, who merits attention as the most frequently maligned of Horace's literary rivals.[13] He too fits the mold of a Fabius or Crispinus. The lugubrious opening of *Satires* 1.2 relates little if anything about Tigellius as a stylist, although it may parody a type of song known from his repertoire. We meet Tigellius again two times in *Satires* 1.3, even though we have just been told of his recent death in 1.2. The second of these two references, *Satires* 1.3.129–30, is a lampoon that parallels the jibe against Alfenus in lines 130–32. This joke, as far as Horace is concerned, captures the essence of Tigellius's character.

The Stoic moralizer who makes such a fool of himself by claiming that the lawyer Alfenus was good "barber," that is, "crook," even though his shop had been closed, makes a similar mistake in the immediately preceding lines (1.3.129–30): *ut, quamvis tacet, Hermogenes cantor tamen atque / optimus est modulator* ("as Hermogenes, even when he is silent, is the best singer and modulator"). As with the joke that follows, the lampoon hangs on the double meaning of a single word, in this case, *modulator*, and we note that, in both instances, the operative word is neatly postponed to the very end of the sentence, serving the purpose of a punchline.[14] The noun *modulator* is extremely rare in Latin literature. It is formed from the verb *modulor*, which means to "measure" or "set limits" to words or sounds. The much rarer noun *modulator* would then seem to connote one possessing this ability, that is, a songwriter. This does not get us very far in understanding the joke, however. The *Oxford Latin Dictionary* cites only two

---

[13] Hermogenes Tigellius receives varying degrees of abuse in *Satires* 2, 3, 4, 9, and 10 of Book 1. There is no consensus among the commentators on Horace as to whether there are two men named Tigellius mentioned in the *Satires* or only one. See, for example, B. L. Ullman, "Horace, Catullus, and Tigellius," *Classical Philology* 10 (1915): 270–96; Rudd, *Satires of Horace*, 292–93; and DuQuesnay, "Horace and Maecenas," 56. I prefer the one-man theory. To this debate, I add that the joke at *Satires* 1.3.129 is based on our knowledge of Tigellius from the beginning of the same satire. Also, my analysis of *Satires* 1.10.18 (later in this chapter) argues strongly against the "separatist" assumption that the Hermogenes mentioned there was a Neoteric.

[14] Note the clever postponement of the punchline in both cases: "ut, quamvis tacet, Hermogenes cantor tamen atque / optimus est *modulator*; ut Alfenus vafer, omni / abiecto instrumento artis clausaque taberna, / *tonsor* erat, sapiens operis sic optimus omnis / est opifex solus, sic rex."

references to the term beyond the one we are considering here, and a check of the Latin files now contained on compact disk (Packard Humanities Institute, CD-ROM 5.3, 1991) gives no further citations. Both other occurrences, one in the *De Re Rustica* of Columella, and the other in Apuleius's *Florida*, suggest that the term carries the sense of an "improviser," that is, one who is able to measure quickly or "adjust" his song. The reference at *Florida* 4 suggests this sense of the word most fully:

> Tibicen quidam fuit Antigenidas, omnis voculae melleus modulator et idem omnimodis peritus modificator, seu tu velles Aeolion simplex sive Iastium varium seu Lydium querulum seu Phrygium religiosum seu Dorium bellicosum.

> There was a certain flute player Antigenidas, in every vocal intonation a sweet voice changer [*modulator*] and likewise an adjuster [*modificator*] skilled in all the modes, whether you prefer the simple Aeolian or the Ionic, full of variety, or the plaintive Lydian, the pious Phrygian, or the warlike Dorian.

The flute player, Antigenidas, is noted for his flexibility; his ability to adjust quickly to every changing vocal inflection and mode. *Modulator*, then, carries the sense of English "modulate," when this is used in a musical context to imply the change from one mode or key to another, put simply, a "key change."

We begin to see the humorous possibilities of the term *modulator*, understood in this sense, when we consider what we already know of Hermogenes Tigellius from the beginning of *Satires* 1.3. The satirist lodges the following complaint (1.3.6–9):

> si collibuisset, ab ovo
> usque ad mala citaret "io Bacchae!" modo summa
> voce, modo hac resonat quae chordis quattuor ima.
> nil aequale homini fuit illi.

> If it suited him, he would recite "Hail Bacchus" from the egg all the way to the apples, first in a low pitch, then in the [high] one that sounds from the lowest of the four strings. The man showed absolutely no consistency.

In the lines that follow (9–19), the satirist expands upon the singer's instability of character, describing how, at one moment, his music imitated the speed of a retreating soldier, while, at the next, it plodded along like a sacred procession. Sometimes, he claims, Tigellius would travel with two hundred servants in tow, while at others only ten. Several other illustrations follow that underscore Tigellius's instability;

he is flighty and, above all, insincere. We begin, then, to see the humorous possibilities of the Stoic's inadvertent reference to Tigellius as an *optimus modulator* at *Satires* 1.3.130. These possibilities are further underscored by Porphyrion's note concerning Tigellius at *Satires* 1.2.2:

> Marcus Tigellius Hermogenes, endowed with knowledge of music, was a close friend [*familiaris*] of the dictator, Gauis Caesar, and later of Cleopatra, because he sang so sweetly and jested with such wit. He also pleased Augustus to the degree that he was included among his household members [*familiares domesticos*].

Hermogenes Tigellius possessed great political savvy as he somehow managed to enjoy the favor first of Julius Caesar, then of Cleopatra, and, finally, Augustus. We can fairly read into the scholiasts' note a certain degree of wonder at Tigellius's remarkable ability to "change keys" or "adjust" himself to the changing political winds of the late Republic, and thus, we further understand the humorous ineptitude conveyed in the Stoic's term *modulator* at *Satires* 1.3.130; what he intended as high praise is heard as a jibe against Tigellius's instability and insincerity. DuQuesnay has added the further possibility that Tigellius had, by the time of this satire, once again "changed keys." He writes:

> One possibility is that Tigellius had defected to Sex. Pompeius. What makes this a possibility is that Tigellius was a Sardinian and in 39 Sardinia had been granted to Sex. Pompeius. If that is so, and if there is only one Hermogenes Tigellius, and if the Fannius of 1.10.80 is related or even identical with C. Fannius, the adherent of Sextus, then the reference to him as *Hermogenis . . . conviva Tigelli* could be a humorous allusion to their billeting arrangements.[15]

Summing up our analysis of Tigellius's character, therefore, we note the favor that Tigellius apparently held among certain Stoics. Porphyrion's note *ad Satires* 1.2.2 suggests that he composed the verses he set to music.[16] The references to Tigellius in *Satires* 1.10 inform us that he was highly critical of Horace and that, at the time this satire was composed, he was employed as a schoolmaster, perhaps having fallen out with Augustus, as Duquesnay suggests.[17] In terms of his

---

[15] DuQuesnay, "Horace and Maecenas," 56.

[16] Pseudacron records, "For this reason Horace said 'of the singer,' because he [Tigellius] was said in his poetry to have pleased with the voice, not with the excellence of his songs" (*Ideo autem dixit cantoris, quia dicebatur in poematibus suis placere voce, non carminum probitate*).

[17] See *Satires* 1.10.18, 80, and 90.

style, we are told only that his music was as flamboyant as the man himself, continually shifting between the wildest extremes.

The final contemporary literary figure criticized in the first four satires of Book 1, concerning whom we are at least moderately well informed, is a certain Fannius, mentioned first at *Satires* 1.4.21: *beatus Fannius ultro / delatis capsis et imagine, cum mea nemo / scripta legat* ("Blessed is Fannius who, unasked, has donated his books and bust, while no one reads my writings"). Fannius is extremely elusive, for, as Rudd has pointed out, the scholiasts' remarks on these lines are inconsistent:

> Here we are told that Fannius presented book-cases to the senate, that the senate presented book-cases to him, that his heirs presented his books to public libraries, and (splendidly) that at the hour of death Fannius begged to be cremated on a pile of his own books.[18]

In a separate article in which he treats these discrepancies in detail, Rudd has concluded that we are to regard Fannius as the donor, who, without being asked, has handed over his writings, along with his portrait, to the public library. Rudd concludes, "The lines will then run something like this: 'Fannius takes a delight in making free donations of his poems, complete with boxes and bust.' "[19] This makes sense, bringing out the full ironic sense of *beatus* and *ultro* in line 21, which stress that Fannius is driven by his own desire to publish his works, not that anyone really wants to read them, and that his wealth alone has made his works known to a broad audience, since he himself made copies available to the various libraries and schools in Rome. Porphyrion, among other possibilities, identifies the Fannius of *Satires* 1.4.21 as Fannius Quadratus, a contemporary writer of satire.[20] The identification, while attractive, is uncertain. Horace gives us little information about the type or style of these works, other than that they required a strong set of lungs in performance. In this he associates Fannius with Crispinus, suggesting that he too wrote in verse, perhaps on the themes of Stoic ethics. We know from *Satires* 1.10.80 that Fannius was, by reputation, a constant dinner companion (*conviva*)—that is, a parasite—of Hermogenes, who was a schoolteacher (perhaps a *grammaticus*, although the specific term is not

---

[18] Rudd, *Satires of Horace*, 132.

[19] N. Rudd, "Horace and Fannius," *Hermathena* 87 (1956): 55.

[20] "Fannius Quadratus was writing satire at that time and he had no sons. The legacy hunters used to carry his books and family busts into the public libraries, though they did not merit public performance" (*Fannius Quadratus eo tempore satyram scribebat et erat sine liberis. Huius imagines et libros heredipetae in publicas bibliothecas referebant, nullo merito dictionis*).

used) and a favorite of the Stoics, and that, at one time he had actively criticized the works of Horace.[21]

Beyond this, little more can be said concerning Fannius. Syme mentions two men named Fannius who were active in politics at the time of the composition of Horace's *Satires*. One, he notes, was a staunch adherent of Sextus Pompey, who was regarded as the champion of the republican cause after Phillipi, and a second, a republican both in family and sentiment, he mentions as the author of a conspiracy against the Caesarian party in late 24 or early 23 B.C.[22] On the basis of the scholiasts' claim that Fannius's books and bust had been housed in the library of Apollo, an honor granted "by the senate's deliberate choice" (*spontanea voluntate senatus*), Tenney Frank has argued for the anti-Caesarian sentiments of the Fannius of *Satires* 1.4.21.[23] Again the contradictory nature of the available evidence precludes any definite assessment of Fannius's political alignment. Suffice it to say that it is likely that Horace's Fannius was aligned with the anti-Caesarians. His *nomen*, at least, carries this stigma.

These, then, are the major contemporary literary figures addressed in the first four satires of Book 1: Fabius, Crispinus, Hermogenes Tigellius, and Fannius. Other names occur, such as Caprius and Sulcius of 1.4.65–66, who were apparently fellow writers of satire, but the glancing nature of their treatment, coupled with the scholiasts' silence and unreliability, has denied these names any definable personality.[24] Concerning those whom we have been able to define in fuller terms, many similar tendencies have been noted. Though beyond proof, their shared sentiments in literature, philosophy, and politics suggest the cohesiveness of a literary circle. That these men were renegade poetasters who applied to no critical standards accepted in their day is dubious at best. They certainly had some fellow feeling among themselves in this regard. To a man, they seem all to have shared some interest in Stoic ethical theory, and this, of a conservative Chrysippean stamp. They were well educated, exhibiting characteristics of wealth and good family. Although Horace himself says nothing about this, they obviously harbored a degree of anti-

[21] Pseudacron, *ad Satires* 1.2.2, suggests that the same was true of Tigellius, who "denied that Horace's songs were *modulated* with sufficient skill" (*negabat satis perite modulata*).

[22] Syme, *Roman Revolution*, 228 and 333–34.

[23] T. Frank, "Horace's Description of a Scene in Lucilius," *American Journal of Philology* 46 (1925): 72–74.

[24] On Caprius and Sulcius as contemporary writers of Satire, see B. L. Ullman, "Horace on the Nature of Satire," *Transactions of the American Philological Association* 48 (1917): 117–18; and Rudd, "Horace and Fannius," 49–50.

Caesarian sentiment among themselves. Some, at least, were competing writers of diatribe or satire, the style of which works merited Horace's most frequent and unsparing abuse. All of this, coupled with an expressive commitment to their cause, which Horace recasts as starry-eyed zealotry, made them an all-too-obvious target for his lampoons.

THE STYLIST OF *SATIRES* 1.4: A MOST UNUSUAL HORACE

Horace skews the portrait of his literary opponents in the opening satires of Book 1, painting them, in his characteristic fashion, in the guise of various comic clowns. This portrait he intends for comic effect, making no claims to accuracy. Nowhere does he seriously engage his opponents in a discussion of the theoretical issues at hand, giving fair weight to the arguments that set them at odds. Although the satirist would have us believe otherwise, these critics were not regarded generally as theoretical illiterates in their day. Horace admits as much when, in carving out a place for his *Satires* within the larger traditions of παρρησία and the liberal jest, he appeals to theories that, he realizes, were well known to his critics from a thorough reading of Greek theory. In facing their objections, the satirist, in a sense, competes on their terms. Although he disagrees with his critics on many basic issues, he knows that their objections have at least some basis in theory. That much the same is true of his opponents as stylists is clear from the two chief passages of *Satires* 1.4 treating theories of style, namely, lines 5–12 directed against Lucilius, and the large central passage, 38–63, glossed over in Chapter 1. Although these passages appear confined to a private debate between Horace and certain obscure, addle-brained opponents, they fit nicely into the context of a much larger, contemporary debate on matters of style, to which both Horace *and* his critics were well attuned. Again, a new understanding of these passages is called for that gives due weight to the cogency of the tenets argued by Horace's critics.

The satirist's central passage on style, *Satires* 1.4.38–63, shows the characteristic marks of conversational logic. The satirist would have us believe that the entire passage is a spontaneous digression prompted by his critics' claim *odere poetas* ("they hate poets") in line 33, to which the response in lines 38–63 is, "Then why hate me? I am no poet." It is in this half-serious, conversational vein that the passage is conveyed, so that one must be wary of accepting at face value the satirist's claim that comedy and satire are not true poetry, which has little if any basis in traditional theory. The passage begins (1.4.38–40): *Agedum, pauca accipe contra. / primum ego me illorum dederim quibus esse poetis / excerpam numero* ("Come now, consider a few arguments to the contrary. I will be the first to exclude myself from the rank of those whom I would concede are poets"). Horace undertakes to prove himself no poet, a bold claim that must be taken in light of the lines directly following (1.4.40–42): *neque enim concludere versum / dixeris esse satis; neque si qui scribat, uti nos, / sermoni propiora, putes hunc esse poetam* ("You would not say that it is enough to close off a verse. Nor would you reckon him a poet if someone should write, as I do, things closer to conversation"). By casting these statements in the second person, Horace makes clear that he is using the tenets of his critics, which are not necessarily his own. The statements that follow, therefore, demand a certain degree of skepticism; they must be weighed against the stylistic tenets to which we know Horace and his circle of friends were sympathetic. Certain of these tenets had, most recently, been reformulated by Cicero in his great theoretical works, the *De Oratore, Brutus*, and *Orator*, and by Philodemus in his *On Poetry* (Περὶ Ποιημάτων). They would soon be treated by Horace himself in his literary epistles, and by Dionysius of Halicarnassus in his *On Word Arrangement* (Περὶ Συνθέσεως τῶν Ὀνομάτων). These, then, along with the more ancient treatises of Aristotle and Demetrius, are the primary sources for the discussion that follows.

The first claim of lines 40–42 poses no problem from the standpoint of traditional theory. Horace would raise no objections to his opponents' claim that true poetry is more than *concludere versum*, putting words into meter. This commonplace is at least as old as Aristotle. Near the beginning of his *Poetics*, Aristotle struggles with the same question as that addressed by the satirist; both seek the peculiar defining characteristic of poetry. Like the satirist and his critics in *Satires* 1.4, on his way to answering this question, he must do away with the common assumption that poetry and meter are synonymous. He argues (*Poetics* 1.1447b9–16):

> For we have no common name to assign the mimes of Sophron and Xenarchus and the Socratic dialogues; nor if someone should make a representation [ποιοῖτο τὴν μίμησιν] in trimeters, elegiacs, or some such meter—except that some men, attaching "the making" [τὸ ποιεῖν] to meter, call them elegy makers and epic makers [ἐλεγειποιούς, τοὺς δὲ ἐποποιούς], addressing them as poets [ποιητὰς] not by virtue of mimesis but, generally, by virtue of meter.

Aristotle shows some consternation at "those men" [οἱ ἄνθρωποι] who make meter synonymous with poetry, thereby denying the "poetic" nature of the prose works of Sophron and Xenarchus, though readily accepting the dry, didactic works of Empedocles as examples of true

poetry. Aristotle would prefer to make *mimesis* the defining characteristic of true poetry, a sentiment he makes explicit at *Poetics*
9.1451b27–29:

δῆλον οὖν ἐκ τούτων ὅτι τὸν ποιητὴν μᾶλλον τῶν μύθων εἶναι δεῖ ποιητὴν ἢ τῶν
μέτρων, ὅσῳ ποιητὴς κατὰ τὴν μίμησίν ἐστιν, μιμεῖται δὲ τὰς πράξεις.

Thus, from this it is clear that the poet should be more a maker of stories
than a maker of rhythms, insofar as he is a poet by virtue of imitation,
and he is an imitator of actions.

Imitation, mimesis, not meter, defines the poet. Poetic imitation, for
Aristotle, is a matter of plot structure, the arrangement of numerous
disparate events to suggest a complete, harmonious whole.[25] At *Poetics* 7.1450b34–51a6 Aristotle compares the beautiful tragedy to a living
creature, whose limbs, though reckoned separately, are integrally
connected to one another and in perfect proportion to the whole. To
alter this arrangement, he suggests, is equivalent to severing the limbs
of a living creature and, thus, destroying or disfiguring the whole.
We see the same thinking at *Poetics* 8.1451a30–35:

So then, just as in the other mimetic arts the imitation is of a single object, so also the plot [τὸν μῦθον], since it is the imitation of an action, is the
imitation of a single, unified action, and the separate "limbs" of these
events should be arranged [τὰ μέρη συνεστάναι] so that, if one part is displaced or removed, the whole is disjoined and dislocated.

Metathesis, the displacement of a single part, destroys the whole. The
double significance of τὰ μέρη, "parts," or "limbs," coupled with the
surgical metaphors that conclude the passage (διαφέρεσθαι καὶ κινεῖσθαι)[26] makes clear that Aristotle again has in mind the analogy between a poem and a living body; what gives life and beauty to both is
the precise organic arrangement (σύστασις or σύνθεσις) of its constituent parts. This, he claims, can suffer no alteration without damage to
the whole.

Emphasis on arrangement, Russell has argued, is central to the
achievement of Aristotle's *Rhetoric* and *Poetics*, distinguishing these
works from the earlier *technai*, which sought only to analyze speeches
into their constituent parts, giving precepts for the composition of
the prooemia, arguments, and so on, without giving much thought to
the internal structure of the whole:

[25] Compare *Poetics* 7.1450b23–24, where Aristotle isolates the "arrangement of the
incidents" (τὴν σύστασιν τῶν πραγμάτων) as "tragedy's primary and most important element" (πρῶτον καὶ μέγιστον τῆς τραγῳδίας).

[26] On διαφέρεσθαι καὶ κινεῖσθαι as surgical metaphors, see Else, *Aristotle's Poetics*, 300.

This is a procedure which Plato ridiculed in the *Phaedrus*, and which Aristotle clearly thought unimportant. Their objection to it was sound and of wide application: Knowledge of parts was only "the preliminary to the art" (*ta pro tes technes*), for the art itself lay in knowing how to put the pieces together to form a coherent whole. This was as true of tragedy as of oratory; and the realisation of it is no doubt the reason why Aristotle in the *Poetics* shows so little interest in the analogous "quantitative" division of tragedy into prologue, episodes, choral parts and *exodos*.[27]

Mimetic art, for Aristotle, involves the organic arrangement of parts to create a living, realistic whole. The tragic poet imitates actions (μιμεῖται δὲ τὰς πράξεις)[28] that, Aristotle specifies, are not real events, "what actually happened" (τὰ γενόμενα), but realistic events, "what could happen and what is possible by likelihood or necessity" (οἷα ἂν γένοιτο καὶ τὰ δυνατὰ κατὰ τὸ εἰκὸς ἢ τὸ ἀναγκαῖον, 9.1451a37–38). This stress on probability and realism, common in nearly all theory after Aristotle, had strong advocates in the Hellenistic period, especially among the Alexandrian poets who actively developed new means for the expression of pictorial realism. Tiny details, the picturing of everyday experience with utmost precision, are at the heart of the Hellenistic aesthetic in all the arts. G. Zanker has defined three main types of realism at work in Alexandrian poetry:

> So realism, as a universal mode, can be observed principally, as far as literature is concerned, in a style which emphasises detail, in a subject-matter which tends towards the everyday and familiar, or in an intellectual approach which pays especial attention to probability or plausibility.[29]

Central to this stress on realism, Zanker argues, is "the desire to relate the objects of literature to the audience's experience of nearby reality," that is, to the common, sometimes petty details of everyday life.[30] At *Rhetoric* 1.1371b4–10, Aristotle makes precisely this point, arguing that the act of "reckoning together" (συλλογισμός), that is, connecting what one knows from nearby experience to what one sees represented (τὸ μιμούμενον) on stage, in a painting or statue, is a source of pleasure for the viewer, even if the thing represented is itself unpleasant. Genre scenes, for example, typical of Hellenistic painting and sculpture, with counterparts in the near trivial domesticity of cer-

---

[27] Russell, *Criticism*, 29.
[28] On the significance of Aristotle's "imitation of actions" to his poetic theory, see P. Simpson, "Aristotle on Poetry and Imitation," *Hermes* 116 (1988): 279–91.
[29] G. Zanker, *Realism in Alexandrian Poetry* (London: Croom Helm, 1987), 8.
[30] Ibid.

tain works of Callimachus, the *Idylls* of Theocritus, and Herodas's *Mimiambi*, are pleasant because the viewer already knows them from personal experience. Although nearly all theory between Aristotle and Cicero is lost to us, the evidence suggests that Peripatetic ideas of probability and pictorial realism dominated the theory and practice of poetry, especially comedy, well into the Roman period.[31] We see, for example, its influence in the first lines of the *Ars Poetica*, where Horace argues that the rules that apply to painting a realistic human portrait with all the "limbs" (*membra*) in their proper place and in the right proportion, apply to the poet's art as well. At lines 153–79 he argues that the good playwright must be a student of human nature, trained in the manners of each age and able to give a suitable tone to subtle shifts in human nature. Again at *Ars Poetica* 317–22, Horace bids the dramatic poet to make verisimilitude his aim:

> respicere exemplar vitae morumque iubebo
> doctum imitatorem et vivas hinc ducere voces.
> interdum speciosa locis morataque recte
> fabula nullius Veneris sed pondere inerti,
> valdius oblectat populum meliusque moratur
> quam versus inopes rerum nugaeque canorae.

I will advise one trained in imitation to look back upon the example of life and manners and to draw from here the sounds of life. Sometimes a story marked by commonplace thoughts and characters well sketched, though lacking in charm and with its mass unworked, gives stronger delight to the crowd and better detains them than verses without substance and sonorous trifles.

Realism, representing the numerous characters and quirks of everyday existence in the humble language of conversation, involved points of honor and rivalry for the Hellenistic poets and the Roman artists, such as Horace, who sought to emulate it. The poets of New Comedy, most notably Menander and Terence, were regarded as unparalleled masters of verisimilitude, and Horace may well have comedy in mind when he speaks of the *speciosa locis morataque recte* in line

---

[31] Menander was acknowledged as the grand master of vivid illustration. Syrianus attributes the following statement to Aristophanes of Byzantium, providing an oblique glimpse into Hellenistic theories of realism applied to comedy: "Oh Menander and Life, which one of you has imitated the other?" (Ὦ Μένανδρε καὶ βίε, πότερος ἂν ὑμῶν πότερον ἀπεμιμήσατο;). Compare Donatus *ad Adelphi* 81, where Terence is judged to be better (*melius*) than his model on the basis of realism. For a general survey of realism in Terence and Lucilius, see W. Krenkel, "Zur literarischen Kritik bei Lucilius," in D. Korzeniewski, ed., *Die römische Satire*, Wege der Forschung 238 (Darmstadt, 1970), 213–27.

319, referring to New Comedy's penchant for pithy moral sentiments.[32] The reference to the *imitatorem* in line 318 draws upon Aristotle's notion of the poet as "imitator," μιμητής (cf. *Poetics* 24.1460b),
alluding, once again, to the Peripatetic theory of realism in imitation.

At *Satires* 1.4.38–63, the satirist makes claims that are wholly out of
character with the *Ars Poetica* and nearly all poetic theory since Aristotle. At *Satires* 1.4.47–48 he disqualifies himself as a writer of poetry,
arguing that, to rank as true poetry, a work must possess "passionate
spirit and power in diction and theme." Comedy and satire fail to
make the grade. An unnamed bystander interrupts at lines 48–52,
arguing that comedy too will at times make passionate rumblings, as
when the "seething father rages" at his prodigal son. The satirist
counters: *numquid Pomponius istis / audiret leviora, pater si viveret?*
("Would Pomponious hear a lecture less stern if his father were
alive?") He dismisses the interlocutor's claim by suggesting that the
"raging father" scene could be witnessed on the streets of Rome any
day of the week, a claim the advocate of Aristotle's mimetic theory
would normally construe as high praise. Here, however, the satirist
takes the role of his critics; he disparages his interlocutor's appeal to
mimetic realism, insisting, against all precedent in traditional theory,
that comedy is not true poetry because its themes and diction are too
lifelike. The claim is brilliantly inept, and Horace's audience certainly
heard it as such.

New qualifications are proposed for the now rarefied "honor"
(*honos*) of the title "poet" (*Satires* 1.4.43–47):

> ingenium cui sit, cui mens divinior atque os
> magna sonaturum, des nominis huius honorem.
> idcirco quidam comoedia necne poema
> esset quaesivere, quod acer spiritus ac vis
> nec verbis nec rebus inest, nisi quod pede certo
> differt sermoni, sermo merus.

If someone should have natural talent, an inspired mind and a voice
suited to singing grand themes, you would grant him the honor of this
name. Therefore, some have questioned whether comedy is poetry, because it lacks a passionate spirit and force in words and themes; if not
for meter, it is pure common talk.

---

[32] Greek New Comedy was especially noted for its moral sententiousness, evidenced
by the inordinately large proportion of *sententiae* in the preserved fragments of Menander. Rawson has made a good case for the comic allusion in Horace's *speciosa locis
morataque recte*. See E. Rawson, "*Speciosa Locis Morataque Recte*," in Michael Whitby,
P. Hardie, and Mary Whitby, eds., *Homo Viator: Classical Essays for John Bramble* (Bristol:
Bristol Classical Press, 1987), 79–88.

The standards proposed, taken at face value, exclude not only the finest works of Menander, Terence, and Lucilius, but also the *Idylls* of Theocritus; Callimachus's *Iambs* and several *Hymns*; most, if not all, of Catullus; much of Vergil, including large sections of the *Aeneid*; Horace's *Satires, Epodes, Epistles*, and a good number of his *Odes*. The list is by no means complete. The standards that would exclude these works are cast in the second person, suggesting that the satirist disclaims responsibility for them. At best he pretends to espouse these views. Even so, I can cite only one substantial analysis of these lines that regards them as anything other than the convictions of Horace himself, his earnest assessment of what it means to write true "poetry."[33] Typical is Brink's analysis:

> The dignity of the name of poet, *nominis huius honorem* (44), should be granted only to the writer of verse who has a certain cast of mind and whose language attains a certain level of style. The sort of mind that is required he describes variously as genius, *ingenium*; inspired mind, *mens divinior* (43), passionate spirit, *acer spiritus*, and force (*vis*) (46). Truly poetic utterance is said to come from a mouth that will speak forth great things, *os magna sonaturum* (43–4); words and matter, *verba* and *res*, will then have the force which critics found wanting in certain kinds of verse (45–8). These lines put in the language of ancient literary criticism certain critical notions of the poet Horace. They show that even at the time of this early satire he envisaged a wider field of poetic production and a larger poetic purpose.[34]

[33] I refer to S. Oberhelman's article (in collaboration with D. Armstrong), "Satire as Poetry and the Impossibility of Metathesis in Horace, *Sermones* 1.4.38b-62," forthcoming in a volume on Philodemus and literary criticism (ed. Dirk Obbink) from Oxford University Press. I am grateful to Professor Oberhelman for allowing me to preview his work, which I consider outstanding in every respect. Put simply, Oberhelman argues that *Satires* 1.4.38–62 must be viewed in light of larger theoretical currents, and that the views espoused in these lines are largely those of Horace's critics, not of Horace himself. He also points out that Horace ironically subverts his surface message, which concerns the alleged irrelevance of word arrangement, by demonstrating his compositional virtuosity in the very lines that deny its importance. Although my own views were formed independent of this article and differ in several details, I make much the same case in the pages that follow.

[34] C. O. Brink, *Horace on Poetry: Prolegomena to the Literary Epistles* (Cambridge: Cambridge University Press, 1963), 162. Brink does add, however, that the passage is rather "extreme and one-sided" and must be accepted with some qualification (pp. 163–64). For similar sentiments, see Grube, *Greek and Roman Critics*, 232; Fraenkel, *Horace*, 126–27; and Hendrickson, "Horace, *Serm.* 1.4," 129–31. DuQuesnay, however, claims in passing that at *Satires* 1.4.39–42 Horace "pretends to deny the status of poetry to his satires," DuQuesnay, "Horace and Maecenas," 26. Likewise Leach recognizes that the claims are disingenuous: "In verses 64–102 he will answer these charges in detail, but first, with characteristic suddenness, he denies that satire is poetry. The denial

Barely concealed here is the well-worn assumption that Horace came into his own as a poet only later in life, with the publication of his *Odes*, and that the *Satires* are early, experimental works that fall short of the standards that, even he as a writer of satire knew, were required of true poetry. Although nearly all commentators on the *Satires* have taken the same view, there is good reason to reject this thesis, for it too readily identifies the convictions of *Satires* 1.4.38–63 with Horace's own views when, in fact, they represent sectarian theories that, though of ancient provenience, were entirely antipathetic to the convictions of Horace and his circle of friends. For example, it is commonly noted among the commentators on these lines that the satirist's disparagement of New Comedy and satire shows awareness of an old critical debate taken up by the Hellenistic critics, perhaps initially by Theophrastus.[35] The only evidence they cite, however, favoring a negative attitude toward New Comedy in ancient theory is a passage from Cicero's *Orator*, which parallels closely the satirist's claims in *Satires* 1.4. *Orator* 67 is enclosed within a larger discussion of the precise defining characteristics of poetry, which Cicero seeks to isolate from oratory. He claims that the matter was in no way settled in his day, and that the poets themselves were concerned with the issue (*Orator* 66): *Nam etiam poetae quaestionem attulerunt, quidnam esset illud quo ipsi differrent ab oratoribus* ("For even poets have asked what that particular thing is by which they differ from orators"). Cicero adds that, at one time, it was thought that rhythm and meter were the real defining characteristics of poetry. But, just as Aristotle and the speaker in *Satires* 1.4, he rejects the thesis, pointing out that, in actual practice, rhythm had become very much a part of oratory.

He continues his search. New criteria are proposed—the convictions of certain unnamed critics (*nonnullis*), who support the satirist's disparagement of comedy and satire in *Satires* 1.4. Cicero writes (*Orator* 67):

> Itaque video visum esse nonnullis Platonis et Democriti locutionem, etsi absit a versu, tamen, quod incitatius feratur et clarissimis verborum luminibus utatur, potius poema putandum quam comicorum poetarum,

---

teases, but should not confuse the reader. As William Anderson observes, Horace is creating an opportunity to define the special qualities of his satiric style." See Leach, "Horace's *Pater Optimus*," 625; and Anderson, *Roman Satire*, 24–25. Slightly different is Armstrong, who argues that the satirist postpones the question of whether satire is poetry to *Satires* 1.10. Armstrong, *Horace*, 46.

[35] Kiessling and Heinze, *Horatius Flaccus*, 76, for example, notes: "Critics of the Hellenistic period, Horace's *quidam*, disputed comedy's right to be valued as poetry. . . . Theophrastus, as Wilamowitz supposes."

apud quos, nisi quod versiculi sunt, nihil est aliud cotidiani dissimile sermonis.

And so I see that, to certain critics, the diction of Plato and Democritus,
even if it lacks meter, nonetheless, because it sweeps along strongly and
makes use of brilliant words, seems more to be reckoned as poetry than
the diction of comic poets in whom, if not for their versicles, there is
nothing dissimilar to everyday speech.

"Brilliant" diction (*locutio*) and a style of delivery that sweeps along
with vigor and excitement certain critics have marked as the essential
criteria of poetry, standards that approximate the *acer spiritus ac vis*
proposed by Horace's critics in *Satires* 1.4. In both cases, New Comedy is excluded because of its *sermo merus*, Cicero's *cotidianus sermo*,
and so we see on what basis *Orator* 67 has traditionally been accepted
as a corroboration of the satirist's negative assessment of comedy in
Satires 1.4. It is very unfortunate, however, that no commentator has
seen fit to follow Cicero's argument through to the end, because it
becomes quite apparent in *Orator* 68 that he rejects the thesis proposed by the unnamed *nonnullis*. Immediately following the lines just
quoted, where all commentators of Horace, without exception, end
their comparison, Cicero adds the disclaimer, "But this is *not*, however, the chief mark of a poet" (*nec tamen id est poetae maximum*). Cicero
disagrees with the theories of the *nonnullis*, and he goes on to offer
his own opinion:

Ego autem, etiamsi quorundam grandis et ornata vox est poetarum, tamen in ea cum licentiam statuo maiorem esse quam in nobis faciendo-
rum iungendorumque verborum, tum etiam nonnullorum voluntate vo-
cibus magis quam rebus inserviunt.

For my part, however, granting that certain poets use grand and figurative language, nonetheless I am convinced that in this they not only enjoy
greater freedom than we in fashioning and joining together words, but
they also, with the approval of some critics, pay more attention to sounds
than to subject matter.

Cicero removes the criterion of poetry from the grandeur and flower
of voice, the *iudicium electioque verborum* ("discernment in the choice
of subject matter and word selection," *Orator* 68) that are the very
qualities sought by Horace's critics in *Satires* 1.4. Such qualities,
though important, Cicero does not regard as unique to poetry.
Forced to give his own opinion, Cicero isolates the essential criterion
of poetry in the poet's greater freedom in the "fashioning and joining
together of words," terminology characteristic of ancient rhetorical

theories of *compositio*, often referred to as *iunctura*. Cicero has, in essence, made the poet's greater facility in *compositio* the single defining characteristic of poetry that isolates his skill from that of the orator. At the same time, he has effectively displaced the criteria by which comedy had been discredited as poetry.

We see, then, that there are several major problems in taking *Orator* 67 as positive support for the satirist's self-deprecating claims in *Satires* 1.4. Against the convictions of the *nonnullis*, Cicero has introduced the criterion of *compositio*, by which, it was understood, New Comedy possessed every legitimate claim to the designation, "poetry." This claim is by no means unique, but stems from a long critical tradition, "as old as Euripides in practice and as Aristotle in criticism," that held that good poetry could be composed of everyday words and themes artfully arranged.[36] Horace was no middling theorist, not even in his earliest works, and he was certainly aware of the problems implied by his claims in *Satires* 1.4. Taking the voice of his critics, he gives no thought to the legitimate claims of *compositio* (σύν-θεσις), so important to Aristotle's mimetic theory and still evident in Cicero's definition of poetry at *Orator* 68. As *Orator* 67–68 demonstrates, the stylistic tenets of Horace's programmatic satires fit neatly within the context not only of a private feud between the satirist and certain obscure critics, but also within the much larger theoretical debates of the late Republic. The topic of *compositio* was central to these debates. A closer look at contemporary theories of *compositio* will demonstrate that the views expressed at *Satires* 1.4.38–63 are not Horace's own, but those of his opponents, and any ancient reader of the *Satires* who was but marginally aware of and sympathetic toward the legitimate claims of *compositio* and traditional theories of euphony would have heard such claims as overtly inept.

SIMPLE DICTION ARTFULLY ARRANGED: SOME THEORETICAL PRECEDENTS

In discussing the proper dictional cast of oratory in the third book of his *Rhetoric*, Aristotle isolates clarity as the chief virtue of style for the orator who wishes not only to dazzle but to be understood (*Rhetoric* 3.1404b1–6):

καὶ ὡρίσθω λέξεως ἀρετὴ σαφῆ εἶναι (σημεῖον γάρ τι ὁ λόγος, ὥστ᾽ ἐὰν μὴ δηλοῖ

οὐ ποιήσει τὸ ἑαυτοῦ ἔργον), καὶ μήτε ταπεινὴν μήτε ὑπὲρ τὸ ἀξίωμα, ἀλλὰ πρέ-

---

[36] L. P. Wilkinson, "The Language of Virgil and Horace," *Classical Quarterly*, n.s. 9 (1959): 191.

πουσαν· ἡ γὰρ ποιητικὴ ἴσως οὐ ταπεινή, ἀλλ᾽ οὐ πρέπουσα λόγῳ. τῶν δ᾽ ὀνομάτων καὶ ῥημάτων σαφῆ μὲν ποιεῖ τὰ κύρια.

And let us define clarity as the virtue of diction. An indication (of its importance) is that the speech, unless it is clear, will not accomplish its proper function. And the diction should be neither mean nor above its rank, but appropriate to discourse. For poetic diction, while perhaps not mean, is appropriate to discourse, but everyday nouns and verbs make the style clear.

To achieve his proper goal, the orator fashions diction (λέξις) from "dominant" or "prevalent" words in everyday use (τὰ κύρια, the *dominantia nomina . . . verbaque* of *Ars Poetica* 240).[37] Even so, Aristotle concedes that a more "poetic" style marked by "exotic language" (ξένη διάλεκτος) possesses a certain persuasive power useful in deliberative speech. He hesitates, however, to recommend such a style, noting that lofty diction is much more suited to the grand themes of epic and tragedy than it is to oratory. He suggests that even poets apply to restrictions of propriety in their use of extraordinary diction: "If a slave should speak in elegant language, or a very young man, or one should do so in speaking of trifles, it would be very unsuitable [ἀπρεπέστερον]." Pulled in opposite directions, Aristotle suggests that the orator should make use of, but cleverly conceal the artifices of poetry within his speech. He adds (*Rhetoric* 3.1404b24–26):

κλέπτεται δ᾽ εὖ, ἐάν τις ἐκ τῆς εἰωθυίας διαλέκτου ἐκλέγων συντιθῇ· ὅπερ Εὐριπίδης ποιεῖ καὶ ὑπέδειξε πρῶτος.

And art is cleverly concealed if one should set together words selected from ordinary language. Euripides does this, and he was the first to set the pattern.

Grube remarks on these lines that "Aristotle is using the technical terms which became stereotyped later, ἐκλέγειν for the choice of words and συντίθεναι for the arrangement of them."[38] These categories, by which Aristotle ordered the initial chapters of Book 3 of his *Rhetoric*, chapters 1–7 treating λέξις as word choice (ἐκλογή), and chapters 8–9 treating λέξις as word arrangement (σύνθεσις), would become the two chief analytical terms in subsequent treatises on style. Word choice, after Aristotle, is only half of the equation. To illustrate the power of arrangement, he gives the example of Euripides, whom he regarded as a consummate stylist, though his diction was not, in

---

[37] See C. O. Brink, *Horace on Poetry: The Ars Poetica* (Cambridge: Cambridge University Press, 1971), 285–86.

[38] Grube, *Greek and Roman Critics*, 95.

itself, out of the ordinary or distinctly "poetic." Rather, Aristotle defines his poetic skill in terms of σύνθεσις, the clever way in which he
shaped and arranged these words. Cicero, we have seen, reached
much the same conclusion at *Orator* 68, making *compositio* the chief
mark of poetry, and the same sentiments can be found in Demetrius,
Philodemus, Dionysius of Halicarnassus, and nearly all theorists after
Aristotle.[39] It was Aristotle who gave rise to this thinking, the first to
address not only the breakdown of a speech or poem into its constituent parts in the manner of the old sophistic *technai*, but also the general principles for arranging these parts. His theory of mimetic realism, stressing probability, unity, and harmony in the overall
construction of a poem or speech, he applied at a much narrower
level to the composition (σύνθεσις) of a single line. Poets, he understood, were masters of σύνθεσις, transforming the most ordinary diction into something truly impressive and "poetic." In the opening
chapters of *Rhetoric* Book 3, he suggests that prinicples of σύνθεσις
were within the province of oratory as well, though, in the interests
of clarity, he insists that they be employed on a much more limited,
"well-concealed" scale.[40]

Dionysius is far more explicit than either Aristotle or Cicero in his
belief that σύνθεσις far surpasses ἐκλογή in its ability to lend expres-
siveness, beauty, and distinction to both poetry and oratory. His most
difficult theoretical work, the *On Word Arrangement*, contemporary
with the later works of Horace himself, is the only ancient treatise
devoted to word arrangement that has come down to us intact, and
thus serves as a key to the theory and practice of σύνθεσις in the age
of Horace. Most important, the treatise gives evidence to a contem-

[39] Centuries later, "Longinus" remarks on the power of σύνθεσις in nearly the same
terms, claiming that many poets who are not "lofty by nature" achieve grandeur using
even the most ordinary language (κοινοῖς καὶ δημώδεσι τοῖς ὀνόμασι) "solely by means of
arranging and fitting together their words" (διὰ μόνου τοῦ συνθεῖναι καὶ ἁρμόσαι). He
lists Philistus, Aristophanes, and Euripides as exemplars of this art, quoting a specific
passage from Euripides' *Heracles*. See *On the Sublime* 40.2. On the semantic effect of
Euripides' word arrangement, see Wilkinson, "Language of Virgil and Horace," 182;
and R.O.A.M. Lyne, *Words and the Poet* (Oxford: Clarendon Press, 1989), 1–2.

[40] Aristotle treats the matter of simple diction again at *Poetics* 22.1458a where, in
contrast to *Rhetoric* Book 3, he seems to harbor a definite prejudice against τὰ κύρια.
We should note, however, that Aristotle does not say that all diction formed of ordinary words is low (noting the contrastive force of μὲν οὖν versus ἀλλά). Rather, he suggests that commonplace diction, while valuable in achieving clarity, has its own virtuous
mean; clear diction, however common, must not wallow in the gutter. He mentions the
poetry of Cleophon and Sthenelus as prime examples of such extremes. What he says
of them does not apply to the practices of Euripides and should not be construed as a
general prejudice against τὰ κύρια. On these lines see S. Halliwell, *The Poetics of Aristotle: Translation and Commentary* (Chapel Hill: University of North Carolina Press,
1987), 160–64.

porary debate raging among the theorists of *compositio* with precise parallels to the satirist's debate with his critics in the early satires of Book 1. In both cases, the debates hinge upon technical, often tedious matters of σύνθεσις.

Dionysius illustrates his theory of the power and distinction of word arrangement in chapter 3 of his *On Word Arrangement*, quoting the first sixteen lines of *Odyssey* Book 16, to which he adds the following commentary (*On Word Arrangement* 3):

> I am sure everyone would testify that these lines allure and enchant the ear, and rank second to no poetry whatsoever, even the most attractive of all. But where does their power to persuade us lie, and what causes them to be what they are? Is it the selection of words or the composition? [διὰ τὴν ἐκλογὴν τῶν ὀνομάτων ἢ διὰ τὴν σύνθεσιν;] No one will say "selection," I am sure: for the whole passage is woven together from the most commonplace, humble words, such as might have come readily to the tongue of a farmer, seaman or artisan, or anyone else who takes no trouble to speak well. Indeed, if the meter is broken up [λυθέντος γοῦν τοῦ μέτρου], these very same lines will appear ordinary and unworthy of admiration. . . . What alternative, therefore, is left but to attribute the beauty of the style to the composition?[41]

Dionysius, adapting, or perhaps mimicking, the manner of Alexandrian critics, such as Eratosthenes, enlists the authority of Homer to prove that σύνθεσις is the chief criterion of poetry. The proof of the power of word arrangement comes in "dissolving the rhythm," metathesis, which leaves the lines trivial and undistinguished. Aristotle, we recall, demonstrated the power of arrangement in very similar fashion at *Poetics* 8.1451a30–35, making metathesis equivalent to killing or disfiguring a living creature.

To the ancient theorist, the term σύνθεσις carried connotations far beyond its apparent sense of "word arrangement." Aristotle, in his analysis of λέξις as σύνθεσις in *Rhetoric* 3.1408b21–1410b4, treats primarily the topics of prose rhythm and the period. The Hellenistic critics gave much greater range to σύνθεσις, so that, by Dionysius's day, the topic included the analyses of letters, their individual sounds, and the arrangement of these sounds within words; the analyses of *cola* and the period, considered both individually and in conjunction; and the study of syllables, meter, and so on.[42] At times *On Word Ar-*

---

[41] The text and translations of Dionysius's *On Word Arrangement*, unless otherwise indicated, are drawn from S. Usher, ed., *Dionysius of Halicarnassus: The Critical Essays II*, with translation (Cambridge Mass.: Harvard University Press, 1985).

[42] On the various theoretical connotations of σύνθεσις in the age of Horace, see Scholz, "Lucilius und Horaz," 360–61.

rangement borders on the trivial and bureaucratic, as in chapter 15, where Dionysius very carefully distinguishes four different "grades" of short syllable. Nonetheless, the topic did not lose its appeal, and it was much studied in Horace's day. Besides Dionysius, Cicero wrote extensively on the topic in his *Orator*, dated to 46 B.C., a work that Quintilian considered nearly the last word *de compositione*.[43] Varro wrote a *De Compositione Saturarum*, now lost, in which he treated technical matters of σύνθεσις, such as those already listed, with specific reference to satire.[44] The literary *Satires* and sections of *Epistles* Book 2 serve as Horace's contribution to the field. Taken together, these works indicate that technical matters of *compositio* were central to the critical debates of the mid to late first century B.C. Cicero's *Orator* takes a very evenhanded approach to the topic, but we know from Tacitus, Quintilian, and, to some extent, Cicero himself that the treatise was regarded as highly controversial in its day.[45] Dionysius is much less successful in concealing the heat of his arguments, for the polemical tone of his *On Word Arrangement*, though it has never received adequate attention, is apparent at all turns, again attesting to the volatile nature of the topic in the late first century B.C. A close study of the treatise shows that the opponents of Dionysius and Horace share much in common, as conservative Stoics (or quasi Stoics), opposed to traditional compositional theory. The parallels are striking. By understanding the give-and-take of these arguments, we move one step closer to defining the critical tenets of Horace's detractors in the opening satires of Book 1 as well as his criticisms of Lucilius in *Satires* 1.4 and 1.10, which need to be considered within the larger context of contemporary compositional theory.

DIONYSIUS'S *ON WORD ARRANGEMENT* AND THE STOIC THEORY OF NATURAL WORD ORDER

In chapter 3 of his *On Word Arrangement*, Dionysius once again makes a case for the power and beauty of σύνθεσις:

[43] See my subsequent discussion.

[44] On Varro's *De Compositione Saturarum*, see Scholz, "Lucilius und Horaz," 359–65; and W. S. Anderson, "Pompey, His Friends, and the Literature of the First Century B.C.," *University of California Publications in Classical Philology* 19, no. 1 (1963): 70–71.

[45] On Cicero's correspondence with Brutus and Calvus, and its relation to the *Orator*, see G. L. Hendrickson, "Cicero's Correspondence with Brutus and Calvus on Oratorical Style," *American Journal of Philology* 47 (1926): 234–58; and "The *De Analogia* of Julius Caesar: Its Occasion, Nature, and Date, with Additional Fragments," *Classical Philology* 1, no. 2 (1906): 97–120.

Every utterance, then, by which we express our thoughts is either in meter or not in meter. Either kind is capable, if accompanied by beautiful arrangement, of conferring beauty upon either verse or prose; but if speech is thrown off carelessly and at random, it destroys the value of the thought in the process. At any rate many poets and prose-writers, both philosophers and orators, have carefully chosen expressions which are very beautiful and suited to their subject-matter, but have reaped no benefit from their efforts because they have given them a haphazard and unmusical arrangement; whereas others have taken humble words which might easily be despised, and by arranging them in a pleasing and striking manner, have succeeded in investing their discourse with great beauty.

In claiming that a noble thought will be drained of its value (τὸ χρήσιμον) unless artfully arranged, Dionysius makes content a function of arrangement, an extreme position with slim precedent in earlier extant theory.[46] Such a stance is best explained as a critical posture in response to the anticompositional theories of his critics, certain unnamed poets and prose writers who, he claims, have "wasted their effort" by ignoring the demands of arrangement. The passage breathes hostility. The point is not that Dionysius's opponents were theoretical illiterates, ignorant of the claims of arrangement, which were as old as Aristotle, but that, to advertise their disdain for such claims, they purposely gave their works a casual, haphazard arrangement, placing all value in content (διάνοια), word choice (ἐκλογή), and propriety (τὸ πρέπον) to the exclusion of compositional refinements, which they regarded as insignificant at best. Their works, which seemed to Dionysius "careless and tossed-off in haphazard fashion" (ἀνεπιστάτως δὲ καὶ ὡς ἔτυχεν ῥιπτομένη), speak not for ineptitude but for rival considerations in theory, real friction between contending critics and writers in the first century B.C.

Dionysius, though he never names his critics, leaves little doubt as to their theoretical leanings. Treating the distinctions of prose and verse in chapter 25 of his *On Word Arrangement*, Dionysius chides the orator who has refused to learn the refinements of arrangement practiced by Demosthenes:

I suspect that certain persons, who have no general education but practice rhetoric on a street-corner level [ἀγοραῖον τῆς ῥητορικῆς μέρος] without method or art, will inveigh violently against these statements. I must defend myself against these for fear of appearing to let the case go by

[46] On Epicurean theories of semantic word arrangement, see my subsequent discussion.

default. No doubt they will argue: "Was Demosthenes such a helpless creature, then, that when he was writing his speeches, he laid out meters and rhythms beside him as his materials, as clay-modellers lay out their moulds, and tried to fit his clauses into them, adjusting the word-order this way and that, keeping a careful watch on his longs and shorts and taking great trouble over the cases of his nouns and the moods of his verbs and everything else affecting the parts of speech?"

Again, Dionysius's opponent proves not so much ignorant of *compositio* as disdainful of it, practicing rhetoric "without method or art" (ὁδοῦ τε καὶ τέχνης χωρὶς), "the marketplace type," if Dionysius can be believed. He introduces the clay-modeling analogy to prove that, unlike a manual craft, *compositio* possesses no well-defined rules in matters such as declension and the consideration of vowel length, denying, in other words, the very premise of Dionysius's work. We see, then, the point of Dionysius's hostility.

Later in the same chapter, Dionysius returns to defend his thesis that the real nature of Demosthenes' achievement lay in his mastery of σύνθεσις as an art, which he compares to a manual skill learned from long study and practice:[47]

> Anyone who argued along these lines would not seem to me to make any unreasonable claims; and he might further add that when Demosthenes was still a lad, and had only recently taken up the study of rhetoric, he naturally investigated all the effects which human application to the art could attain; but after long training [ἄσκησις] had led to the acquisition of a greater mastery [ἰσχὺν], and imprinted on his mind marks and impressions [τύπους τινὰς . . . καὶ σφραγῖδας] of all that he had studied, he henceforth produced his effects with the greatest of ease from sheer force of habit.

Nature stamps its impression on the mind of the young orator, just as a seal ring fashions a perfect image of itself in unworked clay. Once the impression takes hold, it becomes a pattern for the orator's art, reproducing itself not from conscious effort, but as an extension of the speaker's disposition. Dionysius's description of the education of Demosthenes is telling, for he describes the process in terms well known to his audience from Stoic epistemological theory, which treated the acquisition of knowledge as somehow analogous to stamping impressions in clay: long training (ἄσκησις) yields strength of

---

[47] The *ars/ingenium* controversy goes back at least as far as Plato's *Gorgias*, stemming initially from the sophistic debates of the mid to late fifth century B.C. The question, as it was debated in Horace's day, is treated by Brink, *Ars Poetica*, 394–400 and 511–13.

mind (ἰσχύς), a permanent ability or disposition (ἕξις) to distinguish true impressions (τύποι) from false.[48] In casting his description in the technical terminology of the Stoics, Dionysius makes compositional expertise a process analogous to the acquisition of knowledge, which the Stoics regarded as a highly regulated, rational process with its own system of checks and balances. He proceeds in chapter 25 to describe the analogous process of learning to read, which he again casts in the technical vocabulary of the Stoics. These arguments, he claims, he has gathered to prove a point "to those who are in the habit of scoffing at the rules of the rhetorical handbooks," that is, technical treatises such as his own *On Word Arrangement*.[49]

In addressing the problem of σύνθεσις as an art, why does Dionysius incorporate the technical jargon of Stoic theories of sense perception and knowledge? Dionysius was no Stoic. Quite to the contrary, he reserves his sharpest and most frequent criticisms for the stylistic tenets of Chrysippus and his contemporary followers in Rome. A closer analysis of these criticisms will demonstrate that Dionysius's chief critics were themselves Stoics, or at least quasi Stoics, of a conservative, Chrysippean stamp, whose anticompositional theories had gained wide support in the mid to late first century B.C. To a significant extent, Dionysius directs his *On Word Arrangement* against these critics, defending arrangement as an art, fully aware that the treatise will be "scoffed at" in certain quarters. In chapter 25 (quoted previously) his proofs are particularly incisive, for he applies the pet epistemological theories of his critics to the development of an art, which they themselves refused to recognize. In contrast to their stance against Dionysius's compositional art, the Stoics regarded the acquisition of knowl-

---

[48] For a brief but lucid introduction to Stoic theories of sense-perception and knowledge see E. P. Arthur, "The Stoic Analysis of the Mind's Reactions to Presentations," *Hermes* 111 (1983): 69–78, especially 70–71, which treat the seal-ring analogy and the terminology associated with it. For further works on Stoic epistemology, see A. A. Long and D. N. Sedley, eds., *The Hellenistic Philosophers*: Vol. 2, *Greek and Latin Texts* (Cambridge: Cambridge University Press, 1987), 499–501. On the terms ἄσκησις, ἰσχύς, τύπος, σφραγίς, and ἕξις in the technical vocabulary of Stoic theory, see especially the Greek indexes to E. V. Arnold, *Roman Stoicism* (Cambridge: Cambridge University Press, 1911); M. Pohlenz, *Die Stoa: Geschichte einer geistigen Bewegung* (Göttingen: Vandenhoeck and Ruprecht, 1948–49); and E. Zeller, *Stoics Epicureans and Sceptics* (London, 1880; repr. New York: Russell and Russell, 1962). For other useful notes concerning Stoic influence on Dionysius's *On Word Arrangement*, see D. M. Schenkveld, "Linguistic Theories in the Rhetorical Works of Dionysius of Halicarnassus," *Glotta* 61 (1983): 67–94. More recent general surveys to be consulted are J. M. Rist, *Stoic Philosophy* (Cambridge: Cambridge University Press, 1969); A. A. Long, *Problems in Stoicism* (London: Athlone Press, 1971), and *Hellenistic Philosophy* (Berkeley: University of California Press, 1974).

[49] *On Word Arrangement* 25.

edge as a highly regulated technique that could, to some extent at least, be learned from rule books, an idea widely ridiculed by their opponents. Dionysius makes the most of this; by way of Stoic theory, he transforms σύνθεσις into a logical process, comparable with the philosopher's pursuit of knowledge, a strict art to which, in the Stoic view, only the wise man (*sapiens*) could hope to attain. The illustration is double-edged, positing a natural bond between Stoic epistemological theory and the compositional refinements recommended by Dionysius; to reject one is to reject both. In turning the Stoics' technical jargon to his own advantage, Dionysius brings the polemical undercurrent of his treatise fully to the surface.

In discussing the history of compositional study at *On Word Arrangement* 4, Dionysius claims that "the ancients" (οἱ ἀρχαῖοι), by which he apparently means pre-Hellenistic writers, once made a serious study of σύνθεσις, the results of which can be seen in the beauty of their "meters, their lyrics and prose-writings" (τά τε μέτρα καὶ τὰ μέλη καὶ οἱ λόγοι). He goes on to name nine historians, all of the third and second centuries B.C., the successors of "the ancients," whom he notes for their utter neglect of the standards of excellence previously set in matters of σύνθεσις. This severe decline in compositional tact Dionysius regards as in no way surprising, for he suggests that even the philosophers who wrote treatises on dialectic were, at this time, "inept in the arrangement of their words" (ἄθλιοι περὶ τὴν σύνθεσιν τῶν ὀνομάτων). He mentions only one name in proof:

> It is sufficient to point to Chrysippus the Stoic as proof of my statement, for beyond that I refuse to go. Of writers who have been judged worthy of renown or distinction, none has written treatises on logic [διαλεκτικὰς τέχνας] with more precision, and none has published discourses which are worse specimens of composition.

The speeches or "discourses" (λόγοι) of Chrysippus Dionysius regards as compositional disasters, devoid of even the most rudimentary refinements in arrangement. He claims that, in preparing his *On Word Arrangement*, he was especially interested in studying Stoic theories of arrangement, aware that "these men pay no small attention to the subject of language." He was singularly disappointed, however, to discover that the various Stoic works entitled "*On the Arrangement of the Parts of Discourse* contained not a rhetorical but a dialectical investigation" ("περὶ τῆς συντάξεως τῶν τοῦ λόγου μερῶν" οὐ ῥητορικτὴν θεωρίαν ἐχούσας ἀλλὰ διαλεκτικήν). Dionysius claims that these works, two by Chrysippus himself, though they dealt with logical aspects of arrangement, such as the groupings of propositions, true and false, and clear and ambiguous, failed to address matters of euphony, "the attractiveness and beauty of style which should be the aim of composition."[50]

Dionysius, though he has little patience for dialectical theories of arrangement, undertakes to examine some of the basic tenets of Stoic theory in order to "avoid the suspicion of having passed it by through ignorance and not from choice."[51] In undertaking this study he proceeds from a basic Stoic premise: "Well, it seemed to me that we should follow nature as much as possible, and to fit together the parts of speech as she demands" (*On Word Arrangement* 5).[52] Nature herself (φύσις) determines arrangement, that is, a natural word order (*ordo naturalis*) taught not by art but by a life attuned to the unseen logical structures at work in the cosmos. The thinking is entirely Stoic. Dio-

---

[50] It seems that, from its very inception, Stoic rhetorical theory was regarded as bizarre and impractical by all non-Stoic rhetoricians. Dionysius's attitudes toward Stoic rhetoric are by no means unusual. For similar sentiments, see Cicero *De Oratore* 2.159–61; *Brutus* 117–19; and Diogenes Laertius 7.59. Besides the standard histories of Stoicism and ancient rhetoric, see F. Striller, "*De Stoicorum Studiis Rhetoricis*," *Breslauer Philologische Abhandlungen* 1 (1887): 1–61; and C. Atherton, "Hand over Fist: The Failure of Stoic Rhetoric," *Classical Quarterly* 38, no. 2 (1988): 392–427.

[51] This final claim proves that the logical, "natural" theories of arrangement tested in *On Word Arrangement* 5 had some precedent in the rhetorical handbooks mentioned at the end of Chapters 4 and 5 (thereby framing the investigation contained in Chapter 5), and that they were not ideas Dionysius somehow hit upon independently. A. Scaglione, *The Classical theory of Composition from its Origins to the Present: A Historical Survey* (Chapel Hill: University of North Carolina Press, 1972), 77, argues the same point: "What no one seems to have underlined or even noticed is that Dionysius attributes all such prejudiced approaches to the very kind of 'manuals on dialectic' exemplified above by the reference to Chrysippus: Such manuals, he concludes, 'are not relevant to the present inquiry, therefore they are not worth studying.' " The point is important and worth emphasizing, for the existence of theories of natural word arrangement (an *ordo naturalis*) along the lines of *On Word Arrangement* 5, though largely ignored in modern scholarship, is well attested in ancient theory, most notably by Quintilian *Institutes* 9.4.23–28 and Demetrius *On Style* 4.198–201. For other examples see Scaglione, *Composition*, 74–96.

The problem comes, then, not in proving the existence of such theories, but in defining their provenance and later history. Although the reference to Chrysippus points to a source in Stoic logic and grammatical theory, it cannot be assumed from this that later Stoics blindly subscribed to the theory or that other schools may not have revised it for their own use. There also arises the problem of discrete sects within a particular school. As Albrecht Dihle has shown, connections between logical/grammatical theories and stylistic preferences are often contradictory and almost always impossible to trace. See A. Dihle, "Analogie und Attizismus," *Hermes* 85 (1957): 170–205. Thus, it is with some hesitation that I refer to the critics of Horace and Dionysius as "Stoics." Given their extreme stance (which seems very much a product of the late first century B.C.) it may be better to think of them as "quasi Stoics" or "neo-Chrysippeans." Even this, however, is beyond conclusive proof.

[52] Usher, *Dionysius of Halicarnassus*, 47, notes: "A procedure of which a Stoic theorist would have approved."

nysius, an expert in "artificial" refinements in composition, claims to have experimented with the "natural" theories of arrangement taught by the Stoic handbooks at some time in his past: "For example, I thought I should place nouns before verbs (since the former indicate the substance, and the latter the accident, and in the nature of things the substance is prior to its accidents)." Nouns must come before verbs in a line because "by nature" (τῇ φύσει) activity assumes the preexistence of that which acts or is acted upon. Dionysius offers in proof several lines of Homer, such as *Odyssey* 1.1, where "a man," the object of the Muse's song, precedes the act of singing, just as *Iliad* 1.1, where Achilles' "wrath" stands first in the line. In each case, Homer shows his Stoic credentials, making it likely that Dionysius has drawn these examples from some Stoic source now lost. He continues his experiment:

> Again, I thought it was better to place verbs in front of adverbs, since that which acts or is acted upon is prior τῇ φύσει to those auxiliaries indicating manner, place, time, and the like, which we call adverbs. I relied on the following examples.[53]

In proof Dionysius again offers several lines drawn from the *Iliad* and *Odyssey*, which appear to support the working of a natural word order, nouns before verbs, verbs before adverbs, and so on. To each example, however, Dionysius adds a counterexample, also from the *Iliad* and *Odyssey*, to prove that the principle, while persuasive (πιθανόν), is false (οὐκ ἀληθές). Each example directly contradicts the principle in question, proving that, in the actual practice of writing poetry—that is, good poetry such as Homer wrote—Chrysippean theory is irrelevant. Its universal claims, Dionysius concludes, are highly exaggerated; his experiment has failed: "But experience upset all these assumptions and showed them to be completely worthless" (*On Word Arrangement* 5). In spite of his best efforts to prove their worth, Dionysius decides that the old Stoic handbooks on arrangement contained nothing of value for the rhetorician or poet attuned to the demands of euphony. Experience (ἡ πεῖρα), he claims, proves them wrong.

For all of its technical vocabulary, rule setting, and attention to detail, Dionysius's treatise is not a pure theoretical work in the manner of a Stoic treatise on logic. Rather, it is an analytical treatise that strives to objectify the sensitivities of an experienced rhetor, historian, and critic. Thus, Dionysius makes few claims that he regards as

---

[53] Usher neglects τῇ φυσει ("by nature") in his rendering of the passage, thus I insert the Greek into his translation.

universally valid. Concerning the shortening and lengthening of clauses, for example, Dionysius lays down no hard and fast rules; instead, he claims, "Experience herself teaches each of these things" (*On Word Arrangement* 7). In the end, long practice and the well-trained ear, not universals, teach the art of σύνθεσις. Opposition to such claims was double-edged, for although the neo-Chryssipean critics defined word order as a natural principle, invariable and independent of the artificial manipulation recommended by Dionysius, at the same time they possessed elaborate rule books that treated arrangement as a division of dialectic, detailing principles learned from nature itself. Dionysius, therefore, counters in like fashion: against his opponents' disdain for a compositional "art" he offers his own book of rules, teaching a well-defined euphonic technique. Against their rule books, however, he recommends experience and the sensitivities of the well-trained ear. Such a stance, though it appears contradictory, is best interpreted as a critical posture necessitated by the unique claims of Dionysius's critics.

By now it is clear that there existed in Horace's day a long critical tradition that defined good poetry in terms of everyday words, artfully arranged. Dionysius's treatise stems from this tradition, fine-tuned and greatly expanded after Aristotle, yet it clearly relates that Peripatetic theories of word arrangement had significant rivals in the Hellenistic period, especially among the followers of Chrysippus who, Dionysius gives us to believe, were every bit as strident and unyielding in his own day. Although Dionysius believes in the superiority of his own approach, he makes clear that the various critical schools in Athens and Rome had long been divided over the topic of word arrangement, and that there existed no general consensus on the topic in the late first century B.C. This was impossible given the sectarian and universalistic nature of Hellenistic philosophy, which considered the general tenets of logic, ethics, and even physics, as coextensive with those of literary theory. Thus, certain Stoics considered that what is good for a human being, that is, a life according to nature, is good for a line of poetry as well.

PHILODEMUS AND LUCRETIUS

Besides the *On Word Arrangement*, the fragmentary works of Philodemus, especially his Περὶ Ποιημάτων (*On Poetry*), support the idea that σύνθεσις had a long, sometimes violent history in Hellenistic theory. Though it is no longer possible to retrace this history, enough survives of Philodemus's critical works for certain important generalizations to be made concerning Epicurean theories of σύνθεσις developed in the Hellenistic period and later adhered to by Philodemus and his followers, arch-rivals of the Stoics, in the mid to late first century B.C. What makes all of this so important for the present study is that Horace, in all likelihood, was familiar with the theoretical works of Philodemus from a very early stage in his career. He may have also known the works of Siro and the Epicureans who frequented Philodemus's retreat at Herculaneum.[54] Although Dionysius came to Rome just after the publication of *Satires* Book 2 (31–30 B.C.), too late to have influenced the *Satires* directly, Horace was certainly familiar with the divergent compositional theories attested by *On Word Arrangement* (published sometime after 20 B.C.), and it is within the context of these same debates that the private quarrels between the satirist and his opponents should be interpreted.

In his *On Poetry*, through a general survey of earlier poetic theory, Philodemus conducts a search for the essential and unique criterion (τὸ ἴδιον, the *poetae maximum* of *Orator* 67) of poetry. Frequently he criticizes his opponents not because what they have identified as a characteristic of good poetry is false, but because it is not unique to poetry.[55] At Sbordone, *Tractatus Tertius*, col. XVI.7–21, for example, Philodemus attacks his opponent's analogy comparing poetry to a manual craft:[56]

> For just as the engraver's peculiar function [ἴδιον] is not the making of a likeness—for this he shares in common with the sculptor and painter—but (making a likeness) in iron and stone by means of engraving, and yet the good [τἀγαθόν] does not lie in making a likeness, a thing he shares with all other (artisans), so also is the poet expected to desire his particular function to lie in arrangement [τὸ μὲν ἴδιον ἐν τῆι συνθέσει βούλεσθαι],

---

[54] On Horace's connections with Philodemus and Siro, see Wilkinson, "Language of Virgil and Horace," 183, n. 4; and J.I.M. Tait, "Philodemus' Influence on the Latin Poets" (Ph.D. diss., Bryn Mawr College, 1941).

[55] Greenberg's comments *ad PHerc.* 1425, fragment 1.26–33 hold true of Philodemus's method throughout *On Poetry*: "The general procedure of Philodemus in this papyrus can already be recognized. He begins each section with a quotation of his opponent's view. Usually this quotation is very short, and lacks its context. He then attempts to point out the absurdities in the statement of the opponent. . . . Philodemus does not absolutely deny the validity of the opponent's statement. What Philodemus is seeking is that element of poetry which is necessarily peculiar to good poetry, and it is on this basis that he criticizes the opponent's statement." N. Greenberg, "The Poetic Theory of Philodemus" (Ph.D. diss., Harvard University, 1955; repr. New York: Garland Publishing, 1990), 15.

[56] Translations of Philodemus are based on F. Sbordone, *Ricerche Sui Papiri Ercolanesi*, Pubblicazione Finanziata dal Consiglio Nazionale delle Ricerche 2 (Naples: Giannini Editore, 1976).

but to hunt out the good in a common fashion [κοινῶς] by means of thought and diction.

Philodemus, while he grants that the peculiar function of the poet is σύνθεσις, refuses to allow his opponent's claim that the materials arranged, iron and stone in the case of the engraver, thoughts and diction in the case of the poet, are irrelevant to the poet's essential talent. Arrangement, which he regards as a mimetic skill (compare the engraver's "making a likeness"), becomes a unique talent (τὸ ἴδιον) only when applied to certain materials, that is, to the stories, maxims, words, and so on that are the common property of all poets.

Arrangement, thought, and diction are inextricably linked in Philodemus's thinking, and he repeatedly criticizes rival theorists who attempted to consider them in isolation or, even worse, to make content wholly extraneous to the definition of good poetry.[57] At *Herculanensium Voluminum Collectio*[2] IV.176 Philodemus addresses the claims of Heracleodorus, a champion of σύνθεσις, who denied that content adds anything to the overall effect of a poem: "The statement that the irrational perception itself delights in the composition, or that the delight comes about without the content, or that the soul is affected [ψυχαγωγεῖν] in any other way, I deny."[58] Similar is Philodemus's opposition to the anonymous κριτικοί, who identified σύνθεσις as the essential criterion of good poetry to the complete exclusion of diction and thought. Like Dionysius, they used metathesis to great effect in proving the power of arrangement (Sbordone, *Tractatus Tertius*, col. XVIII.25-XIX.5):[59]

> For they are accustomed to reproduce innumerable verses of Homer and the other epic poets as differing by variations [κατὰ τὰς ἐναλλαγὰς παραφέρειν]. However, we must assert that the thought becomes better or worse through the metatheses [τὸ νόημα βέλτιον ἢ χεῖρον γείνεσθαι διὰ τὰς μεταθέσεις].

[57] At *On Poems* 5.12. 1–17, for example, Philodemus faults Neoptolemus for his famous *poiema/poiesis* distinction, which assumes a break between form and thought: "And [Neoptolemus holds that] only the *synthesis* of the *lexis* partakes of the *poiema*, but that the underlying thoughts, actions and characterizations do not." Compare also Sbordone, *Tractatus Tertius*, col. XVIII.12–17: "That the *synthesis* enchants us [ψυχαγωγεῖν] by itself, introducing no other good quality, is unconvincing."

[58] The translation is that of Greenberg, "Philodemus," 146.

[59] "Clearly the practice of metathesis was well known, even though the fragments of Philodemus have preserved only the one example cited. This passage also sounds the tonic note of Philodemus' objections to the practice. In his opinion, metathesis does not isolate the composition but rather invariably has some effect upon the content." N. Greenberg, "Metathesis as an Instrument in the Criticism of Poetry," *Transactions of the American Philological Association* 89 (1958): 267.

Philodemus rejects the idea that the same thought can be expressed in many ways, for a shift in word order, he claims, brings about a corresponding alteration of thought. To rearrange Homer is to destroy not only the beauty of his verse, but his content as well. Word arrangement, sound, and thought are entirely corresponsive.[60]

We recall from Dionysius that the theory of an *ordo naturalis*, so hostile to the demands of euphony, stems from much broader ideas concerning the universal compulsion of nature, which, certain Chrysippean critics believed, orders not only the stars, seasons, and the lives of men, but individual lines of poetry as well. Good poetry, in other words, reflects the nature of reality. Although beyond proof, it seems likely that Philodemus's insistence on the unbreakable bond of arrangement and meaning stems also from larger Epicurean theories concerning the nature of reality, namely, atomic theory, which takes arrangement as the primary creative principle of the cosmos.[61] The

[60] At Sbordone, *Tractatus Tertius*, col. XII.19–24, Philodemus links form and content in defining the essential quality of good poetry: "For choosing proper expressions and arranging them for the clarification of a specific rational content is the essential talent of the poet." On these lines see Greenberg, "Philodemus," 155–57. Compare also Scaglione's summary: "[Philodemus] detached himself from the most established currents of literary scholarship by insisting that the work of art can only be understood and appreciated when seen in the totality of its aspects. This is as close as ancient theory ever came to an 'organic' view of art." Scaglione, *Composition*, 51. The most recent and best study of Philodemus's compositional theory within in its Hellenistic critical context is E. Asmis, "The Poetic Theory of the Stoic Aristo," *Apeiron* 23, no. 3 (1990): 147–201. Asmis points out that the criticisms of the Stoic Aristo in Book 5 of *On Poems* premise the same organic view of art and art criticism that informs Philodemus's judgments throughout the treatise. The specific criticisms addressed against Aristo concern the Stoic theory of two types or stages of apprehension (κατάληψις) in the analysis of poetry. Asmis writes (pp. 188–89): "S. [Aristo] maintains that poetic composition is judged by hearing, even though it must express thought, which is judged by reason. Philodemus objects that composition must be judged by reason, in conjunction with hearing, because composition cannot be considered separately from the thought that it expresses. Whereas S. divided a poem into two components, thought and composition, each judged by means of a different faculty, Philodemus believes that a poem is a unitary object: composition is joined inextricably with thought, and the whole must be judged in a single act of judgement, combining reason and hearing." The controversy was still hotly disputed in Horace's day (compare *Orator* 177 and 183, where Cicero takes up the question of rational versus sensory judgment), and it is likely that Horace's criticisms against the compositional practices of his Stoic opponents stem from similar theoretical concerns. On Horace as Epicurean theorist, see my subsequent discussion.

[61] My observations on the connections between Epicurean physics and poetics I owe to J. Snyder, *Puns and Poetry in Lucretius' De Rerum Natura* (Amsterdam: Grüner, 1980) and David Armstrong, "Lucretius, Philodemus, and the Poetics of Atomism," Panel on Philodemus and Poetry, Annual Meeting of the American Philological Association, Boston, 30 December 1989.

best evidence for such thinking among the Epicureans is found in the *De Rerum Natura*, where Lucretius frequently draws attention to the atomic nature of language, making language a miniature version of nature herself. He argues that, like nature, language is formed of a fixed number of component parts, *elementa* ("letters"), which, like atoms (also known as *elementa* in the Epicurean system), combine in various ways to form single words, phrases, books, and eventually the entire cosmos of literature. At *De Rerum Natura* 1.820–27, for example, Lucretius proves the power of arrangement in the creation of plants, animals, and so on, by comparison with the world of language:

> namque eadem caelum mare terras flumina solem
> constituunt, eadem fruges arbusta animantis,
> verum aliis alioque modo commixta moventur.
> quin etiam passim nostris in versibus ipsis
> multa elementa vides multis communia verbis,
> cum tamen inter se versus ac verba necessest
> confiteare et re et sonitu distare sonanti.
> tantum elementa queunt permutato ordine solo.

And often it makes a great difference with what substances and in what position the basic elements are held together, as well as what motions they give and take among themselves. For the very same elements make up sky, sea, earth, rivers, and sun, the same make up crops, trees, and animals, yet they move differently when mixed with different elements and in a different way. Moreover, you see even in my verses many letters common to many words, yet you must admit that the verses and words differ among themselves both in meaning and in the sound they give forth. So great is the power of letters when nothing is changed but their arrangement.

The analogy comparing letters to atoms recurs with enough frequency in the *De Rerum Natura* to suggest that the idea was known to Epicurean theories of diction and arrangement.[62] Later in the same book, Lucretius repeats the analogy, illustrating the power of arrangement in the creation of the natural world by the clever collocation of *ignis* ("fire") and *lignum* ("wood") (*De Rerum Natura* 1.907–14):

> iamne vides igitur, paulo quod diximus ante,
> permagni referre eadem primordia saepe
> cum quibus et quali positura contineantur
> et quos inter se dent motus accipiantque,

---

[62] See also *De Rerum Natura* 2.686–99 and 2.1007–22.

atque eadem paulo inter se mutata creare
ignis et lignum? quo pacto verba quoque ipsa
inter se paulo mutatis sunt elementis,
cum ligna atque ignes distincta voce notemus.

Do you see now, just as I said a little while ago, that it often makes a tremendous difference with what other elements and in what position the basic elements are held, and what motions they give and take among themselves, and that the very same elements, slightly altered among themselves, create fires and wood? In the same way these very words [that is, *lignum* and *ignis*] consist of letters slightly altered between them, while we differentiate wood from fire by means of a distinct sound.

The addition of a single letter turns fire (*ignis*) into wood (*lignum*), a process in the world of letters that, Lucretius claims, reflects the power of arrangement in the material realm as well, where the slightest change in the arrangement of atoms brings about an entirely new substance.[63] Arrangement and substance, sound and thought are entirely corresponsive in Epicurean theory. Behind this stands the idea, shared with the Stoics, though with vastly different results, that good literature is somehow a mirror image of nature itself. Philodemus, although he makes no explicit reference to the atomistic nature of letters (στοιχεῖα) in his extant theoretical works, constantly appeals to the power of σύνθεσις in the creation of sound and thought, which he refuses to allow any separate existence. The thinking is thoroughly Epicurean, based ultimately in the same atomistic theory of literature as that espoused by Lucretius, a theory that was perhaps as old as Epicurus himself.

Very similar to the passage just examined is *Ars Poetica* 46–49, Horace's famous plea for the power of arrangement. Parallels between this passage and the illustrations of Philodemus and Lucretius are immediately apparent, suggesting that Horace learned his theory of arrangement from some Epicurean source, perhaps from Philodemus himself:

in verbis etiam tenuis cautusque serendis
dixeris egregie, notum si callida verbum
reddiderit iunctura novum.

Moreover, in setting out words in rows, you will express yourself with care and refinement, if a skillful arrangement renders a known word new.

---

[63] Compare *De Rerum Natura* 2.1021–22: "Juxtapositions, movements, order, position, shapes; when these are changed, the substances themselves must also be changed" (*concursus motus ordo positura figurae / cum permutantur, mutari res quoque debent*).

As so often in Horace, the lines serve as an immediate illustration of theory, demonstrating the very principles they seek to prove. Besides the obvious "skillful arrangement" of the final clause (a-b-a-b-a), there is an oblique reference to Epicurean theories of arrangement contained in the juxtaposition of *notum* and *novum*, where, as in Lucretius's *ignis/lignum* illustration, the slightest alteration of a single *elementum*, namely, the *t* in *notum* to the *v* in *novum*, creates an entirely new meaning, proving the power of the *callida iunctura*.[64] The illustration beautifully suits Horace's theory of the semantic effect of arrangement, the inviolable bond of form and meaning, which, it seems likely, he drew straight from Epicurean theory. Whether or not he considered himself an Epicurean theorist, it is obvious that Horace adhered to the long theoretical tradition that considered arrangement the essential criterion of poetry, transforming even the most ordinary words into elegant verse. As a final illustration of this, compare *Ars Poetica* 240–43:

> ex noto fictum carmen sequar, ut sibi quivis
> speret idem, sudet multum frustraque laboret
> ausus idem: tantum series iuncturaque pollet,
> tantum de medio sumptis accedit honoris.

I will pursue a song fashioned from the familiar, whose style anyone might hope to copy. Those who attempt it, however, simply waste their effort and sweat: such is the power of order and arrangement, so great is the honor that attends the everyday.

ANSWERING THE EXTREMISTS: A NEW LOOK AT *SATIRES* 1.4

Basic to a study of Horace's satiric program is a clear understanding of the factional nature of literary criticism in the first century B.C. In his *On Word Arrangement*, Dionysius grapples with the most volatile

---

[64] Horace's *novum verbum* recalls Lucretius's discovery of "new words" (*novis verbis*) to illustrate the obscure findings of his Greek predecessors. Minyard has noted that the thrust of *De Rerum Natura* 1.136–48 concerns "the redeployment of old words, not the creation of new ones. The style of the *De Rerum Natura* is inventive and even idiosyncratic. It is characterized by new coinages, *hapax legomena* which are probably quite often Lucretian in origin, and borrowings from Greek vocabulary. What is to the present point, however, is that much of the invention and idiosyncracy does not involve the creation of a new vocabulary, and so is irrelevant to understanding the passage, and that so little of what is new in the words involves the language of philosophical analysis." J. D. Minyard, *Lucretius and the Late Republic* (Leiden: E. J. Brill, 1985), 44–45. Like Horace, Lucretius understood the power of *iunctura* to achieve new semantic effects from standard Latin vocabulary.

theoretical issue of his day, giving every indication that his opposition enjoyed equal, if not superior influence in the rhetorical schools of Augustan Rome. In turn, the treatise sheds much-needed light on the polemical context of the programmatic satires, in which the satirist argues the same theoretical issues against similar, if not identical, opponents. The similarities shared between the two works are striking. In each case, the critics addressed are Stoics (or quasi Stoics) of an extreme Chrysippean stamp. Both Horace and Dionysius indicate that their rivals elevate the merits of natural talent (the *ingenium* of *Satires* 1.4.43) over art, stressing the importance of a grand, "poetic" vocabulary against the claims of commonplace diction. Grandiloquence of theme, diction, and delivery they considered the distinct characteristics defining true poetry. Most important, both groups show a definite prejudice against the claims of an artificial, euphonic arrangement. In the disparagement of arrangement at *Satires* 1.4.53–62, for example, Horace puts the anticompositional sentiments of his critics in the baldest terms:

> ergo
> non satis est puris versum perscribere verbis,
> quem si dissolvas, quivis stomachetur eodem
> quo personatus pacto pater. his, ego quae nunc,
> olim quae scripsit Lucilius, eripias si
> tempora certa modosque, et quod prius ordine verbum est
> posterius facias, praeponens ultima primis,
> non, ut si solvas "postquam Discordia taetra
> Belli ferratos postis portasque refregit,"
> invenias etiam disiecti membra poetae.

Therefore, it is not enough to write out verse in simple words that, rearranged, any real-life father could use in raging at his son, just as the father in the play. Now concerning the verses I now write, which Lucilius wrote at one time, if you should take away their fixed rhythms and meters, making the word earlier in line later and putting last things before first, you would not discover the limbs even of a dismembered poet as (you would) by breaking down "Once foul Discord had broken back the brazen posts and gates of war."

Disregard for mimetic realism matched by gross insensitivity toward matters of arrangement mark these lines as most uncharacteristic of Horace. The idea that "simple words" (*puris verbis*) cannot constitute good poetry makes no sense from the standpoint of traditional theory; only Stoic zealots, committed to theories of grand, "poetic" diction and natural word order allowed such extremes. In these lines, then, Horace voices theories of his critics, countering the precedent set by Aristotle, Philodemus's κριτικοί, and others, by employing metathesis (marked by *si dissolvas*, line 55, and *si solvas*, line 60) not to prove the power of arrangement but its irrelevance. The idea is unknown in earlier extant theory.[65] To paraphrase the satirist: "If you dissolve the contexture of these lines of Ennius, you will find evidence of true poetry in what remains"—that is, in their noble martial theme ("foul discord"), grandiloquent diction ("brazen posts," and so on), the personification of *Discordia*, and the metaphor equating warfare with a temple or fortress.[66]

The most glaring defect in these sentiments is their total disregard for matters of arrangement, so important to Aristotle, Philodemus, Cicero, and certainly to Horace himself. No educated reader in Horace's day would have failed to note this and to understand that the satirist was speaking in the guise of his Chrysippean opponents. Yet, it is also clear that in its clever word arrangement and in the concluding quip, *disiecti membra poetae*, the passage in lines 53–63 belies all that it says in defense of Stoic/quasi-Stoic theory. For in claiming that the verses of comedy and satire, when metathesized, possess nothing to mark them as distinctly poetic, the satirist implies that his satires are nothing, if not arrangement, and he demonstrates the power of arrangement beyond any doubt in lines 58–59, where the clever placement of words carries a definite semantic effect, undermining the surface meaning of the lines, which speak in defense of anticompositional theory. We note that Horace has placed "the word earlier in line" (*quod prius ordine verbumst*) in front of the "later" word (*posterius*), just as his meaning suggests, only to reverse the arrangement as the metathesis (*praeponens*) is carried out at the end of line 59, placing "last things" (*ultima*) before "first" (*primis*) in the actual configuration of the line. The syntax is mimetic, an exact mirror image of meaning.[67] Had it been his intention to prove, as the lines superficially sug-

---

[65] For the standard version of the metathesis proof, see, for example, *On Style* 1.11 and 1.31.

[66] Oberhelman, "Satire as Poetry," has noted that the word order of the Ennian passage "is a perfectly commonplace prose arrangement," standing in sharp contrast to the highly contrived verses that precede it. He adds, "if we *do* metathesize, that is, put Horace into the unmetathesized imaginary text and metathesize the prosaic Ennius lines, much is lost in Horace but little in Ennius."

[67] Oberhelman, "Satire as Poetry," has noticed a similar syntactic trick in line 39, where Horace elides *primum* into *ego* (*primego*) and *me* into *illorum* (*millorum*), thereby firmly ensconcing himself into the group of poets from whose "number" (*numero*, also the word for "rhythm") he claims to exclude himself. Likewise Nilsson has suggested that in line 46, "Horace has consciously composed a bad verse in order to illustrate comedy's lack of *acer spiritus et vis*. The unaccented spondaic word in the first foot

gest, that arrangement is dispensable and that the qualities of good poetry remain even after the intended arrangement has been destroyed, Horace could have chosen no worse illustration, for he has built into these lines a message on the importance of arrangement, a glaring incongruity between extremist anticompositional theory and the highly suggestive, "artificial" shape of the lines themselves. In the end, the arrangement of the words in lines 58–59 speaks much louder than their superficial meaning.

Besides arrangement, the final phrase, *disiecti membra poetae*, undermines Stoic/quasi-Stoic theory by calling attention to the ability of metathesis not to isolate but to "destroy" or "butcher" the characteristics of good poetry. At one level, the lines appear to say nothing more than, "If you metathesize my verse, unlike rearranging the verse of Ennius, you will be unable to discover the vestiges of poetry in theme and diction"; yet, the metaphor buried in the phrase *disiecti membra poetae* is much more descriptive and violent, playing off the double meaning of *membra*, which, like Greek κῶλα and μέρη, refers not only to the "parts" or "clauses" within the period, but also to "limbs," the various "parts" of the human anatomy.[68] Thus the lines read, "If you metathesize my verse, it will not be like rearranging the verse of Ennius, in which case you will discover the limbs of a poet even after he has been torn apart [*etiam disiecti*]." In other words, to dissolve the contexture of verse is to "butcher" the poet. To avoid the metaphor, Horace could have rearranged line 63 to read "of a poem" (*poematis*), which is what we expect, rather than "of a poet" (*poetae*), yet the idea that metathesis destroys a living thing is, of course, exactly what Horace has in mind. The metaphor is at least as old as Aristotle who, in

---

before the punctuation is without counterpart in the *Satires*." See N. Nilsson, *Metrische Stildifferenzen in den Satiren des Horaz*, Studia Latina Holmiensia 1 (Uppsala: Almquist & Wiksells Boktryckeri, 1952), 77. Especially obvious are the broken, hacking sounds of the phrase *acer spiritus ac vis* (Nilsson reads the softer *et vis*), defects that illustrate not comedy's lack of force, as Nilsson suggests, but the compositional defects of the inflated style favored by Horace's critics, who alone are responsible for these inept claims. The postponement of *excerpam* to line 40 is also significant, for line 39 by itself reads: "I myself the first of those to whom I would allow to be poets." The satirist's position as "first among the poets" is only sluggishly reversed with the *excerpam* ("would exclude") beginning the next line. Again, word order seems to subvert, or at least toy with, the satirist's ostensible meaning. For similar instances of mimetic word order in Augustan poetry, see D. Lateiner, "Mimetic Syntax: Metaphor from Word Order, Especially in Ovid," *American Journal of Philology* 111, no. 2 (1990): 204–37.

[68] Cicero, at *Orator* 211, notes that *membrum* literally translates the Greek κῶλον, adding that, in all arts, "necessity compels us either to invent a new word or to use a metaphor" (*necessitas cogat aut novum facere verbum aut a simili mutuari*). The Roman ear was very alive to the "limb" metaphor in Cicero's day. For an earlier example see *Ad Herennium* 4.26.

his *Poetics*, frequently compares the beautiful poem to a living creature, whose limbs, though distinct, are integrally connected to the whole. Compare *Poetics* 8.1451a30–35:

> So then, just as in the other mimetic arts the imitation is of a single object, so also the plot [τὸν μῦθον], since it is the imitation of an action, is the imitation of a single, unified action, and the separate "limbs" of these events should be arranged [τὰ μέρη συνεστάναι] so that, if one part is displaced [μετατιθαμένου, "metathesized"] or removed, the whole is disjoined and dislocated [διαφέρεσθαι καὶ κινεῖσθαι].

Disiecti in *Satires* 1.4.63 is the Latin equivalent to Aristotle's διαφέρεσθαι, which, along with κινεῖσθαι, G. Else has defined as "surgical metaphors" describing dissection.[69] In both cases, metathesis is described as a "butchering" or "dismembering" of a living whole. Horace knew the metaphor from ancient theory, perhaps from these lines of Aristotle, which graphically confirm the creative power of arrangement, a point already demonstrated by the satirist in the clever arrangement of lines 58–59. Thus, only superficially do word choice and theme win out over the claims of arrangement, for what, at one level, speaks in defense of anticompositional theory, at another level proves its own ineptitude; the claims of arrangement are, in the end, ironically vindicated.

Only a theorist of the most extreme Stoic type, such as a Fabius or a Crispinus, would adhere to the stylistic tenets of *Satires* 1.4.38–62. The evidence of Aristotle, Demetrius, Philodemus, Cicero, Dionysius, and Horace's own *Ars Poetica* (and later, certainly Quintilian and Longinus) speaks strongly against taking these lines as an accurate description of Horace's own sentiments. Horace, time and again in his works, proves himself a consummate stylist, trained in the technical refinements of arrangement so important to ancient theory. Even in his *Odes*, some of the most elevated and highly wrought poems of antiquity, Horace relies almost exclusively on arrangement to achieve his stunning effects. Compare Armstrong's assessment:

> Horace deals in a Latin vocabulary that is restricted, even commonplace. It is significant that of all Latin writers he is the most sparing with superlatives, as if the suffix *-issimus* was sufficient in itself to make a thought overstated and vulgar. . . . But this simple vocabulary is made poetic by elaborate juxtapositions and interlockings, so that successive words color and illuminate one another like pieces of a mosaic; in Nietzsche's deservedly famous judgment, a "mosaic of words, in which every word, by sound, by placing, and by meaning, spreads its influence to the right, to

[69] See Else, *Aristotle's Poetics*, 300.

the left, and over the whole; this minimum in extent and number of symbols, this maximum thereby achieved in the effectiveness of the symbols, all this is Roman, and believe me, elegant par excellence."[70]

Likewise Marouzeau once deemed Horace an "assembleur de mots," claiming that, in the "arrangement of the sentence in terms of verse-structure," Horace "possessed the art of verbal construction to the point of virtuosity."[71] His examples, drawn from every period of Horace's career, bear out this assessment, demonstrating that the *Satires*, against much scholarship that suggests otherwise, do not simply represent some experimental "pre-*Odes*" stage of Horace's career; they are some of his finest works. It was, in all likelihood, the *Satires* that earned Horace a place among the friends of Maecenas, marking him as one of the finest theorists and poets of his day.[72]

LUCILIUS AND THE ATTICIST THEORY OF A RUGGED STYLE

Although nearly thirty years separate Cicero's *Orator* from *On Word Arrangement*, the similarities between the two treatises demonstrate that Cicero's "Atticists" adhered to some form of Stoic anticompositional theory as early as 46 B.C. At *Orator* 232–38 Cicero broods over the fallen state of oratory in his day, making a final plea for refinements of composition against the "rugged," "offhand" theories espoused by Brutus and his fellow Atticists. These, significantly, are his last words as a rhetorical theorist. His arguments are reminiscent of *On Word Arrangement*, suggesting some fellow feeling shared between the Atticists and Dionysius's unnamed Chrysippeans. Anticompositional theories, unknown to most earlier theory, including *De Oratore* of only nine years earlier, gained increasing support in the early 40s B.C., especially among the Stoics, who somehow identified a rugged, natural style of arrangement, such as that which they knew from Lucilius, with Stoic virtue and the bygone values of the old Republic. Word arrangement quickly became the chief theoretical issue of the late Republic, pitting Stoics against Epicureans and Peripatetics, old

[70] Armstrong, *Horace*, 69. For Nietzsche's assessment of Horatian word arrangement, see also D. West, *Reading Horace* (Edinburgh: Edinburgh University Press, 1967), 88.

[71] See J. Marouzeau, "Horace assembleur de mots," *Emerita* 4 (1936): 1.

[72] Quintilian notes at *Institutes* 9.4.28 that Maecenas was especially fond of certain refinements of *compositio*. He claims that Maecenas abused the device of *transgressio*, or hyperbaton, in certain cases (which he quotes) "because his word arrangement jests, though the subject matter is sorrowful" (*quia in re tristi ludit compositio*). He places Maecenas among those authors who play such tricks with their composition "in order to give their lines a skipping, playful rhythm" (*ut exultent atque lasciviant*).

republicans against Caesarians, and, as we shall see, the advocates of Lucilius (*fautores Lucili*) against Horace and the members of his circle.

At *Orator* 232 Cicero uses the metathesis proof in its typical sense to indicate the unique powers of arrangement:

> Quantum autem sit apte dicere, experiri licet, si aut compositi oratoris bene structam collocationem dissolvas permutatione verborum; corrumpatur enim tota res.

> You can experience the importance of close-fitting speech if you dissolve the carefully structured arrangement of an orator attuned to word order. By changing the sequence of his words, the entire meaning is destroyed.

Cicero proceeds to quote a passage from his *Defense of Cornelius*, making some slight alterations in arrangement that destroy the effect of the sentence. He asks (*Orator* 233):

> Videsne ut ordine verborum paululum commutato, isdem tamen verbis stante sententia, ad nihilum omnia recidant, cum sint ex aptis dissoluta?

> Do you not see how, when the word order is slightly changed, even when the thought consists of the very same words, these collapse into nothing, since they have been broken free of their proper arrangement?

Neither the words (*verbis*) nor the thought expressed (*sententia*) give the passage its power; both are second to arrangement (*ordo verborum*). Cicero makes this point a second time by reordering a line from a speech of Gaius Gracchus, this time making alterations for the better (Gaius Gracchus was apparently no expert in matters of composition). He comments on the improved arrangement (*Orator* 234):

> Hoc modo dicere nemo umquam noluit nemoque potuit quin dixerit; qui autem aliter dixerunt hoc assequi non potuerunt. Ita facti sunt repente Attici.

> No one was ever unwilling to speak this way, and no one who could speak thus ever refrained from doing so; moreover, those who have undertaken to speak otherwise have simply failed to attain this. And so, all of a sudden, they have become "Atticists."

Cicero directs his plea for an artificial arrangement against the so-called Atticists, who practiced a style of oratory, which he found "loose and broken" (*diffluens ac solutum*), an effect that, he claims, they consciously sought to achieve.[73] The Atticists, in other words, like

---

[73] Cicero directs the analogy of Phidias's shield (*Orator* 234) against "those who find broken things more pleasant" (*magis delectant soluta*). Compare the comments of the

their Chrysippean counterparts in Horace and Dionysius, strove to "break apart" (*dissolvere*) the smooth collocation of words within the period, and anything else that might suggest that their oratory had undergone some type of artificial refinement.[74] Cicero has no patience for what he regarded as the Atticists' perverse delight in the "broken" sounds of unworked oratory. He writes (*Orator* 235):

> Isti autem cum dissolvunt orationem in qua nec res nec verbum ullum est nisi abiectum, non clupeum sed, ut in proverbio est—etsi humilius dictum est tamen simile est—scopas ut ita dicam mihi videntur dissolvere.[75]

> Moreover, when they break apart an oration in which themes and words are simply "tossed off," they seem to me not to be taking apart the shield (of Phidias); rather, as the proverb relates—if I may be allowed a rather humble illustration—they are untying a broom.

In their speech writing, the Atticists made a conscious effort to *dissolvere orationem*, that is, to break apart the smooth collocation of words so important to theorists after Aristotle. They wanted their every

Elder Seneca at *Controversiae* 7.4.8, addressing the compositional effects sought by Calvus, an avowed Atticist: "Also the word arrangement in his speeches aims toward Demosthenes' example. In it there is nothing calm, nothing smooth. Everything is agitated and fluctuating" (*Compositio quoque eius in actionibus ad exemplum Demosthenis riget: nihil in illa placidum, nihil lene est, omnia excitata et fluctuantia*). It is certainly not to be assumed from this that Calvus sought similar effects in verse (unless, perhaps, as required by certain types of verse invective). Such jarring effects were apparently not sought by all the so-called Atticists even in speeches. Compare *Brutus* 274, where Cicero commends the smooth flowing *comprehensio verborum* of M. Calidius, usually regarded as the oldest of the Atticists. Even within the *Brutus* and *Orator* the evidence points to several varieties of Atticism rather than a single, unified movement. On this point, see A. D. Leeman, *Orationis Ratio: The Stylistic Theories and Practice of the Roman Orators Historians and Philosophers* (Amsterdam: Adolf M. Hakkert, 1963; repr. 1986), 159.

[74] The standard histories of ancient rhetoric discuss the debates between the Asianists and the Atticists. See especially Leeman, *Orationis Ratio*, 136–67. The following works also have some bearing upon the topic: G. L. Hendrickson, "Correspondence" (1926), "*De Analogia*" (1906), and "Cicero *De Optimo Genere Oratorum*," *American Journal of Philology* 47 (1936): 109–23; M. B. Ogle, "Horace an Atticist," *Classical Philology* 11 (1916): 156–68, and "*Molle Atque Facetum*," *American Journal of Philology* 37 (1916): 327–32; and Ullman, "Horace, Catullus, and Tigellius," 270–97.

[75] The lines contain a play on the word *scopas*, "broom." The shield of Phidias is contrasted with a broom, which happens to have the same name as the late Classical sculptor, Scopas, whose work was famous in antiquity for the manner in which it "breaks with the Classical tradition of benign, serene features and prefigures later Hellenistic art." See H. Gardner, *Art through the Ages I: Ancient, Medieval, and Non-European Art*, 8th edition (New York: Harcourt Brace Jovanovich, 1986), 165. Thus, the broom is a clever foil to the shield of Phidias.

word to appear "tossed off" (*abiectum*), that is, rugged and unstudied. Such negligence, Cicero claims earlier in the treatise, is perfectly acceptable at the outset of a speech, where the orator strives to show himself a simple man, "restrained and plain, imitating everyday speech" (*summissus est et humilis, consuetudinem imitans*). Part of this effect, he claims, is gained through word arrangement (*Orator 77*):

> Verba etiam verbis quasi coagmentare neglegat. Habet enim ille tamquam hiatus et concursus vocalium molle quiddam et quod indicet non ingratam neglegentiam de re hominis magis quam de verbis laborantis.

> He should avoid, as it were, fitting together his phrases word by word, for hiatus and the clash of vowels possess a certain ease that indicates a welcome negligence on the part of the speaker, who is more concerned with his subject matter than with words.

Offhand composition is a sign of character, real substance versus ostentation. The thinking is entirely Stoic, the perfect expression of Seneca's dictum, *talis hominibus fuit oratio qualis vita* ("speech reflects life").[76] Word arrangement, in other words, reflects the composition of one's soul: rugged, jarring sounds indicate an inner ruggedness of character, whereas a "smooth fitting" collocation of words, points to dishonesty, flash versus substance. Words, like the man (compare Socrates), should be outwardly plain, even ugly, but possess a depth of substance within. Cicero can accept this "Attic" ruggedness within a context that demands the plain style (*tenuis oratio*), such as the beginning of a deliberative or forensic speech; yet, he adds that one can maintain intellectual integrity without discarding all attention to style: "there is such a thing as careful negligence" (*etiam neglegentia est diligens, Orator 78*). Ruggedness, in other words, demands art. This is

---

[76] At *Moral Epistles* 114.15, Seneca demonstrates that he was not as zealous in the pursuit of Stoic ruggedness as other rhetoricians of his day: "Let us turn to word arrangement. Shall I relate to you how many errors are committed in this? Some approve an arrangement that is broken and harsh, and they purposely disarrange anything that flows too smoothly. They want only rugged connections. They think that word arrangement that strikes the ear with unevenness is brave and manly." Seneca disapproves, though, at *Moral Epistles* 114.4–7; he argues that Maecenas's "loose manner of speech" (*oratio soluta*) and his "loose manner of dress" (*ipse discinctus* and *solutis tunicis*), are signs of effeminacy, a lack of manliness stemming from the loose, ill-composed condition of his soul. Compare also *Moral Epistles* 115.18: "Words cleverly woven together and oration that flows smoothly will not steer you through to that happiness so solid that no storm disturbs it. Let words proceed as they please, provided that your soul is firm in its own arrangement [*eant, ut volent, dum animo compositio sua constet*]." Though not as strict as certain Stoic rhetoricians of his day, Seneca adheres to the old Stoic tenet that words and their arrangement are extensions of the soul.

the basic message of the *Orator*, which defends the artificial refinements cultivated in more elevated styles of oratory against the unbroken, cerebral ruggedness of the so-called Attic orators. Even ruggedness, Cicero claims, is an artificial accomplishment.

Although Brutus and his fellow Atticists appreciated the limitations of Stoic rhetorical theory (see *Orator* 117–21) and should not, therefore, be classified simply as neoconservatives, after the manner of Fabius and Crispinus, it seems likely that their hostility toward refinements in composition stems ultimately from Stoic theories of "rugged" word order. Cicero suggests as much when, at *Orator* 113–16, he argues that the orator should possess a good background in logical theory, learned from Aristotle or Chrysippus, but, in speech writing, he should "unclench the fist," loosening, in other words, the compact deductive modes of dialectic (*Orator* 115):

> Haec tenenda sunt oratori—saepe enim occurrunt—sed quia sua sponte squalidiora sunt, adhibendus erit in his explicandis quidam orationis nitor.

> The orator must grasp these things (logical principles)—for they often turn up—yet because in themselves they are rather harsh, a certain elegance of speech must be used in unfolding them.

Cicero elaborates the lesson of Zeno's unclenched fist (*Orator* 113), reminding his Atticist rivals that rhetoric is a more outward, "unfolded" version of logic, demanding artifices of style unknown to Stoic handbooks on dialectic.[77] The Stoics, he claims at *Brutus* 118–19, are "found to be unresourceful" (*inopes reperiantur*) in oratorical presentation "because their entire attention is absorbed in dialectic" (*quod istorum in dialecticis omnis cura consumitur*). Dionysius's critics, we recall, were equally reluctant to separate rhetoric from dialectic.

Cicero's Atticists and the Stoic extremists maligned by Horace and Dionysius, though not identical, shared much in common, especially in the area of compositional theory. In simplest terms, members of each group sought, in their own way, to remove from their speech anything suggesting artificiality, even if the end result should fail to caress the ear. Harshness, Cicero's "welcome negligence," they regarded as the chief aim of arrangement, the mirror image of the rugged soul. This said, it should be added that Brutus and his fellow Atticists adhered to theories of word arrangement that, while certainly of Stoic provenience, made significant concessions to tradi-

---

[77] Compare also *Brutus* 120, where Stoic oratory is described as "too tight and closely packed for a popular audience" (*astrictior . . . et contractior quam aures populi requirunt*).

tional, nondialectical theories, which acknowledged a technique of arrangement, with fixed rules for attaining desired results. Cicero makes clear that, unlike Dionysius's Stoics, the Atticists sought a ruggedness that was anything but unstudied, that there was method to their madness. At *Brutus* 119–21, for example, he congratulates Brutus for following the example of his uncle Cato who, "though a Stoic through and through" (*perfectissimo Stoico*) cast his net outside Stoic waters (*Brutus* 120):

> Quo magis tuum, Brute, iudicium probo, qui eorum [id est ex vetere Academia] philosophorum sectam secutus es, quorum in doctrina atque praeceptis disserendi ratio coniungitur cum suavitate dicendi et copia.

> All the more do I approve of you, Brutus, since you have followed the school of those philosophers [that is, those of the Old Academy] in whose teaching and precepts the method of logical discourse is joined with the charm and fullness of rhetorical expression.

Cicero proceeds to name the old Attic masters, Plato, Aristotle, and Theophrastus, as models of Brutus's cerebral, yet pleasant oratorical style. Brutus, in other words, knew the ancient theorists, the Academic and Peripatetic traditions, which, while always skeptical of deceptive flourishes of rhetoric, respected the power of art and logic properly combined. Elsewhere Cicero relates that the Atticists had gone too far in imitating the Old Attic masters, attempting by artificial techniques of arrangement to jar the ear, giving the pretense of unstudied ruggedness.[78] The end result seemed to him "disjointed and pared down" (*infracta et amputata*), an all-too-studied imitation of the more austere features of Attic writers, such as Thucydides, Xenophon, and Lysias.

Quintilian alludes to the artificial aspects of Attic ruggedness when, at *Institutes* 9.4.76, he mentions the care that Brutus invested in the cadences of his periods, noting his penchant for iambic sentence closures:

> Illi minus sunt notabiles, quia hoc genus sermoni proximum est. Itaque et versus hi fere excidunt, quos Brutus ipso componendi durius studio saepissime facit.

> Those closures are less noticeable because that meter [iambic] best approximates speech. Therefore, verses of this type generally "tumble out." Brutus makes these verse endings because of his passion for arranging words in a rather harsh fashion.

[78] See especially *Brutus* 284–91.

Ruggedness (*duritia*) is a function of word arrangement (marked by *componendi*).[79] Unlike his Chrysippean counterparts, advocates of the *ordo naturalis*, which, if Dionysius is correct, dictated arrangement by rules of logic, Brutus knew the techniques of arrangement taught by traditional compositional theory, and he consciously employed them to achieve his jarring effects. The Stoics, though from a different premise, sought similar effects, as we see at *Brutus* 113–18, where Cicero discusses the appeal of rugged composition in Stoic thinking. Concerning P. Rutilius Rufus (consul 105), whom Cicero regarded as a Stoic of the first order ("a pupil of Panaetius, all but perfectly trained in Stoic doctrines," *Panaeti auditor, prope perfectus in Stoicis*), and a second orator, M. Aemilius Scaurus (consul 115), not a Stoic, but a devotee *in antiquis*, Cicero writes: "Rutilius, however, was involved in a certain somber and severe type of oratory. Both men were by nature forceful and harsh" (*Rutilius autem in quodam tristi et severo genere dicendi versatus est. Erat uterque natura vehemens et acer*). Cicero recognizes that both Rutilius and Scaurus cultivated a style of oratory that, they felt, somehow reflected their own sturdy and unaffected nature. Likewise, in speaking of the Stoic Quintus Aelius Tubero, Cicero adds (*Brutus* 117): "But as in life, so in oratory was he rugged, unstudied, and harsh" (*Sed ut vita sic oratione durus incultus horridus*). This is the perfect encapsulation of the Stoic creed, which saw oratory as a mirror image of the soul and ruggedness as the ideal expression of life according to nature.

Theories of "rugged" arrangement espoused by the conservative Stoics and Atticists in the late first century B.C. are of central importance to the programmatic satires, for it is immediately apparent from the opening criticisms of *Satires* 1.4 that Horace's Stoic rivals saw Lucilius not only as the champion of anti-Caesarianism inherent in old republican *libertas*, but also as the perfect "rugged" stylist of satire. The satirist writes (*Satires* 1.4.7–10):

> facetus,
> emunctae naris, durus componere versus.

---

[79] Quintilian makes clear that he does not intend *componendi* in the generic sense of "composing" or "writing." Throughout Book 9 of the *Institutes*, *componere* refers to the process of setting words side by side for euphonic effect. Besides the advocates of Atticist theory, still prominent in his day, Quintilian addresses conservative Stoics in Book 9; he begins his discussion "on word order" (*de ordine*), at *Institutes* 9.4.23, by addressing the theory of a natural word order. He complains, in paragraphs 24 and following, that certain theorists (*quorundam*) are far too extravagant in their strict rules which insist that nouns precede verbs, verbs adverbs, and so on. All of this he regards as "excessive superstition" (*nimiae superstitionis*), and he goes on to list other precepts of this type, which are certainly Stoic in origin.

> nam fuit hoc vitiosus: in hora saepe ducentos,
> ut magnum, versus dictabat stans pede in uno.

He was witty, keen-scented, rugged in verse composition. For in this he was defective: he would often dictate two hundred verses in an hour while standing on one foot, as if that were some great feat.

The edition of Kiessling and Heinze annotates the phrase *durus componere versus* as follows: "*duritia* is apparent in the *compositio*, σύνθεσις, of his verses."[80] The suggestion makes perfect sense within the theoretical context of the late Republic. Put simply, the satirist's debate with the pro-Lucilian Stoics centers on technical theories of arrangement. H. Rackham noted that the phrase "rugged in verse composition," normally taken as a straightforward negative assessment, stands at the end of a series of positive qualities conceded to Lucilius, serving, then, as a parallel construction, not an adversative. The line reads "*and* (not *but*) rugged in verse composition," implying that in his rugged word arrangement, just as in his clever, stinging wit, Lucilius consciously imitated the Attic masters of Old Comedy mentioned at *Satires* 1.4.1, showing all the traits of a good Atticist.[81] This suggestion was rather tentatively discussed by Rudd, but has since been rejected by Brink.[82] On the basis of what we know of Horace's critics, however, the phrase *durus componere versus* could well have been heard as a positive assessment by certain members of his audience.[83] Brutus, we recall, was zealous in his pursuit of *componendi durius* (*Institutes* 9.476), and the same is certainly true of the Stoic theorists lampooned in *Satires* 1.4. The immediate disclaimer of line 8, "for in this [his rugged arrangement of verse] he was defective," removes any doubt as to the satirist's own view of the matter. Later, in *Satires* 1.10, we learn that Horace considered the Old Comic poets as unparalleled masters of word arragement, and he chides his critics for imitating certain features of Old Comic composition without ever having studied them seriously.[84] We see, then, that from the standpoint of ancient theory the seemingly unsuggestive claim, "he was rugged in verse composition," is packed with meaning.

---

[80] Kiessling and Heinze, *Horatius Flaccus*, 71.

[81] H. Rackham, "Notes on Horace," *Classical Review* 30 (1916): 224. The paraphrase is made by Brink, *Prolegomena to the Literary Epistles*, 158, n. 1.

[82] See Brink, *Prolegomena to the Literary Epistles*, whose reasons for rejecting Rackham's reading I cannot follow.

[83] The phrase is ambiguous by design. For similar instances of deliberate ambiguity in the *Satires*, see M. Wigodsky, "Horace's Miser (*S.* 1.1.108) and Aristotelian Self-Love," *Symbolae Osloenses* 55 (1980): 37–42.

[84] See *Satires* 1.10.16–19.

As with the lines preceding, the next passage (*Satires* 1.4.11–13) carries its full suggestive meaning only when considered within the context of a larger critical debate. Horace writes of Lucilius:

> cum flueret lutulentus, erat quod tollere velles,
> garrulus atque piger scribendi ferre laborem,
> scribendi recte; nam ut multum, nil moror.

Since he flowed muddy, there was much you would like to remove. He was wordy, and too lazy for the hard work of writing—of writing correctly, that is. For I do not care how much one writes.

Lucilian composition Horace compares to a turgid river, full of mud and debris of every kind. Commentators inevitably regard these lines as a clever allusion to Callimachus's jibe against the writers of epic in the grand style at *Hymn to Apollo* 108, a sensible claim considering the closeness of the parallel.[85] One must also consider, however, that Horace uses the flooded-river analogy numerous times throughout his various works, and only here does it match the Callimachus passage with much precision.[86] Without discarding the Hellenistic allusion, which seems secure, one should also grasp the analogy's more immediate referent in the contemporary rhetorical debates centering on word arrangement, which, we have seen, is the central issue dividing the satirist from his pro-Lucilian critics. To understand the analogy's use in these debates is to understand with greater precision the nature of Horace's criticisms of Lucilius.

The river analogy was a favorite among theorists of word arrangement, employed with tremendous flexibility to argue either for or against various "watery" characteristics of style. At *Brutus* 316, for example, Cicero uses the analogy to describe the Asianist excess that characterized the oratory of his youth, later checked by the Atticist Molo at Rhodes. Molo, he claims, kept his oratory from "overflowing its banks" (*supra fluentis*). Flooded speech, here, is equivalent to Asian-

---

[85] Like the satirist, Callimachus employed the metaphor against the "flooded" style of certain obscure critics and rival poets. I agree with Williams who argues against relating these lines to some alleged quarrel between Callimachus and Apollonius. See F. Williams, *Callimachus: Hymn to Apollo* (Oxford: Clarendon Press, 1978), 2 and 91–92.

[86] Other images of the swollen river we see at *Satires* 1.1.59; 1.7.26–27; 1.10.36–37, 50–51, and 62; *Epistles* 2.2.120; and *Odes* 4.2.5. Ever since Hesiod, fountains, streams, and rivers were taken as symbols of the poet's inspirations. Recent studies on water imagery in Augustan poetry include N. B. Crowther, "Water and Wine as Symbols of Inspiration," *Mnemosyne* 30 (1979): 1–11; P. Knox, "Wine, Water, and Callimachean Polemics," *Harvard Studies in Classical Philology* 89 (1985): 107–19; J. J. Clauss, "Vergil and the Euphrates Revisited," *American Journal of Philology* 109 (1988): 309–20; and F. Dunn, "Horace's Sacred Spring (*Ode* 1.1)," *Latomus* 48 (1989): 97–109.

ist bombast. At *Orator* 97, however, Cicero describes his perfect orator, that is, the orator of the "third style," who draws upon both the grand and simple styles, as one whose eloquence "rushes along with the roar of a mighty stream," a highly positive assessment. The stream in this case is not flooded, but full and vigorous, maintaining the proper "third style" balance between lack of vigor (often termed "dryness") and turgid Asianist excess.

Besides the *Orator*, Seneca's literary epistles outline a theory of arrangement that, while perhaps softer than that espoused by Dionysius's Stoics, shows distinct vestiges of Stoic theory. Among the most telling of Seneca's letters on style is *Moral Epistles* 100, which demonstrates the peculiar serviceability of water metaphors, especially the river analogy, to ancient theories of arrangement, both Stoic and non-Stoic, and thus the epistle serves as a unique commentary on the satirist's criticisms of Lucilius in *Satires* 1.4 and 1.10.[87] In the letter, Seneca responds to his friend, Lucilius, who has criticized the philosophical writings of a certain Fabianus, claiming that his words simply "poured forth" without noticeable regard for arrangement. Seneca rebukes his friend: "You find fault with his word arrangement forgetting that you are dealing with a philosopher" (*oblitus de philosopho agi compositionem eius accusas*). Against the charge of faulty arrangement he adds (*Moral Epistles* 100.1–2):

> Multum enim interesse existimo, utrum exciderit an fluxerit. Adice nunc, quod in hoc quoque, quod dicturus sum, ingens differentia est: Fabianus mihi non effundere videtur orationem, sed fundere.

> I think that it makes a great difference whether one's speech should "fall out" or "flow." Moreover, consider the tremendous distinction in what I will now say: Fabianus seems to me not to "gush forth" but to "pour."

One man's flood (*effundere*) is another man's flow (*fundere*). Unlike Lucilius, Seneca respected the word arrangement of Fabianus on the grounds that it was natural and "fluent" (*Moral Epistles* 100.5):

> electa verba sunt, non captata nec huius saeculi more contra naturam suam posita et inversa, splendida tamen, quamvis sumantur e medio.

[87] On Seneca's adherence to Stoic stylistic doctrines, see C. N. Smiley, "Seneca and the Stoic Theory of Literary Style," *University of Wisconsin Studies in Language and Literature* 3 (1919): 50–61. Atherton, "Hand over Fist," 418, n. 58, makes the following cautionary notes: "It would be rash to employ Seneca straightforwardly either as an authority for or as an example of approved Stoic style. On the one hand, he can be starkly critical of Stoic style; on the other, the question of the sources for Seneca's style is a vexed and complicated one. It is rather a matter of saying that such-and-such a piece of Senecan writing or Senecan stylistics betrays signs of Stoic influence."

His words are chosen, not "hunted down" or, in the manner of the present day, arranged contrary to their nature and inverted; yet they are
brilliant, even though they are taken from ordinary speech.

Seneca speaks as a Stoic, defending Fabianus's offhand rhetoric by
reference to "natural" theories of selection and arrangement. These
sentiments Seneca shared fully with Horace's Stoic critics who, in all
likelihood, fashioned their defense of Lucilius in similar if not identical terms. Like the Atticists and neo-Chrysippeans of the previous
century, Seneca admits that Fabianus's "natural flow" of words will
not always smoothly caress the ear (*Moral Epistles* 100.2): "that man is
an arranger of morals, not words, and he writes them for minds, not
ears" (*Mores ille, non verba composuit et animis scripsit ista, non auribus*).
For the conservative Stoic attuned to the harsh beauty and power of
ruggedness, this neglect of the traditional sensitivities toward euphony poses no problem: the Stoic theorist or the Atticist could claim
that his diction "flowed" naturally and with vigor, like a mountain
current in spring. His critic, such as Horace, with an ear more attuned to traditional notions of euphony, would counter that this
"flow" of words was, in fact, more of a raging "flood."

Quintilian's lengthy study of word arrangement in Book 9 of the
Institutes contains numerous references to the river analogy within a
technical analysis of arrangement, and thus it serves to demonstrate
the untold variety and serviceability of the metaphor in ancient compositional theory. His own study of *compositio*, Quintilian suggests,
looks back to the debates of the mid to late first century B.C. (*Institutes*
9.4.1):

De compositione non equidem post M. Tullium scribere auderem . . .
nisi et eiusdem aetatis homines scriptis ad ipsum etiam litteris reprehen-
dere id collocandi genus ausi fuissent.

I would not venture to write on the topic of word arrangement after
Marcus Tullius (Cicero) . . . had not men of his own age dared censure
that type of arrangement even in the letters they wrote to him.

In undertaking his study of word arrangement, Quintilian refers to
the letters of the Atticists, Calvus and Brutus, mentioned by Tacitus
at *Dialogus* 18. Although the letters have since disappeared and must
always remain obscure, Quintilian points out that they focused on
technical matters of word arrangement, which he recognized as the
chief theoretical issue dividing Cicero from his Atticist opponents.
Word arrangement, he gives us to believe, continued to divide the
theorists of rhetoric even in his own day.

In mentioning Cicero's works *de compositione*, Quintilian must have in mind primarily the *Orator*, for of the sixteen references to *compositio* within the Ciceronian corpus, where the term is used as a technical designation in the analysis of various arts, ten are contained within the *Orator*.[88] The last chapters of this treatise were especially influential upon *Institutes* Book 9. After a brief introduction to his topic, Quintilian launches into a vigorous defense of compositional refinements, suggesting that the old Stoic/Atticist prejudices against euphony were still very much alive in his day, a full century and a half after Cicero. He writes (*Institutes* 9.4.3–4):

> Neque ignoro quosdam esse, qui curam omnem compositionis excludant, atque illum horridum sermonem, ut forte fluxerit, modo magis naturalem, modo etiam magis virilem esse contendant. Qui si id demum naturale esse dicunt, quod natura primum ortum est et quale ante cultum fuit, tota haec ars orandi subvertitur.

> And neither am I unaware that there are certain critics who exclude entirely attention to word arrangement, and they contend that rugged speech, as it chances to flow forth, is both more natural and, in fact, more manly. If they mean that only that is natural which arises directly from nature and receives no subsequent refinement, the entire art of speechmaking is turned upside down.

Quintilian's critics, though unnamed, are certainly Stoics, extremists hostile to the idea of an "art" of oratory, advocating a rugged, "natural" eloquence, "as it chances to flow" (*ut forte fluxerit*). The phrase makes "fluency" a positive character of style, suggesting the image of a strong, untamed current. Quintilian counters with the following (*Institutes* 9.4.5–8):

> Verum id est maxime naturale, quod fieri natura optime patitur. Fortius vero qui incompositum potest esse quam vinctum et bene collocatum? . . . Ceterum quanto vehementior fluminum cursus est prono alveo ac nullas moras obiiciente quam inter obstantia saxa fractis aquis ac reluctantibus, tanto, quae connexa est et totis viribus fluit, fragosa atque interrupta melior oratio. Cur ergo vires ipsa specie solvi putent, quando res nec ulla sine arte satis valeat et comitetur semper artem decor?

> That is most natural, however, which nature permits to attain perfection. How, then, can that which lacks orderly arrangement be stronger than that which is fastened and neatly set together? . . . But just as the current

---

[88] This assessment is based on a check of the *Thesaurus Linguae Latinae* files (still incomplete) now contained on compact disk. For an overview of ancient theories of sentence structure and word order, see Scaglione, *Composition*, 1–96. Scaglione identifies the *Orator* as Cicero's most definitive text on sentence structure and word order.

of rivers is more vigorous when the channel is steep and holds no obstructions to slow it down, than when its waters are broken and struggle against rocks holding them back, so is oration better when it is continuous, flowing at full force, than when it is broken and choppy. Why then should strength be thought to dissolve on that pretext [smooth arrangement] when nothing else reaches its full strength without art and when beauty always accompanies art?

Quintilian counters his critics' claims to "fluency" by objecting that their river of language is full of debris, which prevents its smooth flow. He offers the picture of a crashing torrent, full of rocks, logs, whatever, whose strength is inhibited by its unkempt condition. The image is very close to that drawn by Horace in *Satires* 1.4 and 1.10 as he describes Lucilian verse as a rushing river, filled with much debris that needs to be removed (*tollenda*).[89] What is important to note here is that Quintilian's image is used in exactly the same context; that is, he illustrates a technical point about the power of a smooth, highly wrought *compositio* against critics who were actively hostile to such refinements. *Satires* 1.4 and 1.10 argue the same point using the same illustration, and this is no accident, for at all turns Horace neatly adapts his criticisms of Lucilius to the much larger world of criticism known to his audience from ancient compositional theory. Only within this larger context can we understand the claims and counterclaims that stand behind the satirist's criticisms of Lucilius, for as much as the river analogy is a learned allusion to Callimachus, it is a well-worn, even trite illustration of ancient compositional theory, designed to make a technical point about the way in which Lucilius set his words side by side. In one motion, the river analogy proves Horace a master of ancient theory and an accomplished practitioner of satire.[90]

[89] The image is, in turn, equivalent to Callimachus *Hymn to Apollo* 108–9: "Mighty is the flow of the Assyrian river [Euphrates], but it draws along its waters much mud and rubbish" (Ἀσσυρίου ποταμοῖο μέγας ῥόος, ἀλλὰ τὰ πολλά / λύματα γῆς καὶ πολλὸν ἐφ᾽ ὕδατι συρφετὸν ἕλκει). In contrast, compare Cratinus fragment 198KA, where the comedian uses the metaphor of cataclysmic waters to describe his own raging, scandalous invective. The fragment is discussed by Rosen, *Old Comedy*, 39.

[90] It is apparent that Horace continued to draw criticism from the Stoics throughout his career. More than a decade later in his epistle to Augustus (*Epistles* 2.1), Horace complains that a certain group of critics despises all poetry "except what it sees far removed from the earth, its days already spent" (*nisi quae terris semota suisque / temporibus defuncta videt*). In lines 44–49 he "uses what his critics grant" (*utor permisso*) in the form of the *sorites* puzzle, a mode of arguing that was particularly associated with Chrysippus. Again, Horace's primary literary opponents, as in *Satires* 1.4, are the conservative Stoics who have no patience for modern *fastidia*. See Brink, *Epistles Book II*, 81. We note also that in the *Ars Poetica*, as in *Satires* 1.10 and 2.1, Horace maintains the golden

THE NEOTERICS AND *SATIRES* 1.10

In *Satires* 1.4, Horace addresses criticisms of certain obscure poets and theorists who, he gives us to believe, were nothing more than short-order literary buffoons, wholly unschooled in the finer traditions of scholarship known from Callimachus, Aristotle, and, perhaps, his own Epicurean tradition. The satirist's picture is, of course, severely skewed, for he never gives us to suspect that, in certain quarters of Roman society, these critics commanded respect as some of the best-trained theorists and poets of their day. Crispinus, Fabius, Tigellius, and Fannius share enough common ground as political advocates, philosophers, and stylists to suggest the cohesiveness of a literary circle, whose theories were very much in vogue in the 40s and 30s B.C. In *Satires* 1.10, the satirist returns to his criticisms of Lucilius, making a second attack upon his advocates, and so it is easy to assume that he has returned to the same group. No commentator on the *Satires* has ever suggested otherwise. This understanding of *Satires* 1.10, however, makes little sense of the substantial differences dividing the two satires, for although some of the same names, such as Tigellius and Fannius, do indeed crop up again in *Satires* 1.10, the piece is directed primarily against a second group of critics who, in spite of their mutual regard for Lucilius and perhaps some shared political feeling with the critics of *Satires* 1.4, otherwise have little in common with them. Their critical principles are far closer to those of Horace himself, and it may well be that, on certain points of style, the two groups in question were more hostile to one another than either was to Horace. This, at least, is what the satirist would have us believe in the opening lines of *Satires* 2.1. He writes:

> sunt quibus in satira videar nimis acer et ultra
> legem tendere opus; sine nervis altera quidquid
> composui pars esse putat similisque meorum
> mille die versus deduci posse.

There are those to whom I seem too impassioned, and to be stretching the genre beyond its limit; a second group thinks that whatever I have

---

mean, occupying the middle ground between "the elders who chase from the stage all that is profitless" and "the proud Ramnes" who disdain all poems devoid of charm and modern refinement (*Ars Poetica* 341–42). The elder poet is inspired. He does not bathe. He wears a philosopher's beard and is incessantly teased by the children of the city who regard him as a madman. The parallels with the dogmatic Stoic described at the end of *Satire* 1.3 are obvious.

set together is "gutless" and that verses like mine could be spun out a thousand per day.[91]

The satirist pictures himself caught between two sets of critics who, he makes clear, approach the writing of satire from opposite premises. Though he pretends to worry over their attacks, the lines cleverly suggest that his own work strikes the perfect balance, the "golden mean," between their opposite extremes.[92] The second group finds his work "gutless," or better yet, "impotent," demonstrating a definite prejudice against the refinements of word arrangement marked by *composui* beginning line 3.[93] We know this group quite well by now, and nothing more need be added here concerning it. Concerning members of the first group, however, those who appeal to the "law of the genre" (*lex operis*), objecting to Horace's use of the grand style (*oratio acer*) in satire, much remains to be said. Their opposing claims are best attested in *Satires* 1.10, which addresses a second set of critics nearly opposite the rugged stylists of *Satires* 1.4.

The opening lines of *Satires* 1.10 neatly recapitulate the critique of *Satires* 1.4: "Yes, I *did* claim that Lucilius's verses run with an ill-composed foot" (*Nempe incomposito dixi pede currere versus / Lucili*), a humorous jibe against Lucilian *compositio*. We see him hobble as he at-

---

[91] On the double meanings buried in these lines and throughout *Satires* 2.1, see Freudenburg, "Horace's Satiric Program." The bawdy, metaphorical language of this piece has precedents in contemporary compositional theory. Only in the hands of a satirist, however, are the humorous possibilities of such language fully exploited. For similar allusions to the sexual/compositional terminology of contemporary theory, see *Epodes* 8.1–2 and 17 (on *vis* and *nervus*); *Epodes* 12.15–16 (*opus*); and *Epodes* 1.7–16 (on warfare and sexual potency).

[92] Rudd, *Satires of Horace*, 118, observes that, "At the beginning of 2.1 Horace divided them [his critics] into two classes. . . . Nothing can be said about the first group. They probably had little in common except the conviction that brawling in public was vulgar and undignified. In the second group we must include the pro-Lucilian critics who had been in opposition to Horace ever since the appearance of 1.4 and perhaps earlier." Rudd despairs of saying anything significant about half of Horace's critics. Something can, in fact, be said about them if we differentiate between the critics of *Satires* 1.4 and 1.10, in which case, the introduction to *Satires* 2.1 reads as a recapitulation of the situation described in his earlier programmatic satires.

[93] The analogy of sexual potency, like the river analogy discussed previously, was very much a part of the vocabulary of contemporary criticism in treating matters of style, especially in terms of *compositio*. We noted already that, at *Institutes* 9.4.3, Quintilian addresses the Stoics' claim that rugged speech is more natural and "more virile" (*magis virilem*). Compare also the previous notes on "effeminacy" in Seneca *Moral Epistles* 114. Tacitus notes that Cicero's style was labeled by Calvus as "loose and limp" (*solutum et enervem*), and again by Brutus as "effeminate and loinless" (*fractum atque elumbem*). Again, Quintilian notes at *Institutes* 12.10.12 that *in compositione*, Cicero was regarded by certain contemporary critics as "extravagant and [an outrageous accusation!] softer than a man" (*exultantem ac paene, quod procul absit, viro molliorem*).

tempts to run with a "bad foot." In *Satires* 1.4, we recall, Lucilius had a similar problem with his feet, composing two hundred verses per hour while "standing on one foot." In both cases, the satirist employs a metaphor well known to ancient compositional theory, signifying a faulty, uneven rhythm. Noteworthy parallels we see at *Orator* 173, where Cicero notes that although the average Roman crowd knows nothing of rhythms or "feet" (*nec vero multitudo pedes novit*), they know a "limp" when they see one (*inconditum . . . curtum . . . claudicans*), and at *Orator* 170, where he berates the Atticists for the intentional choppiness of their periods:

> si inanibus verbis levibusque sententiis, iure; sin probae res, lecta verba, quid est cur claudere aut insistere orationem malint quam cum sententia pariter excurrere?

> That's fine if the words are empty and the sentences frivolous; if, however, the subject matter is serious and the words well chosen, what reason should they have for preferring oratory that "limps" or "comes to a halt" rather than oratory that runs at an even pace with the thought?[94]

The satirist has Lucilius "halting" on one foot in *Satires* 1.4 and "limping" in *Satires* 1.10. Similar is *Epistles* 2.1.170–76, where Horace pictures Plautus "running across the stage in a loose shoe" (*non adstricto percurrat pulpita socco*). Again, we see him hobble as he runs, eager to drop a coin in his coffers and "careless of whether the play should collapse or stand on a straight ankle" (*securus cadat an recto stet fabula talo*). The metaphor concerns rhythm, the process of welding words together in creating the overall sonic effect of the line. Lucilius, Horace suggests, is "slipshod," a "limper."

We assume from the opening lines of *Satires* 1.10 that the criticisms of *Satires* 1.4 met with astonishment, designed as they were to shock the Lucilius scholars of Horace's day, and that some unnamed critic has come to the defense of Lucilian word arrangement. The question to ask is just what type of critic is this likely to have been? From what we have seen, it is most unlikely that Stoic theorists, such as Fabius and Crispinus, wedded to the belief that "the ill-composed is stronger" (*fortius quod incompositum est*), should have defended Lucilius on his euphonic technique or should have taken offense at the idea of his slipshod composition, yet throughout *Satires* 1.10, the satirist is careful to use the technical terminology of compositional theory that only those who were sympathetic to such matters would have understood. A new audience is suggested. For example, in lines 8–10

---

[94] Both passages occur within a larger discussion of matters related to *compositio*, *Orator* 149–238.

Horace argues his case for the "listener" (*auditor*) and for diction that caresses the ear. In lines 23–24 he makes his critic sing the praises of *sermo* that is "neatly arranged" (*concinnus*) and "sweeter" (*dulcior*), and again in line 44 he praises the works of his friend Vergil on the grounds that they are "soft and subtle" (*molle atque facetum*). In lines 58 and following he speculates as to why Lucilius's verse was not "more highly wrought and softer moving" (*magis factos et euntis mollius*). The list continues. The terminology is Callimachean/Neoteric, indicating a shift in the satirist's audience from the Chrysippeans of *Satires* 1.4, who were hostile to the "soft," "unnatural" effects recommended in such terms, to a second set of critics who understood and exploited the euphonic possibilities of an artificial word order.[95]

Beginning at line 20 of *Satires* 1.10, we learn that Horace's critics cultivated a hybrid diction, freely mixing Greek and Latin to achieve the sonic quality desired of their lines. This practice found its most extreme expression in certain works of the *Appendix Vergiliana*, of which the *Lydia* is particularly noteworthy because of the possibility, admittedly remote, that it was written by Valerius Cato, the satirist's chief rival in *Satires* 1.10.[96] In contrast, Horace and his literary friends, such as Messalla, were much more sparing in their use of Greek diction, which is especially sparse in the *Satires* and *Epistles*.[97]

[95] Compare Scodel, "Callimachean Polemic," 204: "Lucilius' defenders are neoterics, and their admiration for Lucilius is somehow an expression of their neotericism. Yet the standards of fine craftsmanship to which Horace appeals in the poem are precisely those he might be expected to share with admirers of Calvus and Catullus." Besides the explicit reference to Calvus and Catullus in line 19, it is likely that the "little book" (*libellus*) of lines 41 and 92 and the "whatever sort they are" *qualiacumque* of line 88, would have been heard as allusions to Catullus 1.1, 8–9. On the Callimachean/Neoteric polemical language of *Satires* 1.10, see Thomas, "New Comedy," 191–92, n. 44. I fail to see the connection Thomas draws between *Satires* 1.4.9–10 and Callimachus *Aetia* fragment 1.3–4 and 17–20. Even granting the connection, the evidence for Neoteric terminology is much stronger in *Satires* 1.10 than in 1.4. Thomas takes seriously the satirist's disparagement of satire and comedy in *Satires* 1.4, lending it some Callimachean precedent. Thus, it is with some surprise that he notes a change of sentiment in the *Ars Poetica*: "The *Ars Poetica* contains material by far less partisan than that in his other works. The influence of Callimachus appears to have retreated as he drew from more conventional literary theory. Most notable in this is the fact that epic and dramatic poetry suddenly seem to be respectable genres. This does not, however, imply that Horace necessarily turned away from Callimachean aesthetics; an *Ars Poetica* simply requires recognition of traditional poetic forms." Although it is true that Callimachus does make claims against the thematic repetition of comedy, and therefore rejects writing it himself, he nowhere denies the genre the status of true "poetry." The critical standards of *Satires* 1.4.38–63 would render some of Callimachus's best works "unpoetic."

[96] On the authorship of the *Lydia*, see R. Robinson, "Valerius Cato," *Transactions of the American Philological Association* 54 (1923): 110–16.

[97] On the use of Greek diction in Horace and Vergil, see L. P. Wilkinson, *Golden Latin*

Vergil freely employs Greek diction in his earlier works, which show much stronger Neoteric tendencies than the *Aeneid*, where Greek intrusions are noticeably few. Horace may have had a hand in this. His disparagement of Neoteric excess in *Satires* 1.10 serves as an opposite foil to the claims of *Satires* 1.4, directed against Chrysippean Stoics who would have found no appeal in the "effeminate" sounds of Greek words and the learned snobbery entailed in their use. Quintilian relates that, as far as their sounds are concerned, Latin letters are "more rugged" (*durior*), a quality that any good Stoic would respect and make the most of, whereas the Greek language possesses sounds that "breathe more sweetly" (*dulcius spirant*, *Institutes* 12.10.27), thus lending themselves to smooth composition. This is precisely the attitude assumed by the critics of *Satires* 1.10, who freely incorporated Greek diction into their works on the grounds that "diction drawn from both languages makes a nice blend and is sweeter, as when Falernian vintage is mixed with Chian" (*at sermo lingua concinnus utraque / dulcior, ut Chio nota si commixta Falerni est*, *Satires* 1.10.23–24). *Concinnus* ("neatly arranged," for Greek ἁρμονία) and *dulcis* ("sweet") are drawn from the language of compositional theory, equally descriptive of euphonic word arrangement as of a smooth blend of wine. Completely absent is the appeal to ruggedness so characteristic of anticompositional theory.

Little patient of the metaphor, the satirist claims that his critics have much to learn from the rhetorical practices of his friends, Pedius Publicola and Messalla Corvinus, who applied themselves to a strict Latin vocabulary in "sweating out" (*exsudet*) their court cases. The rules of *sermo* ("oratory"), in other words, apply equally to *sermo* ("satire"). Horace was very alive to the double meaning of the term, and it is perhaps on the basis of this double meaning that he freely avails himself of rhetorical theory in developing his own satiric program. Thus he restricts the writing of *sermo* to pure Latin diction, which is clear and unpretentious. This is not to say that Publicola and Messalla did not possess the same depth of feeling for matters of euphony as the critics of *Satires* 1.10. Quite to the contrary, Quintilian relates at *Institutes* 1.10.23 that Messalla Corvinus actually wrote a treatise on the letter *s*, and at 1.10.35 he suggests that he did the same for other letters as well.[98] Messalla had a sharp ear for matters of euphony, a concern he shared fully with the critics of *Satires* 1.10. In

---

Artistry (Cambridge: Cambridge University Press, 1963), especially 9–34. For Lucilius, see W. Korfmacher, "*Grecizing* in Lucilian Satire," *Classical Journal* 30 (1935): 453–62. On Roman bilingualism, see N. Horsfall, "Doctus Sermones Utriusque Linguae," *Echos du Monde Classique* 22 (1979): 85–95.

[98] See Fiske, "Lucilius and Horace," 342–43.

contrast, however, Messalla refused to give up on the Latin language in his attempts to achieve the desired charm of *compositio*.[99]

Unlike the critics of *Satires* 1.4.38–63, the opponents of *Satires* 1.10 seem also to have shared a desire to write in the slighter genres. We note their shared regard for Calvus and Catullus, self-proclaimed writers of *nugae*. The satirist designates their works "Greek verse-lettes" (*Graecos versiculos*, 31–32), the diminutive stressing the slightness of the genre, perhaps elegy. Rudd has noted that the Neoterics of *Satires* 1.10 may well have looked upon Lucilius as a pioneer in the field of elegy. We know that Lucilius wrote elegies in Books 22–25, and that his *Satires* included love poems on at least two different girls. Rudd speculates that:

> Although there is nothing in any of these pieces to suggest the passionate intensity of the Lesbia poems, and although the tone was probably more hearty than that adopted by the Neoterics, it is still a fair guess that his frank subjective treatment of *amor* was one of the features which commended Lucilius to followers of Calvus and Catullus.[100]

Beyond this, *Satires* 1.10 contains an entire list of new names, such as Demetrius, Pitholeon, Alpinus, and Pantilius, nowhere attested in the first four satires of Book 1. Yet because some of the old names have resurfaced in 1.10, most notably Tigellius and Fannius, scholars have been tempted to lump them all together, taking them as members of a single, cohesive movement. Such a conclusion, however, is unnecessary and problematic. Consider, for example, the case of Tigellius, whom we have seen before and who is mentioned again at *Satires* 1.10.18, where the satirist lodges the following complaint against him and some unnamed "ape" (*Satire* 1.10.17–19):

> hoc stabant, hoc sunt imitandi: quos neque pulcher
> Hermogenes umquam legit neque simius iste
> nil praeter Calvum et doctus cantare Catullum.

> They [the Old Comic poets] relied on this [compositional variation] and in this they are to be imitated. Neither has "pretty" Hermogenes ever read them, nor that ape of yours, the expert who sings nothing but Calvus and Catullus.

Rudd has taken this passage as positive evidence that Hermogenes was a devotee of Calvus and Catullus, thus making him into a Neo-

[99] The Elder Seneca records of Messalla (*Controversiae* 2.4.8): "Messalla was a man of very precise talent in every area of his studies, and a most diligent guard of Latin diction" (*fuit Messala exactissimi ingenii in omni studiorum parte, Latini utique sermonis observator diligentissimus*).

[100] Rudd, *Satires of Horace*, 122.

teric.[101] We know, however, that Calvus at one time sharply lampooned Tigellius, and so Rudd, following the majority of scholars since Kirchner, has been forced to make his case for two men, namely, the Sardinian Tigellius of *Satires* 1.2.3 and 1.3.4 as distinct from a second Tigellius of *Satires* 1.3.129, 1.4.72, 1.9.25, and 1.10.18, 80, and 90.[102] Rudd's entire argument hinges upon the assumption, which has never really been challenged, that the passage just quoted proves the Hermogenes of *Satires* 1.10 a Neoteric, yet the lines in question claim only that Hermogenes never read the Old Comic poets.[103] It is the unnamed "ape," probably Demetrius, Pitholeon, or Furius Bibaculus, not Tigellius, who is accused of "singing" only the works of Calvus and Catullus. The passage draws no direct link between Hermogenes and the "ape." On the contrary, the tenor of the preceding lines suggests that the satirist intends Hermogenes as his opposite foil. Beginning at line 9, the satirist's remarks on the proper compositional cast of satire exhibit an antithetical character, balancing arguments for grandeur and augmentation (*amplificatio*) against arguments for concision (*brevitas*), the poet and rhetor versus the sophisticated wit (*urbanus*). The passage in lines 17–19 fits into this same scheme, rounding off the antithesis before a new theme is introduced in line 20. Within this scheme, we understand that Hermogenes, far from being directly associated with the Neoterics, is men-

---

[101] Ibid., 292–93. The question of the identification of the "ape" (*simius*) in line 18 is extremely vexed, and, as Hendrickson has suggested, "no one can offer a conclusive answer to this riddle of identification." The Elder Seneca relates at *Controversiae* 9.3.12 that overzealous imitation makes an "ape" (πίθηκος) of the poet Argentarius. This seems to be the thrust of *Satires* 1.10.18 as well. G. L. Hendrickson, "Horace and Valerius Cato II: The Adversarius of *Serm.* 1.10, and Other Personal Allusions,"*Classical Philology* 12 (1917): 86–87, makes a case for Furius Bibaculus against the scholiasts' claim that the "ape" was Demetrius. Either possibility is acceptable. I would add Pitholaus as a third possibility, based on the assumption that, when the name was adapted for the hexameter and changed from Pitholaus to Pitholeon, Horace may have realized the humorous possibilities of such a change, making the name itself into a half-Greek, half-Latin hybrid (Pitholeon = Greek πίθων, "ape" + Latin *oleo*, "I smell of"). Thus, Horace disparages the mixing of Greek with Latin by saying, "Oh late learners [*seri studiorum*, itself a studious avoidance of the Greek ὀψιμαθεῖς], do you really think it difficult and marvelous what happens to *Pitholeon* of Rhodes," that is, as exemplified by his name.

[102] Cicero records at *Ad Familiares* 7.24.1 that Calvus made a sharp attack against Tigellius. Obviously the relationship between the two men was not a friendly one. Porphyrion *ad Satires* 1.3.1 credits Calvus with the taunt, "the stinking head of Tigellius the Sardinian comes" (*Sardi Tigelli putidum caput venit*).

[103] Good Attic writers whose merits, as *Satires* 1.4 suggests, the Stoics vaunted in order to disparage the works of Horace. Ullman, "Horace, Catullus, and Tigellius," 295–96, does indeed question the assumption, but his solution (taking *cantare* in the sense of "satirize") has found very little acceptance among subsequent commentators.

tioned as their opposite foil, noted for his flamboyant amplification against the reverse extreme of strict Neoteric brevity. Such an interpretation removes entirely the need for a second, otherwise unknown, Tigellius, while at the same time avoiding the needless extremes of Ullman and Fairclough, who have insisted that the *cantare* of line 19 must convey some otherwise unattested pejorative sense.

The eight-line introduction to *Satires* 1.10 found in several manuscripts of Horace, though probably non-Horatian, is generally accepted as an accurate description of the satire's main premise, drawn from some source contemporary with Horace himself.[104] From these lines we learn that Valerius Cato and his Neoteric advocates are the chief critics addressed in *Satires* 1.10, the defenders of Lucilius's compositional style. The lines read:[105]

> Lucili, quam sis mendosus, teste Catone,
> defensore tuo, pervincam, qui male factos
> emendare parat versus, hoc lenius ille
> quo melior vir et est longe subtilior illo,
> qui multum puer et loris et funibus udis
> exoratus, ut esset, opem qui ferre poetis
> antiquis posset contra fastidia nostra,
> grammaticorum equitum doctissimus. ut redeam illuc.

Lucilius, I will prove how faulty you are with Cato, your defender, as my witness. He has in mind to emend verses poorly fashioned. He [fashions verse?] more smoothly to the extent that he is a better man and far subtler than that one who often, as a child, was "persuaded" by straps and wet ropes to rescue the great poets of the past from our modern-day nitpicking, he the most learned of the knights' professors. Let me return to my previous point.

The grammar is vague, the hypotaxis elaborate and uncharacteristic of Horace. The lines elude any universally acceptable interpretation. Even so, they clearly posit two sets of critics, opposite types among the advocates of Lucilius. The one type, represented by Valerius Cato, does something, perhaps "writes verse" or "emends Lucilius," "more smoothly" (*lenius*), a concession to his expertise in matters of euphony. He is regarded as far more fastidious (*subtilior*) and attentive to the fine points of his art than a second critic, unnamed, who harshly punishes the student under his tutelage, coercing him to res-

---

[104] The standard view is expressed concisely by Brink: "I regard the passage as spurious but contemporary." See Brink, *Prolegomena to the Literary Epistles* (1963) 167, n 1.

[105] For these lines I prefer the text of F. Klingner, *Horatius Opera*, 6th ed. (Leipzig: Teubner, 1982).

cue the old Latin poets from all such modern "nit-picking" (*fastidia nostra*). The final appellation, "most learned of the knights' professors," though ironic, suggests that this second defender of Lucilius was, like Cato himself, a highly trained *grammaticus*, a paid professor of language and literature.[106] In general, then, the lines argue for two distinct types of Lucilian scholar, just as the opening lines of *Satires* 2.1 argue for opposite types among the critics of Horace. The satirist has already addressed the criticisms of the second type in *Satires* 1.4, where he makes a defense of modern "nit-picking" (*fastidia*) in matters of word arrangement. In *Satires* 1.10 he undertakes to address criticisms of a far different type, leveled by none other than Valerius Cato and his Neoteric adherents. Their theories of word arrangement were much in keeping with his own, and so the satirist must tread lightly. He refashions his criticisms of Lucilius in terms that make sense within the Callimachean/Neoteric tradition they both share.

In terms of their arrangement and attention to euphony, the evidence of Lucilius's *Satires* is strangely mixed, suggesting qualities both the Neoterics and Chrysippeans of Horace's day would find attractive. Concerning the first satire of Book 5, for example, Aulus Gellius writes (18.8):

> ὁμοιοτέλευτα . . . ceteraque huiusmodi scitamenta, quae isti apirocali, qui se Isocratios videri volunt, in collocandis verbis immodice faciunt et rancide, quam sint insubida et inertia et puerilia, facetissime hercle significat in quinto saturarum Lucilius.

> Homoeoteleuta . . . and other dainties of this type, which those tasteless ones who wish to appear "Isocratean" practice in their lawless, nauseating word arrangement, how stupid, artless, and puerile these things are Lucilius points out with tremendous wit in the fifth book of his *Satires*.

Gellius goes on to quote the opening lines of this satire (W186–93), where Lucilius chides a friend/critic for failing to visit him while sick because he has somehow found fault with the poet's use of the words "would not" (*nolueris*) and "could" (*debueris*), whose sounds were perhaps too glutinous for the fastidious critic. Such "Isocratean" refinements, he suggests, are nothing more than "trash" (*lerodes*, for Greek ληρῶδες) and "childishness" (*meiraciodes*, for Greek μειρακιῶδες). In the same fragment we see both the Stoic's disdain for compositional re-

---

[106] Hendrickson takes the phrase *grammaticorum equitum doctissimus* as referring to the *Catone* of line 1, in spite of the intervening lines, which suggest that the appellation belongs to a second critic. See G. L. Hendrickson, "Horace and Valerius Cato I: The Original Opening of *Serm*. 1.10," *Classical Philology* 11 (1916): 267–69.

finements and the clever blend of Greek and Latin the Neoterics found so attractive.

The evidence of W84–86 is equally two-sided, for here the poet, in the person of Quintus Mucius Scaevola, mocks both the compositional refinements of Albucius as well as his penchant for obscure Grecisms. The fragment is preserved by Cicero within a technical discussion of word arrangement at *Orator* 149:

> quod vel maxime desiderat diligentiam—ut fiat quasi structura quaedam nec tamen fiat operose; nam esset cum infinitus tum puerilis labor; quod apud Lucilium scite exagitat in Albucio Scaevola: "quam lepide λέξεις compostae ut tesserulae omnes arte pavimento atque emblemate vermiculato!" Nolo haec tam minuta constructio appareat.

> This [the "cohesion" of words] requires the greatest care—the end result should be a certain "structure," as it were, without overdiligence. For one's labor then becomes not only endless, but childish. This is the quality that Lucilius cleverly satirizes in Albucius: "How charmingly he arranges *les mots*, all like close-fitting little tiles in a mosaic or an inlay with a wriggly pattern!" I would not have the construction appear in such minute detail.

The mosaic metaphor coupled with *compostae* ("set together"), which refers explicitly to Albucius's art of *compositio*, suggests that, in oratory at least, Lucilius preferred the rugged native talent of Scaevola to Albucius's lilting periods interspersed with learned Grecisms. This said, the evidence of Book 9 of the *Satires*, where, besides his famous *poema/poesis* distinction, Lucilius discusses rules of spelling, the sound qualities of each letter of the alphabet starting with *a*, as well as their value in arrangement, suggests that he was an expert in compositional theory.[107] His ruggedness, if that is, in fact, what he chose to affect, is studied ruggedness taught by the rules, the sign of a good Atticist. W417–18 from Book 10 of the *Satires* confirms this, integrating word placement into Lucilius's definition of "poetic judgment" (*iudicium*).[108] Taken together, the evidence appears odd and some-

---

[107] At W389–92, for example, Lucilius comments on the sonic qualities of the letters *r* and *s*: *"r"; non multum est hoc cacosyntheton atque canina / si lingua dico; nihil ad me; nomen enim illi est. / "s" nostrum et semigraeci quod dicimus "sigma" / nil erroris habet* ("As for *r*, it makes little difference that the letter is cacophonous, or if I growl like a dog when I say it. I am not responsible for it, since the letter's name belongs to the sound. Our *s*, and what we half-Greeks call sigma, contains no fault").

[108] *Horum est iudicium, crisis ut describimus ante; / hoc est, quid sumam quid non, in quoque locemus* ("Such persons possess judgment, *crisis* as we called it earlier; that is, what word we should choose, what word reject, and where we should place it"). Chirius Fortunatianus 3.6 makes euphony the criterion of Lucilian *iudicium* (see W417–18).

what contradictory, yet it fits nicely with the testimony of the *Satires* and Cicero's rhetorical treatises, which suggest that the Stoics, Atticists and Neoterics (and the various combinations of these that certainly existed) all found something worthy of emulation in Lucilius. In the mid to late first century B.C. he was perceived as an advocate of Stoic εὐθυρρημοσύνη ("straight talk"), equivalent to old republican *libertas*, which played itself out in both his rugged style and unsparing wit.[109] He may well have studied Stoic rhetorical theory under his friend Panaetius, regarded as the founder of Roman Stoicism. Yet he was also perceived as a precursor of Catullus, emulated among the Neoterics of Horace's day, who knew him as a philhellenist, a searing satirist, and an experimenter and fellow writer of "trifles," as well as an exceptional stylist, trained in the best traditions of Greece and Alexandria. It is no longer possible to determine how all of these qualities could have been contained in one man, yet the evidence of Horace and of Lucilius himself suggests that they were, and that Lucilius was the most innovative poet of his age, fully deserving of such emulation. Horace, in spite of his famous criticisms against Lucilius's flooded style, explicitly mentions or invites comparison with him in all but one or two satires, knowing that, if he cannot at least approximate the works of Lucilius, he cannot write satire. Horace was, in the end, Lucilius's greatest admirer.

SATIRES 1.10 AND LUCILIAN SCHOLARSHIP IN THE FIRST CENTURY B.C.

Throughout his treatise *On Word Arrangement* Dionysius shows that the critical debates of his age were conducted on the most minute, often "bureaucratic" level. Minutiae, such as Dionysius's four

---

[109] Trebonius celebrated his new-found *libertas* by writing Lucilian invective against some unnamed opponent, probably Mark Antony. On these verses see my Chapter 2, n. 55. He writes to Cicero in May 44 B.C. (*Ad Familiares* 12.16.3): "If I seem in these verses too straightforward [εὐθυρρημονέστερος *videbor*] with certain words, the foulness of the character against whom I rather openly level my attacks will vindicate me. . . . Again, why should Lucilius be allowed to enjoy greater freedom (*libertatis*) than we?" The Greek adjective refers to the concept of "straight talk" (εὐθυρρημοσύνη). The term is rare and decidedly Stoic in its connotations. At *Ad Familiares* 9.22.5, for example, Cicero chides Paetus for his pursuit of obscene diction in the name of Stoic *libertas* (see *Stoicorum Veterum Fragmenta* 1.22.28): *Habes scholam Stoicam*, ὁ σοφὸς εὐθυρρημονήσει ("Here is the sum total of the Stoic school: 'the wise man will tell it straight' "). In describing himself as εὐθυρρημονέστερος, Trebonius betrays his Stoic leanings and, rightly or wrongly, he makes Lucilius speak for the same creed. Compare also Marcus Aurelius *Meditations* 11.6, where the term is connected with Old Comedy.

"grades" of short syllables, as strange as it may seem, comprised some
of the most burning issues of the day. Although little survives of Lucilian scholarship from the period roughly contemporary with Horace's early career, the scant evidence we do possess suggests that the
study of Lucilius was conducted at an equally minute level.[110] One
case relevant to the question of Lucilian word arrangement we see at
Institutes Book 9, where Quintilian relates that a certain Luranius
once found fault with a second critic, Servius, equally obscure, on a
technical point of composition.[111] Luranius criticized Servius's habit
of dropping the final *s* in cases where the word following began with
a consonant, which he practiced in order to avoid the clustering of
consonants, "slurring" the final *s* into the initial sound of the following word. This is obviously a fine point of *compositio*. Quintilian further relates that Messalla, the same Messalla with whom Horace
aligns himself in *Satires* 1.10, actively defended Servius's practice of
dropping the final *s* (*Institutes* 9.4.38–39):

> quod reprehendit Luranius, Messala defendit. Nam neque Lucilium pu-
> tat uti eadem ultima, cum dicit "Aeserninus fuit" et "dignus locoque," et
> Cicero in Oratore plures antiquorum tradit sic locutos.

> What Luranius censures, Messalla supports. For he does not think that
> Lucilius makes use of the final *s* when he says *Aeserninus fuit* and *dignus
> locoque*, and Cicero relates in his *Orator* that many of the ancients spoke
> in this way.

Messalla, whom we know to have written an entire treatise on the
letter *s*, defends the practice of Servius by claiming that Lucilius, even
in writing *Aeserninus fuit*, would not have retained the final *s* in pro-
nunciation. The point seems tedious, but it demonstrates that the
technicalities of Lucilian word arrangement were debated with near
bureaucratic officiousness in the age of Horace. Horace's primary
complaint against Lucilius, that he was "rugged in setting together his
verses" (*durus componere versus*), is generally regarded as a sweeping
negative assessment of Lucilian verse, and it is commonly assumed
from this that Lucilius was guilty of the most obvious blunders of a
loose, rapid-fire style which would have been all too apparent to Horace's audience. Judging from Messalla's interchange with Luranius,
however, one must admit the possibility that the principles by which
Horace made this assessment were of a much more mundane sort,

[110] On the resurgence of Lucilian scholarship in the first century B.C., see Scholz,
"Lucilius und Horaz," 357.
[111] It is possible that this is the same Servius mentioned favorably by Horace at *Satires*
1.10.86.

and that his critique, "he was rugged in setting together his verses," may have stemmed from something as slight and exasperating as his attitude toward Lucilius's use of the letter *s*.

The "spurious" opening lines of *Satires* 1.10 suggest that the countercriticisms of this piece were leveled against Valerius Cato, the great Neoteric grammarian and poet who, at the height of his career, was extremely influential among the *litterati* of Rome.[112] What little is known of Valerius Cato is drawn primarily from a précis of his career in Suetonius's *De Grammaticis*. R. P. Robinson compiled all the known facts only to conclude: "Our information is too meager and too vague to admit of definite conclusions."[113] Despite the scanty evidence concerning his life and career, several notable facts about Valerius Cato are reasonably certain and speak directly to the interpretation of *Satires* 1.10. At *De Grammaticis* 2, for example, Suetonius relates that Valerius Cato took great pride in having studied the works of Lucilius under Vettius Philocomus, a personal friend of the poet. He was, in other words, a self-proclaimed Lucilius scholar, perhaps the leading authority of his day on matters that pertained to the works of Lucilius. The spurious opening lines of *Satires* 1.10 confirm this, mentioning that Cato had recently undertaken to "emend" the works of Lucilius, signifying some type of noteworthy scholarly activity. Hendrickson took this to imply the following:

> Cato, it appears, was editing Lucilius, and naturally his work would conform to the usage established by Hellenistic practice. His edition would contain prolegomena, in which the editor would set forth such information concerning the poet's life as was available, and express judgments, either of his own, or derived from his predecessors, concerning his author's models, his originality and dependence, the characteristics of his nature and of his style. The general manner is pretty well known from the Greek introductions which have come down to us, and from similar matter prefaced to the commentaries of Servius and Donatus.[114]

Such claims, though they may well be true, Hendrickson has extracted from the terse "he is undertaking to emend verses" (*emendare parat versus*), which may mean something much more or much less. A

[112] Suetonius at *De Grammaticis* 11 quotes the following anonymous verses, attributable perhaps to Bibaculus: "Cato the professor, the Latin Siren, who alone selects and makes poets" (*Cato grammaticus, Latina Siren, / Qui solus legit ac facit poetas*). These lines, though certainly exaggerated, testify to Cato's unparalleled influence among the Neoterics at Rome.

[113] Robinson, "Valerius Cato," 116.

[114] G. L. Hendrickson, "Horace and Valerius Cato II: The Adversarius of *Serm.* 1.10, and Other Personal Allusions," *Classical Philology* 12 (1917): 77–78.

brief survey of the term *emendare* in the theoretical works roughly contemporary with *Satires* 1.10 shows that the verb "to emend" was commonly used in a much more restricted sense, as one of the catchwords of the "anomalists" and the "analogists" in their debates over the natural versus conventional aspects of language. Something of this sense may well be implied in Cato's scholarly activity toward Lucilius.

At *Brutus* 258, Atticus addresses the oratorical style of Julius Caesar and the related question of his "Latinity" (*Latinitas*):

> Solum quidem, inquit ille, et quasi fundamentum oratoris vides, locutionem emendatam et Latinam, cuius penes quos laus adhuc fuit, non fuit rationis aut scientiae, sed quasi bonae consuetudinis.

> "The ground," he said, "and, so to speak, the foundation of oratory is, you see, flawless Latin diction. Up to now, if some have possessed this distinction, it has been a matter of good usage, not of reason and science."

Cicero's three great technical treatises on oratory contain only four occurrences of words with the stem *emend-*, three of which occur within the immediate vicinity of this passage, from *Brutus* 258–61, treating the topic of proper Latin diction. A fourth instance occurs at *Orator* 155, within a similar context. This pattern, coupled with the absence of the term in the massive *De Oratore* of only ten years earlier, suggests that "emending," when used to imply a type of scholarly/linguistic activity, was narrowly limited to the debates concerning proper Latin diction, which had become so prevalent in the 50s and 40s B.C. in the wake of the analogist/anomalist controversy.[115] Atticus alludes to these debates when he insists against the basic tenets of analogy that "impeccable Latin diction" (*locutionem emendatam et Latinam*) results from good usage, not from theory or science. He goes on to elaborate his point, offering the negative example of Sisenna, a strict analogist whom he describes as "you might say, an *emender* of usage" (*quasi emendator usitati*). In a case against Gaius Hirtilius, he says, Sisenna once described certain accusations as "spitabilical" (*sputatilica*), a monster of a word designed to match the Greek κατάπτυστα and somehow built on analogy with words ending in the suffixes *-ilis* and *-icus*.[116] The result is an odd hybrid indeed, and one wonders whether Sisenna ever intended his "spitabilical" to be taken seriously. In any event, Atticus uses it as an example of the worst abuses of

---

[115] F. H. Colson, "The Analogist and Anomalist Controversy," *Classical Quarterly* 13 (1919): 24–36, remains a basic study of these issues.

[116] See Hendrickson and Hubbell's Loeb edition of the *Brutus* (Cambridge, Mass.: Harvard University Press, 1952), 224, n. *a*.

analogy against all precedent in usage. In contrast, he reserves high praise for Caesar who, he claims, strikes a fine balance between the competing demands of rational theory and everyday usage (*Brutus* 261): "Caesar, however, applies rational theory to *emend* flawed and corrupt usage by means of pure, uncorrupt usage" (*Caesar autem rationem adhibens consuetudinem vitiosam et corruptam pura et incorrupta consuetudine emendat*).[117] Caesar occupies the middle ground.[118] This is the third and final occurrence of "emend" in the *Brutus*, where each case refers the term directly to the debates of the anomalists and the analogist, who sought, each in their own way, to "emend" the Latin language of their day and standardize an "impeccable diction."

The final occurrence of *emendare* within the rhetorical treatises of Cicero is of special interest to our study because it is used within a larger discussion of euphonic word arrangement, with specific reference to the Latinity of Lucilius, suggesting perhaps something of the tedious nature of Cato's "emendation." *Orator* 152–55 discusses various contemporary attitudes toward the use of contraction in adjoining words. Among other examples, Cicero cites the case of *multi' modis* for *multis modis*, where final *s* is dropped before a following consonant. We noted that Messalla devoted himself to this very question and, as we have come to expect, Cicero mentions that certain critics opposed the practice, which was itself quite old, and had undertaken to restore the fuller forms (*Orator* 155): "And, in fact, antiquity is even now at this late stage being *emended* by certain critics who find fault with these practices" (*Atque etiam a quibusdam sero iam emendatur antiquitas, qui haec reprehendunt*).

We subsequently learn that these "emenders" were strict analogists, whose various offenses against good usage included a preference for *pertisum* against the usual *pertaesum*, a case that presents peculiar possibilities for the "emending" work of Cato because we happen to know exactly how Lucilius stood on the matter.[119] At W983–84, he chides his friend Scipio Africanus:

> Quo facetior videare et scire plus quam ceteri
> "pertisum" hominem non "pertaesum" dicere
> ferum nam genus.

[117] On these lines, which concern the grammatical side of the Atticist/Asianist debates, see Scaglione, *Composition*, 8–18, especially p. 16, n. 10.

[118] It is often assumed that Julius Caesar was a strict analogist because he published a work, now lost, entitled *De Analogia*. This passage, however, suggests that if he was indeed an analogist, he was a very innovative and moderate one. On the stylistic doctrines of Julius Caesar, see Hendrickson, "The *De Analogia* of Julius Caesar, 97–120.

[119] Those who favored *pertisum* could cite the analogy of *concisum* for *concaesum* (*Orator* 159).

> You seem so much smarter and to know more than the rest in calling someone *pertisum* rather than *pertaesum*, for that style is uncivilized.

Lucilius apparently had little patience for the nit-picking of the strict analogists, even when the "emender" was none other than Scipio himself. Though the evidence of this passage suggests that the members of the Scipionic circle, in their famous pursuit of pure Latin diction, tended to favor the analogical view, it also suggests that Lucilius applied to some other standard, perhaps equally strict, but more in line with the commonsense approach of the anomalists.[120] Even in his own day Lucilius openly challenged the more extreme practices of those who sought to correct everyday usage. In the controversy of *pertaesum* versus *pertisum*, we again see how trivial these debates could be.

A final reference to the technical debates of *compositio* at *Orator* 161 yields special insight into the "emending" work of late republican Neoterics, referring specifically to certain technical deficiencies in Lucilian verse composition that any good Neoteric, such as Cato, would have seen fit to emend. Within a larger discussion of euphony, in which Cicero argues a case for the well-trained ear (*causa aurium*), he mentions in passing that at one time it seemed "rather refined" (*politius*) to drop the final *s* in words ending in *-us*, unless the following word began with a vowel. Obviously, the case of final *s*, which from the distance of time seems inconsequential to the larger, more compelling questions of theory, was considered important enough to make real enemies among the theorists of Cicero's day. He proceeds to mention that the practice of dropping the final *s* was, in his own day, regarded as "rather rustic" (*subrusticum*), adding the very significant note, "now the *New Poets* flee the practice" (*nunc fugiunt poetae novi*). For our purposes, the note is important because of the example that follows: Cicero relates that, while at one time it was considered proper to write *vita illa dignu' locoque*, the more recent trend was to restore the fuller form, *dignus*. The example is taken from a line of Lucilius, and thus provides a specific case where a good Neoteric, such as a Valerius Cato, would have found it necessary to "emend" the verse of Lucilius. The point is extremely subtle, hinging upon the use of a single letter. Yet, the compositional debates of the late Republic were based in just this type of unforgiving subtlety. Any attempt to understand the programmatic satires should keep this in mind, for Horace was very much a product of this same age. His crit-

---

[120] On the question of diction in the Scipionic circle, see G. Fiske, "The Plain Style in the Scipionic Circle," *University of Wisconsin Studies in Language and Literature* 3 (1919): 62–105; and Krenkel, "Lucilius," 202–10.

icisms of Lucilius may, in the end, have stemmed from theoretical technicalities just as trivial as those that informed the "emending" work of the Neoterics.

In *Satires* 1.4 Horace draws a most unflattering and exaggerated image of Lucilius as a stylist, which the fragments of Lucilius's *Satires* tend not to support. In his own day and for many decades to come, Lucilius was regarded as an exceptional stylist fully attuned to the fine points of composition taught by Greek theory. His rough treatment in *Satires* 1.4 was without precedent, and it comes as no surprise that these criticisms prompted a very strong reaction from the Neoterics, led by Valerius Cato. Even a century later Quintilian, an expert on technical matters of word arrangement, made a point of dismissing Horace's criticisms as unwarranted, an opposite extreme counterbalancing the effusive praise that Lucilius received from certain quarters of Roman society, where he was regarded as nothing less than Rome's greatest poet.[121] In *Satires* 1.10, the satirist's tone is conciliatory, but he stands by his former criticisms. Here he seems, for the first time, to acknowledge the exaggerated nature of his earlier claims, and so in lines 46–71 and elsewhere, he attempts to explain the true spirit in which they were intended, maintaining that, like the unnamed *doctus* of 52, probably Valerius Cato, his criticisms were comparable with those of a *grammaticus* who "censures" the older poets "not as if he were any greater than the ones censured" (*non ut maiore reprensis*, 55). He makes clear that he regards himself as "second to the inventor" (*inventore minor*), and he concedes that Lucilius did have at least some feel for euphonic arrangement, referring to him in line 65 as "more polished" (*limatior*) than those earlier writers who had not studied Greek models. Even so, the satirist claims that the standards of Lucilius's day made defects inevitable—that his compositional faults were, in the end, defects cultivated by his entire age.[122]

In spite of this conciliatory tone, Horace does not beg off his earlier criticisms of Lucilian arrangement; rather, he restates them with greater precision, demonstrating in turn his own expertise in technical matters of euphonic word arrangement. Comparison with Dio-

---

[121] See *Institutes* 10.1.94.

[122] Porphyrion summarizes the satirist's disclaimer *ad Satires* 1.10.1: "He responds to those by whom he had been censured because he condemned the verses of Lucilius in the previous satire. . . . Now, however, he says that he did not disapprove of the poet, but of his verses, which he [Lucilius] made rugged not from some defect in himself, but from a defect of his entire age (*Respondet his, a quibus inculpatus erat, quod Lucilii versus damnasset in ea satura, quam supra habuit. . . . Nunc autem dicit non se poetam improbrasse, sed versus eius, quos non suo vitio duros, sed saeculi fecit*).

nysius's treatise *On Word Arrangement* demonstrates that Horace's assessment of Lucilian *compositio* is not the sweeping negative gesture that it is often assumed to be. In the end, his objections to Lucilius are actually quite minute. He summarizes his case (*Satires* 1.10.7–14):

> ergo non satis est risu diducere rictum
> auditoris (et est quaedam tamen hic quoque virtus):
> est brevitate opus, ut currat sententia, neu se
> impediat verbis lassas onerantibus auris;
> et sermone opus est modo tristi, saepe iocoso,
> defendente vicem modo rhetoris atque poetae,
> interdum urbani parcentis viribus atque
> extenuantis eas consulto.

Therefore, it is not enough to elicit a grin from the listener, though there is a certain virtue in this as well. There is need for brevity, in order that the thought might run along and not trip itself on words that overload tired ears. And there is need for dialogue that is at once harsh, often humorous, sustaining the part of rhetor and poet, and from time to time that of the clever wit, who purposely holds back and thins out the full force of his speech.

The satirist bases his case against Lucilius on a technical point of *compositio*, isolating his failure in the matter of euphonic "variety" (ποικιλία, Latin *varietas*).[123] Dionysius devotes chapter 19 of his *On Word Arrangement* to this topic, arguing that, unlike many poets, the writer of "foot-going diction" (ἡ πεζὴ λέξις), that is, "prose," enjoys the leisure to diversify his word arrangement, thereby avoiding monotony and the appearance of artificiality. Plato and Demosthenes, he claims, were especially skilled in their ability to diversify the compositional effects of their works. Concerning Isocrates and his followers, however, Dionysius writes (*On Word Arrangement* 19):

> ἀλλὰ καίπερ ἡδέως καὶ μεγαλοπρεπῶς πολλὰ συνθέντες οἱ ἄνδρες οὗτοι περὶ τὰς μεταβολὰς καὶ τὴν ποικιλίαν οὐ πάνυ εὐτυχοῦσιν· ἀλλ' ἔστι παρ' αὐτοῖς εἷς περιόδου κύκλος τις, ὁμοειδὴς σχημάτων τάξις, φυλακὴ συμπλοκῆς φωνηέντων ἡ αὐτή, ἄλλα πολλὰ τοιαῦτα κόπτοντα τὴν ἀκρόασιν.

They composed much that is attractive and impressive, but they are anything but felicitous in their use of change and variation. Their style is based on a single periodic cycle, a monotonous order of figures, a uniform care in blending of vowels, and many such devices which weary the ear.

---

[123] Compare Nilsson, *Metrische Stildifferenzen*, 1, who correctly sees that these lines treat metrical variation rather than the issue of the poet's *libertas*, applying ancient theories of satiric variety (*Mannigfaltigkeit*) to compositional technique.

Although he admits that Isocrates was a true master at "composing" lines full of charm and grandeur, Dionysius faults Isocrates for failing to vary his periods. Sameness destroys the beauty and distinction of the many compositional refinements mastered by Isocrates (*On Word Arrangement* 19): "For it is always possible to have too much of even beautiful things, as of things sweet to taste, when they retain their sameness." When used without regard for variety, compositional refinements tend only to "fatigue the ear."

Something very close to this comprises Horace's final assessment of Lucilian *compositio* in *Satires* 1.10. In the passage quoted previously, Horace points out that the individual sentence (*sententia*, 9) in Lucilius is invariably long, a compositional feature suited to the grand style, but failing the requirements of good middle style *sermo* that blends the best features of both the grand and simple styles. He claims that the sentence "trips itself" on cumbersome words that "overload tired ears" (*verbis lassas onerantibus auris*, 10). The preponderance of final *s*'s in this line can only be intended to create the toilsome slurring effect that the words themselves malign. We also note that Horace has chosen the perfect word to describe the effect of Lucilian *compositio* on the ear: *onerantibus*, both in its size and in the heavy, liquid texture of its sounds, is bloated and "onerous," demonstrating that when Horace makes the claim, "there is need for brevity" (*est brevitate opus*) in line 9, he means this to apply not simply to the size of the satire taken as a whole, but to the individual sentence, to the words within that sentence, and to the individual sounds contained in these words. Although Lucilius understood the refinements of *compositio* taught by his age, the satirist concludes that the sonic effects of his verse, his vowel blending, rhythms, cadences, and so on, are too predictable; he leans too heavily on one "foot."

Satire, like good middle-style oratory, is a patchwork, interspersing short periods with long, the euphonic with the rugged, precision and balance with neglect. Horace adapts these ideas from rhetorical theory, yet he knows that his demands for compositional variety stem ultimately from generic considerations, that is, from the Protean nature of satire itself, a genre defined by fullness and variety, which, ironically, are its only reliable hallmarks.[124] Thus, the *Satires* of Lucilius and Horace are at once "diatribe" (*sermo*), a motley combination of parodies, fables, anecdotes, character sketches, quotations of poetry, digressions, the polite and the obscene, the serious and the ridiculous (τὸ σπουδαιογέλοιον); and they are "satire" (*satura*), an elusive

---

[124] On the relation of satire's formlessness and heterogeneity to ancient theories of the genre, see C. J. Classen, "Satire, the Elusive Genre," *Symbolae Osloenses* 63 (1988): 95–121.

term that, whatever its actual derivation, implies mixture and fullness. Pseudacron, who derives the term from the *satura lanx*, concludes:

> Ergo et hoc carmen propterea satyram nominarunt, quia ita multis et
> variis rebus refertum est, ut audientes saturet.

> And for this reason, furthermore, they have named this poetry "satire,"
> because it is filled with such a great number of varied themes that it
> "sates" the audience.[125]

Quintilian too makes variety the hallmark of satire (*Institutes* 10.1.95):

> Alterum illud etiam prius saturae genus, sed non sola carminum varie-
> tate mixtum condidit Terentius Varro, vir Romanorum eruditissimus.

> The other well-known type of satire—one that arose even before Lucil-
> ius [that is, the Ennian satire of varied meter]—was exploited by Varro,
> but now with a variety given not merely by metrical changes [but by an
> admixture of prose to the verse].[126]

Variety defines the genre. To innovate as a satirist, Quintilian suggests, is to inject more chaos into the jumble. Varro achieved special
distinction by adding prose to the already disordered metrical
scheme of Ennian satire. His diction, Relihan suggests, was equally
haphazard, "a mad mixture of Latin and Greek, archaism and neol-
ogism, everday speech and rhetorical prose, homely proverbs and
technical terms of art."[127] At all levels, Varro sought to achieve the
"full plate" effect, which he knew the genre demanded.

We see, then, that from the standpoint of ancient theory, the opponents of *Satires* 1.10 had good reasons for defending the hybrid
diction of their favorite, Lucilius; for blending Greek and Latin was
not only preferred Neoteric practice, it was good satiric jumble as
well. Horace, however, insists that variety is a much subtler entity,
whose traces can be seen not only at the most obvious levels of Greek/

---

[125] See Pseudacron's preface to *Satires* Book 1, Keller, *Pseudacronis Scholia*, 2.

[126] Following Relihan, I quote Winterbottom's translation of these lines, which make
clear that Quintilian regarded Varro's *Menippeans* as a type of Ennian satire, not a
separate genre to itself. See J. Relihan, "A History of Menippean Satire" (Ph.D. diss.,
University of Wisconsin at Madison, 1985), 9.

[127] Relihan, "Menippean Satire," 105. Compare *Acad. Post.* 1.9, where Cicero addresses the literary achievements of Varro's *Menippeans* largely in terms of variety (I
quote Relihan's translation, p. 106): "You have brought much light to our poets and to
Latin literature and language as well, and have yourself made a multiform and elegant
poetic work in nearly every meter [*atque ipse varium et elegans omni fere numero poema
fecisti*]." In spite of this praise, Cicero goes on to add that he considered the *Menippeans*
"insufficient for instruction" (*ad edocendum parum*).

Latin, prose/verse, and so on, but in the variation of periods, clauses, words set side by side, and even individual sounds, principles learned from rhetorical theories of word arrangement. The same thinking is evident at *On Word Arrangement* 26, where Dionysius discusses the type of arrangement appropriate to a class of poetry that consciously seeks to resemble "foot-going diction" (τὴν πεζὴν λέξιν). He has in mind primarily those writers of hexameters and iambic verse who, unlike many lyric writers, were unable to vary their meter. They strove, nonetheless, to convey the feeling of conversation in all its variation, breaking up the monotonous effect of their unrelenting rhythmic scheme:

ὥσθ' οἱ μὲν τὰ μονόμετρα συντιθέντες ὅταν διαλύσωσι τοὺς στίχους τοῖς κώλοις δι-
αλαμβάνοντες ἄλλοτε ἄλλως, διαχέουσι καὶ ἀφανίζουσι τὴν ἀκρίβειαν τοῦ μέτρου, καὶ ὅταν τὰς περιόδους μεγέθει τε καὶ σχήματι ποικίλας ποιῶσιν, εἰς λήθην
ἐμβάλλουσιν ἡμᾶς τοῦ μέτρου.

Thus when the writers of single-meter verse break up their lines by dis-
tributing them into clauses in various ways at different times, they destroy and eliminate the regularity of the meter; and when they vary the
length and the construction of the periods, they make us forget the
meter.

The poet who seeks to imitate prose must efface the regularity of his meter by diversifying the size and internal balance of his periods. Dionysius connects diversity, "giving variety to the periods" (τὰς περιό-δους . . . ποικίλας ποιῶσιν), to poetry that seeks to approximate "foot-going diction," sentiments that perfectly match the satirist's advice to his critics in *Satires* 1.10. When Horace refers to his works as "conversations creeping along the ground" (*sermones repentes per humum*) at *Epistles* 2.1.251, and again as the "foot-going muse" (*musa pedestris*) at *Satires* 2.6.17, he very literally translates the Greek ἡ πεζὴ λέξις, "foot-going diction." What applies to prose, in other words, applies equally to satire, which Horace understood as a special type of versified *sermo* subject to the same rules of compositional variety as any good middle style speech. In the end, it is on a very technical point of composition (synthetic ποικιλία) that he objects to the stylistic qualities of Lucilius's *Satires*.

Musa Pedestris is an oxymoron: muses do not walk, they fly. The idea of poetic prose is equally incongruous, for to make poetry of prose is to destroy all that made it prosaic, the unregulated, free-flowing character that differentiates prose from poetry. Their mixture, then, is odd and impossible, yet this is precisely what Horace proposes to write in his *Satires*, a genre that has always prided itself in oxymorons: the "unified diversity" implied by the *farrago* and *satura lanx*, the "seriocomic" (τὸ σπουδαιογέλοιον), "prosimetry," in the case of Menippean satire, and so on. This is not to say, however, that Horace viewed satire simply as a bundle of opposites, a renegade genre subject to rules known only to itself, for the conundrum of the "walking muse" brings us round once more to the question of satire's relationship to comedy. Horace begins a brief discussion of the proper dictional cast of comedy and tragedy at *Ars Poetica* 89, arguing that comic diction should approximate the speech of everyday life, to which he refers at line 95 as "foot-going speech" (*sermone pedestri*). Comedy and satire, in other words, have this fully in common; they are inspired by the same muse. Horace makes this point numerous times in the great programmatic passages of *Satires* 1.4 and 1.10, as he consistently isolates the best analogy for satire in the great works he knew from the comic stage. The analogy needs to be taken seriously as central to Horace's satiric program, every bit as important as his debt to Lucilius and the Callimachean/Neoteric tradition.

Comedy, like satire, conveys the full variety of life and everyday speech, for just as in life, comedy occasionally, though not often, impresses us with its grandeur. Horace writes (*Ars Poetica* 93–94): "Sometimes, however, even comedy raises its voice, and Chremes in his rage *delitigates* with high-flown speech" (*interdum tamen et vocem comoedia tollit / iratusque Chremes tumido delitigat ore*). This was a commonplace of ancient theory, which had long recognized comedy's ability to adapt its style to the shifting dictates of the plot. When Demetrius undertakes to differentiate between the separate styles of the "graceful" and the "laughable" at *On Style* 3.163, he has a particular problem in classifying comedy. At 3.166–67 he relates that Sappho, when she sings of beauty, employs a "graceful" style that exhibits all the most elegant refinements of diction and arrangement. When, however, she "lampoons the clumsy bridegroom," she uses a simple diction that is not arranged in an elegant musical fashion. Thus, Demetrius makes his case for two separate styles of the graceful and the laughable, the highly crafted and the artless. These are wholly distinct, he claims, and are nowhere found together except "in satire and comedies" (ἐν σατύρῳ καὶ ἐν κωμῳδίαις, *On Style* 3.169). Comedy, like satire, shows its Protean character. It is the perfect model for Horace's *Satires*. According to theorists trained in the Aristotelian tradition, it demanded the consummate stylist, one who could move freely from slapstick and lampoon to a touching reunion or the tirade of an angry father. Such are the shades of life, the living colors of comedy and satire.

CHAPTER FOUR

Callimachean Aesthetics and the Noble Mime

MORALS AND AESTHETICS IN THE *SATIRES*

Commentators on the *Satires* traditionally interpret the larger structures of Books 1 and 2 according to the general themes treated in
individual satires, moving from the moral lessons of the diatribes—
avarice and ambition (*Satires* 1.1), sex (1.2), friendship (1.3)—to literary criticism (1.4 and 1.10), scenes from the poet's life with Maecenas (1.5 and 1.6), miniature dramas (1.7, 1.8, and 1.9), and so on.
Because the satirist preaches, the theme of each satire is self-appar-
ent. Given literary precedents that are equally obvious, the reader
naturally assumes that Horace intends his *Satires* in the same self-con-
scious moralizing vein as Bion, or that aesthetic considerations,
though more important to Horace than to Lucilius, are somehow an-
cillary to his aims as a preacher of moral reform. Consequently, little
attempt has been made to see the *Satires* as high art after the manner
of the *Odes* or Vergil's *Eclogues*. Yet even the diatribes, which seem, at
times, half-witted, the most unsophisticated of all the poems of Horace, conceal a second side, a metaphorical dialogue exposing the aesthetic values of the poet and his commitment to writing elegant,
highly allusive poems in the Callimachean tradition. Here again we
see the gulf that separates scholarly consensus on the *Satires* from the
more involved approach to Horace's later works, especially his *Odes*,
where the elusive multivalence of individual poems has long been appreciated and studied. Concerning *Odes* 1.17, for example, scholars
since Klingner have understood that Horace's landscapes and his love
for Tyndaris possess symbolic, literary connotations, as mirror images of the poetic world of the *Odes*. We understand, then, that the
poem is as much about art as it is about a girl named Tyndaris and
the blessings of country life.[1] The same is true of *Odes* 1.14, where it
was obvious even to Quintilian that the ship invoked is much more
than a ship.[2] It is, among other possibilities, the symbol of Rome em-

---

[1] For a review of modern interpretations of *Odes* 1.17 with bibliographical notes, see
F. M. Dunn, "An Invitation to Tyndaris: Horace Ode 1.17," *Transactions of the American
Philological Association* 120 (1990): 203–4; and H. G. Edinger, "Horace, *C.* 1.17," *Clas-
sical Journal* 66 (1971): 306–7.

[2] See *Institutes* 8.6.44.

barking on new wars, a girl taking a new lover, or even a poet attempting a new genre.[3]

Less obvious, but equally important, are the references to the poet's life-style that fill the *Odes*; lessons on eating, drinking, simplicity, friendship, and so on, which J. V. Cody and H. J. Mette, among others, have identified as metaphors of poetic style.[4] Concerning *Odes* 1.38, for example, Cody notes: "It will be seen that not only does the *genus tenue* refer to Horace's preferred style of writing but also is associated with the poet's preferred style of living. A 'slender' aesthetics is seen to be a fitting correlative of the poet's 'slender' ethics."[5] The metaphor equating ethics to aesthetics, Cody claims, is consistent throughout the *Odes* and central to Horace's poetic program: "Horace's own poetry, avoiding mere Callimachean aestheticism, interrelates life and art, ethics and aesthetics, moral goals and literary canons."[6] In reading the *Odes*, then, it is both fair and necessary to ask whether a ship is simply a ship, a girl a girl, and a rustic meal a rustic meal, for to read these poems only at their surface level, to ignore the power of metaphor so important throughout—the literary judgments contained in such terms as *tenuis* ("thin"), *deductum* ("fine-spun"), and *acer* ("impassioned")—is to deny them the highly allusive, multilayered character that marks them as poems in the Callimachean tradition.

In spite of scholarly consensus on the *Odes* and the incessant invitations of the satirist to look beneath the surface of his work, to see a second side to his stated moral objectives, the metaphorical possibilities of the *Satires* remain virtually unexplored. Literary metaphors, after all, are sportive, snobbish, and inconsistent with the satirist's avowed moral objectives. The evidence of the *Satires* themselves, however, suggests that, just as in the *Odes*, the speaker's ethical principles are fully consistent with his aesthetic principles, so that every lesson he teaches on the proper style of life contains a second literary application on the proper style of poetry. Life-style and style in Horace are one and the same.[7]

[3] For the various symbolic possibilities of *Odes* 1.14, see A. J. Woodman, "The Craft of Horace in *Odes* 1.14," *Classical Philology* 75 (1980): 60–67 (bibliography nn. 2 and 6); and H. D. Jocelyn, "Boats, Women, and Horace *Odes* 1.14," *Classical Philology* 77 (1982): 330–35 (bibliography n. 20).

[4] See H. J. Mette, "*Genus Tenue* und *Mensa Tenuis* bei Horaz," in H. Oppermann, ed., *Wege zu Horaz* (Darmstadt: Wissenschaftliche Buchgesellschaft, 1972), 220–24; and J. V. Cody, *Horace and Callimachean Aesthetics*, Collection *Latomus* 147 (Brussels: Latomus Revue d'Études Latines, 1976).

[5] Cody, *Horace and Callimachean Aesthetics*, 36.

[6] Ibid., 45.

[7] Which he considered more important it is impossible to say. It is likely, however,

Horace, it seems, is always writing about writing, for even his most straightforward preaching has a second side that neatly exposes literary judgments and the aesthetic aims of his work. *Satires* 1.1, for example, beneath its moralizing mask, introduces the *Satires* as poetry, setting off the aesthetic values of the poet from those of his rivals, and thus it is much more akin to an *Aetia* prologue or to a Catullus 1 than it is to a straightforward ethical treatise. Commentators on the *Satires*, however, traditionally underscore the stated moral aims of the piece, either excluding or, at best, glossing the Callimachean dialogue that runs beneath the surface, and thus little attempt has been made to see *Satires* 1.1 as something more than versified preaching. Typical is van Rooy: "Horace's main reason for putting this satire at the beginning of his book should now be clear. He placed it first because, within the implicit moral function of his Satires, it dealt with what he (and other Roman authors before him, viz. Lucretius and Sallust) regarded as the first among the cardinal vitia of man."[8] Such an approach, while not patently false, concedes nothing to the real sophistication of this piece, which consists not in the moral lessons themselves, but the clever manner in which Horace manipulates these lessons to serve aesthetic aims without ridiculing or subverting their moral intent. Consider, for example, lines 54–60, addressing the fool who vaunts the capacity of his granaries:

> Ut tibi si sit opus liquidi non amplius urna
> vel cyatho, et dicas "magno de flumine mallem,
> quam ex hoc fonticulo tantundem sumere." Eo fit,
> plenior ut si quos delectet copia iusto,
> cum ripa simul avolsos ferat Aufidus acer.
> At qui tantuli eget, quanto est opus, is neque limo
> turbatam haurit aquam neque vitam amittit in undis.

It's as if you should have need of water, no more than a jar or cup, and you would say "I prefer to drink from a great river than to draw the same amount from this piddling stream." And so it happens that if some

---

that Horace had objectives beyond the Callimachean playfulness that he knew from Catullus and Valerius Cato and their imitators. Epicurean compositional theory, we recall, demanded the perfect expression of meaning through arrangement, content through form. The end result, according to Philodemus, not only caresses the ear, but "wins the soul" (ψυχαγωγεῖν). See Greenberg, "Philodemus," 158–64. Persius, a poet very dependent on Horace, is explicit in the coherence of moral and aesthetic principles in his first satire. See J. Bramble, *Persius and the Programmatic Satire* (Cambridge: Cambridge University Press, 1974), 67–142.

[8] C. van Rooy, "Horace's *Sat.* 1.1 as Prooemium and Its Relation to Satires 2 to 10," in W. Kraus, A. Primmer, and H. Schwabl, eds., *Latinität und Alte Kirche: Festschrift Rudolf Hanslik* (Vienna: Hermann Böhlaus, 1977), 265.

enjoy abundance beyond what is just, the raging Aufidus carries them away, plucked off along with the riverbank, while the one who desires only what he needs neither drinks water churned with mud nor loses his life in the flood.

Horace knew an altered form of this illustration from diatribe where typically, as here, the Cynic objects that the size or external appearance of the package is superfluous, since humans can only eat or drink so much at one sitting, no matter how much is served; food from clay vessels tastes the same as that served on silver platters, and a peacock, once its feathers have been removed, looks and tastes the same as any other roasted fowl. Summarized in the words of Ofellus, the Cynic of *Satires* 2.2: "When hard work has dispelled your finicky tastes, go ahead and despise cheap food" (*Satires* 2.2.14–15). The Cynic symbols of ostentation, where packaging supplants substance, were numerous, but some of the most common were large granaries, golden cups, and outlandish, ornamental foods, such as the peacock of *Satires* 1.2.116.[9] Nowhere, however, in the extant remains of diatribe do we see the profligate insist on drinking from a raging river as here.[10] The shift is slight but significant, for it demonstrates that Horace has something more in mind than repeating the centuries-old illustrations of diatribe; he knew, of course, that ever since Hesiod and Pindar, rivers were exploited for their metaphorical significance, taken as symbols of poetic inspiration. *Hymn to Apollo* 108–12 demonstrates that the metaphor was active in Callimachean polemics: "For Callimachus, the filthy streams of the Euphrates symbolize lengthy and inelegant verse whereas the pure water of a sacred fountain carried by bees represents its opposite."[11] As the recent works of Crowther, Knox, Clauss, and Dunn have shown, the Augustan poets were extremely sensitive to the various symbols of poetic inspiration favored by Callimachus, frequently adapting them to their own programmatic aims.[12] This is perhaps most true of Horace: "Wine, shade trees and water do not just reflect Horace's personal tastes; he regularly uses these to symbolize his poetic values."[13] The Bandusian spring is an obvious example. Armstrong writes of *Odes* 3.13:

[9] For examples in diatribe, see Oltramare, *Diatribe romaine*, 52, themes 38 and 38a.

[10] Usually the fool drinks from a golden cup. Compare *Satires* 1.2.114–15: *num, tibi cum fauces urit sitis, aurea quaeris / pocula?* ("When thirst parches your throat you don't demand golden cups, do you?"). In contrast, it was understood that Cynics drank water from earthenware vessels or from their hands as evidence of their unassuming, natural disposition. See previous note and Gerhard, *Phoinix*, 199 and 282.

[11] Clauss, "Euphrates Revisited," 309.

[12] For citations, see Chapter 3, n. 86.

[13] Dunn, "Horace's Sacred Spring," 99.

Horace is talking about a real fountain, almost certainly at his farm. But more than a fountain is meant: the Callimachean "pure fountain" of poetry is symbolized here. The bloodshed is the sacrifice of reality to create art from it, the fountain is a natural object from which art is created. . . . Horace, as poet and patron, is the creator of a "noble" fountain, the equal of the sacred poetic fountains of Greece.[14]

Likewise, the man reclining "at the source of a sacred spring" (*ad aquae caput sacrae*) in *Odes* 1.1, must be assigned some programmatic significance; he is, according to Dunn, a symbol of the poet himself.[15]

Only a fool, the satirist suggests, would prefer the hazardous current of the Aufidus, muddy from tearing at its own banks, to the waters of a pure, small spring—that is, simple diction neatly arranged. Besides the shift from diatribe's golden cups to a raging river, Horace buries other clues in the illustration to suggest that he intends the image metaphorically, as a jibe against the wild, unrestrained verbiage of his poetic rivals: there is the double significance of *copia* in line 57, which besides implying the "abundance" of some specified object is also the regular Latin term for profuseness of language and full command of the resources of oratory;[16] likewise *acer* ("fierce," "impassioned"), describing the agitated state of the river Aufidus, is one of rhetorical criticism's most common designations of the grand style.[17] The "mud" of line 59, repeated in the epithet *lutulentus* ("full of mud") applied to Lucilian style at *Satires* 1.4.11, is a metaphor known from Callimachus as well as from contemporary composi-

[14] Armstrong, *Horace*, 109.

[15] Likewise it seems necessary to assign some symbolic significance to the water imagery of *Odes* 3.30, the last poem of Horace's first published set of *Odes* (3.30.10–14):

> Dicar, qua violens obstrepit Aufidus
> et qua pauper aquae Daunus agrestium
> regnavit populorum, ex humili potens
> princeps Aeolium carmen ad Italos
> deduxisse modos.

Where the churning Aufidus crashes and where Daunus, poor in water, ruled over rustic peoples, I will be mentioned as a powerful leader from humble origins, the first to have brought Greek songs into Latin measures.

The imagery suggests that Horace has attained the mean between "flooded" and "parched," the "grand" and the "humble."

[16] See especially *De Oratore* 2.151, where Antonius connects "abundance" (*copiose*) with "overflowing" (*abundanter*) in arguing against the existence of an art of oratory. For other examples, see Leeman's Latin index and *copia* entries 1c and 6 in the *Oxford Latin Dictionary*.

[17] On *acer* as a designation of the grand style, see *acer* in Leeman's Latin index, and Freudenburg, "Horace's Satiric Program," 188–91.

tional theory.[18] Imagery and diction conspire in this case to suggest that a river is much more than a river; the Aufidus, with its muddy waves and savage current, Horace intends as a symbol of poetic incompetence, an unthinking lust for inelegant verse. Greed has taken on a distinctly poetic color.

Horace follows the Aufidus illustration with the story of an Athenian "rich man" (*dives*) who, though hated by all because he despised the "opinions of the people" (*voces populi*), took consolation in surveying the "cash in his coffers" (*nummos in arca*). Again, the terms chosen carry a humorous double significance, for in the language of rhetorical criticism words, just as people, possess both wealth and social status.[19] Thus, the man who despises the "opinions of the people" also despises their "language" or "expressions," alternate meanings of *voces*. He is, in other words, a poet who aims at a grand, esoteric vocabulary, a second version of the snob swept away by the Aufidus. In counting the money in his coffers he reminds us of Plautus, at *Epistles* 2.1.175–76, "anxious to drop a coin in his cash-box, careless of whether the play should fall or stand with a straight ankle." Just as his unsound ankle, Plautus's greed symbolizes the compositional defects of his verse. *Loculus*, after all, enjoys the double sense of "cash-box" and "writing tablet."[20]

Besides rivers and wealth, hunger, thirst, fatness, and thinness were common metaphors for style within the parlance of both rhetorical theory and Callimachean polemics. All are involved in the Tantalus illustration of lines 68–70:

> Tantalus a labris sitiens fugientia captat
> flumina—quid rides? Mutato nomine de te
> fabula narratur.

Tantalus in his thirst seeks to draw in the rivers fleeing from his lips— why do you laugh? With the name changed the fable speaks about you.

Why laugh indeed? There is nothing funny about the Tantalus exemplum, other than the triteness of the illustration or perhaps the weak play upon *tantuli* in line 59, until one sees that the "you" ad-

---

[18] See my discussion in the section on Lucilius and Atticist theory in Chapter 3.

[19] On wealth and social status applied to diction, see L. Van Hook, "The Metaphorical Terminology of Greek Rhetoric and Literary Criticism" (Ph.D. diss., University of Chicago, 1905), 27–28. The "Attic" orator, Cicero suggests at *Orator* 83–84, was a spendthrift (see *parcus* and *parsimonia*) when it came to his use of ornaments of diction and thought. See also *De Oratore* 3.185.

[20] The metaphor may be based on an etymological connection (either real or supposed) between *nummus* ("money") and *numerus* ("rhythm"). Compare *numerare* in the sense of "make payment" and its neuter past participle *numeratum*, "cash," "coin."

dressed by these lines refers to rival poets; their words, Horace suggests, "flee from their lips" faster than the rivers pursued by Tantalus. The illustration cleverly combines metaphors of greed, food, drink, and rivers in a cutting jibe against the satirist's literary rivals. Morals, in this case, seem secondary at best to the satirist's literary aims. Against this portrait of insatiate verbal greed the satirist posits his own creed in lines 78–79, playing off the metaphorical possibilities of "poverty" (*paupertas*), which often carries the sense of verbal deficiency:[21] "Of such blessings I might wish to be poorest of the poor" (*Horum / semper ego optarim pauperrimus esse bonorum*).

In the lines that follow, Horace makes the most of yet another metaphor of style (80–83):

> At si condoluit temptatum frigore corpus
> aut alius casus lecto te adfixit, habes qui
> assideat, fomenta paret, medicum roget, ut te
> suscitet ac reddat gnatis carisque propinquis?

> But if your body has suffered, afflicted by a cold, or some other mischance has confined you to bed, do you have some one who will stay at your side, who will prepare the poultices and call the doctor so that he might raise you up and restore you to your children and dear kinsmen?

Horace certainly knew the metaphorical possibilities of "cold" or "chill" (*frigor*) designating bombast, the vice of the grand style.[22] We recall that Catullus was daring enough to imagine Amor sneezing in poem 45, suffering from a head cold brought on by the "chilling," windy conditions of the rhetoric of Septimius and Acme, and in the previous poem (Catullus 44) he himself suffers, laid up by the icy drafts of Sestius's speeches.[23] The lampoon of Furius, at *Satires* 2.5.39–41, demonstrates that Horace too understood the humorous possibilities of the metaphor, and it is likely that he has the same type of lampoon in mind in the passage just quoted.[24] Especially humorous is the reference to "poultices" (*fomenta*) in line 82, which derives from the verb *fovere*, "to make warm." Thus the lines read: "When

---

[21] For examples, see *Paupertas* entry no. 2 in the *Oxford Latin Dictionary*, especially Quintilian 8.3.33, on the "poverty" of Latin vocabulary in contrast to Greek.

[22] Besides *frigor*, Horace may intend us to hear literary connotations in *casus* and *lectus*, line 81.

[23] On the "frigidity" joke of Catullus 45, see M. F. Williams, "Amor's Head-Cold (*Frigus* in Catullus 45)," *Classical Journal* 83 (1988): 128–32. For similar jokes see *Pro Caelio* 25 and (possibly) Lucilius W686. On the metaphor of "frigidity" in ancient theory see L. Van Hook, "Ψυχρότης ἢ τὸ Ψυχρόν," *Classical Philology* 12 (1917): 68–76.

[24] See Freudenburg, "Horace's Satiric Program," 195, n. 18.

the chill [bombast] has afflicted you, do you have someone who will act as critic [*adsideat*] and prepare the 'warmers'?"

Here, as throughout *Satires* 1.1, the moral themes of diatribe serve the demands of a thinly veiled, Callimachean dialogue treating the literary values of the poet and the aims of his satire as poetry. The execution is perfect, for the satirist's moral lessons stand on their own as valid Cynic/Epicurean preaching, a call to observe nature's mean in all areas of life, and nowhere does the satirist give us to suspect that his lessons in morality, though trite and, at times, inept, are somehow extraneous to his satiric mission. Rather, it is in the sustained tension between the apparent and implied meanings of these lessons, that is, the manner in which literary values make themselves felt through moral values without ridiculing or subverting them, that the real sophistication of *Satires* 1.1 is apparent. The preacher, a Bion in Epicurean guise, teaches his lessons concerning nature's mean, moral lessons, which apply at a metaphorical level to the writing of poetry. Thus the moralist is also a good Callimachean who, as he must, introduces his reader to the aesthetic principles of his art in the first poem of his book.

The best illustration of this balance between ethics and aesthetics in *Satires* 1.1 we see in the last lines, in the exemplum of the full dinner guest (117–21):

> Inde fit, ut raro, qui se vixisse beatum
> dicat et exacto contentus tempore vita
> cedat uti conviva satur, reperire queamus.
> Iam satis est, ne me Crispini scrinia lippi
> compilasse putes, verbum non amplius addam.

And so it happens that rarely do we find one who claims to have lived a blessed life and, content with the time passed, will move away from life like a full dinner guest. Enough now, and lest you suppose that I have ripped off the bookcases of bleary-eyed Crispinus, I will add not another word.

The final sentences return us to the question of line 1, "why is it, Maecenas . . . ?" In the end, the satirist follows the conventions of diatribe in concluding that avarice, Bion's "metropolis of evil," is responsible for discontent. As mentioned previously, the abrupt "enough now" (*iam satis est*) of line 120 links the satirist's stylistic principles, his hesitation to add another word, to the traditional moral values he has preached throughout; to be happy with nature's mean, *quod satis est* ("what is enough"), is, in other words, to write good Callimachean satire. The *conviva satur* of line 119, by sharing the name of the genre itself (*satura*), becomes a symbol for the satirist who, only two lines later, abruptly rises from the table and leaves off writing satire. *Iam satis est* then carries connotations of "I'm full now," or better, "It's satire now." In contrast, we see in Crispinus a version of the miser of lines 70–78, Tantalus grasping at rivers, or the snob who loses his life in the muddy waves of the Aufidus. Like the fool of line 110, he sees the "fuller udder" (*distentius uber*) of his neighbor's goat and becomes dissatisfied with his own lot in life. He wants more, and he demonstrates his greed through inelegant, long-winded poetry. In the end, the satirist concludes that discontent and poor verse stem from the same cause: greed, the desire for more. His own practices exemplify contentment; he refuses to add another word.[25]

Like the first diatribe of Book 1, the second also conceals a programmatic focus beneath the conventions of diatribe. Trained in rhetorical theory, Horace knows the metaphorical terms whereby sex becomes a symbol for style, and he freely avails himself of these to set off his aesthetic values against those of his rivals.[26] Different types of women, in this case, symbolize different types of verse, as the Cynic satirist once again calls his listener to avoid extremes, to despise the outward trappings of wealth and status (high-class matrons) as well as outright degradation (prostitutes), and to pursue the middle course.[27] Freedwomen (*libertinae*), pursued within limits, or even household slaves he recommends as natural, safe objects of one's de-

---

[25] Note the mimetic syntax of the final promise: *verbum non amplius addam*. Nothing can follow the satirist's claim "I will not add" without, in turn, making a liar of him. Thus *addam* is the poem's last word.

[26] See especially *Orator* 78–79, where Cicero compares the charm of the Plain Style to women whose beauty requires no enhancement:

Nam ut mulieres pulchriores esse dicuntur nonnullae inornatae quas id ipsum deceat, sic haec subtilis oratio etiam incompta delectat; fit enim quiddam in utroque, quo sit venustius sed non ut appareat. Tum removebitur omnis insignis ornatus quasi margaritarum, ne calamistri quidem adhibebuntur. Fucati vero medicamenta candoris et ruboris omnia repellentur: elegantia modo et munditia remanebit.

For just as certain women are said to be more beautiful when unadorned, since this itself becomes them, so also does this subtle type of oratory give pleasure even when disheveled. There is something in each that enhances beauty while remaining unseen. Every obvious embellishment, pearls as it were, will be removed. Not even the curling irons will be allowed. All the artificial powders of white and red will be rejected; only elegance and neatness will remain.

[27] Consider, for example, line 27 where the opposite extremes of sexual preference and smell represented by Rufillus and Gargonius become compositional/phonetic extremes as Horace posits the lilting *pastillos Rufillus* against the harsh *Gargonius hircum*. I owe the observation to J.G.W. Henderson, "When Satire Writes 'Woman,'" in S. Braund, ed., *Satire and Society in Ancient Rome*, University of Exeter Studies in History 23 (Exeter: University of Exeter Press, 1989), 108.

sires. This all seems very typical of Cynic moralizing, but again the satirist leaves sufficient clues for us to suspect that his lessons concern literature at least as much as they concern morals. Consider, for example, the interlocutor's objection to the young man who earned Cato's praise for choosing to frequent a house of prostitution rather than "grind away at" (*permolere*) other mens' wives (35–38):

> "nolim laudarier" inquit
> "sic me" mirator cunni Cupiennius albi.[28]
> audire est operae pretium procedere recte
> qui moechis rem vultis, ut omni parte laborent.

> "I would rather not be praised for this" says Cupiennius, the admirerer of a high-class cunt. It is worth your while, you who desire the adulterers' steady success, to hear how they face difficulty on every side.[29]

Rudd has suggested that Cupiennius is a significant name chosen on account of its derivation from *cupere* ("to desire"), a claim that makes sense given the aptness of the name to the adulterer described in these lines.[30] Yet the second half of the name, -*ennius*, is equally significant, for line 37 is a direct quote from the *Annals* of Ennius.[31] It can be no accident that the satirist should choose to deride an otherwise unknown "Ennius-lover" with a parodic allusion to Ennius's *Annals* 494–95. The pretentious infinitive *laudarier* in line 35, a piece of grand, archaic diction, suggests that "Ennius-lover," whoever is intended, well deserves his name, and that his love for high-class matrons somehow corresponds to a like preference for diction with a pedigree. These two preferences are really two sides of the same coin, for high-class matrons, throughout this piece, are understood as symbols of literary exuberance, equivalent to the deranged misers of *Satires* 1.1. The literary connotations of *albi, recte*, and *laborent*, ending lines 36–38, serve to confirm the metaphorical reading of these lines.[32]

---

[28] Shackleton Bailey (following Markland) reads *alti* for *albi*.

[29] Similar is Diogenes Laertius 6.88–89 where, standing before the brothel, Crates urges his son Pasicles to avoid the extremes of adultery on the one hand, and taking up with prostitutes on the other. Significantly, he contrasts these extremes in terms of opposed literary types: "The affairs of adulterers belong to tragedy [τραγικούς], entailing exile and destruction, while the affairs of those who take up with prostitutes belong to comedy [κωμικούς], for from luxury and drunkenness comes madness."

[30] Rudd, *Satires of Horace*, 143.

[31] On Cupiennius, see Henderson, "When Satire Writes 'Women,' " 105.

[32] All three terms are attested as stylistic metaphors in the language of late first century rhetorical/literary criticism. At *Controversiae* 7.pr.2 the Elder Seneca relates that Asinius Pollio used to call "white" (*albas*) sentences that were "simple" (*simplices*) and "clear" (*apertae*). Horace himself uses *recte* in reference to compositional style at *Satires*

The end of *Satires* 1.2 proves extremely fertile for a study of Horace's metaphorical technique, for here the satirist allows his implied literary focus to break fully to the surface by setting an epigram of Callimachus directly beside the dictates of Philodemus, a second elegist whose sexual mores represent the aesthetic values that he and Horace share. The satirist prefaces his Latinized version of Callimachus by contrasting the inaccesibility of the matron, dressed in a heavy mantle and surrounded by various low-life attendants, to the open availability of the prostitute, wearing Coan silks, which allow the prospective client "to view her as if nude, and to check against a bad leg [*crure malo*] or an unsightly foot [*pede turpi*]." Either Horace is not much of a lover, as he keeps his eyes fixed on the legs and feet of a prostitute who, otherwise, has nothing to hide, or he realizes that lines of poetry, unlike a prostitute, have no silken hair, breasts, buttocks, or whatever (at least none of which I am aware); they have been known, however, to "limp" from time to time, having a bad "leg" or "foot," metaphors for a faulty compositional technique. He proceeds against the matron-lovers (103–8):

> An tibi mavis
> insidias fieri pretiumque avellier ante
> quam mercem ostendi? "Leporem venator ut alta
> in nive sectetur, positum sic tangere nolit,"
> cantat et adponit "Meus est amor huic similis; nam
> transvolat in medio posita et fugientia captat."

Or would you rather be taken in and have the price snatched from you before the merchandise is shown? "As a hunter pursues the hare amid deep snows, but refuses to touch it when ready at hand," he drones on and adds "so my love is similar; for it flitters past those things set in the middle and makes for things that flee."

Fugientia captat, ending line 108, is not simply a translation of Callimachus' τὰ μὲν φεύγοντα διώκειν; it also recalls the Tantalus exemplum of *Satires* 1.1 where, in line 68, the satirist describes Tantalus in precisely the same terms: "he seeks to draw in the rivers fleeing from his lips

---

1.4.13, claiming that Lucilius was too lazy to undergo the toil of "straight writing" (*scribendi recte*, for Greek ὀρθογραφία, a synonym for Ἑλληνισμός). Compare *Brutus* 262, where Cicero lauds the compositional style of Caesar's *Commentaries*: "Certainly they are without cover, straight and lovely, as if all of oratory's embellishments, like a garment, have been stripped away" (*nudi enim sunt, recti et venusti, omni ornatu orationis tamquam veste detracta*). Here *rectus* refers to a spare, straightforward compositional technique devoid of grand style embellishment. For the same sense in later criticism compare Pliny *Epistles* 9.26.1. For negative literary connotations of *laborare* compare Horace *Satires* 1.10.73 and *Ars Poetica* 25.

[*flumina . . . fugientia captat*]."[33] These rivers, we recall, are rivers of words, symbols of literary excess.[34] We wonder, then, whether in recalling the greed of Tantalus the satirist intends something more in his adaptation of Callimachus (*Epigrams* 31 Pfeiffer) than a lesson against vain amorous pursuits. If rivers fleeing the lips of greedy Tantalus can be words, so can animals as they flee the hunter who pursues but refuses to overtake them. Equally suggestive is the lover's claim to deliberately pass by "those things set in the middle" (*in medio posita*), for in the language of theory, themes and words were commonly spoken of as drawn "from the middle" (*de medio*), that is, from everyday stock.[35] The lover of lines 105–8, we understand, has poetic pretensions, a disdain for everyday themes and diction, to match his amorous pursuits. The satirist responds with an Epicurean objection, claiming that "such drivel" (*hiscine versiculis*) is useless for removing cares from the heart; that nature has established a certain "mean" (*modus*, also the word for a rhythmic pattern, "meter"), a limit to human desires.

At lines 120–24, the satirist makes the Epicurean's case for an "easy" or "attainable" (*parabilem*, for Greek εὐπόριστον) lust, one that respects nature's limits:[36]

> Illam "post paullo"; "Sed pluris"; "Si exierit vir"
> Gallis, hanc Philodemus ait sibi, quae neque magno
> stet pretio neque cunctetur, cum est iussa venire.
> Candida rectaque sit, munda hactenus, ut neque longa
> nec magis alba velit quam dat natura videri.

That one who says, "a little later," "it'll cost you more," or "if my husband leaves" is for the Gauls, says Philodemus; for himself he prefers a woman who neither costs too much nor delays when asked to come. Let her be fair and straight, refined to the point that she appears neither taller nor whiter than nature permits.

Unlike the Callimachean of lines 105–8, Philodemus prefers an "easy Venus," something between the prostitute and the matron. Philodemus is, of course, the perfect foil for Callimachus, for he too was heralded in Rome as an elegist and theorist of the first order. His

---

[33] On these lines, see Cody, *Horace and Callimachean Aesthetics*, 113–19.

[34] On *captare* applied to word selection and arrangement, compare *Moral Epistles* 100.5 (quoted previously in Chapter 3), where Seneca defends Fabianus by asserting that his words are "selected" (*electa*), not "hunted down" (*captata*).

[35] Compare the *ex medio* of *Epistles* 2.1.168, on comic themes, and *de medio* of *Orator* 163, on word choice.

[36] On the relation of *Satires* 1.2 to Epicurean theories of "natural" and "necessary" desires, see Fiske, *Lucilius and Horace*, 260–64.

reputation as an Epicurean womanizer does not seem to extend beyond these lines for, in the end, his sentiments have far more to do with poetry than they do with sex. We see, for example, that the adjectives chosen to describe the perfect, natural object of one's lusts, namely, a woman who is *candida, recta, munda, longa,* and even *alba,* all possess literary connotations, enjoying a second life in the metaphorical terminology of Latin literary criticism.[37] The perfect lover, then, is also the perfect poem, drawn within means dictated by nature. Poems outside of these means, Philodemus claims, are "for the Gauls" (*Gallis*). The claim has all the markings of a sophisticated literary jibe, playing off the multivalence of *Gallis*; for as a plural form of *Gallus,* couched in a distinctly elegiac context, the expostulation would be heard as not only a reference to the castrated priests of Cybele but also as an allusion to Gallus himself, Rome's most famous elegiac poet to date and a famous emulator of Callimachus.[38] "For the Gauls," then, becomes "for the Galluses," as a type of woman becomes a type of poetic pursuit. To make love to this type of woman is to risk punishment at the hands of her husband. The satire ends with doors crashing and dogs barking as the adulterer attempts to flee for his life. We see him struggle to gather his "loose tunic" (*discincta tunica*) attempting to run, significantly, "with a bare foot" (*pede nudo*).[39] From the metaphorical terminology of Greek and Roman literary criticism Horace understood that, like an adulterer on the run, poorly constructed lines of poetry could be imagined as "loose" or "disheveled," "hobbling along" at an uneven pace. As a parting shot he suggests

[37] On *recta* and *alba* as stylistic metaphors, see my n. 32. For *candor* and *candidus* as designations of a smooth compositional technique, compare *Orator* 53, where Cicero contrasts Atticist harshness (*duritia* and *severitas*) with the "smoothness" (*lenitas*) and "evenness" (*aequabilitas*) characteristic of a "pure and clear style of speech" (*puro et candido genere dicendi*). At *Institutes* 10.1.113 Quintilian describes Horace's friend M. Messala Corvinus as "polished and clear" (*nitidus et candidus*) in contrast to the more rugged, "archaic" Pollio. *Mundus,* in contrast, is used of a plain compositional style. Compare the literary range of *munditia* at *Orator* 79 (quoted in n. 26) and at *Attic Nights* 10.24.2, where Gellius refers to Augustus as "a follower of his father's purity of speech" (*munditiarum patris sui in sermonibus sector*). On the metaphorical possibilities of a "long foot" (*pede longo,* line 94), see Hinds, *Persephone,* 16–17, especially his reference to the *pes longior* of Ovid *Amores* 3.1.8. For other references to these terms as metaphors of style, see the Latin indexes to Van Hook, "Metaphorical Terminology," and Leeman, *Orationis Ratio.*

[38] For a second jibe against Gallus at *Satires* 2.1.13–15, see Freudenburg, "Horace's Satiric Program," 194, n. 15.

[39] On the "loose tunic" (*solutus* and *discinctus*) as a metaphor for compositional deficiency, compare Seneca *Moral Epistles* 114.4. He says of Maecenas: *Non oratio eius aeque soluta est quam ipse discinctus?* ("Was not his oratory every bit as loose as the unbelted man himself?").

that Fabius, a writer of Stoic diatribes, knows just how bad it can be to be caught with one's tunic down (1.2.134): "It is miserable to be caught: I could win this case even with Fabius serving as judge" (*Deprendi miserum est: Fabio vel iudice vincam*).

The metaphorical readings proposed for *Satires* 1.1 and 1.2 make sense of these poems as something more than simpleminded moralizing, the early experiments of a poet struggling to hit his proper stride. As highly allusive, fine-spun verse, *Satires* 1.1 and 1.2 are as good as anything Horace ever wrote. While neither of the readings proposed has pretensions to completeness or final judgment on the satirist's programmatic aims, they do demonstrate that the diatribes contain complex metaphorical possibilities, which have been previously unnoticed. As descriptions of the satirist's poetic values they are, in the end, every bit as important as *Satires* 1.4 and 1.10, traditionally regarded as the only "literary" or "programmatic" satires of Book 1. The literary message buried in these pieces does not undermine or mock the satirist's moral intent. Rather, as we have seen, the universal nature of ancient theory demands that what is true of a good line of poetry must also in some sense be true of a good human being. There can be no discrepancy. Horace makes the most of this thinking in the first two satires of Book 1.

IMAGES OF THE SATIRIST AND THE STRUCTURE OF BOOK 1

Horace understood the power of arrangement at all levels. From individual sounds set side by side, to adjacent words, clauses, sentences, and finally entire poems, he actively sought to convey meaning through the placement of disparate parts, making a living creature, a book of *Satires*, from lifeless limbs. In spite of much study, the larger structures of the *Satires* have eluded any generally acceptable interpretation. Book 1 is an obvious case in point, for here, among other possible arrangements, commentators have found evidence for a ring structure,[40] a pattern of responsion around the fifth poem,[41] and divisions into halves,[42] pairs,[43] and triads,[44] all of which possess merit,

---

[40] H. Dettmer, *Horace: A Study in Structure*, Altertumswissenschaftliche Texte und Studien 12 (Hildesheim: Olms, 1983), 34.

[41] R. Rambaux, "La composition d'ensemble du Livre I des *Satires* d'Horace," *Revue des Études Latines* 49 (1971): 179–204. See also Zetzel, "Horace's *Liber Sermonum*," 67 and n. 48.

[42] Fraenkel, *Horace*, 101.

[43] C. A. van Rooy, "Arrangement and Structure of Satires in Horace, *Sermones*, Book 1, with More Special Reference to Satires 1–4," *Acta Classica* 11 (1968): 38–72.

[44] H. Ludwig, "Die Komposition der beiden Satirenbücher des Horaz," *Poetica* 2 (1968): 304–35.

though the best of these is weak and carries no appreciable semantic force.[45] From a traditional structural standpoint, we can only conclude that Horace intends a whole system of correspondences to be felt in Book 1 rather than a single, fixed structure, which it simply does not possess.

Perhaps the most persistent problem in identifying the structural aims of the poet concerns not the poems themselves but the methods of commentators who hunt out structural clues at all levels (dictional, thematic, metrical, and so on) simultaneously, making no serious effort to limit themselves to criteria that are generically similar from poem to poem. Some look for a balance of themes, beginning with the obvious corresponsion of the "literary" pieces 1.4 and 1.10, whereas others find meaning in smaller, less obvious connections, such as the appearance of the satirist's father (1.4 and 1.6), the journey motif (1.5 and 1.9), sexual content (1.2 and 1.8), or, even slighter, the word *rex* in lines ending *Satires* 1.3 and 1.7 or the reference to the Jews (*Iudaei*) linking *Satires* 1.4 to 1.5. Given this method, who is to say that the satirist has not actually organized his poems according to his use of words ending in the letter *s*? Certainly a better approach must be sought, and Zetzel has made significant progress in this direction by focusing on the persona of the satirist, a criterion that, however subjective, can at least be studied from poem to poem.[46]

In spite of obvious methodological difficulties, certain patterns, however weak, do emerge from even a superficial reading of Book 1. We can be sure, for example, that Horace intended some correspondences between the invocations of Maecenas in the opening lines of *Satires* 1.1 and 1.6, dividing the book into halves after the manner of the *Eclogues*. The correspondence hints at symmetry, perhaps even an interlocking pattern as some have suggested.[47] Yet, in the end, the satirist fails to deliver. The obvious balance of *Satires* 1.4 and 1.10 constitutes the most obvious break in the pattern. More successful is the triadic division favored by most critics, but here again the satirist only hints at a structure, which he ultimately fails to deliver, for the diatribes, we have seen, have as much to do with literary theory as they do with morals, and thus the lines that have traditionally been

[45] For a survey of the various arrangements proposed for Book 1 since Heinze, see Rambaux, "Livre I des *Satires* d'Horace," and Dettmer, *Horace*, 32–35, especially n. 36. Oberhelman's "Satire as Poetry," which contains useful notes on previous scholarship, is the best overall study of the structure of Book 1, treating satires 5–9 as sequential and corresponsive exemplars of the *res/verba, ars/ingenium* theories of *Satires* 1.4 and 1.10.

[46] Compositional technique, so important to the program pieces 1.4 and 1.10, might well lend itself to similar study.

[47] On the so-called ring structure of *Satires* Book 1, see Dettmer, *Horace*, 34.

used to set off *Satires* 1.1–1.3 from 1.4–1.6, the strictly "moral" from the "literary," become severely blurred. The triads, though they exist in some fashion, have no appreciable semantic significance; they are loose and suggestive rather than neatly set off.[48]

Numerous patterns suggest themselves in Book 1, so that as we stand back from individual poems to view the book as a whole, we see the intricate, blended patterns of a mosaic or an embroidered cloth, Zetzel's "structure of ambiguity," not the rigid symmetries of the Doric order. Analogies with needlework, paintings, and mosaics were well known to the ancient theorists of composition, including Horace, who favored representations of living creatures to architectural models, as proper symbols of compositional expertise.[49] Zetzel was the first to break from the architectural mode in the study of Book 1, insisting that the satirist's elusiveness is apparent not only in individual poems, but in the shape of the book as a whole, forming a "coherent pattern of incoherence." Rigid symmetries do not make for good satire, at least as far as Horace is concerned, so that whatever pattern he offers he is quick to undermine. This is the logic of conversation at the level of the entire book, and as with conversation, the only way to follow the speaker's train of thought is to begin where he begins and end where he ends. Zetzel writes: "the only significant chronology in a *liber* of this sort is that of unrolling the book: that we are to read the first poem before the second, the second before the third. . . . Any interpretation that takes the poems out of order separates them from the literal unrolling of time and ignores the poet's clear intention."[50] Individual satires, in other words, are perfectly "placed," blending into the contexture of the surrounding poems. They are larger versions of the Epicurean's *callida iunctura*, the well-placed word whose sound and sense both influence and recieve influence from the words to the left and right. Following this model, the challenge comes in seeing an individual satire, such as *Satires* 1.10, not only as a piece of architecture, a balanced response to its thematic counterpart, 1.4, but as a tile in a mosaic, adapted to the shape of neighboring poems, blurring into the contexture of *Satires* 1.9.

[48] On the triadic arrangement of *Satires* Book 1, see especially Ludwig, "Die Komposition der beiden Satirenbücher des Horaz," 304–35.

[49] Compare the opening lines of the *Ars Poetica* in which Horace compares a poorly arranged poem to a grotesque painting filled with fantastic, hybrid creatures "as in a sick man's dreams" (*velut aegri somnia*). Where architectural models are in fact used (see especially *On Word Arrangement* 6), stress is given to the knitting together of stone to stone, brick to brick, rather than to the arrangement of composite units (columns, doors, etc.) or to the overall structure.

[50] Zetzel, "Horace's *Liber Sermonum*," 63.

A clear example of such contextual arrangement we see in the placement of *Satires* 1.5, which both adds meaning to and takes meaning from the poems that surround it. Several scholars have noted that *Satires* 1.5, as the most obvious imitation of Lucilius in the entire book, responds to the criticisms of 1.4, inviting the reader to compare Lucilius and Horace not only at the level of theory but in the actual practice of writing satire.[51] In *Satires* 1.4 Horace claims that Lucilius is a "muddy" composer and that there is much "to be removed" (*tollenda*) from his verse. In 1.5, therefore, he illustrates this critique by taking an entire book of Lucilius, Book 3, which contained only one satire, and condensing it into a mere 104 lines. Classen has studied the fragmentary remains of the Lucilian model to indicate the radical shift in focus and tone that marks the Horatian version of the trip: Horace strips his account to the bare essentials, eliminating the verbal excess, repetitions, and elaborate descriptions that are apparent in nearly all the extant remains of Lucilius Book 3. Even an introduction and conclusion Horace regarded as extraneous. Several times in the poem Horace pokes fun at his own brevity, underscoring the studied nature of his reductions. By the end of line 1, for example, he has covered the sixteen miles from Rome to Aricia, and by line 3 he has reached Forum Appi, another twenty-seven miles. Even so, he apologizes for the sluggish pace of the opening leg of his trip (*Satires* 1.5.5–6):

> Hoc iter ignavi divisimus, altius ac nos
> praecinctis unum; minus est gravis Appia tardis.

> Lazy, we divided this leg of the trip, which is a one-day journey for those girded higher than we; the Appian Way is less taxing for those who take it slow.

[51] Classen observes: "Certainly *Satire* 1.5 does not follow 1.4 by chance; it seeks not only to describe a journey of Horace and to depict modes of human relationships in terms of personal experiences and thereby to incite reflection, it seeks at the same time to exemplify Horace's critique of Lucilius, or at least to illustrate it through its own individual character and form, which is Horace's aim." See C. J. Classen, "Die Kritik des Horaz in den Satiren I 4 und I 5," *Hermes* 109 (1981): 341. The single best treatment of *Satires* 1.5 (with a summary review of scholarship) is K. Sallmann, "Die seltsame Reise nach Brundisium. Aufbau und Deutung der Horazsatire 1,5," in U. Reinhardt and K. Sallmann, eds., *Musa Iocosa: Arbeiten über Humor und Witz Komik und Komödie der Antike* (Hildesheim: Olms, 1974), 179–206. Sallmann has demonstrated that the *aemulatio Lucilii* is but one of the satirist's many aims in *Satires* 1.5 and should not, therefore, be singled out as the satire's "primary" or "only" intention. In contrast to many earlier studies of 1.5, which take the satire as straightforward emulation of Lucilius, epic parody, or even political allegory, Sallmann makes clear that reading a Horatian satire is a synesthetic event, an experience inseparable from the text and only weakly conveyed by abstract studies of the author's "intention."

Perhaps Lucilius, in the earlier version of the journey, had been "girded higher," making the trip in one day rather than two. The joke here is that Horace, at the same time as he "divides" the trip to Forum Appi, extending it to two days, "divides" his account of the trip, cutting it in half or less.[52] The next leg of the journey, day 3, requires a full twenty-four lines as opposed to the nine lines traversed in days 1 and 2. The pace of the description, in this case, is dictated by the ruggedness of the terrain, the Pomptine marshes, and the three-mile "crawl" (*repimus*, 25) from Lucus Feroniae to Anxur. Even so, the pace of the satirist's account is relatively brisk, calling attention to itself in the *tota abit hora* ("an entire hour passes") of line 14. An entire hour passes in five syllables, hastened by the elision between *tota* and *abit*. Here again, the satirist calls us to take note of his technique, which he continues to underscore throughout the piece, such as in the omission of *est* and the double service of *praebuit* in lines 45–46, or the *paucis* lacking its *verbis* in line 51. He concludes in the last lines with a final allusion to the brevity he has sought throughout: "Brundisium concludes both a long page and a long journey" (*Brundisium longae finis chartaeque viaeque est*). The trip certainly was long, requiring fifteen days for what is normally a five-day journey, but its description by Horace fills not an entire book, like its Lucilian model, but a single "long page."[53]

Besides the studied brevity of this piece, Rambaux, following Nilsson, has noted that *Satires* 1.5 and 1.10 are the most metrically complex poems of Book 1, suggesting that Horace has made attention to compositional technique, the central focus of his critique of Lucilius in 1.4, one of the primary aims of the satire. Horace intends us even to hear a distinct rhythmic improvement upon his model.[54] Here again, we see that *Satires* 1.5 has been carefully placed. It could not possibly precede *Satires* 1.4 and carry the same significance, inviting attention to its clean, brisk lines and the compositional savvy, which set it off from the muddy verse of its model. This is the critique of

---

[52] Considering the metaphorical range of *discinctus* (see n. 39), *praecinctis* in line 6 may well allude to the satirist's compositional technique.

[53] On the excessive length of Horace's journey, see W. Ehlers, "Das 'Iter Brundisinum' des Horaz (Serm. 1,5)," *Hermes* 113 (1985): 70.

[54] See Rambaux, "Livres I des *Satires* d'Horace," 184. For useful notes on the structure of *Satires* 1.5, see Sallmann, (1971) "Horazsatire 1, 5," 186–94, who argues that, in the narrator's constant shift of tense, perspective, and style, Horace employs a studied varietal technique in order to obscure the careful arrangement of the satire, which Sallmann divides into two similar halves containing a large episode followed by smaller concluding episodes, the first headed by a nine-verse introduction, the second followed by a nine-verse "coda."

Satires 1.4 made real. Talk about satire has become the genuine article.

Besides looking back to 1.4, *Satires* 1.5 provides a context for the poem that follows, adding meaning to the satirist's autobiographical statements in 1.6. Ever since the opening lines of *Satires* 1.1, the position of the satirist in the circle of Maecenas has been left curiously ambiguous; he appears as an outsider in *Satires* 1.1 and 1.2, a preacher haranguing his audience in the streets and a most unlikely candidate for inclusion among the friends of Maecenas. In 1.3 he pictures himself on close terms with Maecenas, a simpleton philosopher in regal company. Though respected as a dear friend, he makes a nuisance of himself by disrupting Maecenas while studying or at rest: "The pest!" Maecenas complains, "He clearly lacks social tact!" (1.3.65–66). The mention of the parasite Maenius at 1.3.20–23 connects the satirist with the gossipmonger who hunts out vices to earn his bread. The charge is raised again and soundly refuted in *Satires* 1.4, where the satirist makes his critics play the parasite's role in lines 78–103;[55] yet, in *Satires* 1.5 he again subjects himself to the charge of being a lackey of Maecenas, a parasite and nothing more. The year is 37 B.C. Rome once again is on the brink of civil war. We might expect some rather deep reflection from the satirist on the gravity of the situation, a description of Sextus Pompey's menacing fleet or an account of the serious counsel he offered Maecenas along the way. Instead, we learn in the satire's first lines that the accommodations offered at Aricia were mediocre (*modico*), at least by the standards of "great Rome" (*magna Roma*), whose comforts, it seems, the narrator knows well and regrets ever having left.[56] In lines 3–4 he complains of some unspecified trouble with "cheating tavernkeepers" at Forum Appi, and in lines 5–6 he admits to being "lazy" (*ignavus*) and "slow moving" (*tardus*) on the first leg of the trip. As the description proceeds, he complains about bad water and an upset stomach (7–8, 49, 88, 91), mosquitoes, frogs, and noisy sailors (14–17), irritated eyes (30, 49, and 80–81), a cheating prostitute (82–85), bad bread (91) and muddy roads (94–97). The largest single description in the satire he reserves for a mock-epic exchange of abuse between Messius and Sarmentus, an oaf and a freed slave. The scene and its characters have precedents in local farce, widely regarded among Romans as the low-

---

[55] On these lines, see especially C. Damon, "Vetus atque Antiquus Quaestus: The art of the Parasite in Ancient Rome" (Ph.D. diss., Stanford University, 1990), 141–46.

[56] Compare lines 45–51, the unfavorable contrast of the "little house" (*villula*) beside the Campanian bridge, offering only the minimum "wood and salt" (*ligna salemque*), with the "well-stocked villa" (*plenissima villa*) of Cocceius, conveniently located above the taverns of Caudium.

est of low humor.[57] Elsewhere he enjoys recalling the misadventures
of a drunken sailor and his mule who sustained beatings at the hands
of an angry traveler, and he remembers how the ravenous dinner
guests and slaves, himself included, hastened to save their meals before putting out a fire in the kitchen at Beneventum.[58]

All of this suggests that the satirist is himself a lowlife, a parasite of
Maecenas brought along for comic relief.[59] He does not discuss the
big issues, the matters of life and death that stand behind the journey, because he is neither interested in them nor can he be trusted
with matters of real importance. Parasites, after all, are notorious for
their "leaky ears." Throughout *Satires* 1.5, the satirist constantly jux-
taposes the high and the low, trivializing his own character in the process.[60] His incessant complaints have a cumulative effect, suggesting
that not only is he a parasite, but a novice who has yet to learn the
finer techniques of milking one's patron. Comparison with *Epistles*
1.17, a lesson on the art of buffoonery, suggests that the satirist's
complaints have been carefully contrived. The poet warns the novice
Scaeva (*Epistles* 1.17.52–57):

> The man who is taken as a traveling companion to Brundisium or pleas-
> ant Surrentum, when he complains about bad roads, bitter cold, and
> rain, or he moans that his case has been broken open and his travel al-
> lowance pilfered, he recalls the well-known tricks of a mistress who
> weeps because a necklace has been stolen from her, often an anklet, so
> that soon no trust remains for losses and sorrows that are true.

Playing the part of a buffoon as yet unschooled in the finer traditions
of his art, the satirist complains about bad roads and rain (lines 94–
96), an all too obvious ploy to win the sympathy of his patron. Although his suitcase seems to have survived intact, his other com-

---

[57] On the relation of the mock-epic contest of *Satires* 1.10 to the *fabula Atellana*, see
Fiske, *Lucilius and Horace*, 363, n. 217.

[58] In lines 72–73 we note with what disdain the narrator mentions the "crummy little
thrushes" (*macros turdos*) served in the "ancient kitchen" (*veterem culinam*) at Beneventum, as if to imply that the host well deserved his harsh treatment from Vulcan.

[59] On the journey as epic parody and the narrator as picaresque hero, see Sallmann,
"Horazsatire 1, 5," 200–6.

[60] This juxtaposition is especially obvious at lines 27–31, set off by the *huc* and *hic*
beginning lines 27 and 30: "For this point [*huc*, that is, Anxur] was bound the most
excellent Maecenas and Cocceius, both sent as legates on important business, old hands
at bringing together friends who were at odds. Here [*hic*] I, for my part, daubed dark
salve on my bleary eyes." Ehlers, "Iter Brundisinum," 71, remarks on these lines:
"There exists a striking contrast between the importance of the two delegations, on the
one hand, and the triviality of Horace's discomforts on the other. Still, Horace's con-
junctivitis is thoroughly framed by the three verses devoted to the delegations."

plaints are equally trivial and unworthy of Maecenas's attention. Throughout *Satires* 1.5 his chief interests concern his own comfort; his eyes, his stomach, a good night's sleep, laughs at the local tavern and a slave girl who keeps her promise. This attitude, coupled with his praise of Maecenas and his friends, which is effusive and disproportionate to the size of the satire as a whole, makes of him the perfect parasite. The portrait, though conventionally accurate and certainly humorous, bears little resemblance to the poet Horace or to the actual status he enjoyed in the circle of Maecenas's friends.

The charge refuted in *Satires* 1.3 and 1.4 is fully supported by the image of the satirist in 1.5. Horace gives no easy answers. As with the various structural arrangements already mentioned, so with his persona, he immediately undermines the pattern he has just created. In *Satires* 1.6 he shifts again, positing himself not as a buffoon, but as Maecenas's noble advisor valued for his friendship and frank advice. The conventional side of this portrait was noted by Fiske:

> In short, the relation of Horace to Maecenas has certain analogies to that of Bion of Borysthenes to Antigonus Gonatas. . . . Bion too sought to disarm attacks upon his humble origin by proudly and frankly acknowledging it and laying stress upon his worth as a man. Hence the text of this satire is essentially that of Bion's famous letter to Antigonus Gonatas.[61]

The most obvious connection linking *Satires* 1.6 to Bion is the repeated *libertino patre natum* ("son of a freedman father") ending lines 6, 45, and 46, a translation of Bion's ἐμοῦ ὁ πατὴρ ἦν ἀπελεύθερος. As with Antigonus, noble birth counts for little with Maecenas who, upon his first meeting with Horace, saw something of value in the humble demeanor and halting words of the freedman's son (*Satires* 1.6.56–62):

> Ut veni coram, singultim pauca locutus—
> infans namque pudor prohibebat plura profari—
> non ego me claro natum patre, non ego circum
> me Satureiano vectari rura caballo,
> sed quod eram narro. Respondes, ut tuus mos,
> pauca; abeo, et revocas nono post mense iubesque
> esse in amicorum numero.

I came into your presence and spoke a few halting lines—for my childish bashfulness kept me from saying more—I did not say that I was the son of a famous father, nor did I claim to ride about the countryside on a

[61] Fiske, *Lucilius and Horace*, 316.

Saturian steed, but I said what I was. In your usual fashion you gave a
brief response. I left, and nine months later you called me back and
asked me to join the number of your friends.

One would never know from this description that the poor freedman's son was well off, enjoying equestrian status and a substantial
income as a *scriba quaestorius* even in the years before his introduction
to Maecenas. *Satires* 1.6 makes clear that by 35 B.C. he was eligible
even for senatorial status, yet throughout this piece he persists in
magnifying the humble origins which he so clearly overcame.[62] Similar are the later program pieces *Odes* 2.20, *Odes* 3.30, and *Epistles* 1.20,
all of which contain references to the satirist's origins and command
special notice as the final poems in their respective books. The theme
obviously has programmatic possibilities, signifying the "sparing
style" (*genus parvum*) of refined Callimachean verse.[63] The satirist humorously suggests that "shame" (*pudor*), not Callimachean brevity,
prevented him from versifying at length during his initial meeting
with Maecenas. His country modesty, in other words, somehow ex-
tended even to his verse. He could not afford an expensive thoroughbred from his home region, the "Saturian steed" of line 60. It is no
accident that the name of the horse is also the name of the genre that
Horace "rode into" the circle of Maecenas; yet, unlike the horse that
goes by its name, satire has no high-flown pretensions. Horace came
to Maecenas, in other words, not claiming to ride a "thoroughbred"
named satire; rather, he wrote verse that somehow reflected his status
as a poor freedman's son. In lines 104–6 he pictures himself riding
about the countryside not on a stallion, but a gelded mule:

> Nunc mihi curto
> ire licet mulo vel si libet usque Tarentum,
> mantica cui lumbos onere ulceret atque eques armos.

As things are now, if I please I can travel all the way to Tarentum on my
gelded mule, with the saddlebag chafing his loins and the horseman his
shoulders.

Horace, the Roman *eques* ("horseman"), rides not the regulation stallion, but a gelded mule which carries him and his meager supplies
"all the way to Tarentum," the breeding place of Saturian steeds.[64]

---

[62] Armstrong, following Gow and Willems, suggests that *Satires* 1.6 may be read as
Horace's refusal to stand for senatorial office after an initial offer of support by Maecenas. See Armstrong, "*Horatius Eques*," 267–77.

[63] On the metaphorical possiblities of the theme, see Mette, "*Genus Tenue*," 223–24.

[64] On the joke of the mule-riding horseman of *Satires* 1.3.104–6, see Armstrong, *Horace*, 19.

The image is as unlikely as it is humorous, an apt foil to the pretensions of Tillius, a fellow freedman's son mocked in the lines that follow. Whether or not Horace was a mule driver in real life, he realized the metaphorical possibilities implied in his unassuming mode of transportation, for in the terminology of rhetorical criticism, horse riding was a common symbol for poetry as opposed to traveling "by foot" (πεζὸς λόγος, *oratio pedestris*), signifying prose.[65] The more haughty the thoroughbred the grander the verse. Horace, we saw in the previous chapter, had no grand style pretensions for satire, which he regarded as a type of versified prose, a "walking muse." The gelded mule is the perfect symbol for this type of verse, for the satirist is indeed a "rider," that is, a versifier, but he remains close to the ground, traveling just above the walker's pace. His diction, like his mule, has no pedigree.[66] The fact that the mule is "gelded" is also significant, for the term *curtus* enjoyed a second life in compositional theory, where it carried the sense of "cut short," or "curtailed."[67] Here again, the humble pretensions of the satirist's life-style make themselves felt in his verse.

Satires 1.6 concludes with the portrait of the Epicurean sage, an image that, as Armstrong has shown, is every bit as conventional as the description of the buffoon in *Satires* 1.5 or the Cynic moralizer of the diatribes.[68] As mentioned in Chapter 1, the satirist offers no consistent image of himself outside of the diatribe satires in Book 1. In 1.4 he denies that he is a *scurra* of Maecenas, the very image he adopts in 1.5, whereas in 1.6 he abandons the frivolous clown of the previous satire to play an Epicurean Bion, noble advisor to Maecenas. In *Satires* 1.7 and 1.8, the unassuming philosopher gives way to two tactless jesters who undermine all the intellectual and social progress that *Satires* 1.6 seems to imply.[69] *Satires* 1.7 tells the story of Rex and Persius, an outcast and a half-breed who staged a slave's battle of

[65] On the metaphors of walking and horsemanship, see Van Hook, "Metaphorical Terminology," 25.

[66] Compare *Satires* 1.1.88–91, where the satirist chides the rich fool: "But if you should wish to hold fast your sons [*cognatos*] and preserve your friends, whom nature [*natura*] has granted to you without effort [*labore*], your hard work would be wasted, just as if one were to teach an ass to heed the reins and run on the Campus." The terms highlighted contain definite literary connotations. Read metaphorically, the passage lampoons an inept writer of satire for his grand, epic pretensions. He has attempted to make an ass (satire) ride on the Campus Martius, the training ground for the Roman cavalry (epic). Note also that lines 113–16 picture the avaricious as drivers in a chariot race.

[67] See Van Hook, "Metaphorical Terminology," 21.

[68] See Armstrong, "*Horatius Eques*," 277–85, on the "Epicurean day" topos.

[69] I owe the observation to Zetzel, "Horace's *Liber Sermonum*," 71.

abuse, comparable with the exchange between Sarmentus and Cicirrus, in a lawsuit tried before Brutus in 43 B.C. The satirist is himself a lowlife, relating in the opening lines that he picked up the story from the gossipmongers and barbers with whom he apparently has regular contact. The entire scene he stages as a gladiator fight, which again reflects negatively on his status.[70] Although the satire is certainly not Horace's best, it deserves more credit than it has traditionally received for its buried literary allusions and aesthetic aims. *Satires* 1.7 is, after all, a battle between modes of rhetoric, the extremes of Atticism and Asianism exemplified in the practices of Rex, a rugged, purebred Italian, and Persius, a half-breed whose dubious birth makes itself felt in his oratory. The entire scene is played out before Brutus, Rome's principal advocate of Atticist oratory and the addressee of Cicero's *Brutus* and *Orator*. Fiske has shown that the satire invites comparison with Lucilius Book 2, the lawsuit lodged by Titus Albucius against Quintus Mucius Scaevola on the charge of extortion in Asia.[71] Like *Satires* 1.5, its Lucilian companion, *Satires* 1.7 reduces an entire book of Lucilius to a single page. In this case, however, the reduction is more pronounced, for the whole of *Satires* 1.7 amounts to no more than thirty-five lines, falling well short of even the fragmentary remains of its Lucilian model. Callimachean brevity, in other words, increases from *Satires* 1.5 to 1.7 as the satirist continues to improve upon his Lucilian models. In *Satires* 1.8 and 1.10 he attempts to Romanize none other than Callimachus himself.[72]

Satires 1.9 once again raises the question of Horace's status in the circle of Maecenas. His answer, Zetzel has shown, reflects the larger ambiguities of the entire book, for in spite of his smug demeanor and secure position among Maecenas's friends, the satirist is not far from the pest whom he despises.[73] Read in the context of its immediate neighbors, we see that the speaker's self-satisfaction in *Satires* 1.9 is tainted; he is himself a social climber, an outsider in *Satires* 1.1 who becomes all things for Maecenas along the way before finally attaining the respectability sought by outsiders in *Satires* 1.9. He is now an *amicus* ("friend") of Maecenas, a position he describes in *Epistles* 1.18 as a virtue between the extremes of the faithless parasite and the Cynic, roles he has played in earlier satires. Even so, his foibles are apparent. Among other suggestions offered in *Epistles* 1.18, Horace

[70] Compare *Satires* 2.7.95–100, where Davus's love for gladiatorial contests is set against Horace's love of fine painting as a conventional indicator of his slave status.

[71] See Fiske, *Lucilius and Horace*, 325–30.

[72] On the Callimachean precedents of *Satires* 1.4, 1.8, and 1.10, see my discussion at the end of Chapter 2.

[73] See Zetzel, "Horace's *Liber Sermonum*," 71.

advises Lollius to "avoid the questioner, for he is also garrulous [*idem garrulus est*] and his ears, always ready to listen, will not retain secrets committed in good faith" (*Epistles* 1.18.69–70). He continues in lines 76–81:

> Qualem commendes, etiam atque etiam aspice, ne mox
> incutiant aliena tibi peccata pudorem.
> Fallimur et quondam non dignum tradimus: ergo
> quem sua culpa premet, deceptus omitte tueri,
> ut penitus notum, si temptent crimina, serves
> tuterisque tuo fidentem praesidio.

Again and again, be careful of what sort of person you recommend [to your patron], lest someone else's blunders cause you shame. Sometimes we are deceived and introduce someone who is unworthy. In that case, once deceived, do not protect him when he is troubled by his own faults. Then, when charges are leveled against one you know well, you may preserve and defend him who relies on your protection.

Perhaps Horace knew from bitter experience the pains associated with committing his patron's secrets to a gossip or recommending to Maecenas an acquaintance who later proved unworthy. Given the parallels between *Satires* 1.9 and *Epistles* 1.18, it is more likely that the advice that he both gives and heeds he did not learn from experience, but as a *topos* from moral treatises "On Friendship." Against this conventional background we see that, though weak and laughable, the satirist succeeds in fending off the "assaults" of the garrulous climber in *Satires* 1.9, proving himself a friend worthy of Maecenas, something more than a clumsy moralizer or parasite, whose traits he has not entirely shaken off.

As mentioned previously, the mosaic model demands that we see *Satires* 1.10 not only as a counterpart to 1.4, but as somehow responsive to its immediate context, wedged into the shape of its neighbor 1.9.[74] Here again the question of precedents becomes very important, for unlike the satires that precede, *Satires* 1.9 has no counterpart in Lucilius, Bion, or Callimachus; rather, it invites comparison with Catullus, whose Neoteric advocates come under fire in the very next poem.[75] The juxtaposition is significant and deliberate (the "bore" is,

---

[74] On the relation of *Satires* 1.9 to 1.10, see V. Buchheit, "Homerparodie und Literaturkritik in Horazens Sat. I 7 und I 9," *Gymnasium* 85 (1968): 519–55; and C. A. van Rooy, "Arrangement and Structure of *Satires* in Horace, *Sermones* Book I: *Satires* 9 and 10," *Acta Classica* 15 (1972): 37–52.

[75] Against Fiske's reconstruction of a Lucilian prototype for *Satires* 1.9, see N. Rudd, "Horace's Encounter with the Bore," *Phoenix* 15 (1961): 90–96.

after all, a Neoteric).[76] *Satires* 1.9 has an obvious counterpart in Catullus 10, which recalls a similar encounter between the poet and the girlfriend of Varus.[77] Like Horace, Catullus claims that he was busy with nothing in particular when he was suddenly dragged off by Varus who was on his way to visit his girlfriend. As in *Satires* 1.9, the pest of Catullus 10 becomes increasingly obnoxious in the course of the poem as the dialogue focuses on the poet's relationship with important political figures and eventually comes around to the question of his ability to seek favors from his patron.[78] The humor of both pieces is directed primarily against the speaker who is too obliging of the pest to say what is really on his mind. We watch both poets squirm as they try to make the best of an embarrassing situation.

More significant is the broken conversational form of each piece, which is marked by the constant shift between direct and indirect speech as well as a full variety of line breaks and shifts in language, tone, and rhythm. Typical is line 9 where, Rudd suggests, "we can hear Horace accelerating in the dactyls *ire modo ocius*, slowing down in the molossus *interdum*, and coming to a halt with *consistere*."[79] The satire is, in other words, a showpiece of compositional variety, a deliberate study of the technique.[80] The literary aims of the piece were obvious even to Porphyrion, who remarks *ad Satires* 1.9.1: *Et totum hunc sermonem dramatico charactere alterno sermone variat* ("And he diversifies this entire satire in a dramatic fashion by means of dia-

[76] Oberhelman, "Satire as Poetry," notes: "The position of 9, the famous 'bore' poem, is intentional: we are prepared for Horace's literary criticism in the next poem through the running battle with this obnoxious person. The 'bore' implicates himself as a member of the Neoterics, a group that evidently admired Lucilius." Among the many connections linking the bore of 1.9 with the Neoterics of 1.10, van Rooy, "Arrangement and Structures," 41–45, 51, notes the implied criticism of compositional technique in the *omnis composui* of line 28 and the Greek/Latin blend parodied in the satire's last verse (*sic me servavit Apollo*). He concludes, "I,9 forms a pair with I,10 . . . in the sense that it reflects its literary theory in a manner which is usually deftly concealed and often extremely ironic."

[77] Rudd, *Satires of Horace*, 284, n. 38, argues that "on the Latin side Horace's poem (*Satires* 1.9) owes much to the cheerful self-revelation of Catullus (especially no. 10) and Lucilius. I am not convinced, however, that there was a 'pest satire' in Lucilius." Quinn also sees similarities between the two poems. See *Catullus, the Poems*, 2nd ed. (London: Macmillan, 1973), 120–21.

[78] Quinn, *Catullus*, 121, notes the change that takes place in Catullus's attitude toward the pest as the poem progresses: "to begin with she was *non sane illepidum neque invenustum*; two thirds of the way through she becomes *cinaediorem*; by the end she is *insulsa male et molesta*."

[79] Rudd, *Satires of Horace*, 77.

[80] On the metrical complexity, variety of language, perspective and incident in *Satires* 1.9, see Rudd, *Satires of Horace*, 76–85.

logue"). Catullus in his version of the bore poem was equally concerned with exposing his compositional expertise (Catullus 10.5–8):

> Huc ut venimus, incidere nobis
> sermones varii, in quibus, quid esset
> iam Bithynia, quo modo se haberet,
> et quonam mihi profuisset aere.

When we arrived we fell to talking in varied conversations. Among these she asked what was going on in Bithynia, how one could get along there and whether I had made any money for myself.

Catullus 10 rambles and shifts because Catullus intends the piece as a case study in "varied conversations," that is, compositional variation.[81] In *Satires* 1.9, then, Horace emulates both the theme and technique of his Catullan model, applying the theories of *Satires* 1.10 to the actual practice of satire. He anticipates the critique of the Neoterics, whom he censures for their lack of compositional variety, with a vivid example of the technique drawn from their favorite, Catullus.

We conclude, then, that *Satires* 1.9 lends meaning to 1.10 just as *Satires* 1.5 responds to 1.4. *Satires* 1.5 improves upon Lucilius in the matter of compositional brevity, the primary critique of 1.4, whereas *Satires* 1.9 improves upon the contemporary imitators of Catullus in terms of their varietal technique, censured in 1.10. This is the Epicurean's *callida iunctura* at the level of the entire book. In the case of Satires 1.9, the tile has been perfectly selected and placed, wedged into the contexture of *Satires* 1.10. Standing back from Book 1, we see the image of the satirist himself. Horace, it seems, bears a striking resemblance to Proteus.

THE LOW-LIFE SATIRIST AND SATURNALIAN EXPOSURE

Throughout the *Satires*, patterns are made to be broken, authority is asserted to be undermined. Strange as it sounds, it is chiefly in his instability and self-mockery that the speaker shows consistency from satire to satire, for in spite of his changing faces, whether he plays the stern Cynic preacher, the parasite, or valued friend, the satirist is always about the business of mocking himself, undermining the authority his lessons or personality assert. This is true even when his lessons concern literature, the one area of his life we know Horace took very seriously. The last lines of Book 1, for example, suggest

---

[81] On the diversified character of Catullus 10, see W. B. Sedgwick, "Catullus X: A Rambling Commentary," *Greece and Rome* 16 (1947): 108–14.

that the theorist of *Satires* 1.4 and 1.10 has played his listener for a fool: *I puer atque meo citus haec subscribe libello* ("Come, boy, and be quick about adding these things to the end of my book!"). The Callimachean poet, so concerned with compositional precision and studied brevity, in the end paints himself as a slipshod poetaster, randomly dictating lines to the slave who has trouble keeping pace. This bit of self-mockery, though certainly false, trivializes not the poetic principles argued in *Satires* 1.4 and 1.10, but the satirist's own character, undermining all the intellectual authority he has built for himself along the way. He must do so, for his models in Iambic poetry, Cynic moralizing, Comedy, both Old and New, even Lucilian satire, demand it. From these precedents Horace understands that the scoffer cannot exempt himself from the degradation he metes out, for his own humiliation is central to his mission of leveling and exposure, a festival mission that concerns the dying nature of all men, the instability of their beliefs and their institutions. Anything that has pretensions to stability in a world where the wheels of life and death are constantly in motion the satirist unsettles, his own self included. In so doing he teaches the pretentious fool how to live, how to join the larger party of the dying, helpless fools who know that wealth is to be spent, wine is to be drunk, and authority mocked because tomorrow brings death. His mockery, despite all appearances, is deeply felt and moral in nature. He preaches the one true, unalterable fact of human behavior, that all must die, and in so doing he teaches us how to live. Such sentiments, of course, one normally associates with Bakhtin and his modern expositors who have taught us to see satire (initially medieval satire) against the backdrop of the Saturnalia and Feast of Fools, popular festivals celebrating man's lower nature, including his ultimate death and decay.[82] In the pages that follow we shall see that Horace himself had some sense of satire's festival origins, and that the consistent degradation of his *personae* in Book 1 is closely attached to a peculiar theory of satire that neatly parallels and, in a sense, anticipates modern notions of "symbolic inversion" and the "material grotesque." For Horace, just as for modern critics after Bakhtin, the satirist's degradation, his consorting with lowlifes and his reveling in death and decay—all prevalent in Book 1—are matters

---

[82] See especially M. Bakhtin, *Rabelais and His World*, trans. H. Iswolsky (Cambridge, Mass.: MIT Press, 1968). Structural studies of symbolic inversion draw freely upon Bakhtin. Of these I have found most useful B. Babcock, *The Reversible World: Symbolic Inversion in Art and Society* (Ithaca: Cornell University Press, 1978); P. Stallybrass and A. White, *The Politics and Poetics of Transgression* (Ithaca: Cornell University Press, 1986); and T. Castle, *Masquerade and Civilization* (Stanford, Calif.: Stanford University Press, 1986).

of theory, the prerequisites of satire, perceived as such from long precedent in the iambographic tradition.

Hipponax is a beggar and Horace the son of a freed slave. The satirist cannot enjoy intellectual or social authority over those whom he lampoons without undercutting his own mission, and thus, writers in the iambographic tradition inevitably portray their protagonists as lowlifes, beggars, and slaves who, in spite of their misfortunes, learn to make the most of what little life has to give, expecting no success and feeling no remorse at failure. Nature, the Cynic knows, has its own bounty for those with eyes to see it. Old Comic heroes, such as Dikaiopolis, Trygaeus, and Strepsiades, are inevitably bumpkins of a sort, unable to control the outward circumstances of their lives, which depend on persons of authority, the various creditors, warmongers, politicians, and philosophers who stumble their way across the Old Comic stage. They want nothing more than to return to their country existence, to enjoy the simple pleasures they once enjoyed. They are powerless, however, to win back what little they had by any normal means because the channels of the state and family connections are closed to them. The solutions they seek, therefore, are impossible in any context outside of Old Comic fiction, and we laugh at them as much for their stupidity as for their genius. Their plans can never work, but in Old Comedy they do: Trygaeus flies a dung beetle to the palace of Zeus and Lysistrata, a woman, disenfranchised and powerless in anything other than a festival context, calls a sex-strike against the warring armies of Athens and Sparta. In festival, the beggar becomes king and the simple joys of sex and wine are restored. This type of regeneration is fundamental to the cult of Dionysus and to its various manifestations in the popular festivals of Rome and medieval Europe.[83] Like the Dionysia, the Saturnalia and Feast of Fools celebrate the fundamentals of human existence, sowing and harvest, growth and death. Dionysus is a god who both dies and gives life.

The Cynic moralizers of the Hellenistic period carry on the legacy of Hipponax and the heroes of Old Comedy. As Horace was aware, Cynics, such as Bion, flaunted their humble origins to prove that wealth and status were extraneous to the happiness they had achieved. Diogenes Laertius (6.5) relates that Antisthenes, the so-called "founder" of the Cynic sect, was once reproached because his parents were not both freeborn: "Neither am I the son of two wrestlers," he replied, "yet I am a wrestler." Family connections, in other words, do not make the man. Likewise, legend relates that Diogenes,

---

[83] On the Saturnalian character of Old Comedy, see K. McLeish, *The Theatre of Aristophanes* (New York: Taplinger, 1980), 64–78.

a pupil of Antisthenes, was captured by pirates and sold as a slave in Crete. When asked by the auctioneer what his specialty was, Diogenes replied, "I rule men" (6.74). The slave becomes master. Next in line, Crates, though of good family, sold his possessions and lived the life of a beggar. Stories are told of him taking donations of bread and wine and being dragged by the ankles from the gymnasium at Corinth (6.90). According to Diogenes Laertius: "He claimed that Bad Reputation and Poverty were his homeland, which Fortune could not take captive" (6.93). Menippus rates equally low. Diogenes begins his account: "Menippus, also a Cynic, was a Phoenician by descent, a slave, according to the *Ethics* of Achaicus" (6.99).

These are the credentials of the Cynic. Horace knew from Menippus, Bion, and perhaps from Lucilius himself that to play the satirist was to play the part of a slave, a parasite, or lowlife. In Book 26 of his *Satires*, commonly taken as his earliest publication, Lucilius, who came from noble Roman stock, pictures himself in the role of a shifty freed slave. The antithesis of *publicanus Asiae* and *libertinus Syrus*, as well as the obvious rhyme and contrastive force of the fragments' last words, *non muto omnia* and *conmuto omnia*, suggests that W650–51 and W652–53 should be read together as a single fragment:

> Publicanus vero ut Asiae fiam, ut scripturarius
> pro Lucilio, id ego nolo et uno hoc non muto omnia. [W650-51]
> At libertinus tricorius Syrus ipse ac mastigias
> quicum versipellis fio et quicum conmuto omnia. [W652–53]

However, to become a tax farmer of Asia, a collector of the pasture tax rather than Lucilius, this I refuse and for this alone I do not receive everything in exchange. Rather, he is himself a Syrian, a triple-skinned freed slave and a scoundrel with whom I exchange my skin and with whom I trade everything.

Lucilius is a Syrian freedman, a "skin-changer" (*versipellis*) who wears the many guises of the slave con artists known from the New Comic stage. Like his Horatian counterpart, he is a character of fiction, and he encourages us in his very first book to understand that, like the various *Syri* of New Comedy, he will play many roles in the fictional world of his *Satires*, occasionally exiting the stage only to reemerge as the greedy parasite, the inept pedagogue, or whatever role the plot demands.

The slaves, beggars, and bumpkins of the Greek iambographic tradition have counterparts in Roman satire, both Menippean and formal verse satire, and in satiric literature of all ages and of all types.[84]

[84] The single extant fragment of the satirist Saevius Nicanor (late second/early first

The medieval satirist known as the "Piers Plowman," for example, is a version of the Cynic of Horace's diatribes, the Ofellus of *Satires* 2.2, or Juvenal's Umbricius (*Satires* 3). A. Kernan writes:[85]

> The pose of simplicity is frequently reinforced by references to humble but honest origins. The typical medieval satirist assumes the mask of the humble plowman working hard in the fields to support his family, close to nature and to God. . . . Somehow the satirist seems always to come from a world of pastoral innocence and kindness: he is the prophet come down from the hills to the cities of the plain; the gawky farm-boy, shepherd, or plowman come to the big city.

Modern satirists show similar traits. Though not a writer of formal verse satire, Garrison Keillor comes to mind as a version of the same type; a kid from Minnesota, somehow displaced to the heart of Manhattan, he is a modern Bion, a beggar in the court of kings.[86] To grow up in the city does not disqualify one as satirist, but it requires different tactics of the speaker. Inevitably, a city-bred satirist, such as Mike Royko, must undercut his status by referring to the poverty of his youth or to his regular converse with pimps, common laborers, and petty thieves. He is, in other words, a version of the New Comic parasite or slave who has regular contact with all elements of his society, both high and low. Though constantly reminded of his lowly status, the slave only pretends to respect the persons of eminence whom he serves, knowing that the lines that separate rich from poor, slave from free are tenuously drawn.[87]

Playing the Cynic, bumpkin, parasite, or slave, the satirist cannot assert his own superiority over those whom he lampoons. His secret is not that he is superior to those whom he lampoons but that they

---

century B.C.), though a mere two lines in length, informs us that he was (or a least claimed to be) a freed slave (*libertus*). On these lines, see C. van Rooy, *Studies in Classical Satire and Related Literary Theory* (Leiden: E. J. Brill, 1966), 58. For theoretical precedents, compare *Poetics* 4.1448b25–28, where Aristotle ranks writers in the iambographic tradition among the εὐτελέστεροι, "those of less substantial character" who represent the deeds "of baser individuals" (τῶν φαύλων). On these lines, see the section on Aristotle on Old Comedy in Chapter 2.

[85] A. Kernan, *The Cankered Muse* (New Haven: Yale University Press, 1959), 17–18.

[86] Will Rogers is a second modern version of the same type.

[87] Mike Royko, columnist for the *Chicago Sun Times* and *Chicago Tribune*, has made a career of voicing the opinions of Slats Grobnik, a fictional working man's guru whom he regularly consults in the taverns of Chicago's Polish district. Like Horace and many other satirists before him, Royko frequently refers to his milkman father as a source of his inspiration and moral indignation. He would, for example, have us believe that his father made a habit of running down criminals in his milk truck. Similar techniques we find in the comic routines of Bill Cosby or David Brenner, both from inner-city Philadelphia.

are his equals.[88] He is, in essence, a slave among slaves, or as Persius prefers, an ass among asses (*Satires* 1.121): *auriculas asini quis non habet?* ("Who does not have asses' ears?"). The satirist's mission, in other words, is to expose all men for what they are; to strip away the trappings of eminence that hide the braying, shitting, dying ass beneath. Bakhtin has argued that "the ass is one of the most ancient and lasting symbols of the material bodily lower stratum, which at the same time degrades and regenerates."[89] To expose the ass, then, is to show that men are in process; that there is a rhythm to life, an "unfinished" character marked by the body's birth, growth, nourishment, excretion, and death, which the ass symbolizes. The festival, the slave's day off, marks this process at its separate stages. The ongoing stability suggested by status, by large, well-built estates, and by money in the bank is for the Cynic a denial of the rhythm of life, and represents the jackass striving toward divine status, dignity, and permanence in a world that guarantees only death. The satirist's role in all of this is to level "eminence" (literally a "jutting out"), forcing his hearer to see life as a process. He demonstrates that pretensions to stability and finish are doomed to exposure, if not by some smaller version of death, such as excretion, warts, fire, or famine, then ultimately by death itself. He reminds us that all are dying creatures, and teaches us, in turn, how to live. Horace, who clearly understood his debt to the Cynics, understood his mission as satirist in these same terms. At *Satires* 2.1.62–65 he claims to follow Lucilius, the first Roman poet to "draw back the skin," referring to the fable of the Ass in the Lion's skin:

> Lucilius ausus
> primus in hunc operis componere carmina morem
> detrahere et pellem, nitidus qua quisque per ora
> cederet, introrsum turpis.

> Lucilius first dared to compose poems of this character and to draw back the skin with which each man glides shining before our eyes, though filthy within.

The satirist's task, in other words, is the exposure of hypocrisy, removing the outward trappings of beauty and stability to expose the dying corpse, the filth within. Compare Rambaux on these same

[88] We recall that during the Saturnalia all celebrants, even the emperor, wore the freedman's cap (see Martial *Epigrams* 14.1). The point is not so much that the slave is king, but that all men, regardless of wealth and family, are slaves who, during the Saturnalia, celebrate the day of their enfranchisement.

[89] See Bakhtin, *Rabelais*, 78.

lines: "For Horace as for Lucilius . . . to attack vice is to distinguish reality from appearance by revealing the mask which deceives and the ugliness which has gone unnoted. It is, then, to expose delusions."[90]

Death, like an Old Comic protagonist, is ugly, offensive, and unimpressed by status. It is, in other words, the ultimate exposer and the surest weapon of the Cynic satirist. Lucian, at *Menippus* 16, compares life to a stage production filled with Creons, Priams, and Agamemnons decked out in all their finery who, for all of their false bravado, must hand in their costumes at the play's conclusion: "Each of them strips off his gold-bespangled robe, lays aside his mask, steps out of his buskins, and goes about in poverty and humility. . . . That is what human affairs are like."[91] The end of the play, Lucian suggests, is death, which finds everyone naked and helpless. Earlier in the same satire, Lucian has Menippus compare life to a parade (πομπή) in which Fortune (Τύχη) hands out costumes at will. Some she clothes as kings and others as slaves. Occasionally she demands that players exchange costumes midway through the parade, so that one might see even a Croesus wearing the dress of a slave. When all is done, however, the costumes are again called in, at *Menippus* 16: "For a brief space she lets them use their costumes, but when the time of the pageant is over, each gives back the properties and lays off the costume along with his body, becoming what he was before his birth, no different from his neighbor." Death levels all, stripping away the trappings of eminence that falsely distinguish one man from another. It is the ultimate Cynic and satirist.

At *Menippus* 12, Lucian describes the connection between death and Cynic laughter, relating that Minos, judge of the dead,

> dealt most harshly with those who were swollen with pride of wealth and place . . . for he resented their short-lived vainglory and superciliousness, *and their failure to remember that they themselves were mortal* [italics mine] and had become possessed of mortal goods. So, after stripping off all their quondam splendour . . . they stood there naked, with hanging heads, reviewing, point by point, their happy life among us as if it had been a dream.

Minos, lord of the dead, is a version of the Cynic Menippus who relates the story. He targets those who would deny their own mortality, forcing them to view the dying side of all that they once held dear.

---

[90] Rambaux, "Livres I des *Satires* d'Horace," 188.

[91] All translations of Lucian, unless otherwise stated, are from A. M. Harmon's *Lucian*, vol. 4 (Cambridge Mass.: Harvard University Press, 1953).

Menippus continues: "For my part I was delighted to see that, and whenever I recognized one of them, I would go up and quietly remind him what he used to be in life and how puffed up he had been then." The Cynic relishes in death's exposure. He alone laughs in the underworld because, unlike the emperor or king, he has always understood that life is a process brooded over by death. Menippus relates of his fellow Cynic Diogenes (*Menippus* 18):

> And good old Diogenes lives with Sardanapalus the Assyrian, Midas the Phrygian, and several other wealthy men. As he hears them lamenting and reviewing their former good-fortune, he laughs and rejoices; and often he lies on his back and sings in a very harsh and unpleasant voice, drowning out their lamentations, so that the gentlemen are annoyed and think of changing their lodgings because they cannot stand Diogenes.[92]

Even in death, Lucian suggests, the Cynic remains faithful to his mission, reminding former tyrants that their glories have ended and that their costumes have been called in. In spite of its grim, malicious appearance, Diogenes' laughter has roots in a deeply philosophical view of life and is not at all "cynical" in the modern sense of the term. His aim is not to inflict needless pain, but to negate the opposition of life to death, which hypocrites, such as Midas and Sardanapalus, have maintained to their own intense distress. His exposure degrades and buries in order to create a new, better human being.[93] For Midas and Sardanapalus, however, the exposure has come too late.

Regeneration, putting to death in order to give life, is at the heart of Cynic lampoon and its antecedents in Old Comedy, set within the festival of Dionysus, the dying god who gives life.[94] It is, perhaps, for

---

[92] Midas and Sardanapalus sharing quarters with Diogenes is reminiscent of several of Gary Larson's "scenes from hell" cartoons. One version of the motif pictures a Maestro receiving his room assignment in hell. Satan, with a sardonic grin, points to a door behind which are seated dozens of smiling accordion players.

[93] Compare *Satires* 1.4.126–29, where Horace treats death and satiric exposure under the same heading:

> avidos vicinum funus ut aegros
> exanimat mortisque metu sibi parcere cogit,
> sic teneros animos aliena opprobria saepe
> absterrent vitiis.

> Just as a neighbor's funeral stuns unhealthy gluttons and compels them with the fear of death to spare themselves, so also do taunts against another man deter young minds from vice.

[94] Compare Bakhtin's account of Cervantes' Sancho, whom he regards as the perfect manifestation of the carnivalesque spirit: "In Cervantes' images of food and drink there is still the spirit of popular banquets. Sancho's materialism, his potbelly, appetite,

this reason that the scoffer, whether Old Comic protagonist, Cynic, or the writer of formal verse satire, is often painted in the guise of the honest country bumpkin who has learned the basic lessons of life and death. He has seen his animals grow and die. His crops he has lost to drought and frost. Life he knows as an unfinished process, a regular cycle of planting and harvest interspersed with festivals, which find him an older man with each passing year. The farmers of comedy and satire see themselves not outside this process but moving within it, and thus they make no pretensions to permanence or finish. Juvenal's Umbricius chides his citified interlocutor at *Satires* 3.168–79:

> It shames you to eat off clay dishes, something that one does not regard as foul when suddenly set among the Marsi or dining at a Sabine table. There he is content to wear a coarse blue hood. Throughout most of Italy, to be perfectly frank, no one wears a toga till the day he dies. Even if the pageantry of the festival days is observed in a grassy theater and a well-known farce is brought back on stage, when the tiny peasant child sits cringing on his mother's lap, afraid of the gaping white masks, there you will see everyone dressed alike, so that the reserved seats resemble the bleachers. Here, white tunics are the dress of high office, suiting even the mightiest of aediles.

The dark blue hood (*veneto cucullo*) was the poor man's costume known from the stage of comedy and, one assumes, from the actual habits of Italian peasants.[95] In the Italian countryside, Juvenal suggests, status loses its meaning, for even during the official feast days, when the regalia of eminence was especially evident and persons of status were expected to advertise their rank, all the trappings of status were absent. Like the naked dead in Lucian's underworld, Juvenal's Italian peasants all resemble one another. Their dress advertises only their sameness and humility.

In the great city of Rome, however, other practices were favored among social climbers and persons of status who sought to advertise their eminence through dress. Juvenal writes (*Satires* 10.33–40):

---

his abundant defecation, are on the absolute lower level of grotesque realism of the gay bodily grave (belly, bowels, earth) which has been dug for Don Quixote's abstract and deadened idealism. One could say that the knight of the sad countenance must die in order to be reborn a better and a greater man. This is a bodily and popular corrective to individual idealistic and spiritual pretense. Moreover, it is the popular corrective of laughter applied to the narrow-minded seriousness of the spiritual pretense. . . . it is a regenerating and laughing death." Bakhtin, *Rabelais*, 22.

[95] On the blue hood in comedy, see E. Courtney, *A Commentary on the Satires of Juvenal* (London: Athlone Press, 1980), 178.

Democritus used to shake his side with a constant laugh, even though there were no togas bordered with purple in those cities, no rods and axes, sedans or raised platforms. What would he have done had he seen the praetor, jutting out from his lofty chariot, standing high amid the Circus's dust in Jove's tunic, draping from his shoulders the Tyrian folds of an embroidered toga and wearing a giant crown's orb, which no neck could bear?

The praetor dressed in "Jove's tunic" presents a ridiculous image to be sure. One should recall, however, that by the time of Claudius Roman emperors were being worshiped as gods. The public display of *dignitas*, Juvenal recognizes, was especially obnoxious at Rome, unlike anything he knew from the Italian countryside, for in the city, the rules regarding the advertisement of status were clearly marked off and could not be breached without severe consequences. Magistrates had their lictors, rods, and axes; freedmen their caps; senators the broad stripe; knights the narrow stripe and gold ring.[96] Rich and poor, slave and free were clearly set off in Rome, where dress itself made it nearly impossible for men of unlike status to respect each other as equals. It is against the backdrop of this fierce battle for dignity and the stifling rigidity of Roman attitudes toward status that the satirist performs his leveling work, stripping away the accoutrements of power and status so important at every level of Roman society.[97]

To perform his leveling task the satirist makes frequent use of obscenity, which is both a mark of supreme honesty and a perfect exposer. Bakhtin writes of obscenity:

[96] Roman matrons possessed female versions of the broad stripe and *fasces* in the hairstyles, clothes, retainers, biers, and so on, which satirists, such as Horace and Juvenal, found utterly obnoxious, not because they were inherently offensive, but because they were intended and perceived as trappings of status and its advertisement.

[97] A poignant, almost pitiful reminder of the Roman preoccupation with status and its trappings we see in the monument of the military tribune L. Appuleius and his parents, which dates to 40–30 B.C. Armstrong, "*Horatius Eques*," 257, describes the monument, which has three figures, a father and mother in Roman dress, with the son in full regalia in the center. Armstrong writes of the parent figures: "Like many other freedmen of the late Republic, they flaunted on their monument with special pride their Roman dress and their status as legal married people (for as slaves they could only live in *contubernium*). Many freedmen also proudly display their children at right or left, frequently wearing the Roman *bulla* that they themselves had been denied as slave children. But here, exceptionally, and because of their son's high rank, Asclepiades and Sophanuba have made him the central figure, with themselves looking at him respectfully on each side. . . . He is in 'heroic' soldierly costume, wearing the *paludamentum* on the shoulder of his bare torso, presenting a sword—displaying prominently on the fourth finger of his left hand, as he does so, a disproportionately oversized equestrian ring which, as Zanker conjectures, was most probably gilded on the monument for extra display."

Modern indecent abuse and cursing have retained dead and purely negative remnants of the grotesque concept of the body. Our "three-storied"
oaths or other unprintable expressions degrade the object according to
the grotesque method; they send it down to the absolute bodily lower
stratum, to the zone of the genital organs, the bodily grave, in order to
be destroyed.[98]

Compare J. Henderson's notes on the power of Old Comic obscenity
to expose and degrade:

The effect of obscenity is to break through social taboos rather than to
escape them in fantasy. Thus obscenity is most often used to insult someone; to emphasize what one is saying in the most forceful possible way;
to make curses; to add power to comedy, jokes, ridicule, or satire. Its
efficacy in all these functions resides in its ability *to uncover what is forbidden*, and thus to shock, anger, or amuse. The pleasure afforded by obscenity lies in our enjoyment at *exposing someone else or seeing someone else
exposed* without having to effect the exposure physically.[99]

Aristotle, at *Politics* 7.1336b12–13, defines obscenity as a type of "slavishness" (ἀνδραποδωδία), an outright degradation naturally unsuited
to the free citizen, whom he urges to use polite speech as a mark of
his rank. Speech, for Aristotle, indicates status, an idea that has clear
applications to rhetorical principles of decorum (τὸ πρέπον). It follows,
then, that in the history of comedy and the larger iambographic tradition, the coarsest sentiments were traditionally conveyed by slaves,
Cynics, or farmer-bumpkins, such as Aristophanes' Dikaiopolis or the
Davus of *Satires* 2.7.[100] The slaves of New Comedy cannot pretend to
any status among themselves or their superiors, and, like their counterparts, the rustics and Cynics, they have learned that life guarantees
only death, perhaps even death by crucifixion, the standard threat of
New Comic masters.[101] Their obscenity, then, is a condition of status,
a reminder of death that forces pretenders, in the guise of various
New Comic spoilsports, to see and deal with this side of their own
nature. Obscene words such as "shit," "fuck," "hell," and "damn" expose the dying, animal side of man, which the pretender would deny,
but which the slave has learned to accept. The gods of Greece and
Rome could not look upon death in any of its various manifestations;
defecation, sickness, sexual intercourse, ill-omened words, all re-

[98] Bakhtin, *Rabelais*, 28.
[99] J. Henderson, *The Maculate Muse* (New Haven: Yale University Press, 1975), 7 (emphasis added).
[100] On ἀγροικία and obscenity, see Henderson, *Maculate Muse*, 6.
[101] Compare the slave's sentiments at *Pseudolus* 683–87, quoted in the next section.

minders of man's "unfinished," dying nature, were restricted from the temple and its surrounding holy space. The gods themselves were undying, not subject to defecation, age, or sickness. Although they ate, drank, and had sex, they did so for enjoyment, not fearing for their own survival. Satirists, Cynics, and slaves, as Lucian suggests, remind us that we are not gods, that the costumes we wear must soon be turned in. In service to his mission, the satirist avails himself of obscenity, invading the sanctuary of human dignity, so obnoxious in the age of Horace and Juvenal, by reminding us that all piss, shit, fuck, and, ultimately, die (hell!). There is no finish or stability here. All pretense is stripped away.

Like Juvenal, Horace knew that the satirist must learn the lessons of the bumpkin, Cynic, or slave, that he must reject the status that he so obviously enjoyed at Rome in favor of the simple offerings of his country estate. His longing for his Sabine villa gives him credibility as a satirist (*Satires* 2.6.65–67):

> o noctes cenaeque deum! quibus ipse meique
> ante Larem proprium vescor vernasque procaces
> pasco libatis dapibus.

Oh, for those nights and godly feasts! My friends and I partake of these before the hearth, and I feed my impudent slaves on the feasts that we have sampled.

His country slaves, Horace suggests, enjoy a near Saturnalian existence. Roles are reversed as the master and his invited guests take their seats in the kitchen, the slave's working space, only sampling the feasts that they set before their servants. This type of leveling is essential to the satirist and his Saturnalian message; a slave himself, he compels his reader to look at the hopeless, dying side of the human condition, not that he should despair, but join in the festival conducted in honor of all the world's dying slaves.

In the end, it is the slave who teaches the king how to live. Menander's old grump Knemon, we recall, only in the last lines of the *Dyskolus* concedes to dance with the slaves who have got the better of him. They have won a Dionysiac or Saturnalian victory, and we, as fellow laughers, are convinced that Knemon is a better, happier man for their efforts. Drawing a rather crude comparison, one recalls the leveling efforts of the Three Stooges, modern versions of the buffoons and slaves of farce and the mime tradition. Inevitably, called on as servants or plumbers, they fumble their way into the mansion of a wealthy aristocrat on the day of an elaborate dinner party. Words are exchanged between them and a pie-fight ensues. The guests, insulted and enraged, take up pies for themselves, taking aim first at the Stooges, then at one another. As the lowlifes bid a hasty retreat out the back door, we expect the pie-fight within to cease, yet it does not; it continues. The dignity and eminence suggested by the mansion, the music, and the costumes have been stripped away, and the elegant guests have shown that, in spite of their pretensions, they too are Stooges of the purest water. Like Knemon, they have learned that the slaves' party has its own pleasures. They have learned to dance. This is Saturnalian exposure, learning to laugh as a slave among slaves.

THE *MIMUS NOBILIS*

Included among the numerous artifacts and documents unearthed at Pompeii that have enhanced the study of Roman religion, Paul MacKendrick mentions in his *Mute Stones Speak* a "cynical *graffito*" he once saw at Agrippa Postumus's villa at Boscotrecase.[102] It reads: "Augustus Caesar's mother was only a woman." The message, however crude, is indeed cynical, at least in a restricted sense, for it exposes the unspoken truth about Caesar's mother, which all the trappings of her status had attempted to hide: she did in fact die. The anonymous writer felt the oppression of his age, the stifling rigidity of a society that knew no limits to eminence and its advertisement, and, with little or no public forum for his discontent, he tells his secret to a wall, which, like Persius's ditch (*scrobis*), cannot hide the grim fact that all, even the divine lights of the emperor's family, are dying asses. We laugh at the graffito, not because it is particularly clever or revealing, at least not in a modern context, but because it is so obvious, artless, and, in a sense, pitiful. The society that could regard such a message as scandalous or worthy of secret publication is a society ripe for satire.

In the Pompeian graffito we see the rough, unworked sentiments of the budding Cynic who has not yet learned the finer modes of exposure known to the laughing satirists of the iambographic tradition. His message is grim, wholly deficient in the sweet side of the seriocomic, the *spoudaiogeloion* that is the hallmark of Cynic exposure. One might also compare the teachings of Christ, which, in spite of obvious affinities to the Cynic tradition, carry an altogether different tone. We see, for example, the basic outlines of Cynic exposure in

[102] See P. MacKendrick, *The Mute Stones Speak*, 2nd ed. (New York: W. W. Norton, 1983), 272.

Christ's censure of the scribes and pharisees at Matthew 23:27: "Woe
to you, the scribes and pharisees, hypocrites! You resemble white-
washed tombs, which are beautiful on the outside, but filled with the
bones of corpses and all impurity within." The hypocrite (ὑποκριτής),
in ancient terminology, is an "actor," one who hides beneath a mask,
pretending to be something he is not. Christ exposes the scribes and
pharisees as dying creatures, attractive tombs filled with rotting flesh,
a very Cynic technique, but his exposure is much more direct and
disturbing than even the blunt assertions of the Pompeian graffito.[103]
He offers no self-mockery, nothing sweet to temper the bitter. In
contrast, the true Cynic, at the same time as he uncovers the secret of
Caesar's mother, invites laughter not only at the object of his exposure but also at himself as a fellow dying creature. Compare the sentiments of Plautus's Pseudolus, the most famous of all New Comic
slaves (*Pseudolus* 683–87):

> For that matter, we're all fools though we don't know it, for running so
> hard after this or that, as if we could possibly tell for ourselves what's
> good for us and what isn't. We lose the certainties while seeking for un-
> certainties; and so we go on, in toil and trouble, until death creeps up on
> us. . . . But enough of this philosophizing [*iam satis est philosophatum*]. I
> do run on, don't I?[104]

Pseudolus, the philosophizing slave, knows the cruelty and bitter
frustrations of enslavement. He brings a grim message to the stage,
the satirist's conviction that all are fools (*stulti*) who, despite their best
efforts to attain security, advance steadily toward death. His sentiments hardly seem worthy of laughter, yet they do evoke a bitter-
sweet smile, for he never allows us to forget that these are the sentiments of a comic clown. The final jibe, "I do run on, don't I?"
reminds us that Pseudolus, even when philosophizing, is a stage character, a typical New Comic slave given to gossip and prattling. Like
the speaker of *Satires* 1.1, he suddenly checks himself, "enough now"

---

[103] Similar is the parable of Luke 12.16–21 where the rich man, in a vain effort to
secure his existence for years to come, tears down his old barns and builds bigger ones
only to hear: "Fool! This night your soul is required of you; and the things you have
prepared, whose will they be?" Death, for Christ and for the Cynic, exposes the myth
of human "security" in any of its various forms (wealth, status, political power, and so
on). Compare the message of the moralizing Cynic of Menander's *Pilots* 301K (the
Greek is quoted in Chapter 1): "Does money, my boy, seem to you capable of supplying
the price of something beyond the daily necessities of life, of bread, meal, vinegar, and
oil? There is no price for immortality, not even were you to gather together the legendary talents of Tantalus. But you will die and leave these things to others."

[104] The translation I take from E. F. Watling's *Plautus, the Pot of Gold and Other Plays*
(London: Penguin Books, 1965).

(*iam satis est*), mocking his own garrulity. The message is grim, but we laugh all the same.

New Comic slaves are crude, self-mocking, and without pretensions to status or even to living beyond the play's end. Even more, they are notorious gossips who, in spite of their best efforts, are unable to keep their masters' secrets for any length of time, especially when drunk at the Saturnalia.[105] The slave is, in other words, an ideal exposer, the mirror image of the Cynic beggar. Consider the secrets of Horace's own slave, revealed in the Saturnalian setting of *Satires* 2.7. Davus claims (*Satires* 2.7.46–61):

> Another man's wife takes you captive. I go for a little whore. Which one of us does a wrong more deserving of the cross? When my passionate nature stiffens me up, whatever woman lies naked beneath the lantern's clear light, receiving the lashes of my swollen tail or playfully riding me like a horse, she sends me home neither with my reputation destroyed nor frightened that someone richer or more handsome might water at the same hole. You, however, when you toss aside the marks of your rank, your equestrian ring and your Roman dress, and you go from being a *iudex selectus* to a stinking Dama with a mantle covering your perfumed head, have you not become the very thing you resemble? You are led into her house frightened. Your bones rattle as your fear wrangles with your desires. What's the difference between going off to be branded with torches and butchered by the sword and being locked in a stinking closet where the maid, in on her mistress' crime, has hidden you, contorted, your head pressed against your knees?

Davus has nothing to hide. In his own obscene, honest fashion, he uncovers the hypocrisy of his master, contrasting his own lurid amusements "beneath the lantern's clear light" (*sub clara lucerna*) with the secretive escapades of Horace who, he claims, makes a habit of hiding in closets and traveling about with his head shrouded in a cloak (*obscurante lacerna*). Davus's secret is not that he is superior to his master, but that Horace is his equal, a "slave" to the desires that strip him of his equestrian status, for as he slinks away to his lover's house, he exchanges the narrow stripe and gold ring of the Roman knight for a hooded mantle, thereby becoming the slave that he resembles. When he arrives at the matron's house, Horace acts out the part of the handsome lover in an adultery mime, hiding in a bedroom closet while the matron attempts to cool her husband's amorous designs and direct him out of the bedroom. His head covering, too, es-

---

[105] On the conventional image of the slave as gossip and revealer of the master's secrets, compare Juvenal *Satires* 9.93–110 and *Miles Gloriosus* 259–65.

tablishes a comic context for the tryst. Compare Seneca's portrayal of Maecenas at *Moral Epistles* 114.6:

> This is the man who would always move about the city in a loose tunic. . . . This is the man who, on the tribunal or rostrum and in every public gathering would appear with his head covered in a cloak [*pallio*], his ears sticking out on both sides like the millionare's fugitive slaves in a mime play.[106]

Davus, like the Cynic of the diatribes, is a stage character, a philosophizing Pseudolus whose exaggeration and garrulity get the better of him, sweetening his abuse with self-mockery. At the end of *Satires* 2.7 he is chased from the scene by his master's threat to transfer him to his country estate, a typical punishment for the city slaves of New Comedy, but before he leaves, Davus invites his master on stage as well, converting the noble Roman knight to a mime actor, a *mimus nobilis*; he is a slave, parading about with his head covered, and an adulterer, the closeted lover of the adultery mime. His technique is precisely that of the satirist of the diatribes, who portrays opponents such as Crispinus in the guise of various characters of comedy, creating a fictional, satiric world filled with the wastrels, stern fathers, misers, haughty matrons, slaves, and buffoons from the stage of popular comedy.

Behind this penchant for dramatization stands a peculiar Roman attitude toward comic acting, which was held in the lowest possible esteem, regarded as the profession of slaves, freed slaves, and aliens.[107] Cornelius Nepos, in the preface to his treatise on foreign generals, contrasts Greek and Roman attitudes toward the acting profession (Nepos, preface 5):

> Throughout nearly all of Greece, it was a matter of great distinction to be cited as an Olympic champion. In fact, among the Greeks it was no disgrace even to go out on stage and appear in a public performance, practices that we consider destructive of one's good name, degrading and without honor.

[106] On slaves as hood-wearers, see also Martial *Epigrams* 10.76 where it is assumed that the *cucullus* belongs to Syrians, Parthians, and "knights from the slave markets of Cappadocia." Plautus *Curculio* 288–95 makes the *capite operto* typical of Greek slaves (*drapetae*) who, with their *sermones*, *sententiae*, and *crepitum polentarium* show all the traits of beggar Cynics. Juvenal *Satires* 6.118 and 8.142–45, perhaps in imitation of Horace *Satires* 2.7.46–61, treat the leveling effect of the adulterer's hood.

[107] On the status of actors at Rome, see R. Reynolds, "Criticism of Individuals in Roman Popular Comedy," *Classical Quarterly* 37 (1943): 38, n. 5; and N. Horsfall, "The Collegium Poetarum," *Bulletin of the Institute of Classical Studies, University of London* 23 (1976): 81, n. 23. Compare also Tacitus *Annals* 14.14 and 14.20–21.

With the possible exception of Livius Andronicus, no Roman writer of comedies is attested to have willingly performed his plays on stage. The stigma attached to the acting profession at Rome simply would not allow it, for in spite of the concealing masks and costumes, the low status of the comic performer beneath the costume was never far from the audience's mind. In the prologue to his *Prisoners*, for example, Plautus plays off the situation of his actors. After pointing out that Tyndarus will play the part of his father's slave, the speaker adds: *haec res agetur nobis, vobis fabula* ("for us, the situation will be played out as fact; for you, it is fiction").[108] Along similar lines, Macrobius records at *Saturnalia* 2.7 that the mime writer Laberius, a member of the equestrian order, was once punished by Julius Caesar, his erstwhile patron, by being "invited" to act in one of his own mimes. It was an invitation he knew better than to refuse, and he complains in his prologue: "For twice thirty years I have lived without reproach and left my household gods today a Roman knight; I shall return home—a mime. In very truth, today I have lived a day too long."[109]

In a Roman context, to play the mime actor's role is to become a slave or, at best, a freed slave or alien. We see, then, the real scandal that Horace's penchant for dramatization entails, for when he converts his opponents into stage characters, he effects their enslavement, fulfilling his satiric aims of exposure and leveling by reducing all to the level of mime actors and comic clowns. Rather than stripping his opponents of the trappings of their status, Horace clothes them in stage costumes, a technique that, given the Roman prejudice against comic acting, accomplishes the same effect. Because the satirist himself has a comic role to play, whether slave, parasite, or Cynic preacher, the enslavement he effects is self-mocking and sweet to the taste, a perfect expression of Cynic *spoudaiogeloion*.

Like Horace, Juvenal understood the leveling force of the *mimus nobilis* motif, sometimes reducing his characters to comic slave actors in order to achieve his satiric aims.[110] Yet, even more popular with Juvenal is the related motif of the *tragoedus nobilis*, the making of tragic comparisons that give an entirely different tone to his lam-

---

[108] The observation I owe to Tim Moore, "Plautus, Brecht, and the 'Alienation Effect,'" an address to the Classical Association of the Atlantic States, Lancaster, Pennsylvania, 30 September 1989.

[109] The translation I take from *Macrobius, the Saturnalia*, translated with introduction and notes by P. V. Davies (New York: Columbia University Press, 1969).

[110] See, for example, *Satires* 6.41–44, where Juvenal converts his friend Postumus into the typical lover-boy of the adultery mime. On these lines, see my comments in Chapter 1.

poons. At *Satires* 6.643–61, for example, he ends his tirade against
Roman women by suggesting that Pontia's brutality in murdering her
children exceeds even that of Medea and Procne:

> Whatever the tragic poets tell us about Medea and Procne may well have
> happened: I won't dispute that. Such women were monsters of daring
> in their own day—but not from the lust for cash. . . . take a morning
> stroll, you'll meet Danaids galore; an Eriphyle or Clytemnestra turns up
> in every street. The only difference is this: whereas Clytemnestra used a
> clumsy great double ax, nowadays an ounce of toad's lung is just as ef-
> fective. But cold steel may have a comeback if our modern Agamemnons
> take a hint from old Mithridates, and sample the pharmacopeia till
> they're proof against every drug.

In contrast to Horace, Juvenal's satiric world is filled with Medeas,
Procnes, Eriphyles, and Agamemnons, and far fewer Davuses, raging
fathers, and wastrel sons. His comparisons, while certainly humorous
and enslaving, carry a tone far more brooding, somber, and "tragic"
than the lighter, "comic" spirit of Horatian satire, so that it has become the common practice of modern critics such as Alvin Kernan
and Northrop Frye to distinguish between the "tragic" and "comic"
modes of later English satire by reference to Juvenal and Horace.[111]
The English Augustans themselves maintained the same distinction,
and it seems quite likely that behind this stand the divergent dramatic
techniques of the two authors, one seeking his models primarily from
comedy, the other from tragedy. At *Satires* 15.30–32, Juvenal suggests that he rifled the canon of tragedy "from Pyrrha onward," that
is, all Greek mythology since the flood, in search of a model in tragedy with which to compare the collective crime that is the premise of
the piece. From the evidence of his *Satires* as a whole, it seems that
Juvenal made a regular practice of searching the tragic canon for his
models, a technique that, while effecting a leveling and enslavement
similar to the *mimus nobilis*, carries a sense of anger and despair absent
from the *Satires* of Horace. Tragic characters, like comic buffoons
and slaves, are dying creatures whose troubled lives point to the fragility of human eminence. The disasters that plague them, however,
are far more mysterious and destructive than the minor troubles
played out on the comic stage, where, in the end, young lovers marry,
old men learn to dance, and slaves are set free.

Foibles of character and the minor "disasters" of the New Comic

---

[111] On the "comic/tragic" distinction between Horace and Juvenal, see H. Weber,
"Comic Humour and Tragic Spirit: The Augustan Distinction between Horace and
Juvenal," *Classical and Modern Literature* 1 (1981): 275–89.

stage are the chief sources of humor in Horace's satiric world, yet even these he manages to color with Old Comic or Cynic modes of exposure, which focus on death and man's unfinished nature, giving real philosophical depth and bite to his lampoons. Among the most memorable of Horace's dramatic set pieces is the story of Priapus and the witches, an episode known from earlier curse literature, the *Priapea*, iambic poetry and mime. The speaker of *Satires* 1.8 is a Roman version of the talking ithyphallic herm of Callimachus's *Iambs* 7 and 9, while the lustful hags, played by Canidia and Sagana, are characters known from Old Comedy and mime. Priapus himself, with his obtrusive phallus and obscenity, resembles the Old Comic protagonist or Cynic who refuses to conceal even the most offensive marks of his unfinished nature.[112] As a symbol of potency and fertility in the heat of life's regenerative process, he very literally "exposes himself" to the world as a life-giving/dying creature, and it is an extension of this same guttural honesty, a prodigious fart, that ultimately shatters the pretensions of the witches Canidia and Sagana. His phallus and his anus, then, effect not only his own degradation but that of the pretenders as well.

Everything about the rites described in *Satires* 1.8 suggests that Canidia and Sagana have somehow learned to control death. We look on as the two women attempt to channel the destructive powers of Hecate and Persephone against an unruly lover (certainly Horace) by the clever manipulation of dead men's bones, herbs, voodoo dolls, and so on. Priapus, aware that he is witness to *arcana*, secret rites harmful to the uninitiated, is duly frightened by all he sees and in his stupidity he suggests that even the moon, to avoid witnessing these rites, hid itself behind the grave markers.[113] Priapus, however, cannot move from his statue base. Forced to look on, then, he takes his revenge, which is far more a condition of his fear and ineptitude than of a conscious desire to expose (*Satires* 1.8.46–50):

> nam displosa sonat quantum vesica pepedi
> diffisa nate ficus: at illae currere in urbem.
> Canidiae dentes, altum Saganae caliendrum
> excidere atque herbas atque incatata lacertis
> vincula cum magno risuque iocoque videres.

[112] On Cynic openness towards sex, compare the stories of public masturbation at Diogenes Laertius 6.46 and 6.69.

[113] Priapus does not realize that the drawing down of the moon was part of the magic rite, a sign of the witches' power. Compare Aristophanes *Clouds* 749–52, Plato *Gorgias* 513a, and Ovid *Heroides* 6.85.

For I farted as loud as an exploding bladder, splitting my fig-wood ass.
But then you might have seen them tear off into town. What fun to
watch Canidia's teeth fall out and Sagana's lofty wig, her potions, and
enchanted love knots tumbling from her arms.

Like the slaves of New Comedy, Priapus has learned the dark secrets
of those who seek to control him, and he exposes them in a fashion
suited to his status.[114] His fart is an obvious injection of Bakhtin's
"material grotesque," the ugly, dying side of his nature, which, as satirist, he cannot suppress. The witches, who made pretensions to con-
trolling even the elemental spirits of the underworld, mistake a fart
for a thunderclap and, as they scramble to save themselves, they are
very literally "stripped" of the magical trappings that made them so
powerful and terrifying. Their exposure is effected as we see the
lion's hide, in the form of Canidia's false teeth, Sagana's wig, her potions and love knots, pulled back to expose the ass within. The teeth
and wig are especially significant because they indicate age, the approach of death and the ugliness it entails, which both women attempted to hide. They are, in the end, exposed as dying creatures,
old hags and hucksters who really exercise no control over the powerful forces of death, which they pretend to manipulate.[115]

The scrambling scene that ends *Satires* 1.8 is laughable for the exposure it effects as well as for the incongruity of the witches' reaction
to the reality of the "disaster" they encounter. It is a fart, after all, a
harmless injection of the grotesque, not a major calamity that sends
them flying, and so we laugh at their confused, feeble efforts to save
themselves. This is good comic practice, for as Aristotle suggests at
Poetics 5.1449a, the laughable (τὸ γελοῖον) is a subcategory of the
shameful or ugly (τὸ αἰσχρόν), that is, it treats the deformities that society compels us to hide or regard as shameful, matters related to sex,
excretion, warts, blunders, and so on, which are evidence of a dying,
unfinished nature. This said, however, Aristotle is quick to point out
that comic laughter, while it stems from the shameful, must not treat
the ultimate taboo, which is death itself: τὸ γὰρ γελοῖόν ἐστιν ἁμάρτημά
τι καὶ αἶσχος ἀνώδυνον καὶ οὐ φθαρτικόν ("For the laughable is a certain
defect and ugliness, which does not inflict pain or destruction").[116]

---

[114] Farting from fear was a gag known from the stage of Old Comedy. See Henderson, *Masculate Muse*, 195–96.

[115] Juvenal's proposition "all old men look alike" (*una senum facies*) treats the leveling
effects of age. See Juvenal *Satires* 10.198–202.

[116] On these lines, see my comments in Chapter 2. A similar stress on "shame"
(αἰσχύνη) as basic to comedy we see at *Rhetoric* 2.1384b9–11: "And men feel shame
before those who preach against the faults of their fellow citizens, such as the mockers

Death and its immediate reminders are, for Aristotle, too strong for the stage of comedy, and he insists that the exposure of fools be conducted at a much less obvious level. Against these dictates stand the Old Comic poets and Cynics who were much less reticent about man's dying nature, making the denial of death a chief target of their lampoons.

Horace's theory of satire balances the demands of two hostile traditions of humor, the Aristotelian and iambographic, giving an aesthetic application to the basic ethical principles of balance and nature's mean, which the satirist preaches throughout. The *mimus nobilis* device (the making of noble mime actors) exemplifies Horace's concern for both traditions; for, while indirect and harmless, as Aristotle demands, the penchant for dramatization ultimately enslaves, effecting the exposure of human frailty and death, which is basic to Cynic lampoon. Similar is the frequent injection of mishaps or *res adversae*, harmless reminders of death in the form of farts (1.8), attacking dogs (2.6), falling tapestries (2.8), and so on, which send the characters of the play scrambling to save themselves, exposing them as lowlifes and pretenders. The concept was known to Horace from philosophical sources, possibly from Lucretius, who comments on misfortune's power to expose at *De Rerum Natura* 3.55–58:

> quo magis in dubiis hominem spectare periclis
> convenit adversisque in rebus noscere qui sit.
> nam verae voces tum demum pectore ab imo
> eliciuntur et eripitur persona: manet res.

So then, it is more useful to inspect character in times of danger and to discern what sort of man one is in adverse circumstances, for then are one's true feelings drawn forth from the very depths of the heart. The mask is torn away, the reality remains.

Lucretius puts this idea into practice in the plague scene that concludes his treatise, where he demonstrates that the real disaster is not the plague itself but man's diseased attitude toward death, the hidden fears, despair, and bitterness, which times of suffering (*res adversae*) expose in those who have neglected the study of nature.[117] Tearing away the mask, that is, the exposure of hypocrisy, is a Cynic procedure, yet Cynic self-mockery is totally absent from Lucretius's grue-

---

and comic poets." Compare Henderson, *Maculate Muse*, 1–29, on Greek concepts of shame in relation to Old Comedy.

[117] Concerning the psychological aspects of the disaster that underlie the so-called lapses in Lucretius's imitation of Thucydides, see Freudenburg, "*Causa Morbi*," 61–63, especially nn. 6 and 8.

some scenes of men castrating themselves, robbing funeral pyres or abandoning loved ones, all in an effort to rescue themselves, or at least a modicum of their former dignity, in the face of death's final and ultimate degradation. The passage in lines 1272–75 describes temples filled with corpses, the pollution of sacred space reserved for the undying and the perfect.[118] The scene, for Lucretius, exposes the epitome of human folly, which is the denial of death, the attempt of dying creatures to tap into the immortal, finished nature of the gods.

Falling tapestries and a spoiled meal, the *res adversae* of Horace's final satire, *Satires* 2.8, seem to admit little if any comparison with the scenes of utter degradation and despair that conclude the *De Rerum Natura*. The two works end in opposite tones, one solemn and disturbing, the other self-mocking and frivolous, yet beneath the surface of each lies a similar intent and technique, for both deal with the shattering of man's foolish gestures toward eminence and stability through the sudden injection of death. In contrast to the plague scene, the *res adversae* that afflict Nasidienus are drawn in comic proportions. They are subtle, harmless reminders of human frailty, and thus they suit Aristotle's strictures against comic applications of pain and destruction. The entire scene, as mentioned in Chapter 1, is drawn from the comedian Fundanius's point of view, so that Nasidienus is drawn in the colors of a braggart cook or *cenae pater* ("father of the feast"), while Porcius ("the pig") and Nomentanus (the "namer" or "pointer") play the parasitic roles suggested by their names, as does Servilius Balatro, the "servile buffoon" who crashes the party along with Vibidius on the coattails of their patron, Maecenas. Even Horace, who was not invited, shows traces of comic coloring. He addresses Fundanius in the opening lines (*Satires* 2.8.1–3):

> Ut Nasidieni iuvit te cena beati?
> nam mihi quaerenti convivam dictus here illic
> de medio potare die.

> How did you enjoy the dinner party of that rich man Nasidienus? Yesterday, when I went looking for you, I was told that you were over there drinking since midday.

Horace, it seems, was not invited, and we rightly percieve in his query a certain regret for having missed out on a "rich man's" (*beati*) lavish dinner and the abundant drinking that commenced at midday. He is, in other words, the uninvited *scurra*, the hungry parasite who expe-

---

[118] Compare Euripides *Hippolytos* 1437–38, where Artemis rushes from the scene claiming, "I am not permitted to look upon the dead nor to pollute my sight with a dying man's final breath."

riences the meal vicariously through the comic descriptions of his friend Fundanius (*Satires* 2.8.4–5): *"dic, si grave non est, / quae prima iratum ventrem placaverit esca"* ("Tell me, if it's not too much trouble, the first dish he used to soothe your growling stomach"). Fundanius describes and Horace listens, scarcely able to check his enthusiasm and regret. He interrupts: "Ah, wealth! What misery!" (*Divitias miseras!*), and he demands to know the names of those lucky enough to have swung an invitation.

Suspended above the entire scene Fundanius is careful to include "tapestries" (*aulaea*), the "stage curtains" that come crashing down on the evening's main course, spoiling the host's moment of glory and putting an end to his unflagging bombast. His reaction to the mishap, like that of Canidia and Sagana in *Satires* 1.8, is wholly incongruous to the event itself, and Varius can scarcely keep from laughing as he watches the interactions of Nasidienus and his favorite parasite (*Satires* 2.858–64):

> Rufus posito capite, ut si
> filius immaturus obisset, flere. quis esset
> finis, ni sapiens sic Nomentanus amicum
> tolleret? "heu, Fortuna, quis est crudelior in nos
> te deus? ut semper gaudes illudere rebus
> humanis!" Varius mappa compescere risum
> vix poterat.

Nasidienus lowered his head and began crying, as if one of his sons had just met an untimely death. Who knows where it would have ended had not Nomentanus, Mr. Philosopher, encouraged his friend with, "Alas, Fortune, what god is crueler to us than you? How you love always to make a mockery of human affairs!" Varius barely succeeded in stifling his laughter with a napkin.

Nasidienus responds to the loss of his fish course as if he had just witnessed the death of a son, and Nomentanus, rather than calling him to his senses, proceeds to expostulate on the cruelty of fortune and the fragility of human affairs, confirming the loss of the fish course as a most "grave" disaster. Balatro, fearing that the feast might be called off, follows in a similar vein, dwelling on all the disasters that hosts encounter but can never anticipate, the burned bread and poorly seasoned sauce that are the bane of the parasite's existence: *haec est condicio vivendi* ("such is the character of life"). He concludes (*Satires* 2.8.71–74):

> "adde hos praeterea casus, aulaea ruant si,
> ut modo, si patinam pede lapsus frangat agaso.

> sed convivatoris, uti ducis, ingenium res
> adversae nudare solent, celare secundae."

"Add besides disasters such as the canopy falling, as happened just now,
or one of the slave boys slipping and breaking a dish. But adverse circumstances often expose the true character of the host, the part you are
playing, while pleasant times hide it."

Balatro, a philosopher-buffoon, applies the sentiments of *De Rerum
Natura* 3.55–58 to the frivolous circumstances surrounding the demise of the fish course, giving cosmic significance to a lost meal,
which is the parasite's worst nightmare. His words are replete with
irony hinging on the double meaning of *ingenium*, which signifies
both "talent" and personal "character." Thus, what the host hears as
a plea to continue the feast, an invitation to show off his true "talent"
in the face of adversity, the audience hears as a reference to the scene
just witnessed, where the falling tapestries have already exposed the
true "character" of the host in all its insubstantial, hypocritical colors.
In the annihilation of the fish course, death injects itself into Nasidienus's dinner party in its most unthreatening, comic form, and as
Balatro ineptly suggests, it uncovers the true character of the host,
exposing him as a fool who has somehow thought that his life could
be controlled, friends made, and respect guaranteed through the
clever manipulation of seasonings and sauces. In the end, Nasidienus's spices, his Venafrian olive oil, and Methymnaean wine, differ
little from the incantations, voodoo dolls, and love knots that Canidia
and Sagana devise in their vain attempts to control the powers of
death.

In the feast of fools described by Fundanius, the "Servile Buffoon"
becomes an expert on hard work and a noble reputation (*labor* and
fama, line 66), and Nasidienus, unaware that Balatro's philosophizing
entails the debasement of his own character, congratulates the uninvited parasite on his moral savvy, dubbing him a "good man" (*vir bonus*) and an "elegant guest" (*conviva comis*). Convinced of Fortune's
instability and his own determination to overcome it, he goes off to
prepare the next dish. Horace, who has been silent since line 19,
breaks in at this point to congratulate Fundanius on the brilliant
piece of playacting he has just concocted (*Satires* 2.8.78–79): "*Nullos
his mallem ludos spectasse; sed illa / redde, age, quae deinceps risisti*" ("No
plays would I rather have watched than these; but come, tell me the
funny details one at a time"). The lines make explicit what we have
suspected all along; namely, that the characters and events of *Satires*
2.8 have been carefully contrived to suggest comic precedents and
the inverted world of the Roman *ludi*. Here, as throughout the *Sat-*

ires, every mask conceals a slave, and the chief slave, the head actor, is the satirist himself.

Satires 2.8 concludes with the return of Nasidienus, rejuvenated, "as if determined," Fundanius suggests, "to remove Fortune's errors by means of his [cooking] skill" (*ut arte / emendaturus fortunam*). In spite of his previous humiliation, Nasidienus has not learned that his culinary mumbo jumbo is powerless against fate, and he proceeds to narrate the "causes" (*causas*) and "natures" (*naturas*) of the food he sets before his guests, adapting the terminology of Epicurean physics to the roasting of blackbirds and pigeons as if these were matters of high scientific discourse. The incongruity again exposes his frivolous character, for although he has some feel for the technical jargon of the *De Rerum Natura*, he knows nothing of its content, which concerns the larger "causes" and "natures" of the universe, which will ultimately demand his death. The satire concludes with the dinner guests taking "revenge" (*fugimus ulti*) on their host by refusing to touch his final course, "as if infected by Canidia, whose breath is more deadly than an African viper's" (*velut illis / Canidia afflasset peior serpentibus Afris*). The final jibe against Canidia and the "revenge" of the guests points back to final scenes of the Priapus episode as well as ahead to the *Epodes*, where Canidia receives a full dose of "African venom," that is, invective in the tradition of Callimachus's *Iambs*. The hasty retreat of the dinner guests alludes also to the last lines of *Satires* 1.1, where the satirist, the "full dinner guest" (*conviva satur*) of line 119, says simply, "Enough now," and within two lines he brings the piece to an abrupt close. Here, however, the meal really has ended, for in the *serpentibus Afris* of line 95 Horace promises to move on to something else, a new genre untried by any Roman poet before him. Never again will he stretch his hand to satire's feast. *Iam satis est.*

Select Bibliography

Adams, J. N. *The Latin Sexual Vocabulary*. Baltimore: Johns Hopkins University Press, 1982.

Allen, A. W. " 'Sincerity' and the Roman Elegists." *Classical Philology* 45 (1950): 145–60.

Anderson, W. S. "Pompey, His Friends, and the Literature of the First Century B.C." *University of California Publications in Classical Philology* 19, no. 1 (1963): 1–87.

———. "The Form, Purpose, and Position of Horace's *Satire* I, 8." *American Journal of Philology* 93 (1972): 4–13.

———. *Essays on Roman Satire*. Princeton: Princeton University Press, 1982.

———. "Ironic Preambles and Satiric Self-Definition in Horace *Satire* 2.1." *Pacific Coast Philology* 19 (1984): 35–42.

Armstrong, D. "Horace, *Satires* I, 1–3: A Structural Study." *Arion* 3 (1964): 86–96.

———. "*Horatius Eques et Scriba: Satires* 1.6 and 2.7." *Transactions of the American Philological Association* 116 (1986): 255–88.

———. *Horace*. New Haven: Yale University Press, 1989.

———. "Lucretius, Philodemus, and the Poetics of Atomism." Panel on Philodemus and Poetry, Annual Meeting of the American Philological Association, Boston, 30 December 1989.

Arnold, E. V. *Roman Stoicism*. Cambridge: Cambridge University Press, 1911.

Arnott, G. "Moral Values in Menander." *Philologus* 125 (1981): 215–27.

Arthur, E. P. "The Stoic Analysis of the Mind's Reactions to Presentations." *Hermes* 111 (1983): 69–78.

Asmis, E. "The Poetic Theory of the Stoic Aristo." *Apeiron* 23, no. 3 (1990): 147–201.

Atherton, C. "Hand over Fist: The Failure of Stoic Rhetoric." *Classical Quarterly* 38, no. 2 (1988): 392–427.

Atkins, J.W.H. *Literary Criticism in Antiquity*. Cambridge: Cambridge University Press, 1934.

Axelson, B. *Unpoetische Wörter: Ein Beitrag zur Kenntnis der lateinischen Dichtersprache*. Skrifter Utgivna av Vetenskaps-Societeten i Lund. Lund, 1945.

Babcock, B. *The Reversible World: Symbolic Inversion in Art and Society*. Ithaca: Cornell University Press, 1978.

Baker, R. J. "Maecenas and Horace *Satires* 2.8." *Classical Journal* 83 (1988): 212–31.

Bakhtin, M. *Rabelais and His World*. Translated by H. Iswolsky. Cambridge, Mass.: MIT Press, 1968.

Benedetto, A. "I giambi di Callimacho e il loro influsso sugli Epodi e Satire di Orazio" *Rendiconti dell'Accademia di Archeologia* 44 (1966): 23–69.

Bennett, C. E. *Horace, the Odes and Epodes*. Cambridge, Mass.: Harvard University Press, 1947.

Bergson, H. *Laughter: An Essay on the Meaning of the Comic*. Translated by B. Cloudesley, and F. Rothwell. New York: Macmillan, 1928.

Bernstein, M. A. "*O Totiens Servus*: Saturnalia and Servitude in Augustan Rome." *Critical Inquiry* 13 (1987): 450–74.

Blänsdorf, J. "Das Bild der Komödie in der späten Republik." In U. Reinhardt and K. Sallmann, eds., *Musa Iocosa: Arbeiten über Humor und Witz Komik und Komödie der Antike*, 141–57. (Hildesheim: Olms, 1974.)

Blickman, D. "Lucretius, Epicurus, and Prehistory." *Harvard Studies in Classical Philology* 92 (1989): 157–91.

Bodoh, J. J. "Unity in Horace *Sermo* 1.1." *L'Antiquité Classique* 39 (1970): 164–67.

Bond, R. P. "The Characterization of Ofellus in Horace *Satires* 2.2 and a Note on v. 123." *Antichthon* 14 (1980): 112–26.

———. "The Characterisation of the Interlocutors in Horace, *Satires* 2.3." *Prudentia* 19 (1987): 1–21.

Botschuyver, H. J. *Scholia in Horatium*. Amsterdam: H. A. Van Bottenburg, 1935.

Bowie, A. M. "The Parabasis in Aristophanes: Prolegomena, *Acharnians*." *Classical Quarterly* 32 (1982): 27–40.

Bramble, J. *Persius and the Programmatic Satire*. Cambridge: Cambridge University Press, 1974.

Brink, C. O. "Callimachus and Aristotle: An Inquiry into Callimachus' ΠΡΟΣ ΠΡΑΞΙΦΑΝΗΝ." *Classical Quarterly* 40 (1946): 11–26.

———. *Horace on Poetry: Prolegomena to the Literary Epistles*. Cambridge: Cambridge University Press, 1963.

———. *Horace on Poetry: The Ars Poetica*. Cambridge: Cambridge University Press, 1971.

———. *Horace on Poetry: Epistles Book II*. Cambridge: Cambridge University Press, 1982.

———. "Horatian Notes IV: Despised Readings in the Manuscripts of Satires Book 1." *Proceedings of the Cambridge Philological Society*, n.s. 33 (1987): 16–37.

Brock, R. "Plato and Comedy." In E. M. Craik, ed., *Owls to Athens: Essays on Classical Subjects Presented to Sir Kenneth Dover*, 39–49 Oxford: Clarendon Press, 1990.

Brown, P. G. McC. "Masks, Names and Characters in New Comedy." *Hermes* 115 (1987): 181–202.

Buchheit, V. "Homerparodie und Literaturkritik in Horazens Sat. I 7 und I 9." *Gymnasium* 85 (1968): 519–55.

Casson, L. "The Athenian Upper Class and New Comedy." *Transactions of the American Philological Association* 106 (1976): 29–59.

Castle, T. *Masquerade and Civilization*. Stanford, Calif.: Stanford University Press, 1986.

Charpin, F. *Lucilius Satires II*. 2 vols. Paris: Belles lettres, 1978–79.

Gardner, H. *Art through the Ages I: Ancient, Medieval, and Non-European Art.* 8th ed. New York: Harcourt Brace Jovanovich, 1986.

Geffcken, K. *Comedy in the Pro Caelio. Mnemosyne* Supplement 30. Leiden: E. J. Brill, 1973.

Gercke, A. "Die Komposition der ersten Satire des Horaz." *Rheinisches Museum* 48 (1893): 41–52.

Gerhard, G. A. "Iambographen." In A. Pauly and G. Wissowa, eds., *Real-Encyclopädie der classischen Altertumswissenshaft.* Stuttgart: J. B. Metzler, 1894–1963.

———. *Phoinix von Kolophon.* Leipzig: Teubner, 1909.

Giangrande, L. *The Use of Spoudaiogeloion in Greek and Roman Literature.* Studies in Classical Literature 6. The Hague: Mouton, 1972.

Glazewski, J. "*Plenus Vitae Conviva*: A Lucretian Concept in Horace's *Satires*." *Classical Bulletin* 47 (1971): 85–88.

Goldberg, S. *Understanding Terence.* Princeton: Princeton University Press, 1986.

Golden, L. "Catharsis." *Transactions of the American Philological Association* 93 (1962): 51–60.

———. "Mimesis and Katharsis." *Classical Philology* 64 (1969): 145–53.

———. "Katharsis as Purification: An Objection Answered." *Classical Quarterly* 23 (1973): 45–46.

———. "The Purification Theory of Catharsis." *Journal of Aesthetics and Art Criticism* 31 (1973): 474–79.

———. "Aristotle on Comedy." *Journal of Aesthetics and Art Criticism* 42 (1984): 283–90.

———. "Comic Pleasure." *Hermes* 115 (1987): 165–74.

Grant, M. A. *The Ancient Rhetorical Theories of the Laughable.* University of Wisconsin Studies in Language and Literature 21. Madison, 1924.

Greenberg, N. "The Poetic Theory of Philodemus." Ph.D. diss., Harvard, University 1955. Reprint. New York and London: Garland Publishing, 1990.

———. "Metathesis as an Instrument in the Criticism of Poetry." *Transactions of the American Philological Association* 89 (1958): 262–70.

———. "The Use of *Poiema* and *Poiesis*." *Harvard Studies in Classical Philology* 65 (1961): 263–89.

Griffin, J. *Latin Poets and Roman Life.* Chapel Hill: University of North Carolina Press, 1986.

Griffith, J. J. "The Ending of Juvenal's First Satire and Lucilius Book XXX." *Hermes* 98 (1970): 56–72.

Grube, G.M.A. "Theophrastus as a Literary Critic." *Transactions of the American Philological Association* 83 (1952): 172–83.

———. *A Greek Critic: Demetrius on Style.* Toronto: University of Toronto Press, 1961.

———. *The Greek and Roman Critics.* Toronto: University of Toronto Press, 1965.

Cherniss, H. "The Biographical Fashion in Literary Criticism." *University of California Publications in Classical Philology* 12 (1943–44): 279–91.

Christes, J. "Der frühe Lucilius und Horaz: Eine Entgegnung." *Hermes* 117 (1989): 321–26.

Classen, C. J. "Horace's Satire on Satire, Some Remarks on *Sat.* 1.4." *Museum Africum* 6 (1977–78): 15–20.

———. "Die Kritik des Horaz in den Satiren I 4 und I 5." *Hermes* 109 (1981): 339–60.

———. "Satire, the Elusive Genre." *Symbolae Osloenses* 63 (1988): 95–121.

Clausen, W. "Cicero and the New Poetry." *Harvard Studies in Classical Philology* 90 (1986): 159–70.

Clauss, J. J. "Allusion and Structure in Horace Satire 2.1: The Callimachean Response." *Transactions of the American Philological Association* 115 (1985): 197–206.

———. "Vergil and the Euphrates Revisited." *American Journal of Philology* 109 (1988): 309–20.

Clayman, D. "Callimachus' Thirteenth *Iamb*: The Last Word." *Hermes* 104 (1976): 29–35.

———. *Callimachus' Iambi. Mnemosyne* Supplement 59. Leiden: E. J. Brill, 1980.

Cody, J. V. *Horace and Callimachean Aesthetics.* Collection Latomus 147. Brussels: Latomus Revue d'études Latines, 1976.

Coffey, M. *Roman Satire.* London: Methuen, 1976.

Cole, T. *The Origins of Rhetoric in Ancient Greece.* Baltimore: Johns Hopkins University Press, 1991.

Colson, F. H. "The Analogist and Anomalist Controversy." *Classical Quarterly* 13 (1919): 24–36.

Cooper, L. *An Aristotelian Theory of Comedy, with an Adaptation of the Poetics and a Translation of the Tractatus Coislinianus.* New York: Harcourt, Brace, 1922.

Corbett, P. *The Scurra.* Edinburgh: Scottish Academic Press, 1986.

Coulter, J. A. "An Unnoted Allusion to Aristotle's *Nichomachean Ethics* in Horace *Sermones* 2.2." *Classical Philology* 67 (1967): 39–41.

Courtney, E. *A Commentary on the Satires of Juvenal.* London: Athlone Press, 1980.

Crowther, N. B. "ΟΙ ΝΕΩΤΕΡΟΙ, Poetae Novi, and Cantores Euphorionis." *Classical Quarterly* 20 (1970): 322–27.

———. "Horace, Catullus, and Alexandrianism." *Mnemosyne* 31 (1978): 33–44.

———. "Water and Wine as Symbols of Inspiration." *Mnemosyne* 30 (1979): 1–11.

Curran, L. C. "Nature, Convention, and Obscenity in Horace, *Satires* 1.2." *Arion* 9 (1970): 220–45.

D'Alton, J. F. *Roman Literary Theory and Criticism.* London: Longmans, Green, 1931.

Damon, C. "Vetus atque Antiquus Quaestus: The Art of the Parasite in Ancient Rome." Ph.D. diss., Stanford University, 1990.

Davies, P. V. *Macrobius, the Saturnalia*. Translated with introduction and notes. New York: Columbia University Press, 1969.

Dawson, C. M. "The Iambi of Callimachus, a Hellenistic Poet's Experimental Laboratory." *Yale Classical Studies* 11 (1950): 3–168.

DeAngeli, E. "A Literary Chill: Catullus 44." *Classical World* 62 (1969): 354–56.

Degani, E. *Hipponactis Testimonia et Fragmenta*. Vol. 1. Leipzig: Teubner, 1983.

DeLacy, P. "The Epicurean Analysis of Language" *American Journal of Philology* 60 (1939): 85–92.

———. "Stoic Views of Poetry." *American Journal of Philology* 69 (1948): 241–71.

Dettmer, H. *Horace: A Study in Structure*. Altertumswissenschaftliche Texte und Studien 12. Hildesheim: Olms, 1983.

DeWitt, N. "The Parresiastic Poems of Horace." *Classical Philology* 30, no. 1 (1935): 312–19.

———. "Epicurean Doctrine in Horace." *Classical Philology* 34 (1939): 127–34.

———. *Epicurus and His Philosophy*. Minneapolis: University of Minnesota Press, 1954.

Dickie, M. W. "The Disavowal of *Invidia* in Roman Iamb and Satire." *Papers of the Liverpool Latin Seminar* 3 (1981): 183–208.

Dihle, A. "Analogie und Attizismus." *Hermes* 85 (1957): 170–205.

Douglas, A. E. *M. Tulli Ciceronis Brutus*. Oxford: Clarendon Press, 1966.

Dover, K. J. *Aristophanic Comedy*. London: B. T. Batsford, 1972.

Duckworth, G. E. *The Nature of Roman Comedy*. Princeton: Princeton University Press, 1952.

Dudley, D. R. *A History of Cynicism*. London: Methuen, 1937.

Duff, J. W. *Roman Satire*. Berkeley, 1936. Reprint. Hamden, Conn.: Archon Books, 1961.

Dunn, F. "Horace's Sacred Spring (*Ode* 1.1)." *Latomus* 48 (1989): 97–109.

———. "An Invitation to Tyndaris: Horace *Ode* 1.17." *Transactions of the American Philological Association* 120 (1990): 203–8.

DuQuesnay, I. M. Le M. "Horace and Maecenas." In T. Woodman, and D. West, eds., *Poetry and Politics in the Age of Augustus*, 19–58. Cambridge: Cambridge University Press, 1984.

Edelstein, L. "The Philosophical System of Posidonius." *American Journal of Philology* 57 (1936): 286–325.

Edinger, H. G. "Horace, *C.* 1.17." *Classical Journal* 66 (1971): 306–11.

Edmonds, J. M. *The Fragments of Attic Comedy*. Vol. IIIa. Leiden: E. J. Brill, 1961.

Eggermont, P.H.L. "*Queritur num Horatius se nuce comparet. Serm.* 2.1.74–80." *Mnemosyne* 10 (1941–42): 69–76.

Ehlers, W. "Das 'Iter Brundisinum' des Horaz (Serm. 1,5)." *Hermes* 113 (1985): 70.

Ehrman, R. "Terentian Prologues and the Parabases of Old Comedy." *Latomus* 44 (1985): 370–76.

Else, G. *Aristotle's Poetics: The Argument*. Cambridge Mass.: Harvard University Press, 1957.

———. *Plato and Aristotle on Poetry*. Chapel Hill: University of North Carolina Press, 1986.

Evans, H. "Horace, *Satires* 2.7: Saturnalia and Satire." *Classical Journal* 73 (1977–78): 307–12.

Fairclough, H. R. "Horace's View of the Relations between Satire and Comedy." *American Journal of Philology* 34 (1913): 183–93.

———. *Horace: Satires, Epistles, Ars Poetica*. Cambridge, Mass.: Harvard University Press, 1929.

Fantham, E. *Comparative Studies in Republican Latin Imagery*. Toronto: University of Toronto Press, 1972.

———. "Roman Experience of Menander in the Late Republic and Early Empire." *Transactions of the American Philological Association* 114 (1984): 299–309.

———. "Mime: The Missing Link in Roman Literary History." *Classical World* 82 (1989): 153–63.

Fiske, G. C. "Lucilius and Persius." *Transactions of the American Philological Association* 40 (1909): 121–50.

———. "The Plain Style in the Scipionic Circle." *University of Wisconsin Studies in Language and Literature* 3 (1919): 62–105.

———. *Lucilius and Horace: A Study in the Classical Theory of Imitation*. University of Wisconsin Studies in Language and Literature 7. Madison, 1920.

———. *Cicero's* De Oratore *and Horace's* Ars Poetica. University of Wisconsin Studies in Language and Literature 27. Madison, 1929.

Flintoff, E. "Naevius and Roman Satire." *Latomus* 47 (1988): 593–603.

Fortenbaugh, W. W. *Aristotle on Emotion*. London: Duckworth, 1975.

Fraenkel, E. *Horace*. Oxford: Clarendon Press, 1957.

Frank, T. "Horace's Description of a Scene in Lucilius." *American Journal of Philology* 46 (1925): 72–74.

Freud, S. *Jokes and Their Relation to the Unconscious*. Translated by J. Strachey. New York: W. W. Norton, 1960.

Freudenburg, K. "Lucretius, Vergil, and the *Causa Morbi*." *Vergilius* 33 (1987): 59–74.

———. "Greek Theories of Comedy and Style in the Satires of Horace." Ph.D. diss., University of Wisconsin at Madison, 1989.

———. "Horace's Satiric Program and the Language of Contemporary Theory in *Satires* 2.1." *American Journal of Philology* 111, no. 2 (1990): 187–203.

Gaiser, K. "Menander und der Peripatos." *Antike und Abendland* 13 (1967).

Gantar, K. "Horazens *Amicus Sibi*." *Acta Antiqua Academiae Scientiarum Hungaricae* 12 (1964): 129–135.

———. "Horaz zwischen Akademie und Epikur." *Ziva Antika* 22 (1972): 5–24.

———. "La Préhistoire d'*Amicus Sibi* chez Horace." *Les Études Classiques* 44 (1976): 209–21.

Guilhamet, L. *Satire and the Transformation of Genre.* Philadelphia: University of Pennsylvania Press, 1987.

Hahn, E. A. "Horace's Use of Concrete Examples." *Classical World* 39, nos. 2 and 3 (1946): 82–86 and 90–94.

Haight, E. H. "Menander at the Sabine Farm, *Exemplar Vitae.*" *Classical Philology* 42 (1947): 147–55.

Halliwell, S. "Ancient Interpretations of ὀνομαστὶ κωμῳδεῖν in Aristophanes." *Classical Quarterly* 34 (1984): 83–88.

———. *The Poetics of Aristotle.* Chapel Hill: University of North Carolina Press, 1987.

Harmon, A. M., trans. *Lucian.* Vol. 4. Cambridge Mass.: Harvard University Press, 1953.

Harrison, G. "The Confessions of Lucilius (Horace *Sat.* 2.1.30–34): A Defense of Autobiographical Satire?" *Classical Antiquity* 6 (1987): 38–52.

Hawtrey, R.S.W. "The Poet as Example: Horace's Use of Himself." In Carl Deroux, ed., *Studies in Latin Literature and Roman History,* vol. 1, 249–56. Collection *Latomus* 164. Brussels: Latomus Revue d'Études Latines, 1979.

Heath, M. "Aristotelian Comedy." *Classical Quarterly* 39, no. 2 (1989): 344–54.

Heinze, R. "Die Horatio Bionis Imitatore." Ph.D. diss., Bonn, 1889.

Heldmann, K. "Die Wesenbestimmung der Horazischen Satire durch die Komödie." *Antike und Abendland* 33 (1987): 122–39.

———. "Trebonius und seine Lucilische Satire aus dem Jahre 44 v.Chr." *Symbolae Osloenses* 63 (1988): 69–75.

Henderson, J. *The Maculate Muse.* New Haven: Yale University Press, 1975.

———. "The Demos and the Comic Competition." In J. Winkler and F. Zeitlin, eds., *Nothing to Do with Dionysus?*, 271–313. Princeton: Princeton University Press, 1990.

Henderson, J.G.W. ". . . When Satire Writes 'Woman.'" In S. Braund, ed., *Satire and Society in Ancient Rome,* 89–125. University of Exeter Studies in History 23. Exeter: University of Exeter Press, 1989.

Hendrickson, G. L. "The Dramatic Satura and the Old Comedy at Rome." *American Journal of Philology* 15 (1894): 1–30.

———. "Horace, *Serm.* 1.4: A Protest and a Programme." *American Journal of Philology* 21 (1900): 121–42.

———. "The Peripatetic Mean of Style and the Three Stylistic Characters." *American Journal of Philology* 25 (1904): 125–46.

———. "The Origin and Meaning of the Ancient Characters of Style." *American Journal of Philology* 26 (1905): 248–90.

———. "The *De Analogia* of Julius Caesar: Its Occasion, Nature, and Date, with Additional Fragments." *Classical Philology* 1, no. 2 (1906): 97–120.

———. "Satura, the Genesis of a Literary Form." *Classical Philology* 6 (1911): 129–43.

———. "Horace and Valerius Cato I: The Original Opening of *Serm.* 1.10." *Classical Philology* 11 (1916): 249–69.

Hendrickson, G. L. "Horace and Valerius Cato II: The Adversarius of *Serm.* 1.10, and Other Personal Allusions." *Classical Philology* 12 (1917): 77–92.

———. "Horace and Valerius Cato III: The Neoteric Poets and the Latin Purists." *Classical Philology* 12 (1917): 329–50.

———. "Cicero *De Optimo Genere Oratorum*." *American Journal of Philology* 47 (1926): 109–23.

———. "Cicero's Correspondence with Brutus and Calvus on Oratorical Style." *American Journal of Philology* 47 (1926): 234–58.

———. "Cicero *De Optimo Genere Oratorum*." *American Journal of Philology* 47 (1936): 109–23.

Hering, W. *Die Dialektik von Inhalt und Form bei Horaz*. Schriften zur Geschichte und Kultur der Antike 20. Berlin: Akademie-Verlag, 1979.

Herter, H. "Zur ersten Satire des Horaz.," *Rheinisches Museum* 94 (1951): 1–42.

Highet, G. *The Anatomy of Satire*. Princeton: Princeton University Press, 1962.

———. "*Libertino Patre Natus*." *American Journal of Philology* 94 (1973): 268–81.

———. "Masks and Faces in Satire." *Hermes* 102 (1974): 321–37.

Hinds, S. *The Metamorphosis of Persephone*. Cambridge: Cambridge University Press, 1987.

Holder, A., and O. Keller, eds. *Scholia Antiqua in Q. Horatium Flaccum*. Vol. 1, *Porfyrionis Commentum* Innsbruck: Wagner, 1894. Reprint. New York: Arno Press, 1979.

Horsfall, N. "The Collegium Poetarum." *Bulletin of the Institute of Classical Studies, University of London* 23 (1976): 79–95.

———. "Doctus Sermones Utriusque Linguae." *Echos du Monde Classique* 22 (1979): 85–95.

Hubbard, T. "The Structure and Programmatic Intent of Horace's First Satire." *Latomus* 40 (1981): 305–21.

Hunter, R. L. "Horace on Friendship and Free Speech." *Hermes* 113 (1985): 480–90.

———. *The New Comedy of Greece and Rome*. Cambridge: Cambridge University Press, 1985.

Irwin, T. *Plato's Moral Theory*. Oxford: Clarendon Press, 1977.

Janko, R. *Aristotle on Comedy*. Berkeley: University of California Press, 1984.

Jensen, C. *Philodemos über Die Gedichte Fünftes Buch*. Berlin: Weidmannsche Buchhandlung, 1923.

Jocelyn, H. D. "Boats, Women, and Horace *Odes* 1.14." *Classical Philology* 77 (1982): 330–35.

———. "Diatribes and Sermons." *Liverpool Classical Monthly* 7, no. 1 (1982): 3–7.

Kaibel, G. "Die Prolegomena ΠΕΡΙ ΚΩΜΩΙΔΙΑΣ." *Abhandlungen der Gesellschaft der Wissenschaften zu Göttingen* 2, no. 4 (1898): 3–70.

———. *Comicorum Graecorum Fragmenta*. Berlin, 1899.

Keller, O, ed. *Pseudacronis Scholia in Horatium Vetustiora*. Vol. 2. Stuttgart: Teubner, 1967.

Kennedy, G. *The Art of Persuasion in Greece*. Princeton: Princeton University Press, 1963.

———. *The Art of Rhetoric in the Roman World.* Princeton: Princeton University Press, 1972.

———. "Two Contributions to Aristotelian Studies." *American Journal of Philology* 111, no. 1 (1990): 86–91.

Kenney, E. J. *Lucretius De Rerum Natura Book III.* Cambridge: Cambridge University Press, 1971.

Kernan, A. *The Cankered Muse.* New Haven: Yale University Press, 1959.

Kiessling, A., and Heinze, R. *Q. Horatius Flaccus: Satiren.* Berlin: Weidmannsche Verlagsbuchhandlung, 1961.

Kindstrand, J. F. *Bion of Borysthenes.* Studia Graeca Upsaliensia 11. Uppsala, 1976.

Klingner, F. *Horatius Opera.* 6th ed. Leipzig: Teubner, 1982.

Knapp, C. "The Sceptical Assault on the Roman Tradition concerning Dramatic Satura." *American Journal of Philology* 33 (1912): 125–48.

———. "Horace, *Sermones* 1.1." *Transactions of the American Philological Association* 45 (1914): 91–109.

Knoche, U. *Roman Satire.* Translated by E. Ramage. Bloomington: Indiana University Press, 1974.

Knox, P. "Wine, Water, and Callimachean Polemics." *Harvard Studies in Classical Philology* 89 (1985): 107–19.

Kock, T. *Comicorum Atticorum Fragmenta.* 3 vols. Leipzig: Teubner, 1880–88.

Korfmacher, W. "*Grecizing* in Lucilian Satire." *Classical Journal* 30 (1935): 453–62.

Koster, W.J.W. *Scholia in Aristophanem, Fasc. Ia.* Groningen: Bouma's Boekhuis, 1975.

Krenkel, W. "Zur literarischen Kritik bei Lucilius." In D. Korzeniewski, ed., *Die römische Satire*, 161–266. Wege der Forschung 238. Darmstadt, 1970.

———. "Horace's Approach to Satire." *Arethusa* 5 (1972): 7–16.

LaFleur, R. "Horace and *Onomasti Komodein*: The Law of Satire." *Aufstieg und Niedergang der römischen Welt* 2.31.3 (1981): 1790–1826.

Langford, P. "Horace's Protean Satire: Public Life, Ethics, and Literature in Satires II." Ph.D. diss., Princeton University, 1989.

Lateiner, D. "Mimetic Syntax: Metaphor from Word Order, Especially in Ovid." *American Journal of Philology* 111, no. 2 (1990): 204–37.

Leach, E. W. "Horace's *Pater Optimus* and Terence's Demea: Autobiographical Fiction and Comedy in *Serm.* 1.4." *American Journal of Philology* 92 (1971): 616–32.

Leeman, A. D. "Die Konsultierung des Trebatius: Statuslehre in Horaz, *Serm.* 2.1." In P. Handel and W. Meid, eds., *Festschrift für Robert Muth*, 209–15. Innsbrucker Beiträge zur Kulturwissenschaft 22. Innsbruck, 1983.

———. *Orationis Ratio: The Stylistic Theories and Practices of the Roman Orators, Historians, and Philosophers.* Amsterdam: Adolf M. Hakkert, 1963. Reprint. 1986.

Lefèvre, E. "*Nil Medium Est*: Die früheste Satire des Horaz (I,2)." In E. Lefèvre, ed., *Monumentum Chiloniense: Festschrift E. Burck*, 311–46. Amsterdam: Adolf Hakkert, 1975.

Lejay, P., and Plessis, F. *Oeuvres d'Horace.* Paris, 1911. Reprint. Hildesheim: Georg Olms, 1966.

Leo, F. "Varro und die Satire." *Hermes* 24 (1889): 66–84.

Long, A. A. *Problems in Stoicism*. London: Athlone Press, 1971.

———. *Hellenistic Philosophy*. Berkeley: University of California Press, 1974.

———. "Socrates in Hellenistic Philosophy." *Classical Quarterly* 38 (1988): 150–71.

Long, A. A., and D. N. Sedley, eds. *The Hellenistic Philosophers*: Vol. 2, *Greek and Latin Texts*. Cambridge: Cambridge University Press, 1987.

Lord, C. "Aristotle, Menander, and the *Adelphoe* of Terence." *Transactions of the American Philological Association* 107 (1977): 183–202.

Lucas, D. W. *Aristotle: Poetics*. Oxford: Clarendon Press, 1968.

Ludwig, H. "Die Komposition der beiden Satirenbücher des Horaz." *Poetica* 2 (1968): 304–35.

Lyne, R.O.A.M. *Words and the Poet*. Oxford: Clarendon Press, 1989.

MacDowell, D. M. "The Nature of Aristophanes' *Acharnians*." *Greece and Rome* 30 (1983): 143–62.

Mack, M. "The Muse of Satire." *Yale Review* 41 (1951–52): 80–92.

MacKendrick, P. *The Mute Stones Speak*. 2nd ed. New York: W. W. Norton, 1983.

MacMullen, R. *Enemies of the Roman Order*. Cambridge, Mass.: Harvard University Press, 1966.

Marouzeau, J. "Horace assembleur de mots." *Emerita* 4 (1936): 1–10.

Martyn, J.R.C. "Satis Saturae?" *Mnemosyne* 25 (1972): 157–67.

Marx, F. *C. Lucilii Carminum Reliquiae*. Leipzig, 1904.

McKeown, J. C. "Augustan Elegy and Mime." *Proceedings of the Cambridge Philological Society*, n.s. 25 (1979): 71–84.

McLeish, K. *The Theatre of Aristophanes*. New York: Taplinger, 1980.

McMahon, A. P. "On the Second Book of Aristotle's *Poetics* and the Source of Theophrastus' Definition of Tragedy." *Harvard Studies in Classical Philology* 28 (1917): 1–46.

———. "Seven Questions on Aristotelian Definitions of Tragedy and Comedy." *Harvard Studies in Classical Philology* 40 (1929): 97–198.

Mendell, C. W. "Satire as Popular Philosophy." *Classical Philology* 15 (1920): 138–57.

Mette, H. J. "*Genus Tenue* und *Mensa Tenuis* bei Horaz." In H. Oppermann, ed. *Wege zu Horaz*, 220–24. Darmstadt: Wissenschaftliche Buchgesellschaft, 1972.

Michels, A. K. "ΠΑΡΡΗΣΙΑ and the Satire of Horace." *Classical Philology* 39 (1944): 173–77.

Minyard, J. D. *Lucretius and the Late Republic*. Leiden: E. J. Brill, 1985.

Moles, J. "Cynicism in Horace *Epistles* 1." *Papers of the Liverpool Latin Seminar* 5 (1985): 33–60.

Moore, T. "Plautus, Brecht, and the 'Alienation Effect.' " An address to the Classical Association of the Atlantic States, Lancaster, Pennsylvania, 30 September 1989.

Motto, A. L. "Stoic Elements in the *Satires* of Horace." In C. Henderson, ed.,

Classical, Mediaeval and Renaissance Studies in Honor of Berthold Louis Ullman, 133–41. Rome: Edizioni di Storia e Letteratura, 1964.

Murley, C. "Lucretius and the History of Satire." *Transactions of the American Philological Association* 70 (1939): 380–95.

Murray, R. J. "Aristophanic Protest." *Hermes* 115 (1987): 146–54.

Musurillo, H. "Horace and the Bore: *Character Dramaticus* of *Sat.* 1.9." *Classical Bulletin* 40 (1964): 65–69.

Nauta, R. R. "Seneca's *Apocolocyntosis* as Saturnalian Literature." *Mnemosyne* 40 (1987): 69–96.

Nilson, N. *Metrische Stildifferenzen in den Satiren des Horaz.* Studia Latina Holmiensia 1. Uppsala: Alumquist & Wiksells Boktryckeri, 1952.

Nisbet, R., and M. Hubbard. *A Commentary on Horace: Odes Book 1.* Oxford: Clarendon Press, 1970.

Ogle, M. B. "Horace an Atticist." *Classical Philology* 11 (1916): 156–68.

———. "*Molle Atque Facetum.*" *American Journal of Philology* 37 (1916): 327–32.

Olivieri, A., ed. *Philodemi* ΠΕΡΙ ΠΑΡΡΗΣΙΑΣ. Leipzig: Teubner, 1914.

Oltramare, A. *Les origines de la diatribe romaine.* Lausanne: Payot, 1926.

Palmer, A. *The Satires of Horace.* London: Macmillan, 1883.

Parker, A. "Comic Theory in the Satires of Horace. Ph.D. diss., University of North Carolina at Chapel Hill, 1986.

Parker, W. *Priapea: Poems for a Phallic God.* London: Croom Helm, 1988.

Pavlovskis, Z. "Aristotle, Horace, and the Ironic Man." *Classical Philology* 63 (1968): 22–41.

Pfeiffer, R. *Callimachus:* Vol. 1, *Fragmenta.* Oxford: Clarendon Press, 1949.

Pohlenz, M. *Die Stoa: Geschichte einer geistigen Bewegung.* Göttingen: Vandenhoeck and Ruprecht, 1948–49.

Quinn, K. *Catullus, the Poems.* 2nd ed. London: Macmillan, 1973.

Rackham, H. "Notes on Horace." *Classical Review* 30 (1916): 223–24.

Radermacher, L. "Die Zeit der ersten Horazsatire." *Wiener Studien* 42 (1921): 148–51.

Radke, G. "Topographische Betrachtungen zum *Iter Brundisinum* des Horaz." *Rheinisches Museum* 132 (1989): 54–72.

Rambaux, R. "La composition d'ensemble du Livre I des *Satires* d'Horace." *Revue des Études Latines* 49 (1971): 179–204.

Randolph, M. C. "The Structural Design of the Formal Verse Satire." *Philological Quarterly* 21, no. 4 (1942): 368–84.

Raschke, W. "The Chronology of the Early Books of Lucilius." *Journal of Roman Studies* 69 (1979): 78–89.

———. "*Arma Pro Amico*—Lucilian Satire at the Crisis of the Roman Republic." *Hermes* 115 (1987): 299–318.

Rawson, E. *Intellectual Life in the Late Roman Republic.* Baltimore: Johns Hopkins University Press, 1985.

———. "*Speciosa Locis Morataque Recte.*" In Michael Whitby, P. Hardie, and Mary Whitby, eds., *Homo Viator: Classical Essays for John Bramble.* Bristol: Bristol Classical Press, 1987.

Relihan, J. "A History of Menippean Satire." Ph.D. diss., University of Wisconsin at Madison, 1985.

———. "Menippus the Cynic in the Greek Anthology." *Syllecta Classica* 1 (1989): 55–61.

Reynolds, R. "Criticism of Individuals in Roman Popular Comedy." *Classical Quarterly* 37 (1943): 37–45.

Rist, J. M. *Stoic Philosophy*. Cambridge: Cambridge University Press, 1969.

Roberts, R. *Dionysius on Literary Composition*. London, 1910. Reprint. New York: AMS Press, 1976.

Robinson, R. P. "Valerius Cato." *Transactions of the American Philological Association* 54 (1923): 98–116.

Rosen, R. M. "Hipponax, Boupalos, and the Conventions of the *Psogos*." *Transactions of the American Philological Association* 118 (1988): 29–42.

———. *Old Comedy and the Iambographic Tradition*. Atlanta: Scholars Press, 1988.

Rudd, N. "Horace and Fannius." *Hermathena* 87 (1956): 49–60.

———. "Horace's Encounter with the Bore." *Phoenix* 15 (1961): 90–96.

———. *The Satires of Horace*. Cambridge: Cambridge University Press, 1966.

———. *Themes in Roman Satire*. Norman: University of Oklahoma Press, 1986.

Russell, D. A. *Plutarch*. New York: Charles Scribner's Sons, 1973.

———. *Criticism in Antiquity*. Berkeley: University of California Press, 1981.

Russell, D. A., and M. Winterbottom. *Ancient Literary Criticism*. Oxford: Clarendon Press, 1972.

Sallmann, K. "Die seltsame Reise nach Brundisium. Aufbau und Deutung der Horazsatire 1,5." In U. Reinhardt and K. Sallmann, eds., *Musa Iocosa: Arbeiten über Humor und Witz Komik und Komödie der Antike*, 179–206. Hildesheim: Olms, 1974.

Sandy, G. N. "Indebtedness, *Scurrilitas*, and Composition in Catullus (Cat. 44,1,68)." *Phoenix* 32 (1978): 68–80.

Saunders, C. *Costume in Roman Comedy*. New York: AMS Press, 1966.

Sbordone, F. *Ricerche Sui Papiri Ercolanesi*. Pubblicazione Finanziata dal Consiglio Nazionale delle Ricerche 2. Naples: Giannini Editore, 1976.

Scaglione, A. *The Classical Theory of Composition from Its Origins to the Present: A Historical Survey*. Chapel Hill: the University of North Carolina Press, 1972.

Schenkeveld, D. M. "Linguistic Theories in the Rhetorical Works of Dionysius of Halicarnassus" *Glotta* 61 (1983): 67–94.

Schetter, W. "Zum Aufbau der Horazsatire I,8." *Antike und Abendland* 17 (1971): 144–61.

Schmidt, P. "Typologische und gattungsgeschichtliche Vorüberlegungen zum sozialen Engagement der römischen Satire" *Lampas* 12 (1979): 259–81.

Scholz, U. "Der frühe Lucilius und Horaz." *Hermes* 114 (1986): 335–65.

Schröter, R. "Horazens Satire 1,7 und die Antike Eposparodie." *Poetica* 1 (1967): 8–23.

Schütrumpf, E. "Traditional Elements in the Concept of *Hamartia* in Aristotle's *Poetics*." *Harvard Studies in Classical Philology* 92 (1989): 137–56.

Schütz, H. *Q. Horatius Flaccus. Satiren.* Berlin: Weidmann, 1881.

Scodel, R. "Horace, Lucilius, and Callimachean Polemic." *Harvard Studies in Classical Philology* 91 (1987): 199–215.

Sedgwick, W. B. "Catullus X: A Rambling Commentary." *Greece and Rome* 16 (1947): 108–14.

Segal, E. *Roman Laughter.* Cambridge, Mass.: Harvard University Press, 1968.

Shackleton Bailey, D. R. "*Vindiciae Horatianae.*" *Harvard Studies in Classical Philology* 89 (1985): 153–70.

Shero, L. R. "The Satirist's *Apologia.*" *University of Wisconsin Studies in Language and Literature* 15 (1922): 148–67.

Sihler, E. G. "The Collegium Poetarum at Rome." *American Journal of Philology* 26 (1905): 1–21.

Simpson, P. "Aristotle on Poetry and Imitation." *Hermes* 116 (1988): 279–91.

Smiley, C. N. "Seneca and the Stoic Theory of Literary Style." *University of Wisconsin Studies in Language and Literature* 3 (1919): 50–61.

Snyder, J. *Puns and Poetry in Lucretius' De Rerum Natura.* Amsterdam: Grüner, 1980.

Solmsen, F. "Aristotle and Cicero on the Orator's Playing upon the Feelings." *Classical Philology* 33 (1938): 390–404.

———. "The Aristotelian Tradition in Ancient Rhetoric." *American Journal of Philology* 62 (1941): 35–50.

Solodow, J. B. "*Raucae, Tua cura, Palumbes*: Study of a Poetic Word Order." *Harvard Studies in Classical Philology* 90 (1986): 129–53.

Stallybrass, P., and A. White. *The Politics and Poetics of Transgression.* Ithaca: Cornell University Press, 1986.

Stone, L. M. *Costume in Aristophanic Comedy.* New York: Arno Press, 1981.

Storey, I. "Old Comedy, 1975–1984." *Echos du Monde Classique* 31, n.s. 6 (1987): 1–46.

Striller, F. "*De Stoicorum Studiis Rhetoricis.*" *Breslauer Philologische Abhandlungen* 1 (1887): 1–61.

Syme, R. *The Roman Revolution.* Oxford: Clarendon Press, 1939.

Tait, J.I.M. "Philodemus' Influence on the Latin Poets." Ph.D. diss., Bryn Mawr College, 1941.

Tate, J. "Horace and the Moral Function of Poetry." *Classical Quarterly* 22 (1928): 65–72.

Taylor, L. R. *Party Politics in the Age of Caesar.* Berkeley: University of California Press, 1949.

Thomas, R. "New Comedy, Callimachus, and Roman Poetry." *Harvard Studies in Classical Philology* 83 (1979): 179–206.

Tillyard, E. M. *The Personal Heresy: A Controversy by E. M. Tillyard and C. S. Lewis.* London: Oxford University Press, 1965.

Tukey, R. H. "The Stoic Use of ΛΕΞΙΣ AND ΦΡΑΣΙΣ." *Classical Philology* 6 (1911): 444–49.

Ullman, B. L. "Horace and Tibullus." *American Journal of Philology* 33 (1912): 140–67.

Ullman, B. L. "Horace, Catullus, and Tigellius." *Classical Philology* 10 (1915): 270–96.

———. "Horace on the Nature of Satire." *Transactions of the American Philological Association* 48 (1917): 111–32.

Usher, S., ed. *Dionysius of Halicarnassus: The Critical Essays II*. Cambridge Mass.: Harvard University Press, 1985.

Ussher, R. G. *The Characters of Theophrastus*. London: Macmillan, 1960.

———. "Old Comedy and *Character*, Some Comments." *Greece and Rome* (1977): 70–79.

———. "The Mimic Tradition of Character in Herodas." *Quaderni Urbinati di Cultura Classica*, n.s. 21 (1985): 45–68.

Van Hook, L. "The Metaphorical Terminology of Greek Rhetoric and Literary Criticism." Ph.D. diss., University of Chicago, 1905.

———. "Ψυχρότης ἢ τὸ Ψυχρόν." *Classical Philology* 12 (1917): 68–76.

Van Rooy, C. A. *Studies in Classical Satire and Related Literary Theory*. Leiden: E. J. Brill, 1966.

———. "Arrangement and Structure of Satires in Horace, *Sermones*, Book 1, with More Special Reference to Satires 1–4." *Acta Classica* 11 (1968): 38–72.

———. "Arrangement and Structure of Satires in Horace, *Sermones*, Book 1: Satires 5 and 6." *Acta Classica* 13 (1970): 45–59.

———. "Horace, *Sermones*, Book 1: Satires 1.4 and 1.10." *Acta Classica* 13 (1970): 7–27.

———. "Arrangement and Structure of *Satires* in Horace, *Sermones* Book I: Satires 9 and 10." *Acta Classica* 15 (1972): 37–52.

———. "Horace's *Sat.* 1.1 as Prooemium and Its Relation to Satires 2 to 10." In W. Kraus, A. Primmer, and H. Schwabl, eds., *Latinität und Alte Kirche: Festschrift Rudolf Hanslik*, 263–74. Vienna: Hermann Böhlaus, 1977.

Verdenius, W. J. "The Principles of Greek Literary Criticism." *Mnemosyne* 36 (1983): 14–59.

Vlastos, G. "Socratic Irony." *Classical Quarterly* 37 (1987): 79–96.

Wallach, B. "A History of the Diatribe from Its Origin up to the First Century B.C. and a Study of the Influence of the Genre upon Lucretius III, 830–1094." Ph.D. diss., University of Illinois, Urbana-Champaign, 1974.

———. *Lucretius and the Diatribe against the Fear of Death: De Rerum Natura III 830–1094. Mnemosyne* Supplement 50. Leiden: E. J. Brill, 1976.

Walsh, G. B. "Philodemus on the Terminology of Neoptolemus." *Mnemosyne* 40 (1987): 56–68.

Watling, E. F., trans. *Plautus, the Pot of Gold and Other Plays*. London: Penguin Books, 1965.

Walz, A. *Des variations de la langue et de la métrique d'Horace*. Studia Philologica 12. Rome: L'Erma di Bretschneider, 1968.

Weber, H. "Comic Humour and Tragic Spirit: The Augustan Distinction between Horace and Juvenal." *Classical and Modern Literature* 1 (1981): 275–89.

Webster, T.B.L. *Studies in Menander.* Manchester: Manchester University Press, 1950.

———. *An Introduction to Menander.* Manchester: Manchester University Press, 1974.

Wellek, R., and A. Warren. *Theory of Literature.* New York: Harcourt, Brace, 1942.

Wendel, C. "Platonios." In A. Pauly and G. Wissowa, *Real-Encyclopädie der classischen Altertumswissenschaft,* col. 2544. Stuttgart: J. B. Metzler, 1894–1963.

West, D. *Reading Horace.* Edinburgh: Edinburgh University Press, 1967.

———. "Of Mice and Men: Horace, *Satires* 2.6.77–117." In T. Woodman and D. West, eds., *Quality and Pleasure in Latin Poetry,* 67–80. Cambridge: Cambridge University Press, 1974.

West, M. *Studies in Greek Elegy and Iambus.* Berlin: Walter de Gruyter, 1974.

Wiesen, D. S. "Two Problems in Horace's Satires." *Mnemosyne* 34 (1981): 87–95.

Wigodsky, M. *Vergil and Early Latin Poetry. Hermes* Einzelschriften 24. Wiesbaden: Franz Steiner, 1972.

———. "Horace's Miser (*S.*1.1.108) and Aristotelian Self-Love." *Symbolae Osloenses* 55 (1980): 33–58.

Wilkinson, L. P. "The Language of Virgil and Horace." *Classical Quarterly,* n.s. 9 (1959): 181–92.

———. *Golden Latin Artistry.* Cambridge: Cambridge University Press, 1963.

Williams, F. W. *Callimachus: Hymn to Apollo.* Oxford: Clarendon Press, 1978.

Williams, M. F. "Amor's Head-Cold (*Frigus* in Catullus 45)." *Classical Journal* 83 (1988): 128–32.

Wimmel, W. *Kallimachos im Rom. Hermes* Einzelschriften 16. Wiesbaden: Franz Steiner, 1960.

Winkler, M. M. *The Persona in Three Satires of Juvenal.* Hildesheim: Olms, 1983.

Wirszubski, C. *Libertas as a Political Idea at Rome during the Late Republic and Early Principate.* Cambridge: Cambridge University Press, 1950.

Wiseman, T. P. "Satyrs in Rome? The Background to Horace's Ars Poetica." *Journal of Roman Studies* 78 (1988): 1–13.

Witke, C. *Latin Satire.* Leiden: E. J. Brill, 1970.

Woodman, A. J. "The Craft of Horace in *Odes* 1.14." *Classical Philology* 75 (1980): 60–67.

Yardley, J. C. "Comic Influences in Propertius." *Phoenix* 26 (1972): 134–39.

———. "Propertius 4.5, Ovid *Amores* 1.6 and Roman Comedy." *Proceedings of the Cambridge Philological Society,* n.s. 33 (1987): 179–89.

Zanker, G. *Realism in Alexandrian Poetry.* London: Croom Helm, 1987.

Zeller, E. *The Stoics, Epicureans and Sceptics.* London, 1880. Reprint. New York: Russell and Russell, 1962.

Zetzel, J.E.G. "Horace's *Liber Sermonum*: The Structure of Ambiguity." *Arethusa* 13 (1980): 59–77.

Cupiennius, 194

curtus, 207

Cynicism, in the *Satires*, 11, 14–16, 35, 36n. 82, 43, 96, 107, 188, 188n. 10, 194, 212, 215

Cynics: in comedy, 32–33, 35, 36, 44, 94, 224n. 103; on death, 216–23, 231; on exposure of hypocrisy, 216–19, 223–26, 229; on free speech and jest, 54, 72, 78–82, 85, 89, 90, 90n. 59; and Old Comedy, 82; social status of, 213–14. *See also* diatribe

Damasippus, 7, 47, 48, 107, 113

Davus, 7, 47, 48, 113, 221, 225, 228

Dawson, C. M., 106

Death, as mode of exposure, 216–23, 229–32, 234

De Comoedia, 76

deductum carmen, 111, 111n. 5, 186

delectare, 102

Demea, 8, 34–39

Demetrius (Hellenistic theorist), 57, 57n. 15, 110, 120, 130, 149

Demetrius (of *Satires* 1.10), 168, 169, 169n. 101

Demetrius of Phalerum, 57

Democritus, 127

Demosthenes, 151–52n. 73; Dionysius on, 133–34, 180

DeWitt, N., 90, 90n.59

diatribe: characteristics of, 7n. 14, 9, 35, 85, 99, 100, 188, 188n. 10; in late republic, 16–21

diatribe satires, definition of, 7n. 14; persona in, 7, 36, 38

Dickie, M., 54, 104–5

diction: in diatribe, 15–16; in the *Satires*, 11, 11n. 21; ancient theories of, 126–29, 166–67

dignitas, 220

Dihle, A., 137n. 51

Dikaiopolis, 72, 213, 221

Diogenes the Cynic, 18, 79, 80, 82, 213–14, 218

Diomedes, 99n. 72

Dionysius of Halicarnassus, 120, 140; on word arrangement, 130–39, 145–46, 149, 173–74

Dionysus, 213; festival of, 213, 218

discinctus, 197n. 39, 202n. 52

doctor ineptus, 8, 34, 38, 47

doctors, in comedy, 41

dogs, as symbol of Cynics, 79; as symbol of parasites, 79n. 44; as symbol of poets, 78

Dolabella, 87n. 55

Domitian, 45

Donatus, 175

Don Quixote, 218–19n. 94

dossennus, 32n. 77

dulcis, 166, 167

Dunn, F., 188, 189

DuQuesnay, I. M., 26n. 67, 86, 113, 116, 125–26n. 34

duritia. See ruggedness

Ehlers, W., 204n. 60

Elder Horace, 8, 34–39

elementa, 143

Else, G., 149

English Augustans, 228

emendare, 175–78

emotions, in Aristotle, 64–65; in Plato, 61–63; in oratory, 59, 60

Empedocles, 120

Ennius, 147, 148, 182, 194

envy, as comic emotion, 63, 65, 91, 105. *See also* technical terms, φθόνος

Epicharmus, 68

Epictetus, 7n. 14

Epicureans: on free speech, 87–90; in the *Satires*, 11, 11n. 22, 26, 35–36, 43n. 96; stylistic theories of, 139–45, 150

Epicurus, 19, 43n. 94

Eratosthenes, 57, 131

ethopoeia, 5n; in comedy, 7, 7n. 15, 29n. 72

ethos, 4–5, 56, 59, 71n. 35

euphony, in Dionysius, 136–37

Eupolis, 66n. 26, 96, 98, 99, 107–8

Euripides, 110, 128, 129–30, 130n. 39

exclusus amator, in the *Satires*, 43, 47, 47n. 103

exempla, as teaching device, 35, 36, 36n. 82

exposure, Cynic modes of, 216–23

Fabianus, 159–60, 196n. 34

Fabius, 15, 20, 38, 104, 109–14, 118, 149, 154, 163, 165, 198

Fairclough, H. R., 170

Fannius, 109, 116–18, 163, 168

Fannius Quadratus, 117, 117n. 20

Oberhelman, S., 125n. 33, 147nn. 66 and 67, 199n. 45, 210n. 76
obscenity, 60; Aristotle on, 65–66; Bakhtin on, 220–21; as Cynic convention, 12, 222
Octavian. *See* Augustus
Ofellus, 7, 188, 215
Old Comedy: Aristotle on, 61–72, 91; and Bion, 39n. 86; and censorship, 22, 22n. 56, 73, 80, 85; characters of, 40, 213; costume of, 70; in the *Satires*, 22, 22n. 58, 40, 96, 98–100, 103, 107–8, 157, 212, 231; and free speech, 89, 173n; and Horace's theory of satire, 52–54, 98–100; and the iambographic tradition, 72–77, 82, 83; and obscenity, 221; Plato on, 61–63, 65; Platonius on, 84; Plutarch on, 90–91
Olivieri, A., 88n
Oltramare, A., 9, 13, 14, 17
oratio pedestris, 183–84, 207. *See also* technical terms, πεζὴ λέξις
ordo naturalis. See Stoics, stylistic theories of
Origo, 43

Paetus, 173n
pain, of jest, 69
Panaetius, 173
Pantilius, 168
parasites: in comedy, 33, 41, 79n. 44, 80, 93–95; and the satiric persona, 203–5, 215, 232–33
Parker, A., 53, 53–54n. 8, 98
parody, in Bion, 39n. 86; in the *Satires*, 17, 26–27; of diatribe, 18–21, 24, 25; of the satiric persona, 21–27
pater ardens, 34, 41, 47, 50
Pedius Publicola, 167
Periplectomenus, 42
Persius (the satirist), 186–87n. 7, 216, 223
Persius (of *Satires* 1.7), 207–8
persona: in the diatribe satires, 14–16, 21–33, 36, 38; in drama, 4; of Horace's father, 34–39; as lowlife in *Satires* Book One, 199–207, 212–16; in rhetoric, 4; theory of, 3–4
personification, 24–25, 24n. 62, 43
Phidias, 151n, 152, 152n. 75
philargyria, 85
Philemon, 30, 42, 42n. 89, 44

Philistus, 130n. 39
Philodemus, diatribes of, 18; on free speech, 88–90; on poetry, 120, 130, 139–42, 147, 149; in the *Satires*, 195–97
Philokleon, 74
Phoinix of Colophon, 18, 21
Phormus, 68
physician metaphor, in Cynic philosophy, 81, 81n; in Old Comedy, 74, 77; in Philodemus, 89
Piers Plowman, 215
Pindar, 188
Pitholaus, 103, 168, 169, 169n. 101
Pitholeon. *See* Pitholaus
pity, as tragic emotion, 62, 63, 65
plain style, 153, 193n. 26
Plato, 47, 59; in ancient criticism, 127, 155, 180; on comedy and jest, 61–63, 65, 71, 72, 83, 91, 92; in the *Satires*, 107–8
Platonius, 66n. 26, 70, 75, 83, 83nn. 51 and 52, 84, 85, 92, 99
Plautus, 31, 33; compositional style of, 165, 190; names in, 49
pleasure. *See* emotions
Plotius Plancus, L., 113
Plutarch, on comedy and jest, 57, 90, 90n. 62, 91, 92
poetry, ancient definitions of, 120, 124–28
polyeideia, 106, 106n. 96
Pompey, 86, 110, 111, 113
Pomponius, 124
Pontia, 228
Porcius, 232
Porphyrion, 47, 113
Postumus, 45, 227n. 110
poverty, as stylistic metaphor, 191, 191n. 21
Priapus, 47, 105, 229–30, 229n. 113
propriety, in ancient criticism, 133, 221. *See also* technical terms, τὸ πρέπον
prostitutes, in comedy, 42, 42n. 89, 47, 50; in satire, 194, 194n. 29
Puelma-Piwonka, M., 53
Pseudolus, 224
Pyrgopolynices, 42, 45n. 98, 49
Pyrrho, 15
Pythagoras, 47